The Chinese Civil Code in the Global Legal Order

Comparative Law in Global Perspective

VOLUME 7

The titles published in this series are listed at *brill.com/clgp*

The Chinese Civil Code in the Global Legal Order

Inner and Outer Perspectives

Edited by

Mauro Bussani, Ivan Cardillo, Marta Infantino and Xue Jun

BRILL | NIJHOFF

LEIDEN | BOSTON

Library of Congress Cataloging-in-Publication Data

Names: Bussani, Mauro, editor.
Title: The Chinese civil code in the global legal order : inner and outer perspectives / edited by Mauro Bussani, Ivan Cardillo, Marta Infantino and Xue Jun.
Description: Leiden ; Boston : Brill/Nijhoff, 2024. | Series: Comparative law in global perspective ; 7 | Includes index. | Identifiers: LCCN 2024024383 | ISBN 9789004704411 (hardback) | ISBN 9789004704428 (ebook)
Subjects: LCSH: Civil law–China. | China. Min fa. English.
Classification: LCC KNQ500 .C4495 2024 | DDC 349.51–dc23/eng/202406023
LC record available at https://lccn.loc.gov/2024024383

Typeface for the Latin, Greek, and Cyrillic scripts: "Brill". See and download: brill.com/brill-typeface.

ISSN 2772-5332
ISBN 978-90-04-70441-1 (hardback)
ISBN 978-90-04-70442-8 (e-book)
DOI 10.1163/9789004704428

This book is printed on acid-free paper and produced in a sustainable manner.

Contents

PART 3
The Outer Significance of the Chinese Civil Code

Notes on Contributors

Grzegorz J. Blicharz
Assistant Professor, Department of Roman Law, Jagiellonian University in Kraków, Kraków, Poland.

Mauro Bussani
Full Professor of Comparative Law, Law Department, Trieste University, Trieste, Italy; Adjunct Professor, Law School, University of Macau, Macau, SAR of the People's Republic of China.

William E. Butler
John Edward Fowler Distinguished Professor of Law, Penn State Dickinson Law, Carlisle, USA; Emeritus Professor of Comparative Law, University College London, London, United Kingdom; Foreign Member, Russian Academy of Natural Sciences, Moscow, Russia; Member, Ukrainian National Academy of Sciences and Ukrainian National Academy of Legal Sciences, Kiev, Ukraine.

Ivan Cardillo
Adjunct Professor holder of the chair of Chinese Law at Trento University, Italy; Adjunct Professor at China University of Political Science and Law, People's Republic of China; Senior Advisor 'Faren' Think Tank of the Chinese Government Ministry of Justice; Director of the Institute of Chinese Law.

Umberto Celli
Full Professor of International Law, University of São Paulo, Ribeirão Preto Law School, São Paulo, Brazil.

Sjef van Erp
Emeritus Professor, Maastricht University, Maastricht, the Netherlands; Visiting Professor at Trento University, Trento, Italy, and at the University of Oldenburg, Oldernburg, Germany.

Ligia Espolaor Veronese
PhD from the University of São Paulo, lawyer in the arbitration field, São Paulo, Brazil.

方新军 *Xinjun Fang*
Dean and Professor of Civil and Commercial Law, School of Law, Soochow University, Suzhou, People's Republic of China.

James Russell Gordley
W.R. Irby Chair in Law, Tulane University Law School, New Orleans, USA.

Marie Goré
Professor, Faculté de Droit, University of Paris Panthéon-Assas, Paris, France; Director of the Institute of Comparative Law, Paris, France.

韩世远 *Shiyuan Han*
Professor, School of Law, Tsinghua University, Beijing, People's Republic of China.

Marta Infantino
Associate Professor of Comparative Law, Department of Political Science, Trieste University, Trieste, Italy.

蒋昊 *Hao Jiang*
Assistant Professor of Comparative Law, Bocconi University, Milan, Italy.

Salvatore Mancuso
Full Professor of Comparative Law, University of Palermo, Palermo, Italy; Honorary Professor of African law, Centre for African Laws and Society, Xiangtan University, Xiangtan, People's Republic of China; Visiting Professor, Somali National University, Mogaishu, Somalia.

Antonello Miranda
Full Professor of Comparative Law, University of Palermo, Palermo, Italy.

Ujal Kumar Mookherjee
Assistant Professor, Symbiosis Law School, Pune, a constituent of Symbiosis International (Deemed University), Pune, India.

Ken Oliphant
Professor of Tort Law, University of Bristol Law School, Bristol, United Kingdom.

Nicoletta Patti
PhD Candidate in System Dynamics (Social Science Stream), University of Palermo, Palermo, Italy.

Pascal Pichonnaz
Full Professor, Faculty of Law, University of Fribourg, Fribourg, Switzerland; President of the European Law Institute (administrative seat Vienna, Austria).

Manjeri Subin Sunder Raj
Knowledge Network Expert, Harmony with Nature, United Nations, New York, USA; Assistant Professor, Christ (Deemed to be University), Bangalore, India.

唐曉晴 *Io Cheng Tong*
Dean and Professor of Law, Faculty of Law, University of Macau, Macau, SAR of the People's Republic of China

王利明 *Liming Wang*
Distinguished Professor, School of Law, Renmin University of China, Beijing, People's Republic of China; Chairman of the Civil Law Society of China, Beijing, People's Republic of China.

汪洋 *Yang Wang*
Tenured Associate Professor, School of Law, Tsinghua University, Beijing, People's Republic of China.

Franz Werro
Full Professor, Faculty of Law, University of Fribourg, Fribourg, Switzerland; Professor of Law, Georgetown University Law Center, Washington DC, USA.

徐涤宇 *Diyu Xu*
Dean and Professor, Law School, Zhongnan University of Economics and Law, Wuhan, People's Republic of China.

薛军 *Jun Xue*
Full Professor, Peking University Law School, Beijing, People's Republic of China.

尹思雨 *Siyu Yin*
PhD student, School of Law, Tsinghua University, Beijing, People's Republic of China.

张家勇 *Jiayong Zhang*
Professor, School of Law, Zhongnan University of Economics and Law, Wuhan, People's Republic of China.

朱晓喆 *Xiaozhe Zhu*
Professor, School of Law, Shanghai University of Finance and Economics, Shanghai, People's Republic of China.

Preface

The book analyses the internal and external impact of the Chinese Civil Code (CCC) that entered into force in China in January 2021. The CCC, which covers the main pillars of Chinese private law – from personhood to personality rights, from property to succession and secured transactions law, from contract to tort law –, represents the final point of arrival of almost forty years of reforms of Chinese law. During this period, Chinese law developed as an original hybrid of norms inspired by selected foreign Western legal traditions and autoctonous rules consonant with historically-rooted approaches to law and legal institutions. The CCC is the civil codification with the largest personal scope of application in human history. Yet, the sphere of influence of the CCC will likely be wider, given the long-standing, historical influence of China in the East Asian region, and the growing economic, technological and cultural power of China beyond that region (as well as the many Chinese business communities operating abroad).

Against this background, the volume offers, we believe, a valuable contribution to the English-speaking literature on Chinese law, by assessing the gist of the provisions in the CCC and their broader impact within and outside China, and by investigating not only the comparative origins of current Chinese rules, but also the influence these rules may have on comparative law scholarship.

The volume is the outcome of a truly joint collaboration of distinguished Chinese and non-Chinese scholars, and it is divided in three parts. The three chapters in the first part ('The Overall Framework of the Chinese Civil Code') place the CCC within the broader historical and comparative perspectives of private law codifications. The fourteen chapters in the second part ('The Inner Contents of the Chinese Civil Code') survey the main contents and novelties of the seven books that compose the CCC. Each book is analyzed by a Chinese and a non-Chinese scholar, in order to provide readers with a reliable picture of inner and outer perceptions about the core features of the CCC. The six chapters in the third part ('The Outer Significance of the Chinese Civil Code'), which are authored by scholars who are not based in mainland China, explore the potential impact of the CCC in Macao and Hong Kong (where the CCC does not apply), India, Russia, Europe, Africa and North America.

We leave the conclusions on this vast survey to the readers. But I cannot leave this page without thanking all the other editors and contributors for the time and energy they spent in bringing this book to fruition.

Mauro Bussani

PART 1

The Overall Framework of the Chinese Civil Code

CHAPTER 1

The Chinese Civil Code in Comparative Perspective

Mauro Bussani and Marta Infantino

1 Introduction

This chapter attempts to place the newly enacted Chinese Civil Code (hereinafter CCC) within a wider historical and comparative framework. When discussing about China in the global competition of legal models, scholars tend to repeat a story that starts at the beginning of the nineteenth century, revolves around Western legal models and, quite unsurprisingly, is deeply Western-centric. Western-centrism explains the time-frame and point of departure chosen for unfolding this story, as well as the emphasis the story poses on post-Westphalian legal institutions, the downplay of pre-existing alternative legal models, its espousal of the idea that the industrialized West is the acme of civilization, and its delicate silence about the crudest forms of Western imperialism and colonialism.[1]

In the limited space available, the chapter aims to tell another version of the same story: a version that begins much before the nineteenth century and takes place on the Eastern side of the Eurasian continent. As such, after summarizing Section 2's contemporary mainstream narratives, Section 3 will briefly recall the significance of Chinese civilization in the world's history from a long-term perspective. Section 4 will confirm such significance through a rapid overview of data historically associated with the Middle Kingdom. As the next two sections will argue, it is against this historical and cultural background that one should appreciate the meaning of the CCC (Section 5) and its contribution to putting China back in its traditional position vis-à-vis the world at large (Section 6). Section 7 will draw some observations on the role that Chinese law is likely to play in what is often dubbed the China century.[2]

---

1 Nina Tzouvala, *Capitalism As Civilisation. A History of International Law* (CUP 2020) 45–84; Thomas Duve, 'What Is Global Legal History?' (2020) 8 Comparative Legal History 73–115; H. Patrick Glenn, *Legal Traditions of the World. Sustainable Diversity in the Law* (5th edn, OUP 2014) 52–57; Werner Menski, *Comparative Law in a Global Context. The Legal Systems of Asia and Africa* (2nd edn, CUP 2006) 37–57.

2 See, for all, David Scott, *'The Chinese Century'? The Challenge to Global Order* (Palgrave 2008).

 | DOI:10.1163/9789004704428_002

2 Western Legal Globalization and China

When examining recent legal developments in the global perspective, scholars often take a timeline starting with the American and French revolution, and from that moment onwards, they follow the adventures of the following three Western legal models that, one after the other, gained prominence in global legal thought: the French, the German and the American model.[3] As is well-known, the temporary leadership of these legal models were epitomized by the worldwide spread (through military conquest, economic dominance or cultural prestige) of what was considered the most famous by-product and vehicle of exportation for each of them: the French Civil Code of 1804, the German Pandectist school, and the American legal thinking and practice.[4] Equally well-known is that, in international relations, the alleged superiority of Western models justified (and was further strengthened by) the way in which the European powers and the United States managed their encounter with other cultures, including those that could not be subjugated to colonial domination. These cultures were deemed by Westerners as uncivilized and undeveloped insofar as they did not respect the basic principles of (Western) civilization. As such, these non-Western 'others' did not deserve equal standing and equal treatment under international law.[5]

This was notably the fate of China after the end of the two Opium Wars (1839–1842 and 1856–1860). The victory of these conflicts by Britain and France obliged imperial China to sign unequal international treaties that required,

3 Duncan Kennedy, 'Three Globalizations of Law and Legal Thought: 1850–2000', in David M. Trubek and Alvaro Santos (eds), *The New Law and Economic Development. A Critical Appraisal* (CUP 2006) 19–73 (who however invert the moment of influence of German and French legal thought); Gianmaria Ajani, 'By Chance and Prestige: Legal Transplants in Russia and Eastern Europe' (1994), 43 Am J Comp L 92–117, esp 94–98; Ugo Mattei, 'Why the Wind Changed: Intellectual Leadership in Western Law' (1994) 42 Am J Comp L 195–218.

4 Mattei (n 3) 200.

5 On the immense literature on the 'standards of civilization', now enshrined in Article 38(1)(c) of the Statute of the International Court of Justice (according to which "general principles of law recognized by civilized nations" are a source of international law), see Tzouvala (n 1) esp 14–15, 45–84; Jedidiah Kroncke, *The Futility of Law and Development. China and the Dangers of Exporting American Law* (OUP 2016) 40–46; Teemu Ruskola, *Legal Orientalism. China, the United States, and Modern Law* (Harvard University Press 2013) 127–130, 186–187; Guido Abbattista, 'Chinese Law and Justice: George Thomas Staunton (1781–1859) and the European Discourses on China in the Eighteenth and Nineteenth Centuries', in Guido Abbattista (ed), *Law, Justice and Codification in Qing China. European and Chinese Perspectives* (EUT 2017) 1–137 (available at <https://www.openstarts.units.it/handle/10077/15690>, accessed 25 May 2024).

among other things, the opening up of specific ports to Western traders and the surrender of the Hong Kong island to the British crown.[6] The victory of Japan in the first Sino-Japanese war (1894–1895) further aggravated the loss of prestige of the Chinese classical tradition. After the fall of the empire in 1912 and the establishment of the Kuomitang-led Republic of China (RoC), the country remained plagued by internal conflicts, and suffered from foreign invasion during the second Sino-Japanese war (1937–1945). Instability only ended in 1949, when the Chinese Communist Party established the People's Republic of China on China mainland – and the RoC institutions relocated in Taiwan.[7]

In this perspective, it should be stressed that during this period – often dubbed as the 'century of humiliation'[8] – every Chinese government attempted to 'modernize' domestic legal architecture, including a codification of private law. In 1910, shortly before its fall, the last Chinese dynasty published a draft civil code inspired by European codes, and in particular by the BGB, which was never adopted.[9] Later on, looking at the German, the Japanese, the French, the Swiss and at many other legislative models, the RoC adopted the Kuomintang Civil Code in 1929–1930; the code (which is still in force in Taiwan nowadays) officially came into operation, although the situation in the mainland largely prevented it from becoming operative.[10]

The quest for legal 'modernization' and for the adoption of a civil code did not end after the foundation of the People's Republic of China. After 1949,

---

6 David C. Kang and Kenneth M. Swope, 'East Asian International Relations over the *Longue Durée*', in Stephen Haggard and David C. Kang (eds), *East Asia in the World. Twelve Events that Shaped the Modern International Order* (CUP 2020) 22–43, at 40–42; Tzouvala (n 1) 15, 46, 50–54; Kroncke (n 5) 35–46, 68–70. The history of Macau was notably different, since the Chinese government recognized the Portuguese right of 'perpetual occupation' of Macao in 1887: Paulo Cardinal, 'Macau: The internationalization of an historical autonomy' (2008) 41 Boletín mexicano de derecho comparado 637–689.

7 On all these developments, Jianfu Chen, *Chinese Law: Context and Transformation* (3rd edn, Martinus Nijhoff 2015) 39–46.

8 See, for all, David Scott, *China and the International System, 1840–1949. Power, Presence, and Perceptions in a Century of Humiliation* (SUNY Press 2008).

9 Marina Timoteo, 'Of Old and New Codes: Chinese Law in the Mirror of Western Laws', in Abbattista (ed) (n 5) 177–192, at 179; Lei Chen and C.H. (Remco) van Rhee, 'Introduction', in Lei Chen and C.H. (Remco) van Rhee (eds), *Towards a Chinese Civil Code. Comparative and Historical Perspectives* (Brill 2012) 1–17, at 2–3.

10 Timoteo (n 9) 179; Chen (n 7) 455 (who, among the sources of the Kuomintang code, cites, besides the BGB, "the Japanese Civil Code of 1896, [...] the French Civil Code of 1804, the Swiss Civil Code of 1907 and the Swiss Code of Obligations of 1911, the Brazilian Civil Code of 1916, the Civil Code of Soviet Russia of 1922, the Siamese Civil Code of 1923–1925, the Turkish Commercial Code of 1926, the draft Italian Commercial Code of 1925 and the never enacted Franco-Italian Code of Obligations and Contracts of 1927").

China repealed the Kuomintang code and turned to Soviet models (which themselves had roots in the civil law tradition).[11] Thus, in 1954, it resulted in a plan which failed to enact a civil code modelled after the 1922 Civil Code of the Russian Soviet Federated Socialist Republic (itself inspired by the BGB).[12] After the deterioration of Sino-Soviet relationships, new draft civil codes were repeatedly prepared, most notably in 1964 and 1982, but they all landed nowhere.[13] Following the piecemeal approach to legislation advocated by Deng Xiaoping, China adopted from the 1980s onwards (besides several special laws concerning civil law matters[14]), the General Principles of Civil Law of 1986, which mixed European continental models and Socialist ideology to provide general rules of civil and commercial law.[15] Pending accession to the World Trade Organization (finalized in 2001), a new project for a civil codification was launched in 1998, but the text proposed in 2002 failed to get approved.[16] In 2014, the Civil Code once again came at the top of the political agenda, ending up in the re-packaging of the many special laws adopted in previous years in

11 Ajani (n 3) 94–96. During the same period far-reaching reforms were adopted in order to forge anew the Chinese society. For example, Articles 1, 2, and 3 of the Marriage Law of the People's Republic of China (1950) ended polygamy, arranged marriage, concubinage, child betrothal, forced remarriage of widows (levirate marriage), and marriage payments (e.g., dowry), and wives gained the right to both own property and inherit it from their husbands. From the same perspective, land reforms were enacted seeking to break down and redistribute the corporate holdings of patrilineal clans. See A. Greif and G. Tabellini, 'The clan and the city: Sustaining cooperation in China and Europe' (2012) J Comp Econ 1–35.

12 Chen (n 7) 459–460.

13 Both the 1964 and the 1982 draft civil codes were, despite their socialist inspiration, somehow modeled after the BGB: Chen (n 7) 459–461.

14 Through time, these acts included the Marriage Law (1980, revised 2001), the Succession Law (1985), the Contract Law (1999), the Real Rights Law (2007), the Tort Law (2009). In addition to the enactment of these statutes, one should also take into consideration the regulatory role played by the Supreme People's Court (SPC). The SPC does not only perform the judicial function, but also supervises and gives guidance to lower courts through different types of texts that occupy a central position in the Chinese system of legal sources. See, for all, Ding Qi, *The Power of the Supreme People's Court: Reconceptualizing Judicial Power in Contemporary China* (Routledge 2020).

15 Cp. Lei Chen and Larry A. DiMatteo, 'History of Chinese Contract Law', in Larry A. DiMatteo and Lei Chen (eds) *Chinese Contract Law. Civil and Common Law Perspectives* (CUP 2018) 3–25, at 4–5; Chen (n 7) 465–493; Rou Tong, 'The General Principles of Civil Law: Its Birth, Characteristics, and Role' (1989) 52 L & Contemp Probls 151–175, 152–154 (1989).

16 Timoteo (n 9) 183–185.

the unified Civil code, which entered into force in mainland China on January 1, 2021.[17]

According to mainstream narratives, the enactment of the CCC therefore represents the final act of a long process which started in the middle of the nineteenth century, experienced several revolutionary moments and changes in momentum, and finally allowed China to get closer to the Western ideal of legal development and civilization.[18] However, these kinds of narratives, being deeply Western-centered, capture only a part of the picture.

3 China and the Rest in the Long Durée

Taking a long-term perspective is a necessity when talking about China. China has the longest continuous history of any country in the world, and is one of the few ancient civilizations that have survived changes of borders and rulers to the present.[19] The origins of imperial China date back to as early as the 3rd century BC; soon after, the empire replaced Legalism with Confucianism as its main orthodoxy. Imbued by these doctrines, the empire rapidly developed a nationwide civil service admission system, which selected members of the imperial bureaucracy on the basis of their knowledge of Confucian classics, and adopted codes that collected rules for the smooth administration of the state and the maintenance of peace.[20]

17 Timoteo (n 9) 185–189. The CCC does apply neither to Macao nor to Hong Kong. Macao and Hong Kong, as former foreign colonies, are formally allowed by the Constitution and special laws to maintain their legal systems (influenced, respectively, by British and Portuguese law). See Article 31 of the 1982 Chinese Constitution, as well as the 1990 Basic Law of the Hong Kong Special Administrative Region and the 1993 Basic Law of the Macao Special Administrative Region. On the Hong Kong and Macau's legal systems, see Ignazio Castellucci, 'Legal Hybridity in Hong Kong and Macau' (2012) 57 McGill L J 665–720 (2012); Jorge Oliveira and Paulo Cardinal (eds), *One Country, Two Systems, Three Legal Orders – Perspectives of Evoluton* (Springer 2009).

18 Lei Chen, 'Continuity and change: some reflections on the Chinese Civil Code' (2021) 29 Asia-Pacific L Rev 287–305 (2021), at 288 ("Overall, the CCC is a milestone of Chinese legislative history towards rule-based governance. This is because the CCC is in line with legitimizing private interests and holding the public power on account"); Timoteo (n 9) 182–188; Chen and van Rhee (n 9) 1–4.

19 Tansen Sen, *India, China, and the World. A Connected History* (Rowman & Littlefield 2017) 1–28; John Wu, 'Reading from Ancient Chinese Codes and Other Sources of Chinese Law and Legal Ideas' (1921) 19 Mich L Rev 502–536, at 502.

20 Cp. Muzhou Li, Haifeng Liu, Wei-Chiao Huang, 'A Historical Investigation and Classification Analysis of Seven Controversies on the Reform and Abolition of the 1300-year Chinese Imperial Examination System' (2022) 114 Int'l J Educ Res 1–9 (2022), available

The Chinese tradition became hegemonic in the East Asian region, providing the script, the vocabulary, the model and the legal paradigms for neighboring tributary countries (such as Korea, Japan, and Vietnam).[21] However, Chinese tradition also proved influential beyond its immediate zone of material contact. At the height of the Enlightenment period, China was for European intellectuals (such as Leibniz, Wolff and Voltaire) a living testimony of an ancient civilization endowed with historical continuity, and was orderly administered by a competent and committed administration. In contrast, Europe was torn apart for centuries by internal religious and political conflicts, instability, and profound societal inequality.[22] Across the Atlantic Ocean, the Chinese tradition played a similar influence on the American Founding Fathers, many of whom looked at China (as an alternative to colonial Europe) as the leading model for institutional and political stability.[23]

Yet, from the end of the eighteenth century in Europe, and from the mid-nineteenth century in the US, the Sinophile attitude of Western élites was gradually replaced by Sinophobe views, which denied the historical continuity of the Chinese empire and criticized its despotism, its reliance on rites, the corruption of its officials and the harsh punishments that the latter could arbitrarily inflict.[24] It is not by chance that this change of attitudes coincided with a period of economic stagnation in China, accompanied by the spread of industrialization in the West and, above all, with a new phase of colonial expansion of European empires. Subsequent developments in China and in the West, including the Opium Wars and the signature of the unequal treaties, nurtured Western self-perceived superiority, along with the diffusion of narratives such as the ones mentioned in the previous section.

---

at <https://doi.org/10.1016/j.ijer.2022.101976> (accessed 25 May 2024); Chen (n 7) 9; Teemu Ruskola, 'The East Asian legal tradition', in Mauro Bussani and Ugo Mattei (eds), *The Cambridge Companion to Comparative Law* (CUP 2012) 257–277, at 264 (noting in particular that "a centralized bureaucratic state […] emerged in China centuries before its European equivalent").

21 Kang and Swope (n 6) 26–40; Hendrik Spruyt, *The World Imagined. Collective Beliefs and Political Order in the Sinocentric, Islamic and Southeast Asian International Societies* (CUP 2020) 831–32; Michele Graziadei, 'Comparative Law as the Study of Transplants and Receptions', in Mathias Reimann and Reinhard Zimmermann (eds), *The Oxford Handbook of Comparative Private Law* (2nd edn, OUP 2019) 442–473, at 445–446; Ruskola (n 20) 264; for an overview of the influence of the Chinese tradition on India, see Sen (n 19) 29–110.

22 Abbattista (n 5) 9–10.

23 Kroncke (n 5) 21–25.

24 Abbattista (n 5) 33–75; Kroncke (n 5) 29–46, 110–112.

4 A Path of Great Numbers

Among the many aspects that mainstream narratives tend to underestimate, there exists a simple fact. Throughout its long history, China has always been a country of great numbers.

From the Bronze age onwards, China, together with its neighbor, India, have accounted for more than half of the world's population.[25] Historical estimates of the gross domestic product (GDP) in the last two millennia suggest that China, alongside India, have always produced more than half of the world's GDP until the early nineteenth century.[26] Between the sixteenth and seventeenth century, China was, in simple terms, the richest country in the world in terms of GDP output.[27] During this entire period, China's technology (which included the 'four great inventions': compass, gunpowder, papermaking, and printing) was much more advanced than that of its neighbors and trading partners along the network of land and maritime routes that allowed commerce, exchange and flow of knowledge across Eurasia.[28]

Likewise, numbers show that after the period of economic stagnation that preceded and followed the encounter with the West, contemporary China has been back at the top of the world. China is currently the second most populous country on earth, with its 1.42 billion population covering 18.5% of the world population[29] (to which one could add the millions of Chinese living abroad).[30] In 2022, China was the number 2 economy in the world (second to the US) in terms of GDP, and the number 1 in terms of both total exports and imports of goods and services;[31] notably, China is number 2 (second to the US) for

25 See <https://ourworldindata.org/grapher/population> (accessed 25 May 2024) (from 4000 BCE to 2021); Angus Maddison, *The World Economy: A Millennial Perspective* (OECD 2001) 28 (Table 1–1), and 241 (Table B–10) (from 0 to 1998).

26 Maddison (n 25) 261 (Table B-18) (from 0 to 1998) and 263 (Table B-20).

27 Ibid. On this point, see also R. Bin Wong, *China Transformed: Historical Change and the Limits of European Experience* (Cornell University Press 1997).

28 Kang and Swope (n 6) 31–34; Spruyt (n 6) 86; Sen (n 19) 38–39; Jialu Fan, Qi Han, Zhaochun Wang, Nianzu Dai, 'The Four Great Inventions', in Yongxiang Lu (ed), *A History of Chinese Science and Technology* (II, Springer 2015) 161–299.

29 See <https://ourworldindata.org/world-population-growth> (accessed 25 May 2024) (chart 'All the people in the world').

30 The number of overseas Chinese is quite unclear. A reasonable estimate is around 40 to 45 million Chinese living outside China: Tan Chee-Beng, 'Introduction', in Tan Chee-Beng (ed), *Routledge Handbook on the Chinese Diaspora* (Routledge 2013) 1–12, at 4.

31 See World Bank, 'GDP', 'Exports of goods and services', 'Import of goods and services' (all 2022 data) at <https://data.worldbank.org/> (accessed 25 May 2024).

artificial intelligence-related research, innovations and implementations.[32] The Belt and Road Initiative could serve as a vast network of programs concerning trade, investments, infrastructures and development aid stretching across Eurasia with branches in Africa, America and the Arctic. It would involve more than 140 countries, and promises to not only further connect China with the rest of the globe (and particularly with developing countries), but to also shape a new world order through economic, smart and soft power with China at its core.[33]

Unsurprisingly, this long history of extraordinary achievements also applies to the law. China has a well-rooted tradition of written legal sources, with archaeological findings confirming the existence of sophisticated laws in the proto-imperial period, which dates back to as early as the 6th century BC.[34] In continuity with that tradition and with the country's history of big numbers, the entry of the CCC into force in 2021 marked another important step along its path. Never before in human history has a civil code been applied to so many people at the same time. In comparison, at the zenith of the French colonial empire the most exported civil code so far – the code Napoléon – nominally applied (albeit often in an adapted or reduced form) to less than 150 million people around the world.[35]

5 Code and Symbols

When seen in this wider perspective, reading the CCC as representation of a further move in China's long march toward legal modernization, rule of law and full inclusion among civilized nations, clearly becomes reductive.[36]

---

32 See Stanford University, '2021 Global Vibrancy Ranking' (last available ranking), at <https://aiindex.stanford.edu/vibrancy/> (accessed 25 May 2024); Tortoise Media, '2023 Global AI Index', at <https://www.tortoisemedia.com/intelligence/global-ai/> (accessed 25 May 2024).

33 Anu Bradford, *Digital Empires* (OUP 2023) 294–297, 316–317, 321–322; Lutz-Christian Wolff, 'Legal Responses to China's "Belt and Road" Initiative: Necessary, Possible or Pointless Exercise?' (2020) 29 Transn'l L & Contemp Probls 249–325 (2020); Julien Chaisse and Mitsuo Matsushita, 'China's "Belt and Road" Initiative: Mapping the World Trade Normative and Strategic Implications' (2018) 52 J World Trade 163–186; Miao Ji, 'Expectations and Realities: Managing the Risks of the "Belt and Road" Initiative' (2015) 1 China Q Int'l Strategic Stud 497–522.

34 Chen (n 7) 8–9.

35 Thomas Piketty, *Capital et idéologie* (Éditions du Seuil 2019) 304–307.

36 Zhongyuan Xu, 'Politicization, nationality, systemization and the Chinese Civil Code' (2021) 8 Renmin Chin L Rev 57–88, esp. at 68 ("the codification of civil law systematizes

As such, that corresponds to the dominant narratives within and outside of China, which on the one hand forgets to emphasize historical continuities in the country's trajectory, and on the other hand embraces too uncritically the Western-centric idea that Western legal institutions (only) are conducive to (economic) development, and that only countries with institutions and qualities resembling those of the West can actually become developed.[37]

This is not to deny that the CCC also aims at providing legal certainty, coherence and uniformity to the regulation of civil relationships, thereby contributing to the satisfying internal and external (more or less Western-centric, more or less well-founded) expectations about how a modern and well-functioning legal system should look like. Of course, the CCC does it. Our point is simply that the symbolic value of CCC goes far beyond this.[38]

A civil code is not only a deeply technical act, but also a deeply political one. Civil codes are associated, inter alia, with stabilizing moments of transition and embodying change, affirming a country's (new or renewed) unity and sovereignty, and solidifying its national legal identity and achievements.[39] The CCC encompasses all these functions. It entrenches and confirms China's commitment to shape a socialist market economy, allowing private initiative under public control, while striving for fairly distributed wealth and promoting long-term, harmonious growth. However, the enactment of the CCC also

---

the code; it is the systemic content presented by the code that promotes the ideals of the modern nation-state that have been practiced and that shows the road to the rule of law has been embarked on"); Timoteo (n 9) 190; Chen and van Rhee (n 9) 3; Randall Peeremboom, *China's Long March Toward Rule of Law* (Cambridge University Press 2002) 141–174.

37 Cp. Mauro Bussani, 'Deglobalizing Rule of Law and Democracy: Hunting Down Rhetoric Through Comparative Law' (2019) 67 Am J Comp L 701–744, at 712–726; Mauro Bussani, 'Geopolitics of Legal Reforms and the Role of Comparative Law', in Mauro Bussani and Lukas Heckendorn Urscheler (eds), *Comparisons in Legal Development. The Impact of Foreign and International Law on National Legal Systems* (Schulthess 2016) 235–248, at 240–245; Taisu Zhang, 'Beyond Methodological Eurocentrism: Comparing the Chinese and European Legal Traditions' (2016) 56 Am J Leg Hist 195–207.

38 We are focusing here on the symbolic value of the CCC because this is actually the level at which the impact of a civil codification is usually discussed, inside and outside the codifying country. It is quite common that provisions contained in newly enacted civil codes have a limited innovative character insofar as they build on pre-existing rules and visions of the law shared by the legal actors (or formants) in that system; whenever a code really innovates, time and efforts are required by those very same actors before the new rules be effectively internalized. Michele Graziadei and Lihong Zhang, 'On Civil Codes: A Twenty-First Century Perspective', in Michele Graziadei and Lihong Zhang (eds), *The Making of the Civil Codes. A Twenty-First Century Perspective* (Springer 2023) 1–16, at 2–5.

39 See, for all, Graziadei and Zhang (n 38) 1–8.

asserts Chinese full maturity in facing and attempting to provide answers to the most compelling social problems – such as the rural-urban divide and the preservation of traditional family bonds, as well as preventing mass incidents and reducing emissions of pollutants. Of course, the choice for a code stands in historical continuity with many of its country-wide codification drafts from the past century, and reinforces the connection with the earlier great codes that have marked important epochs of Chinese history, and with their tradition of Confucianism and Legalism.[40]

In the outer perspective, the decision to adopt a civil code confirms what previous codification attempts also demonstrated: that the Chinese legal system sees itself as more consonant, among Western legal cultures, with legal systems whose origins can be traced back to continental Europe rather than to common law jurisdictions. After all, the idea that authoritative written texts are the main source of the law is a foundational mythology of the civil law tradition. Underlying the Chinese consonance with civil law tradition is not only a shared belief in written laws, but also the preference for top-down regulation and for an overtly centralized system of legal sources, the desire to keep the role of judges and jurists limited within the reach of social expectations, and the penchant for State-led interventions in promoting collective values, such as good faith and solidarity. All these features are notoriously absent or minimal in the basic architecture of common law jurisdictions, in which lawmaking is by definition decentralized, state apparatuses are relatively small, and the room for limiting individual action for social purposes is scant.[41]

This affinity between contemporary Chinese legal culture and the Romano-Germanic legal tradition is hardly surprising, but is particularly meaningful in current times. From the end of World War II onwards, dominant narratives and discourses, fueled by the prestige associated with the global prominence of US law, have relentlessly advocated the superior efficiency of the common law models vis-à-vis civil law ones.[42] Against this context, the reaffirmation of

---

40 Lihong Zhang, 'A Brief Analysis of Cryptotypes in the Chinese Civil Code: Legalism and Confucianism', in Graziadei and Zhang (eds) (n 38) 365–383; Chen (n 18) 297–298.

41 See, for all, Glenn (n 1) 132–179, 236–286; Konrad Zweigert and Hein Kötz, *An Introduction to Comparative Law* (trans. by Tony Weir) (3rd edn, OUP 1998) 63–72.

42 Suffice it to remind how, in the private law field (especially contract and property law), the World Bank has, in the last twenty years, promoted the view that the common law is more business-friendly and overall conducive to economic growth than the civil law, through the publication of its yearly 'Doing Business' Reports (at https://www.doingbusiness.org/): see Marta Infantino, 'Quantitative Legal Comparisons: Narratives, Self-Representations and Sunset Boulevards' (2019) 6 J Int'l & Comp L 287–306; Gerard McCormack, 'Why 'Doing Business' with the World Bank May Be Bad for You' (2018) 19 Eur Bus Org L Rev 649–676; Guy Canivet, 'Le débat common law versus civil law sur la

China's belonging to the civil law tradition is a confirmation that the tradition is alive and well, and perfectly compatible with economic growth.[43]

Moreover, within the group of civil law countries, the CCC now stands as one of the youngest and most up-to-date civil codifications in the world. History has repeatedly shown that, within that group, the latest codifications are usually kept in the highest regard by those who follow in the steps of drafting a new civil code or updating an existing one, insofar as they are regarded as an updated summa of the best solutions available until that moment (and all the more so whenever the country adopting the code is imbued with political, economic and technological power[44]). This implies that the CCC is likely to become a reference point for forthcoming codification efforts, and to further strengthen the capacity of China to dialogue with the many jurisdictions having a civil law legacy in Asia, Africa and the Americas.[45]

6 One Law, Many Models

A codification never occurs in a vacuum. Every civil code, no matter how revolutionary, stands on the shoulders of giants – that is, of previous (own and others') practices, experiments and failures.[46] From this point of view, every codification can be read as the result of a selection, among the many options that are available at the time of the drafting, of those that are deemed optimal in light of the perceived needs of the country and of the outcomes that the reform seeks to achieve.[47]

In this regard, the CCC is not an exception. The text entered into force on January 2021, reorganizes and systematizes in a unified body of rules, the legal

performance économique du droit est-il pertinent?' (2018) 129 Rev d'écon financière 31–51; Bénédicte Fauvarque-Cosson and Anne-Julie Kerhuel, 'Is Law an Economic Contest? French Reactions to the Doing Business World Bank Reports and Economic Analysis of the Law' (2009) 57 Am J Comp L 811–829.

43 Mauro Bussani, 'A Streetcar Named Desire: The European Civil Code in the Global Legal Order' (2009) 84 Tulane L Rev 1083–2003, at 1087–1089.

44 Sital Kalantry, 'Reverse Legal Transplants' (2020) 99 NC L Rev 49–99, at 64–70 (suggesting with empirical evidence that legal transplants occur from richer to poorer countries, and not viceversa).

45 Chen (n 18) 300; for similar observations, but with regard a possible continental European civil code, Bussani (n 43).

46 On this point, it is needless to recall the historically supported argument of Portalis that "[l]es Codes des peuples se font avec le temps, à proprement parler on ne les fait pas": J.-E.-M. Portalis, 'Discours préliminaire', in 1 *Recueil complet des discours prononcés lors de la présentation du Code Civil* (Firmin Didot Frères 1838) 1, 6.

47 Chen (n 18) 300; Graziadei (n 21) 448–451.

architecture that the Chinese government had built in a fragmented fashion throughout the last forty years of piecemeal reforms. As such, the CCC has inherited the combination of foreign-inspired transplants, traditional solutions and original creations that characterized the multi-layered, pre-existing pieces of legislation. However, the CCC also reworks these inherited materials in a comprehensive and novel way, often introducing brand new approaches and rules that are pioneering without being disruptive.

Chapters in Part 2 of this book explore in detail the inner contents of the CCC, from both the internal and the external perspective. Suffice it to recall that the list of foreign-inspired transplants that made their way into the CCC include many civil law principles and rules, such as the inclusion of a Book One on general provisions, the doctrine of '*numerus clausus*' of rights in rem, and the centrality of good faith in the law of obligations.[48] One can add to this list a few remnants of the influence of Soviet law, that are still visible, for instance, in the regulation of collective and state ownership, in the limitations to the parties' freedom of contract, and in the liability in equity rule for accidents that cannot be attributed to anybody's fault.[49] Besides Romanistic transplants, the CCC also bears the imprint of common law systems (mostly of US law). This is evident in Book Seven on tort law, which allows punitive damages and juxtaposes to open-ended clauses on tort liability a somewhat pigeonhole system of nominate liability regimes.[50] Moreover, in Book Three on contracts, the CCC has additionally inherited from pre-existing statutes the distinctive influence of some international legal sources, such as the Convention on Contracts for the International Sale of Goods (CISG) and the UNIDROIT Principles of International Commercial Contracts.[51]

At the same time, the CCC contains many autochthonous elements, some of which are rooted in traditional Chinese law and some of which are innovative and forward-looking. Traditional postures are visible in the law of personhood and residence, in the regulation of family and succession law, and in the

48 See, in this book, chapters on Books Two, Three and Seven.

49 See Gianmaria Ajani, 'Chinese Civil Law and Soviet Influences: What Is Left', in Hao Jiang and Pietro Sirena (eds), *The Making of Chinese Civil Code: Promises and Persistent Problems* (CUP 2023) 292–307; Zhang (n 40) 374–377; James Gordley, Hao Jiang, Arthur Taylor von Mehren, *An Introduction to the Comparative Study of Private Law* (2nd edn, CUP 2020) 520–525, 581–584.

50 Mauro Bussani, 'The Aims of Tort Law across China and the West', in Jiang and Sirena (eds) (n 49) 197–213; Timoteo (n 9) 188–189.

51 Lihong Zhang, 'Chinese Report', in Salvatore Mancuso and Mauro Bussani (eds), *The Principles of BRICS Contract Law* (Springer 2022) 241–296, at 242, 251.

general approach to remedies.[52] Innovations are no less evident in the creation of an autonomous book (Book Four) devoted to personality rights,[53] as well as the inclusion of several sustainability/pro-environment obligations throughout the whole text of the CCC.[54]

As this minimal list already makes clear, and as chapters collected in Part 2 of this book further show, the CCC provides its own optimal mix for regulating civil law relationships. This mix is obviously grounded in Chinese ancient and recent legal culture, but also takes inspiration from (what was deemed to be) the best of other experiences to comprehensively deal with the country's old and new problems. The question naturally arises about what influence the CCC is likely to have outside of mainland China, in the Asian region and beyond. Chapters in Part 3 of this book aim to answer precisely to that question.

7 Conclusions

The aim of this chapter was to show that any interpretation of the CCC as a further step in China's move from a lawless society to a 'civilized' one is, at best, biased and oblivious of the country's past.

It is biased as it projects (recent) features of Western law on a non-Western culture, on the implied assumption that Western law epitomizes the highest possible point of development for any legal system. However, the same interpretation is also oblivious of the past because it forgets (not only whatever happened in the West before colonial ventures and industrialization, but also) the millennial continuity of China as one of the world's cradles of human civilization, its historical position in the Asian region, and its longstanding role of an exporter of culture, technology and rules.

Instead, the CCC can be seen as a confirmation of the long-term centrality of China in the geopolitics of legal reforms. Now that the 'sleeping giant' has awakened, in a world that is much more interconnected than it used to be two centuries ago, it is reasonable to wonder what role its law will play in the global

52 Cp. Zhang (n 40) 372–374, 378–379; Chen (n 18) 295–296; see chapters on Books One, Five and Six.

53 Liming Wang and Bingwan Xiong, 'Personality Rights in China's New Civil Code: A Response to Increasing Awareness of Rights in an Era of Evolving Technology', in Jiang and Sirena (eds) (n 49) 41–76; Liming Wang, 'System Innovations: Characteristics and Contributions of the Chinese Civil Code', in Graziadei and Zhang (n 38) 341–364.

54 Sabrina Lanni, 'New Civil Codes and the Environment: The Contributions of China and Argentina', in Graziadei and Zhang (n 38) 385–404.

competition of legal models, and whether the CCC will become part of the Chinese export. With certainty, language is a formidable barrier for a broad circulation of the Code. Yet, soon after the adoption of the CCC, the government released its complete English translation,[55] making it not only the civil codification applying to the widest number of people in human history, but also the fastest one to be translated.

55 Available at <https://english.www.gov.cn/archive/lawsregulations/202012/31/content_WS5fedad98c6d0f72576943005.html> (accessed 25 May 2024).

CHAPTER 2

The Chinese Way to the Civil Code

Ivan Cardillo

1 Introduction

In the words of Xi Jinping, "[t]he Civil Code systematically integrates the civil legal norms formed by the long-term practice of the People's Republic of China over the past 70 years, has absorbed the excellent legal culture of the Chinese nation of more than 5,000 years, and borrowed from the beneficial achievements of humanity in the construction of a civilization of rule of law".[1] There are three sources of inspiration for the Civil Code: Socialism and its Chinese practice, Chinese legal tradition, and the West with the transplant of its legal institutions. The Code symbolizes the completion of a specific idea of legal order. Not by chance, the final act that resulted in the adoption of the Code was, precisely, the 'Decision of the Central Committee of the Communist Party of China on Several Major Issues Concerning Comprehensively Advancing the Rule of Law'.[2] The Code is considered to be a milestone in the process of modernization of the Chinese legal order, a "modernization in Chinese style" ("中国式现代化"), and a Chinese contribution to legal modernity, based on the integration of the three original elements mentioned above. The Code has been welcomed as an 'Encyclopedia of Social Life' ("社会生活的百科全书"), because it offers a new 'method'[3] for the people, legal experts and the

1 Xie Hongfei, 'The Civil Code has a profound cultural background' (谢鸿飞, 民法典具有深厚文化底蕴) available at <http://www.npc.gov.cn/npc/c30834/202206/6e885087dd40432984568331942f615c.shtml>, accessed 8 July 2023.

2 Original title '中共中央关于全面推进依法治国若干重大问题的决定', available at <https://mp.weixin.qq.com/s?__biz=MjM5NzUzNjE2MA==&mid=200972492&idx=1&sn=482eb708c0a092887a400760545e9143&scene=27>, accessed 8 July 2023.

3 Here the reference is to Mao's definition of method: "We must not only set out the task but also solve the problem of the method of accomplishing the task. Our task is to cross the river, but we cannot cross the river without a bridge or a boat. Without solving the bridge or boat problem, crossing the river is empty talk. Without solving the method problem, the task is just nonsense". See Mao Zedong, 'Caring about people's lives, paying attention to working methods', in *Selected Works of Mao Zedong* (People's Publishing House 1967, 1) 125 ('关心群众生活,注意工作方法', 《毛泽东选集》, 第一卷, 人民出版社).

 | DOI:10.1163/9789004704428_003

government to accomplish the task of "developing socialism with Chinese characteristics".[4]

The Code marked the beginning of the its era in the history of Chinese law. For the first time, a law is called 'code'. Such achievement is the final result of collective efforts over almost two centuries in order to "gather the wisdom of the multitude, and turn it into the great code".[5] 'Multitude' refers to several generations of not only Chinese scholars, but also of Western scholars whose ideas have been translated into China.[6] We can consider the newly adopted Code as the final product of a long period of legal reforms attempts. This process started in the second half of the XIX century, which was a time of great codifications in Europe and an epic transformation in the history of China; as well as a period of experiments, whose final result is epitomized by the Chinese Civil Code. The Chinese Code is the XXI century's version of a code as the source of law, with the *Bürgerliches Gesetzbuch* leading the XX century and the *Code Civil* leading the XIX century.[7]

2 The Codification Experience in Late Imperial China and in Republican China

In the late Qing dynasty, the codification marked the beginning of the legal modernization movement, which can be considered part of the codification movement initiated in Western countries in the XVIII century, characterized by peculiar problems, some of which still challenge Chinese society today.[8]

Around 1840, a movement of law revision began in China, carried forward by the Law Revision Office ('修订法律') and by the Ministry of Law Revision

4 'Decision of the Central Committee of the Communist Party of China on Several Major Issues Concerning Comprehensively Advancing the Rule of Law' (n 2) article 1.

5 In Chinese '聚万众智慧，成伟大法典'. See Wang Liming, 'Jiang Ping's Important Contribution to the Compilation of the Civil Code' (王利明, 江平先生对民法典编纂的重要贡献), available at <http://www.aisixiang.com/data/121926.html>, accessed 8 July 2023.

6 See Marina Timoteo, 'Of Old and New Codes: Chinese Law in the Mirror of Western Laws', in Guido Abbattista (ed), *Law, Justice and Codification in Qing China. European and Chinese Perspectives. Essays in History and Comparative Law* (EUT 2017) 177–192.

7 For an analysis of the code as a source of law in a comparative perspective, see Michele Graziadei and Lihong Zhang (eds), *The Making of the Civil Codes. A Twenty-First Century Perspective* (Springer 2023).

8 Liang Zhiping, 'Law, Politics and Social Change: Codification in China since 1902', in Paolo Cappellini and Bernardo Sordi (eds), *Codici. Una riflessione di fine millennio* (Giuffrè 2002) 402.

('修律大臣'). The movement had to face the challenge of confronting the legal tradition, judging it, and setting a path of reforms in order for the country to gain back full sovereignty of its territory.[9] Such a path implied a double shift of paradigm, one concerning the idea of legislation and the other concerning the idea of civil law. China had a tradition of law codification and a method of legal studies similar to the Western positive method.[10] The main difference laid in the principle behind legislation, i.e., the unity 'of all laws, with no distinction between civil and penal law',[11] and between substantial law and procedural law.[12] Therefore, the first step down the path of legal modernization was to distinguish what belonged to penal law from what belonged to civil law, thus reviewing the tradition according to the new categories imported from the West.

In 1898, Zhang Zhidong published his famous 'Exhortation to Learning' ('劝学篇'), in which he reaffirmed his faith in Confucianism, but detailed the measures needed for the acquisition of Western knowledge such as studying abroad by Chinese students, the establishment of a school system, translation of Western and Japanese books, and acquisition of knowledge from foreign newspapers. His motto was 'Chinese learning as substance, Western learning for application'.[13] Zhang, along with many Chinese scholars, believed that China should have maintained its own Confucian style of learning as the basis ('substance', '体') of society while, at the same time, using Western learning for 'practical application' ('用') to develop China's infrastructure, military, and economy. Reformers had to 'refer to the written laws of other countries and observe China's code of rites and the conditions of the people',[14] where observing the conditions of the people implied an investigation of customs and habits.[15] The purpose was to revise all Chinese statutes and sub-statutes

---

9 F. T. Cheng, 'Law Codification in China' (1924) 6(4) J Comp Legis & Int'l L 283.

10 Liang Zhiping, *Searching for Harmony in the Natural Order: A Study of Chinese Traditional Legal Culture* (China University of Political Science and Law Press 1997) 307–325 (梁治平, 寻求自然秩序中的和谐: 中国传统法律文化研究, 中国政法大学出版社).

11 In Chinese '诸法合体、民刑不分'.

12 See Li Xiandong, *On the Model Transformation from the Codex of the Qing Dynasty, to the Civil Code – Concurrently on the Open Law Norm System of Proper Civil Law in Ancient China* (People's Public Security University Press 2003) (李显冬, 从《大清律例》到《民国民法典》的转型--兼论中国古代固有民法的开放性体系, 中国人民公安大学出版社).

13 In Chinese '中学为体, 西学为用'.

14 In Chinese '参考各国成法，体察中国礼教民情'.

15 See chapter 579, published in the Guangxu 33rd year (1907), the fifth day of September, in *Veritable Records of Qing Dezong* (Zhonghua Book Company 1987) 66 (《清德宗实录》, 卷五七九, 中华书局).

in reference to the laws of the foreign countries in "order to have the laws of the empire recognized by foreign countries".[16] This led to the '礼法之争', meaning the struggle between the ritualist school (礼教派) represented by Zhang Zhidong and Lao Naixuan, and the legal theorist school (法理派) represented by Shen Jiaben, who was more open to western legal categories.[17]

On the first of May of the 33rd year of Guangxu, i.e., in 1907, in 'A Memorial to the Emperor about Appointing Ministers to be in Charge of Civil Law Making', Zhang Renfu, minister of the Supreme Court, 'Da Li Yuan' ('大理院'), discussed the importance of civil law making. He said that "there is only one law in China, i.e., the criminal law and the affairs like marriages and land disputes are also included in it, which shows that the laws are far from complete. Moreover, the mixture of criminal law with civil law has especially been criticized by foreigners. So, what is most important in law revision is firstly to study the distinction of the nature of laws".[18] For Liang Qichao, the lack of private law in China constituted "the most unfortunate event in China's legal world".[19]

On October 4, 1908, Shen Jiaben submitted a memorial in his capacity as Minister of Law Revision, reporting on the Japanese jurists' division of the law into criminal law, civil law, and criminal and civil procedure law. In addition, he also suggested sending personnel to investigate the civil and commercial habits of each province and pointed out that the revision of the civil and commercial laws should not only adopt the laws of other countries, but should also not violate China's rites and people's sentiments.

In 1911, the 'Draft of the Civil Law of Great Qing' ('大清民律草案') was completed and presented as "the first draft of civil law in history".[20] However, it was never enforced because the Qing Dynasty soon perished. The first three chapters of the first draft of the civil law were mainly based upon the Japanese

16 Shen Jiaben, 'Deletion of heavy law in statutes and sub-statutes', in *Examination of the Criminal Law of Past Dynasties* (Zhonghua Book Company 1985) 150 (沈家本,《删除律例内重法折》, 载历代刑法考, 附寄簃文存, 中华书局).

17 Li Guilian and Li Qicheng, *Three Thousand Years of Chinese Legal History* (*A brief history of legal thought*) (China Democracy and Legal Publishing House 2016) 300 (李贵连, 李启成, 中华法史三千年 (法律思想简史), 中国民主法制出版社).

18 *The Historical Files for the Preparation of Constitutionalism during Late Qing Dynasty*, II, compiled by the Ming and Qing Archives Department of the Palace Museum (Zhonghua Book Company 1979) 835 (故宫博物院明清档案部汇编, 清末筹备立宪档案史料, 中华书局).

19 Fan Zhongxin, *The Collected Legal Works of Liang Qichao* (China University of Political Science and Law Press 2000) 174 (范忠信, 梁启超法学文集, 中国政法大学出版社).

20 Yang Honglie, *The Development of Chinese Legal History* (China University of Political Science and Law Press 1930) 250 (杨鸿烈, 中国法律发达史, 中国政法大学出版社).

civil law made in the 29th year of Meiji. Meanwhile, references were also made to the German and Swiss civil laws.[21]

Article 1 of the Draft stated: "When civil affairs are not regulated by this law, then apply customary law, and in their absence then apply general principles of law".[22] The code of rites and the conditions of the people entered the new civil law in the form of customs. Yu Liansan, Minister of Law Revision, expressed that "in ancient times, China's civil law was not specifically codified. But it was outlined in some detail in the Rites of Zhou".[23]

At this point in the evolution of civil law in China, it became impelling to collect all customs followed by the people. In 1923, the Ministry of Justice and Administration revised the reports on civil customs collected by legal offices and judicial organs in various provinces and regions, and compiled them into 'The Complete Book of Civil Customs in China' ('中国民事习惯大全') edited by Shi Peisheng, Bao Yinxuan, and Wu Guichen. In the same year, a second collection was published, 'The Complete Book of Commercial Customs in China' ('中国商业习惯大全'). The collections were based on a survey designed according to modern Western civil codes' doctrines and codification style. They classified the customs of Chinese regions into the categories of their Western-style questionnaires – forcing China's local customs into paradigms imported from the West.[24] In the preface of the collection, Yang Yuanjie pointed out that "since the beginning of the reform of the Qing dynasty, people are idolized by means of Europeanization and learning from Japan. Therefore, the drafts of civil laws are mostly German and Japanese copies and detailed textual research of the native civil customs and habits of our country [have] not been included. Consequently, it has not been put into practice until more than ten years later".[25]

---

21 See Zhang Jinfan, *The Tradition and Modern Transition of Chinese Law* (Springer 2014) 652.

22 Huai Xiaofeng (ed), *Historical Materials of Legal Reform in the Late Qing (2 Volume)* (China University of Political Science and Law Press 2010) 510 (怀效锋主编，清末法制变革史料 (下卷) 中国政法大学出版社). On the relation between customs and codified law see Zhang Sheng, 'Investigation of Civil Customs in the Late Qing Dynasty and Compilation of "Draft of the Civil Law of the Great Qing"' (2007) Chinese J L 125–134 (张生, 清末民事习惯调查 与 "大清民律草案" 的编纂, 《法学研究》).

23 *A Memorial to the Emperor about the Completion of the First Three Chapters of the Civil Law* (奏呈编辑民律前三编草案告成折), quoted in Zhang Jinfan, 'Thoughts from the "Inherent Civil Law Theory" of Law Revision Officials in the Late Qing Dynasty' (2011) 4 Contemp L Rev 3 (张晋藩：从晚清修律官"固有民法论"所想到的, 《当代法学》).

24 Liang Zhiping, 'The Vernacularization and Localization of Civil Law in China' (2021) Ancilla Iuris 189, 192.

25 Ministry of Justice and Administration of the former Nanjing National Government (ed), *Records of the Investigation Report of Civil Custom* (China University of Political Science

The Civil Code published in 1930 was supplemented by a rich collection of customary laws or popular habits concerning civil and commercial matters.[26] At that time, readers of Savigny and his advocation for customs recollection, could not accept a Chinese codification without first a recollection work of Chinese customs.

Roscoe Pound, a Western scholar and an acute observer of the evolution of Chinese law, praised the use of customs for their ability to make and keep the code in touch with the life of Chinese people, and as "a body of received ideals that can give to the interpretation and application of the Chinese codes a truly Chinese character".[27] Customs, as a product of Chinese legal history and legal philosophy, could "not only enable a wise choice from among conflicting interpretations and applications disclosed by comparative law, but may well suggest new ones more adaptable to Chinese life".[28] Pound could not imagine the collapse of the Republic of China, and the codification process started in 1949 with the foundation of the People's Republic of China. Thus, for this reason, he considered accomplished the function of comparative law as a study and research of foreign laws, and advocated for the study of Chinese legal history in order to prove the bearing of that history upon the ideal elements of Chinese law and their impact on the administration of justice.

3 The Codification Experience in Socialist China

A new codification period started with the foundation of the People's Republic of China (PRC), and the beginning of the Socialist experience of building a modern legal system. The journey to the civil code passed through five drafts in total.

---

and Law Press 2001) 11 (前南京国民政府司法行政部 编, 民事习惯调查报告录, 中国政法大学出版社).

26 Customary laws were considered the heart of civil law. The definition of 'customary law' is subject to the same uncertainty that affects the notion of 'civil law'. Bourgon defines customary laws as popular habits in China, avoiding referring to Western categories. Bourgon also argues that customary laws were created as substitutes for civil laws. See Jerome Bourgon, 'Uncivil Dialogue: Law and Custom did not Merge into Civil Law under the Qing' (2002) 23(1) Late Imperial China 50–90.

27 Roscoe Pound, 'Comparative Law and History as Bases for Chinese Law' (1948) 61 Harv L Rev 757, 758.

28 Ibid at 759.

3.1 *Before the Reform and Opening-up: The First and Second Draft*

The PRC was established in 1949, and the first constitution was adopted in 1954. That same year, the National People's Congress Standing Committee (NPCSC) formed a special panel charged with the drafting of the Civil Code, which completed the work only in December 1956. The draft was composed by the following parts: general principles, property, obligations, and inheritance, for a total of 525 articles. Since then, due to the expansion of the 'rectification and anti-rightist' movement, legislative activities have been terminated. This first draft was heavily influenced by the Soviet civil code.

In 1962, the drafting of the Civil Code was put on the agenda again, and a draft (trial draft) was completed in 1964. The draft was structured into three parts, namely: general principles, property ownership, and property transfer. However, soon after the release of the draft, the legislative work stopped again; this time due to the 'Socialist Education Movement' that developed into the 'Cultural Revolution'.

Besides political reasons, economic circumstances obstructed the codification too. China was implementing a planned economic system based on a single public ownership system. Under the planned economic system, there is no economic and social condition for the existence of civil law as a superstructure. Such an economic system relies on administrative power, administrative levels, and administrative means (including mandatory plans) to organize and arrange the entire economic life, including the production, circulation, distribution, and consumption of products, and as such there is no need for civil laws or civil codes. Industrial and agricultural production strictly follows the mandatory plan; living consumption also strictly follows the plan.

Therefore, the planned economic system implemented by the government at that time, was the root cause of the failure of the previous two drafting of civil law.

It is worth mentioning that both attempts were not called 'Civil Code' ('民法典'), but rather 'Civil Law' ('民法').

3.2 *After the Reform and Opening-up: The Third and Fourth Draft*

With the Reform and Opening-up, a new trend for the legislative agenda began, which also affected the civil codification. The development of civil law was instrumental to the transition from a planned economy to a more market-oriented economy. In this perspective, the legislator chose to adopt a model of "specific statutes on specific contracts",[29] but on a parallel track, the discourse over a comprehensive codification kept going on.

On December 13, 1978, Deng Xiaoping delivered a speech, 'Emancipate the Thoughts, Seek Truth from Facts, and Look Ahead in Unity' at the Central Work Conference, where he proposed to concentrate efforts on enacting criminal law, civil law, procedural law, and other necessary laws. Following that path, on July 1, 1979, Ye Jianying proposed, in the closing speech of the Second Session of the Fifth National People's Congress (NPC), that it was necessary to organize all forces to speed up the formulation of various laws such as civil law, marriage law, and contract law. Such an approach, focusing on single laws, better fit the political agenda of rebuilding a socialist legal order after the nihilist period of the 'Cultural Revolution'. A few days later, Peng Zhen, director of the Legislative Affairs Committee (LAC), opened the discussion about the drafting of the Civil Law with relevant officials. Peng Zhen concluded that, with regard to the scope of civil law, legal circles had different opinions. Thus, it appeared necessary to understand the relevant situation of civil law in various countries, and collect and study some reference materials before opening an internal debate.

On November 2, 1979, the LAC formally established the Civil Law Drafting Group,[30] which was led by Yang Xiufeng and Tao Xijin, deputy directors of the LAC, and saw the participation of more than thirty legal experts from judicial organs, economic departments, and legal teaching and research institutions. In his speech at the inaugural meeting of the Civil Law Drafting Group, Peng Zhen pointed out that civil legislation should adopt the policy of 'walking on two legs' ('两条腿走路').[31] The purpose of the codification was to develop social justice, commodity production and commodity exchange in line with the economic development agenda.

The following year, the Civil Law Drafting Group completed the draft Civil Law (draft for comments), and sent it to the Standing Committees of the People's Congresses of all provinces, autonomous regions, and municipalities directly under the Central Government and relevant central departments for comments. From mid-August to mid-October of that same year, the Civil Law

29 Lei Chen and C.H. (Remco) van Rhee, 'Introduction', in Lei Chen and C.H. (Remco) van Rhee (eds), *Towards a Chinese Civil Code. Comparative and Historical Perspectives* (Brill 2012) 4.

30 'Civil Law' was still the word used to imply 'civil code'.

31 The 'policy of walking on two legs' is Mao Zedong's image pretty effectively summarizing China's socialist construction policy based on the principle of simultaneous development, i.e., to promote comprehensive development of the legal, social and economic sphere.

Drafting Group was divided into six groups and went to thirteen provinces and cities to directly listen to opinions. In the spring of 1981, the Drafting Group revised the draft based on opinions from various parties and formed the draft civil law (the second draft), which consisted of six parts, 42 chapters, and 226 articles. On May 27th, 1981, Peng Zhen presented at the symposium on the Draft Civil Law the second draft based on three main opinions: proceed from China's reality, investigate and study the actual reality and historical reality; conduct investigation and research, listen to the opinions of cadres, workers, farmers, experts, intellectuals, etc.; the enactment of civil law should go hand in hand with the enactment of separate laws.

From July 31, 1981, to June 1982, the Civil Law Drafting Group revised the draft civil law (the third draft), and sent it to the Standing Committees of the People's Congresses of all provinces, autonomous regions, and municipalities directly under the Central Government and relevant central departments for comments. The draft civil law (third draft) was divided into eight parts: tasks and basic principles; civil subject; property ownership; contract; intellectual achievement; family relatives; Civil Liability; other Provisions. On May 7, 1982, Xi Zhongxun, father of Xi Jinping and director of the LAC, during a meeting to discuss the drafting of the Civil Law, proposed that due to the difficulty of drafting the Civil Law Code, the code should not be passed all at once, but separate laws should be enacted one after the other. On June 3, 1982, Xi, after presiding over a meeting again to hear a report on the draft civil law (fourth draft), which consisted of eight parts and 465 articles, decided to abolish the Civil Law Drafting Group.

The imperfection of the market economy and the instability of social relations which characterized this historical period did not help the codification process. Nevertheless, although the draft was not formally passed into law, it laid down the foundations of the General Principles of Civil Law, promulgated in 1986.

A turning point occurred in 1992, with Deng Xiaoping declaring, in a speech on a tour to the South of the country, that the implementation of the socialist market economic system was confirmed. Such a declaration paved the way for the beginning of civil codification rooted in a new and stable socio-economic path.

The work for the drafting of the fourth civil code draft began on January 13, 1998, with Wang Hanbin, then vice chairman of the NPCSC, meeting with several civil law scholars, who agreed that the conditions for drafting the Code were met. Such conditions were summarized in the following way: the socialist market economic system being established; the market economy being developed to a considerable extent; the trend of civil law development being advanced enough; the development of legal education having cultivated a group of talents, and the courts having accumulated considerable experience in civil judgment practice.

In line with the legislative plan to formulate the Code, Wang resumed the drafting work, which was suspended in 1982, without the need to report it to the Party Central Committee. The Standing Committee, thus, authorized Wang Jiafu and others to form a drafting group. The members of the drafting group were Wang Jiafu, Jiang Ping, Wei Zhenying, Wang Baoshu, Liang Huixing, Wang Liming, Fei Zongyi, Xiao Xun, and Wei Yaorong. During the first meeting, the drafting group decided on the general plan to formulate the Civil Code, the so-called 'three-step process', as proposed by Professor Jiang Ping. The first step was to complete the unification of the contract law and realize the unification of market transaction rules; the second step was to formulate the property law and improve the basic rules for property relations; the third step was to complete the remaining parts of the Civil Code in about 10 to 15 years. On September 3, 1998, Hu Kangsheng, deputy director of the LAC, presided over a symposium to study the Civil Code outline drafted by the Chinese Academy of Social Sciences, Renmin University of China, and China University of Political Science and Law.

In 2002, the last year of the Ninth NPC, a major event happened, i.e., China's accession to the World Trade Organization, which required an improvement to the domestic legal environment. Therefore, Li Peng, Chairman of the Ninth NPCSC, requested to speed up the drafting of the Civil Code.

On January 11th, 2002, Gu Angran, director of the LAC, presided over an expert seminar on the drafting of the Civil Code. This was attended by the following: Jiang Ping and Wu Changzhen from China University of Political Science and Law, Wei Zhenying from Peking University, Wang Baoshu from Tsinghua University, Wang Liming from the Renmin University of China, Wang Jiafu, Liang Huixing, and Zheng Chengsi from the Institute of Law of the Chinese Academy of Social Sciences, and Tang Dehua from the Supreme People's Court. Gu pointed out in particular that 'the Civil Code is a collection, not a separate draft, but additions, deletions, revisions, and improvements based on the original General Principles of the Civil Law'. He used the word 'compilation/collection' ('汇编').[32] Thereafter, the Legal Committee of NPCSC invited a number of scholars to submit their own proposals. The first draft of the Civil Code submitted on December 17, 2002, consists of 1,209 articles,

32 For the relative debate, see Liang Huixing, 'Let's Talk About Some Issues Concerning the Compilation of the Civil Code—and Respond to the So-called "Decodization and Uncodification"' (梁慧星，再谈民法典编纂的若干问题—兼回应所谓"解法典化、

divided into nine parts: general provisions, personality rights, property rights, contracts, intellectual property rights, tort, marriage and family, inheritance, and application of laws to foreign-related civil relations.

In June 2003, with the establishment of the Tenth NPC, the Standing Committee issued a new legislative plan. Due to the fact that the Property Law was not yet enacted, coupled with the large differences in understanding the draft of the code, the Civil Code was finally shelved. The work of civil legislation continued in the form of enactments of separate laws, and the Property Law took four years to be adopted.

3.3 *The Final Draft*

In November 2014, the Fourth Plenary Session of the Eighteenth Central Committee of the Communist Party of China proposed the compilation of the Civil Code as an important task for China's reform. In the 'Decision of the Central Committee of the Communist Party of China on Several Major Issues Concerning Comprehensively Advancing the Rule of Law',[33] the Party used the word 'compilation' ('编纂') and not 'drafting' ('起草') or 'formulation' ('制定'). This choice is meant to systematically sort out and integrate existing civil laws and systems such as property rights, contracts, personality rights, marriage and family, inheritance, and tort liability. At the same time, legislation and judicial experience was to be used in order to make the necessary improvements and innovations to the existing normative texts in line with the new needs of the country.

In March 2015, the agenda for the compilation work adopted a 'two-step' approach: the first step was to publish the general provisions; the second step was to publish the special provisions. In June 2016, the 21st meeting of the Twelfth NPCSC reviewed the draft of the general provisions of the Code for the first time, marking the beginning of the legislative process that led to the Civil Code. This time, the Code's draft compiled had seven books: General Provisions, Property Rights, Contracts, Personality Rights, Marriage and Family, Inheritance, Tort Liability, and Supplementary Provisions, with a total of 1,260 articles.

On March 8, 2017, Li Jianguo, vice chairman of the NPCSC, made a speech on the draft of the General Provisions explaining that, since 1979, China's civil legislation has been fruitful and that a relatively complete system of civil laws

---

非法典化"), available at <http://www.aisixiang.com/data/90909.html>, accessed 8 July 2023.

33 'Decision of the Central Committee of the Communist Party of China on Several Major Issues Concerning Comprehensively Advancing the Rule of Law' (n 2).

has been taking shape, laying a good legal and practical foundation for the compilation of the Civil Code. For this reason, the compilation of the Code should have consisted in scientifically sorting out the existing civil laws. A few days later, the Fifth Session of the Twelfth NPC adopted the General Provisions.

In December 2019, the NPCSC decided to submit the draft Civil Code, formed by the merger of the General Provisions and the draft of separate books, to the third session of the Thirteenth NPC for consideration. The complete version of the draft Civil Code was presented to the world for the first time.

On May 22, 2020, Wang Chen, Vice Chairman of the NPCSC, reiterated at the Third Session of the Thirteenth NPC that the aim of the Civil Code's codification was to systematically integrate, compile and revise the existing norms to form a code that met the requirements of the development of a Socialism with Chinese characteristics in the new era. Some days later, Xi Jinping signed Presidential Decree No. 45 related to the Third Session of the Thirteenth NPC's decision to adopt the Civil Code, with an effective date on January 1, 2021. According to statistics, in the process of compiling the Civil Code, the LAC has publicly solicited opinions through the NPC's website ten times and has received a total of 1.02 million opinions and suggestions from 425,000 people.

The task of codifying the Civil Code has thus been successfully completed after a long journey. The Civil Code has become the first law named 'code' since the founding of the PRC and constitutes the law with the largest number of articles, and therefore is known as 'an encyclopedia of social life'.

As for the systematization of civil law, the adoption of the Code explicitly abolished separate laws which were adopted on a parallel path to that of the compilation of the code itself, such as the Marriage Law (1980), the Economic Contract Law (1981), the Trademark Law (1982), the Patent Law (1984), the Inheritance Law (1985), the Foreign Economic Contract Law (1985), the General Principles of Civil Law (1986), the Adoption Law (1991), the Security Law (1995), the Contract Law (1999), the Real Right Law (2007), the Tort Liability Law (2009), and the Law Applicable to Foreign-related Civil Relations (2010). Ideally, the use of judicial interpretations, the recurring tool of the Supreme People's Court to supplement legislation, should be restricted because it is contrary to the idea of consistency of the Code.

4 Conclusions

The codification journey followed Deng Xiaoping's motto, 'crossing the river by feeling the stone' ('摸着石头过河') suggesting one step at a time after careful consideration. Such method was the only possibility, due to the many uncertainties over the general development direction of the country. As such, preference has been given to a problem-oriented pragmatic legislation.[34] In terms of legislative policy, it implied a 'better vague than detailed, better short than long, when it is ready, draft it'[35] legislation. With these words Deng Xiaoping attempted to teach how to deal with historical problems, i.e. by looking at the big picture and not at the details, by focusing on the short period of time and by adopting special laws for specific issues based on social needs and practices, without aiming at formulating a general and comprehensive law at once.

Led by the 'crossing the river by feeling the stone' approach, China's civil and commercial laws and judicial interpretations showed clear traces of political orientation. For example, article 6 of the General Principles of the Civil Law stated that "civil activities must abide by the law; if the law does not provide for it, it shall abide by state policy", providing the basis for policy intervention in civil justice. However, due to the unclear definition of the scope of policies and their distinction from the law, judges in practice often encountered problems such as a lack of supporting provisions, confusion, and difficulties in reasoning when applying policies to adjudication. For this reason, article 10 of the Civil Code removed the reference to state policy as a source of civil law and established a two-tier legal source system of "law and custom".

The core goal of compiling the Civil Code was to realize the systematization and to scientize civil and commercial legislation, as well as building a unified and authoritative source of law, focusing on the modernization of China's governance system and capacity.[36] But the 'crossing the river by feeling the stone' approach limited the integration of special laws into the Code to the ones embedded in the books of the Code. Besides the Code, there are still a large number of legal sources such as special commercial laws, civil and commercial judicial interpretations, documents of the nature of judicial interpretations, and guiding cases. It is foreseeable that future civil and commercial practices will still require the use of such legal sources. This will inevitably dissolve the

---

34 Zhu Guangxin, 'The History and Features of the Codification of Civil Law' (2020) 3 China L Rev 18 (朱广新, 民法法典化的历程与特色, 《中国法律评论》).

35 In Chinese '宜粗不宜细、宜短不宜长、成熟一个制定一个' See *Chronicle of Deng Xiaoping's Thought (1975–1997)* (Central Party Literature Press 1998) 98 (《邓小平思想年谱（1975–1997）》中央文献出版社).

36 Wang Qicai, 'Methodological Reflections on China's Codification in the New Era' (2023) 7 L & Soc Dev 41–57 (王奇才, 新时代中国法典化的方法论思考, 《法制与社会发展》).

authority of the Code to a certain extent as a systematic source.[37] Besides, the Supreme People's Court (SPC) already adopted several judicial documents for the correct application of the Civil Code such as: the 'Several Provisions of the SPC on the Retroactivity in the Application of the Civil Code of the PRC' (2020), the 'Interpretation of the SPC for the Application of the Relevant Guarantee System of the Civil Code of the PRC' (2020), the 'Interpretation (I) of the SPC on the Application of the Book Real Right of the Civil Code of the PRC' (2020), the 'Interpretation (I) of the SPC on the Application of Book Six Succession of the Civil Code of the PRC' (2020), the 'Interpretation (I) of the SPC on the Application of the Marriage and Family Book of the Civil Code of the PRC' (2020), the 'Interpretation by the SPC of Several Issues Concerning the Application of Book One General Provisions of the Civil Code of the PRC' (2021), the 'Notice by the SPC regarding Issuing the Meeting Minutes on the Implementation of the Civil Code by Courts Nationwide' (2021), the 'Nine Model Civil Cases of Judicial Protection of Personality Rights after the Issuance of the Civil Code' (2022), the 'First Group of Model Cases on the People's Courts' Implementation of the Civil Code' (2022), and the 'Second Group of Model Cases on the People's Courts' Implementation of the Civil Code' (2023).

The legislative issues that the Code wanted to solve are appearing again after its promulgation.[38] The legislative landscape is getting back to the fragmented state in which it existed before the promulgation of the Code. It is safe enough to say that the Chinese way of formulating civil law in the systematic form of the code is far from its final stage; if such a stage, auspicated by the government at the beginning of the journey, was ever a realistic goal.

---

37 Jiang Ping, 'Some Reflections on the Compilation of the Civil Code of China' (江平, 中国民法典编纂的的几点思考), available at <http://www.aisixiang.com/data/80555.html>, accessed 8 July 2023.

38 Xue Bo, 'Reflection on the Negative Effects of China's Civil Code Compilation Method' (薛波, 我国民法典编纂方法的消极效应反思), available at <http://www.aisixiang.com/data/139073.html>, accessed 8 July 2023.

CHAPTER 3

Highlighting the Significance of the Chinese Civil Code

王利明 *Wang Liming*

1 Introduction

The Civil Code of the People's Republic of China (hereafter referred to as the 'Civil Code') was adopted by the 13th National People's Congress of the People's Republic of China on May 28, 2020 and came into force on January 1, 2021. The Civil Code consists of 1260 articles, which are divided into seven books: General Provisions, Real Rights, Contracts, Personality Rights, Marriage and Family, Succession, and Tort Liability. Since the establishment of the People's Republic of China, the codification of Chinese civil law has been initiated four times but without success. In 2014, the legislature restarted the codification process by taking a 'two-step' approach: firstly, the adoption of General Principles of the Civil Law of the People's Republic of China on March 15, 2017, which marked a key moment in the codification of the Chinese civil law; secondly, following the publication of the General Principles, the codification of the other books was fully launched. All this work led to the final promulgation of the Civil Code in 2020. Article 1260 of the Civil Code states that "[t]his Code shall come into force on January 1, 2021. The Marriage Law of the People's Republic of China, the Succession Law of the People's Republic of China, the General Principles of Civil Law of the People's Republic of China, the Adoption Law of the People's Republic of China, the Security Law of the People's Republic of China, the Contract Law of the People's Republic of China, the Real Right Law of the People's Republic of China, the Tort Liability Law of the People's Republic of China, and the General Provisions of Civil Law of the People's Republic of China shall be repealed at the same time".

The implementation of the Civil Code has already immensely impacted many sectors of Chinese society, including commercial practices, governmental administration, dispute resolution, as well as academic research. In addition, the codification of Chinese civil law has been a long-cherished wish of several generations of Chinese private law scholars. The Civil Code is not only a great legislative achievement, but also a hallmark of the progress in the academic development of Chinese civil law.

 | DOI:10.1163/9789004704428_004

Both the structure and provisions of the Civil Code, which was born in this new century, emphasize that the codification of the Chinese civil law is centered on the protection of private rights. Article 1 of the Civil Code clearly states that its essential purpose is to "protect the lawful rights and interests of the parties to civil legal relations". The aforementioned seven Books of the Code are elaborated around the main line of protecting private rights. The initial Book (General Provisions) establishes the fundamental principles for the protection of private rights. Book Two to Book Six contain the basic rules regarding the exercise and protection of real rights, rights in contract, personality rights, rights arising from marriage and family relationship and succession. The seventh and last book, on Tort Liability, establishes a body of remedial rules in case of infringement of civil rights and interests, which covers the protection of all private rights. It provides remedies for the infringement of persons' civil rights under the other Books, with the exception of contractual claims, covered in Book Three. Therefore, it is evident that the concept of private rights protection permeates the entire Civil Code, which is essentially a law of rights and a manifesto for the protection of civil rights.

The Civil Code is the culmination of more than forty years of China's civil law legislation. On the one hand, the Civil Code builds on the previous legislative experience, both domestically and abroad. On the other hand, it takes special attention to respond to the present demands of China's society. Overall, the Civil Code reflects China's legislative progress from the beginning, as well as the features of Chinese society in contemporary times.[1] It can be argued that the system design and structure of the Civil Code (Section 2), its values (Section 3) and the choices it makes in terms of contents (Section 4), all closely fit China's civil society's current needs.

2 Significant Innovations in the System Design of the Civil Code

In terms of system design, the Civil Code draws heavily on the past legislative wisdoms of civil law legal systems, such as the achievements embodied in the German Civil Code. Thus it is constructed according to a logical system which starts from a general concept and concludes with detailed rules. The most noteworthy innovations in the overall design of the Civil Code, are the following: Book Three's inclusion of contracts of themany general rules on

1 See Chen Lei, 'Continuity and change: some reflections on the Chinese Civil Code' (2019) 29(2) Asia Pacific L Rev 287–305.

obligations (Section 2.1), and the introduction of two separate books for personality rights (Section 2.2) and tort law (Section 2.3).

2.1 *The Book on Contracts as the Provider of General Rules on Obligations*

The Book on Contracts in the Civil Code is divided into three parts (General Rules, Nominate Contracts and Quasi-contracts), with 526 articles which account for more than 40% of the total articles in the Civil Code. Book Three therefore has a pivotal position in the Civil Code. The section on General Rules provides the principles of contract law, including contract formation, validity, performance, preservation, modification and assignment of contracts, termination of contractual rights and obligations, and liability for breach. The section on Nominate Contracts provides a detailed regulation for the nineteenth nominate contracts and builds the sub-rules of the contract law system. Thus it epitomizes the logical structure of the Book on Contracts, whereby general principles are established first and specific rules of contract law are then derived from general principles.

Unlike many classic civil codes in civilian jurisdictions, such as the German Civil Code, the Chinese Civil Code does not have an independent book detailing the general provisions governing the law of obligations. Instead, the general rules on obligations that materially overlap with the general rules of contract have been absorbed in the general rules concerning contracts. Firstly, chapter four of the Book on Contracts provides the main categorizations for obligations, dividing them into joint and several obligations, divisible and indivisible obligations, obligations involving third parties, performance, assumption, and subrogation of obligations, monetary obligations, and so on and so forth. Secondly, according to article 468 of the Civil Code, for creditor-debtor relationships not arising from a contract, the provisions of laws relating to such relations shall be applied. In the absence of such provisions, the general provisions of the Book on Contracts shall apply, unless the nature of the creditor-debtor relationship precludes their application. Thirdly, in the chapter on Performance of Contracts, the general rules of contract performance include the obligations owed to third parties, distinguishing between authentic and non-authentic contracts with third party beneficiaries. Fourthly, many rules in the Book on Contracts make a distinction between the concepts of claim and debt, and the concepts of contractual rights and obligations. When a provision refers to parties' contractual rights and obligations, the wording makes it clear that the article is only applicable to contractual relationships. By contrast, when a provision uses the notions of claim and debt, the choice indicates that the scope of application of the article is no longer limited to contractual relationships, but rather extends to other forms of debtor-creditor relationships. Fifthly, the rules on quasi-contractual obligations, such as unjust enrichment and *negotiorum gestio* (the former inspired from the common law tradition and the latter from French law), are provided in the last part of the Book on Contract as an independent third subpart. Through this legislative design, the Book on Contracts functions as the foundation of general provisions on the law of obligations. The choice helps maintain the integrity of the general system of contract law and avoids repeating the same rules in an independent body of general rules on obligations. It is therefore more convenient for the legislature and judiciary to interpret and apply the Book on Contracts.

The Book on Contracts also summarizes the achievements and experience of China's recent years of contract law reform and opening up to the development of a market economy, and aims to respond to the demands of China's economic life and transaction practice. The extent to which Book Three builds on the experience of previous Chinese judicial practice is for instance made clear by rules on preliminary contracts (article 495), contracts not yet into force (article 502), breaking the deadlock of a contract (article 580, paragraph 2), and direct indemnity in subrogation cases (article 537). Moreover, many provisions in Book Three take inspiration from international conventions and model laws, such as the United Nations Convention on Contracts for the International Sale of Goods, the Unidroit General Principles of International Commercial Contracts, and the European Draft Common Frame of Reference, as well as the advanced experience of other legal systems on contract legislation.[2]

The Book on Contracts further implements the principles of party autonomy, encouraging transactions, as well as civil and commercial fairness. In order to respect party autonomy, a legally formed contract is always protected by the law (article 465). Therefore, most provisions of the Book on Contracts are default rules. Likewise, the Civil Code establishes a series of complete contract rules from contract formation to contract termination, with the goal of encouraging transactions and striving to reduce the transaction costs for parties. In addition, the Civil Code protects the rights of creditors, establishes comprehensive rules for remedying contract breaches in order to strengthen the protection of creditors and to increase the likelihood of performance. The Civil Code also emphasizes the significance of the principle of good faith and contract fairness by providing rules on standard clauses (articles 496, 497 and

2 See Wang Liming, 'The Civil Code with an International Perspective Contract Book Legislation', Economic and Trade L Rev (2021) 4: 69–97 (王利明, 具有国际化视野的〈民法典〉合同编立法,《经贸法律评论》), article number 2096-6180, at http://law.uibe.edu.cn/docs/2021-09/1e198f346ab94234bfbdeb5a4d627bb0.pdf.

498), mandatory contracts (article 494), the continuity of the rights of lessees on leased property after the change of ownership in the property (article 725), the lessee's right of first refusal in case of sale of a leased house (article 726), the right of continuing a lease even after the expiration of its term (article 734), and the right of co-occupants to continue the lease after the death of the lessee (article 732). The provisions on leases clearly strengthen the protection of the lessee as the vulnerable party. Furthermore, the Civil Code establishes a variety of nominate contracts, regulating factoring contracts, financial leasing contracts and other new types of contracts so as to guide the parties in negotiating these agreements, protecting their expectations and reducing their transactional costs. As such, the Civil Code promotes a healthy business environment. The Book on Contracts in particular contains several rules on the right of transferring and retaining ownership for security purposes, in coordination with the rules on security in Book Two on Real Rights.

2.2 *A Separate Book for Personality Rights*

Unlike all the civil codes that have appeared throughout human history, the Chinese Civil Code devotes a separate book for personality rights. As I have argued elsewhere,[3] there are profound socio-economic meanings underlying a technical departure from the classic structure of civil codes in the civil law tradition. On the one hand, the stand-alone part on personality rights is the fruit and embodiment of the rising right-consciousness of personality in Chinese civil society. On the other hand, the Book provides a new legislative model to comprehensively tackle the pervasive challenges raised by technology against the protection of the personal sphere, which is entangled with the rising right-consciousness over personality in China. The Book on Personality Rights in the Civil Code is designed to implement the constitutional principle of 'inviolability of the human dignity of citizens' and to comprehensively protect the personality rights of natural persons, legal persons and unincorporated organizations for legislature proposes.

Including the general principles and specific rules, the Book is composed of six chapters and fifty-one articles. The first chapter provides the general rules for the exercise and protection of personality rights. Chapters two to six deal with the following personality rights: the right to life, inviolability and integrity of the person, health, name, likeness, reputation, honor, privacy and personal information. Not only does it affirm these specific personality rights, but also

3 Wang Liming and Bingwan Xiong, 'Personality Rights in China's New Civil Code: A Response to Increasing Awareness of Rights in an Era of Evolving Technology' (2021) 47(6) Modern China 703–739.

sets up a general provision in article 990(2) to protect all the other personality rights and interests associated with the personal freedom and dignity enjoyed by natural persons, thus emphasizing the openness of the system of personality rights' protection.

Among the rights that are explicitly regulated by the Code, preferential treatment in the system of personality rights is given to life, health and inviolability and integrity of the person. This is highlighted by article 110 of the Civil Code, which lists the material personality rights (the right to life, to corporeal integrity and to health) prior to the spiritual personality rights. The same happens in Book Four, which prioritizes the right to life, inviolability and integrity of person and health, and confirms the superiority of material personality rights over spiritual ones. In the event of conflict between material and spiritual personality rights, the former shall be prioritized.

With specific regard to spiritual personality rights, the Civil Code takes seriously the heightened risk of their infringement in modern society, for instance through online defamation, personal information disclosure and 'human flesh search'. To cope with these challenges, the Civil Code has developed different mechanisms, the most important of which are the remedies of injunction, deletion and correction. Firstly, the Civil Code stipulates the right of any concerned person to request that the author of the attack to personality assumes liability. Article 995(1) of the Civil Code provides that "[a] person whose personality rights are infringed upon has the right to request the actor to bear civil liability in accordance with the provisions of this Code and the other laws. Where the said person exercises his right to request the actor to stop the infringement, remove the nuisance, eliminate the danger, eliminate the adverse effects, rehabilitate his reputation, or extend apologies, the provisions on limitation periods shall not apply". Secondly, article 997 of the Civil Code provides that, whenever personality rights are being infringed or are in the danger of being infringed, the same person can request the court to issue an injunction to prevent or stop the infringement.[4] The article provides the victim with a timely remedy and a mechanism to prevent further infringements before the trial, which encourages the prevention of infringements to personality rights and offers a procedural protection to the exercises of personality rights. In addition to natural persons whose personality rights are in danger, online platforms may also apply injunctions against the infringements by taking emergency measures, such as removing, blocking or disconnecting a user's account and links, before the intervention of a court. The injunction performs a deterrent

4 Wang and Xiong (n 3) 717–718.

effect on the infringing party and has the potential to prevent the infringement of the personality rights of other persons. If the infringing party disputes the injunction, it will be up to the court to decide whether to revoke or uphold the injunction. Thirdly, article 1028 of the Civil Code provides unique remedies for spiritual personality rights such as correction and deletion. The conditions for applying these remedies require any person whose right is infringed by an inaccurate mediatic content, to request for either correction or deletion of the content, no matter whether the author of the content was or not at fault. In terms of the procedure, the person who requests correction or deletion can do so without resorting to courts. These substantive and procedural advantages contribute to the timely prevention of infringements, to strengthen the protection of victims, and to limit the harmful consequences of accidents.

2.3 *A Separate Book for Tort Liability*

Prior to the enactment of the Civil Code, the Chinese legislature adopted the Tort Liability Law in 2009. The statute is now incorporated into the Civil Code as a separate book, Book Seven, on Tort Liability, although with some amendments and additions.

The same structure described above with regards to Book Three (from general principles to specific rules) applies to the Book on Tort Liability. Book Seven was mainly constructed around the issue of damages which forms the rules of liability. The first chapter sets out the main general provisions governing tort liability, such as the scope of liability rules, the ordinary principle of fault liability, joint liability, causation and damage. While the second chapter focuses on damages awards, chapter three contains specific provisions on assumption of liability, and chapters four to ten deal with special imputation principles. Specifically, rules on assumption of liability mainly consist of liability for the acts of others, such as vicarious liability rules. Special imputation principles are liability regimes based on presumed fault and strict liability, such as those applying to damages caused by defective products, motor vehicle traffic accidents, medical malpractice, environmental pollution and ecological damage, ultra-hazardous activities, domesticated animals, buildings and objects falling therefrom.

The most common way to approach tort liability is through an award for damage compensation. This can be seen in the second chapter of the Book, which is entirely devoted to the basic rules for assessing damages. However, article 1167 of the Book provides that, "[w]here a tortious act endangers another person's personal or property safety, the infringed person has the right to request the tortfeasor to bear tort liability such as cessation of the infringement, removal of the nuisance, or elimination of the danger". Therefore, the Book emphasizes damage compensation, but also recognizes the importance of harm prevention, thus striving to perform the dual function of providing victims with adequate relief and preventing accidents. The structure of this Book also stresses the legislative purpose of creating an intimate connection between rights and remedies. In particular, Book seven adopts a diversified relief mechanism in the liability for motor vehicle traffic accidents in Chapter 5, which combines a system of compulsory insurance liability in article 1213 with the establishment of a Social Assistance Fund for Road Traffic Accidents in article 1216 thus providing comprehensive remedies for victims. This also exemplifies how the idea of adequate remedies for victims pervades the Book.

The Civil Code provides a variety of new types of torts. In response to the proliferation of online torts in the Internet era, the Civil Code provides the safe harbor rule (article 1195), the counter notice rule (article 1196), and the knowledge rule (article 1197) for online tort liability. In response to the infringements by omission, it provides the liability for breach of the duty of maintaining safety (article 1198). For harm caused by defective products, the Civil Code provides a strict liability rule for the producer (article 1202), measures of preventive derisking of defective products (article 1205), a warning and recall system (article 1206), and the award to victims of punitive damages in special circumstances (article 1207). With regard to medical malpractice, the Civil Code provides that the medical staff has a duty to inform patients (article 1219), that medical institutions are under a duty to offer emergency assistance and are liable for medical malpractice under a rule of presumed fault (article 1222), and that, in case of defective medical products, the holder of the marketing for the products, their manufacturer and supplier, as well as the medical institution, are strictly liable for the harm caused (article 1223). Article 1254 of the Civil Code further modifies and completes the liability for damage caused by throwing or falling objects from buildings. First, the provision clearly prohibits throwing objects from buildings, and anyone who violates this obligation shall be held liable. Second, where the incident occurs, the relevant authorities, such as the public security department, shall conduct investigations in accordance with the law and identify the responsible person(s). Third, if the accident occurred due to a lack of necessary security measures, the manager of the building, such as the property management service enterprise, shall be liable for neglecting to implement the necessary security measures. Fourth, any user of the building who may have caused the damage shall make compensation. The provision strengthens the protection of victims, aims to prevent and reduce the occurrence of such accidents, and promotes the uniformity of judicial decisions and dispute resolution processes.

3 The Highlights of the Chinese Civil Code in Terms of Value System

In terms of the value system, the Civil Code implements the principle of private autonomy, adhering to the principle of people-oriented law (Section 3.1) and advocating the respect for traditional Chinese virtues (Section 3.2).

3.1 *Adhering to the Principle of People-Oriented Law*

In 'The Spirit of the Law', Montesquieu pointed out that "in the motherly eyes of the civil law, each individual is the whole nation".[5] This is a profound expression of the spirit of humanism that the civil law should uphold and that has inspired the codification of Chinese civil law, as demonstrated by the structure and value system embraced by the Civil Code.

The Civil Code strengthens the protection of human dignity. Human dignity refers to the personality rights and interests that the law should recognize and respect. Traditionally, the civil codes of civil law countries have focussed more on property rights and treated these rights with priority over people, thus overestimating their value. On the contrary, the Chinese Civil Code has established separate books for personality rights and tort liability, with the aim to strengthen the protection of personality rights and safeguard human dignity. From this point of view, the Civil Code attempts to fix the systemic defects affecting traditional civil codes.

As noted above, the Civil Code has designed a complete system for protecting personality rights through a series of new provisions, such as article 990 of the Civil Code, which recognizes the general personality rights of natural persons in terms of personal freedom and human dignity. The rule on general personality rights in Book Four aims to preserve the dignity of people and to foster their personal development. Not only does it strengthen the protection accorded to each specific personality right, but it also provides the possibility of protecting newly emerged personality rights and interests. Likewise, with regard to the specific personality rights already recognized in the Civil Code, the provisions concerning them reflect the demand of heightened protection of human dignity. For example, article 1002 of the Civil Code does not only recognize people's right to life, but also interprets the scope of right to life as to include the concepts of safety and dignity of life. These concepts may also be predicated for the protection of embryos, fetuses, and human remains. Similarly, article 1011 of the Civil Code guarantees the freedom of the person

5 Montesquieu, *The Spirit of the Laws*, vol 2 (Commercial Press 1997, Chinese translation by Zhang Shenyan) 190.

and prohibits illegal searches on persons, which also strengthens the protection of human dignity.

In addition, the Civil Code establishes the principle of maximizing the interests of minors. As a contracting state to the United Nations Convention on the Rights of the Child, China is obliged to maximize the interests of minors. Traditionally, the guardian of a minor is mainly obliged to supervise and instruct the ward. However, article 34(1) of China's Civil Code now provides that "[t]he duties of a guardian are to carry out juridical acts as an agent of the ward, and to protect personal rights, property rights, as well as other lawful rights and interests of the ward". This emphasizes that the guardian's first priority is to protect the personal rights, property rights, and other lawful rights and interests of the ward. Moreover, where adoption is concerned, article 1098 of the Civil Code requires that the adoptive parents have "no criminal record unfavorable to the healthy growth of the adoptee", which also aims to protect minors.

As such, the Civil Code creates additional duties of protection and care vis-à-vis vulnerable groups to respond to the need of achieving substantive justice and equality. For example, considering the lack of judgment of minors, the Book on Personality Rights establishes special protection rules of their personal information. In addition, in order to emphasize the significance of the people's well-being, the Book on Contracts contains a specific chapter devoted to contracts for property management service. It recognizes the preliminary property management service contract, the owner's unilateral right to rescind the contract and the service provider's duty of maintaining safety. For example, article 944 provides that "[t]he property management service provider may not collect the property management fees by such means as shutting off power, water, heat, or gas". However, it should be noted that the pursuit of substantive justice and equality by the Civil Code, does not imply ignoring the need of ensuring procedural justice and equality. In fact, the pursuit of the former is often based on serious distortions of the latter. In this situation, the Civil Code embraces the idea of formal equal protection as the adequate means to protect the majority, and allows the adoption of substantive justice and equality only to ensure that vulnerable groups will be adequately protected.

3.2 *Advocating Traditional Chinese Virtues*

Article 1 of the Civil Code emphasizes core socialist values as one of the purposes for the codification. These values embody traditional Chinese virtues, many of which are now incorporated in the Civil Code.

For example, the Civil Code emphasizes the significance of family relationships, promotes the harmony of the family, and stimulates the cultural and ethical advancement in family. Under Chinese civil law, the relationship between husband and wife is neither contractual nor associative; the conjugal relationship is rather established by the ethical identity of the spouses. Article 1043 of the Civil Code distinctly reflects this by stating that "families shall establish good family values, promote family virtues, and enhance family civility. Husband and wife shall be loyal to each other, respect each other, and care for each other. Family members shall respect the elderly, take care of the young, help each other, and maintain a marital and familial relationship of equality, harmony, and civility".

Likewise, the Civil Code adopts a principle of inheritance that is different from the one widespread in Western countries, where succession is mainly based on blood lineage. The succession under the Civil Code emphasizes the interrelationship and interaction, such as maintenance and support, between members of the family. Therefore, article 1129 of the Civil Code provides that "[w]idowed daughters-in-law or sons-in-law who have made predominant contributions in supporting their parents-in-law shall, in relationship to their parents-in-law, be regarded as successors first in order". In addition, article 1131 provides that "[a]n appropriate share of the estate may be given to a person, other than a successor, who has made considerable contributions in supporting the now decedent". It is thus evident that, compared with the succession principle based on blood lineage, the Civil Code also takes into consideration the maintenance of marital and familial support, assistance, and harmonious relationship between family members when determining the scope of heirs and distributing inheritance in intestate succession. This reflects traditional virtues in Chinese culture.

The Civil Code also embraces a traditional Chinese virtue, the principle of mutual help and mutual concern, which is in line with the spirit of Confucianism and the idea that 'the benevolent loves others'. Many rules in the Civil Code promote this traditional virtue. In the Book on General Provisions, article 184 exempts from liability for the harm caused the person who engages in a rescue attempt in an emergency situation. Article 183 also provides that "[w]here a party is injured for protecting the civil-law rights and interests of another person, the tortfeasor shall bear civil liability, and the beneficiary may make appropriate compensation to the injured person". In the Book on Personality Rights, article 1005 provides that "[w]here a natural person's right to life, right to corporeal integrity, or right to health is infringed upon or otherwise in peril, the organization or individual who is legally obligated to aid shall promptly extend rescue". Similarly, in the Book on Marriage and Family, article 1043 provides that "[h]usband and wife shall be loyal to each other, respect each other, and care for each other. Family members shall respect the elderly, take care of the young, help each other, and maintain a marital and familial relationship of equality, harmony, and civility".

Furthermore, the Civil Code aims to strengthen the spirit of honesty and trust. Honesty and trust are part of traditional virtues of the Chinese nation, and they are also promoted by Confucianism as a fundamental principle to be a member of the society. These traditional virtues are deeply embedded in the spirit of contract law and have influenced several rules of the Civil Code. The latter does not only embrace the principle of good faith in article 7 by providing that "[w]hen conducting a civil activity, a person of the civil law shall, in compliance with the principle of good faith, uphold honesty and honor commitments", but also embeds this principle into many other provisions. For instance, with regard to the performance of contract, article 509 provides that "[t]he parties shall comply with the principle of good faith, and perform such obligations as sending notices, rendering assistances, and keeping confidentiality in accordance with the nature and purpose of the contract and the course of dealing". Article 142 on contract interpretation highlights good faith as the main principle to interpret ambiguous terms in contracts. Article 533 establishes the rule of *rebus sic stantibus*, according to which, when a change of circumstances occurs in the performance of contract and causes an imbalance of interests between the parties, the parties shall be allowed to modify or rescind the contract. Article 558 recognizes that parties bear post-contractual obligations based on the good faith principle, such as the duty to send notification, render assistance, keep confidentiality, and retrieve used items according to trading customs.

4 Features of the Civil Code in Terms of Content

The most peculiar features of the Civil Code are those addressing problems and needs relating to the specificity of Chinese reality, as well as practical challenges and urgent developments posed by contemporary times. In particular, the emphasis on China's situation means that the Civil Code is based on the reality of the current basic national conditions of the country, and therefore it upholds the basic economic system, promotes its core socialist values and protects the basic rights of the people. The attention to practical issues implies that the Civil Code aims to solve real-world problems, especially those arising out from the social transformation process. The significance of contemporary challenges entails that the Civil Code strives to respond to the demands of people, as well as the new issues raised by current and future developments.

These features are reflected throughout the entire body of the Civil Code and are particularly epitomized by the regulation of the following aspects: usufruct rights (Section 4.1), protection of privacy, personal information, data and virtual property (Section 4.2), electronic commerce (Section 4.3), security interests (Section 4.4), sexual harassment (Section 4.5) and ecological and environmental protection (Section 4.6).

4.1 *Effective Resource Allocation through Usufruct Rights*

The Civil Code does not only protect state and collective land ownership, but also provides for a comprehensive system of usufruct rights, achieving an organic combination of public ownership in the market economy. According to the Chinese Constitution, land ownership cannot be transferred. But in order to develop a market economy, it is necessary to bring land, the most important resource, into the market. To solve such a dilemma, article 206 of the Civil Code confirms that land is either state-owned or collectively-owned and systematically establishes the usufruct rights as the legal solution to introduce market mechanisms into the institution of public ownership. The usufruct rights could bring land resources into the market, and maximize their value by allowing parties to negotiate and compensate each other for their uses.

4.2 *Protection of Privacy, Personal Information, Data and Virtual Property*

The Civil Code strengthens the protection of a number of rights that are at risk in the rising digital world.

The most serious challenge raised by modern high-tech society is most likely the protection of privacy. The Civil Code has been adapted to this need by specifying for the first time the scope of privacy, which consists of private peace of mind, private space, private activities and private information. It is significant that for the first time, article 1032 of the Civil Code protects the peace of private life as an important element of privacy. In order to effectively reduce the invasion to private peace of mind, article 1033 of the Civil Code clearly prohibits various acts that may threaten one's privacy, such as spamming, junk mail, surreptitious photography, voyeurism and trespassing.

Activities such as spamming, flesh search, information leakage and illegal selling in the informational society have actually become social nuisances of our contemporary times. In response to these problems, the Civil Code provides detailed rules for the protection of personal information. Regarding the scope of personal information, article 1034 expands the scope of personal information to include not only information relating to personal identity, but also information relating to personal actions such as digital traces. The article adopts a combination of specific enumeration and general cover-all provisions to maintain the notion of personal information open. Further, article 1034 extends the idea of personal information to matters such as biometry, health and whereabouts. In addition, with regard to those who bear the duty of protecting personal information, article 1039 provides obligations of confidentiality for state authorities and agencies with administrative functions on the privacy and the personal information of natural persons, which are known to them during the performance of their responsibilities.

A further technology-related issue on which the Civil Code intervenes concerns the protection of data and virtual assets. Along with the development of digital technology, data and virtual property have now become new relevant assets, although their nature and means of protection are still largely unclear. To fill this gap, article 127 in the Book on General Provisions of the Civil Code provides that "[w]here there are laws particularly providing for the protection of data and online virtual assets, such provisions shall be followed". The article provides for the protection of data interests by stipulating that they belong to the category of civil rights and by providing a legal basis for any future lex specialis; further, the provision recognizes virtual assets as property. This implies that such assets call for the application of property rules rather than rules about personality rights, and that non-patrimonial damages cannot be awarded in case of their infringement.

In addition, in order to protect the dignity of individual persons, article 1019 of the Civil Code prohibits the forgery of other people's image by utilizing information technology. Furthermore, article 1023(2) explicitly recognizes voice as a new type of personality interest worthy of legal protection. With regard to scientific research related to human genes and human embryos, article 1009 sets the basic rule by stating that "[a] medical and scientific research activity related to human genes, embryos, or the like, shall be done in accordance with the relevant provisions of laws, administrative regulations, and the regulations of the State, and shall not endanger human health, offend ethics and morals, or harm public interests". As such, the provision effectively regulates medical and scientific research activities and guarantees the legitimacy of their operation, but also safeguards human dignity, the dignity of life, and intergenerational interests.

4.3 *New Rules on Electronic Commerce*

In recent years, electronic commerce (or e-commerce) has developed dramatically in China, which is now leading the industry globally. In order to meet the needs raised by e-commerce, the Book on Contracts devotes specific rules for electronic transactions. For example, in consideration of the paperless and data-based characters of electronic contracts, article 469(3) provides that "[a] data message in any form, such as electronic data interchange and e-mails, that renders the content contained therein capable of being represented in a tangible form and accessible for reference and use at any time shall be deemed as a writing". Article 491(2) further states, in case of contracts made through the Internet, that " [w]here the information about goods or services published by a party via information network, such as internet, satisfies the conditions for an offer, unless otherwise agreed by the parties, a contract is formed at the time when the other party chooses such product or service and successfully submits the order". Furthermore, article 512 provides a special rule for the delivery time of the subject matter under an electronic contract concluded through an information network. All this satisfies the demands of the e-commerce era.

4.4 *Achieving Modernization of Security Interests in the Property*

In order to further improve the business environment, the Civil Code establishes a series of complete and unified rules of security interests of the property.

First, the Civil Code unifies the system of registration of security interests in movable assets and rights. While the original Chinese property law had scattered rules for registration authorities of security rights in movable assets, the Book on Real Rights in the Civil Code unifies both the conditions for registration and the department competent to receive registration requests, thus promoting the integration of registries of security interests over movable assets. The Civil Code also establishes a priority system based on registration, thus eliminating the shadow security and promoting the overall efficiency of the security system.

Second, the Civil Code simplifies the registration requirements of mortgaged property in mortgage contracts to make it more efficient and convenient, with the only requirement for registration now being a description of the name and quantity of the mortgaged property.

Third, the Civil Code dictates additional rules on agreements for the creditor's satisfaction. After entering into such agreements, the debtor must enter into a liquidation procedure when the debt is not duly paid off. The procedure is divided into two categories. The first one is the liquidation of disposition, whereby the creditor has priority to be paid from the proceeds obtained from the auction or sale of the secured property. The second category is ownership liquidation, whereby the mortgagee acquires the ownership of mortgaged property and then refunds the debtor or gets compensation from the debtor in case of difference between the value of the property and the debt.

Fourth, the Civil Code determines the priority of payment in case of multiple security interests over the same property.[6] Under article 414 of the Civil Code, where a property is mortgaged to two or more creditors who have all registered their mortgages, the order of payment from the proceeds obtained from auction or sale of the mortgaged property is based on the priority in time of registration.

Fifth, the Civil Code expands the scope of the security contract, which is of great significance to recognize innominate security rights, following the approach embraced by the Uniform Commercial Code in the U.S. to widen the use of property as security. The Civil Code recognizes that the retention of ownership, financial leases, factoring contracts and other methods of using property as a security function are to be included in the scope of security interests after their registration. All these measures have helped achieve the modernization of security interests law.[7]

Sixth, the Civil Code expands the scope of secured property to encourage the development of new forms of securities, and further recognizes security interests in assembled property and in future property.

4.5 *Rules to Regulate and Prevent Sexual Harassment*

The special provisions for sexual harassments under the Civil Code has attracted much attention both domestically and internationally.[8] Sexual harassment is defined as any act committed against another person's will by oral or written language, images, physical acts, or the like with sexual orientation and degrading to his or her dignity,[9] which is now explicitly prohibited by article 1010.

---

6 See Gao Shengping, 'On the Relative Prohibition of Lex Commissoria', (2018) 1 J Pol Sci and L (2018) 1:72–82 (高圣平, 论流质契约的相对禁止,《政法论丛》).

7 See Jing Zhang, 'Functional Reform of the Chinese Law of Secured Transactions in Movables from a Comparative Perspective' (2022) 86 RabelsZ 119–165.

8 "Over the years, there have been important legislative and judicial reforms. On gender equality, I welcome revision of the Law on Protecting Women's Rights and Interests, which should bring about several improvements for protection of women's rights. I also commend the recent reform of the Civil Code that introduced provisions on sexual harassment as well as the anti-domestic violence law that provides for restraining orders to protect women and children at risk. Of course, as in every country, implementation is key, so it will be important for the authorities to be vigilant in that regard and respond to concerns about how the law is applied in practice". Statement by UN High Commissioner for Human Rights Michelle Bachelet after official visit to China, https://www.ohchr.org/en/statements/2022/05/statement-un-high-commissioner-human-rights-michelle-bachelet-after-official (last visited: December 1, 2022).

9 See Christian von Bar, Eric Clive, Hans Schulte-Nölke, *Principles, Definitions and Model Rules of European Private Law: Draft Common Frame of Reference* (DCFR) (Sellier 2009).

The Civil Code specifies the following essential elements for establishing sexual harassment. First, the harassment must be realized through a verbal, written, graphic, or physical act relating to sex, such as sending another person a text, a voice-message or a recorded material having sexual content or sexual innuendo. Second, the harassment must be directed to a specific person. The term "against another person" refers to acts addressed deliberately at a specific person. Third, the act must be realized "against the will of the victim", meaning that it should not correspond to the interests of the victim or be expressly rejected by the latter. The consent of a victim under coercion shall be regarded as the act against the will of the victim.

In addition, the Civil Code also emphasizes the obligation of the entities to take preventive measures so as to prevent harassment. Article 1010(2) clearly provides that State organs, enterprises, schools and other organizations have the obligation to prevent sexual harassment and therefore to adopt reasonable prevention measures. All of which promote the protection of the legitimate rights and interests of those employees, as well as students, in order to achieve comprehensive multi-level social prevention of sexual harassment.

4.6 *The 'Green Principle' and Enhanced Ecological and Environmental Protection*

The Book on the General Part of the Civil Code establishes the so-called 'Green Principle' as one of the underlying fundamental principles, stressing the need to save natural resources and to strengthen ecological and environmental protection. The Green Principle is further enshrined by several rules, especially in the Books on Real Rights, on Contracts and on Tort Liability. It is in the latter where most significant provisions in this regard are to be found.

Book Seven of the Civil Code now provides many rules on liability for ecological and environmental damage. Under the Tort Law of 2009 that was previously regulating the issue in China, the chapter on liability for environmental pollution mainly aimed to protect private interests, and therefore did not respond to the need for establishing a comprehensive protection of the environment and the ecology. This need is addressed by the rules on liability for environmental pollution and ecological damage in the Book on Tort Liability of the Civil Code. Although pollution often harms private interests, such as those holding a contractual right over a piece of land when the soil is polluted, it is actually more harmful to the public interest, insofar as it entails a decrease of the quality of the ecological environment.[10] Consequently, the

10 See Gong Gu, 'Reflections on the Nature of Environmental Civil Public Interest Litigation' (2019) 3 Chinese J L 127 (巩固, 环境民事公益诉讼性质定位省思,《法学研究》).

Book on Tort Liability establishes a public interest litigation rule with regard to environmental damage.

The Civil Code also provides for a duty of restoration to the original conditions. Under article 1234 of the Civil Code, restoration can be provided either by the tortfeasor himself or by State authorized agencies (directly or through others). Given the facts that the restoration of ecological damage is often a technically complex activity, which may cause extra damages, it is often feasible that restoration is carried out by State authorized agencies, subject to reasonable cost and necessity. Any reasonable expense thus incurred shall be borne by the tortfeasor.

Finally, it is very well-known that in this field it often happens that enterprises gain profit by polluting the environment, while the government pays for environmental restoration. Therefore, article 1232 of the Civil Code now provides for punitive damages in case of environmental pollution and ecological damage. According to this article, tortfeasors who violate the provisions of laws and intentionally cause environmental pollution or ecological damage, resulting in serious consequences, shall be liable for punitive damages.

5 Conclusion

The development of civil law in China needs to follow, and respond to, domestic culture, customs and economic situations. To this purpose, classic rules and principles enshrined in the Civil Codes of many civil law jurisdictions can be transplanted into the Chinese legal system, but then have to be transformed and even transcended. Even when some legal provisions are literally borrowed from other legal systems, their meaning cannot but be construed and applied in light of the specificities of the context to which they apply. In other words, legal borrowing in the Civil Code is not a mere imitation of established institutions, but a process of learning, adaptation and innovation that reflects the interests of people and the evolving needs of society through time.

Since the implementation of the Civil Code, the previous statutes dealing with civil law issues, such as the Contract Law and the Real Right Law, were repealed, while the related judicial interpretations have been gradually renovated. The Chinese legislature has already initiated the annulment, enactment, modification and interpretation of other statutes to align them with the Civil Code. Meanwhile, the Supreme People's Court has also made efforts to renovate previous judicial interpretations and issuing new judicial interpretations according to the Code. Chinese scholars, officials, judges and lawyers are working to implement the Civil Code and to promote its integration and systematic application. Predictably, the body of civil laws in China will be further enriched and completed in the years to come, responding to the practical demands of China and further promoting the scientific prosperity of Chinese civil law.

PART 2

The Inner Contents of the Chinese Civil Code

CHAPTER 4

The General Part of the Civil Code of the PRC: Formulation, Structure and Features

薛军 *Xue Jun*

1 Introduction

The Civil Code of the People's Republic of China, promulgated on May 28, 2020 (hereinafter, unless otherwise specified, referred to as the 'Civil Code', with the Civil Codes of other countries expressly indicated), is divided into seven books. Book One contains the General Part, while the other books deal with Real Rights, Contracts, Personality Rights, Marriage and Family, Succession, and Tort Liability. The so called 'general part-specific parts' structure of the Civil Code is obviously influenced by the German Civil Code. But how did such influence occur? What changes have been made to the general part of the German style during the process of compilation in China? How should we evaluate these changes? What are some distinctive contents in the General Part of the Civil Code that have been highly valued theoretically? These questions are all worthy of further research. To answer these questions, this paper will describe the context, the features and the debates around Book One.

2 History of the General Part

Historically, modern China learned from the European civil law model to formulate its own Civil Code in the process of reforming the Chinese traditional legal system. In 1907, the Qing government attempted to compile a European-style Civil Code and regarded it as the most important measure for the reform of its traditional legal system. In 1911, the Draft Civil Code of the Qing Dynasty was completed. However, the 1911 Revolution overthrew the Qing Dynasty, and this Draft was not officially promulgated.[1] The compilation of a civil code based on the Civilian tradition, finally succeeded during the period of the Republic of China government. From 1929 to 1930, the Republic of China Government

1 Zhang Jinfan, *The Tradition and Modern Transition of Chinese Law* (Springer 2014) 652.

 | DOI:10.1163/9789004704428_005

promulgated the complete Civil Code. This Civil Code, which was heavily influenced by the German Civil Code, is still in force in the Chinese special territory, Taiwan. Meanwhile, in 1949 when the People's Republic of China was founded, all laws promulgated by the Republic of China Government, including the Civil Code, were abolished. Therefore, after 1949, China once again needed to compile a new civil code. Unfortunately, all the attempts to do so, failed due to different causes at the time. After the 1990s, especially from 1992 onwards, when the Communist Party of China proposed the goal of "building the socialist system of laws with Chinese characteristics", Chinese legislators began to expedite their work in the civil and commercial fields. The Contract Law[2] formulated in 1999 was an important achievement concerning legislation in the field of civil law sector. Following the promulgation of this law, scholars were highly encouraged to study the compilation of the Civil Code. Around 2000, Chinese civil law scholars discussed the compilation of China's Civil Code, which eventually led to the establishment of a "Civil Code Drafting Working Group"[3] by the Chinese legislator. A draft of the civil law was formulated in 2002, and a formal deliberation took place at the Standing Committee of the National People's Congress.[4] However, this deliberation was more important symbolically than practically, because the legislative work in this regard went back to the previous model of 'separate legislation' (under which 'a law will be formulated only after its previous one becomes well-established') at a later time. For example, after the promulgation of the Contract Law in 1999, the Property Law was formulated in 2007, and the Tort Liability Law was put in act

2 The Contract Law promulgated in 1999 superseded the previous Economic Contract Law, Technological Contract Law, and Foreign Economic Contract Law, and thus is called as Uniform Contract Law.

3 On January 13, 1998, Wang Hanbin, the then Vice Chairman of the Standing Committee of the People's Congress, invited civil law scholars including Wang Jiafu, Jiang Ping, Wang Baoshu, Liang Huixing and Wang Liming to start a panel discussion over the Civil Code's drafting. All attendees unanimously believed that the conditions for drafting the Civil Code were present. Wang Hanbin, therefore, decided to immediately resume the Civil Code's codification, and entrusted Wang Jiafu, Jiang Ping, Wei Zhenying, Wang Baoshu, Liang Huixing, Wang Liming, Fei Zongyi, Xiao Xun and Wei Yaorong to form the Civil Code Drafting Working Group, and so to draft the Civil Code.

4 On December 23, 2002, the 31st session of the 9th Standing Committee of the National People's Congress considered the draft civil law for the first time. This draft was composed of 9 books, namely the General Part, Property Law, Contract Law, Personality Right Law, Marriage Law, Adoption Law, Law of Succession, Tort Liability Law and Law on Choice of Law for Foreign-related Civil Relationships, with 1,209 articles in total. Among others, the Contract Law, the Marriage Law, the Adoption Law and the Law of Succession are prevailing laws, while the Property Law, the Personality Right Law and the Tort Liability Law are new ones.

in 2009. With the promulgation of a series of separate laws in the field of civil law sector, the necessity of codifying a civil code was obviously reduced. In 2010, China had in place several separate and special laws such as the Marriage Law, the Law of Succession, the Contract Law, the Property Law, and the Tort Liability Law, in addition to the General Principles of the Civil Law formulated in 1986. These separate laws covered all the fields a traditional Civil Code could cover. Around 2014, although some civil law scholars still called for the codification of the Civil Code, most scholars believed that it was an impractical idea and of little practical significance considering the real situation.

The turning point came on October 20–23 in 2014, when the Fourth Plenary Session of the 18th CPC Central Committee was held. At this session, the Resolution of the Central Committee of the Communist Party of China on Major Issues Concerning the Enhancement of all-round Law-based Governance was approved. This resolution explicitly brought forward the task of 'codifying the Civil Code'. After this, the codification of the Civil Code proceeded rapidly, and a specific timetable was given. As a result, the previous debate over whether it was necessary to codify China's Civil Code ended abruptly. Scholars focusing on civil law immediately threw themselves into the work of the codification. This suggests that the codification had a prominent 'political-driven' feature. When politicians set the codification of the Civil Code as a political task to be accomplished within a given period, the relevant academic discussions could only be carried out on this established premise. This special background, which profoundly influenced the choices made during the codification of the Civil Code in many aspects, has a bearing on the current features of the Civil Code.

At the beginning of the Civil Code's codification, a 'two-step' project was determined. According to this project, the codification of the Civil Code's General Part was first finished in 2017, while that of its specific books finished in 2020, after which both parts were combined together to compose a complete Civil Code. Seemingly tight, this deadline was not as difficult to meet as imagined. Regarding these specific books, with the exception of the book of Personality Rights, which was totally new, the rest went through partial revision and perfection based on their previously existing separate legislation. Likewise, the Civil Code's General Part was codified on the basis of the General Principles of the Civil Law formulated in 1986.

As such, there is a world of difference between the nature and functions of the General Principles of the Civil Law, and the Civil Code's General Part. The former was formulated under a special context. In the early 1980s, China embarked on reform and opening, when its rule of law system was re-established. At that time, there were several abortive attempts to codify the Civil Code in the field of civil legislation. The main cause for their lack of success is that the nature of the Civil Code made it unable to adapt to the fast changing social and economic systems. To meet the needs of the social and economic activities for basic rules of civil law, legislators at that time decided to formulate the General Principles of the Civil Law, which functioned as a 'minimalist version' of a Civil Code, with only 156 articles in total. Now that separate works on Property Law, Contract Law and Tort Liability Law have been subsequently formulated, those parts in the General Principles of the Civil Law involving real rights, contract and tort liability are no longer applicable.

Nonetheless, the main content of the General Principles of the Civil Law, namely the provisions on civil subjects (natural persons and legal persons), juristic acts and limitation of action, share similarities with those in the German Civil Code's General Part. This explains why the General Principles of the Civil Law has been selected naturally as a basis for codifying the Civil Code's General Part. This is also reflected in the fact that the basic structure of the Civil Code's General Part is roughly identical to that of the General Principles of the Civil Law, despite their total divergence on the matters they respectively handle.

This further leads to a question: why could the General Principles of the Civil Law be used as a reference, almost as a whole, to the Civil Code's General Part? Historically, at the time of their drafting, the General Principles of the Civil Law were influenced by the following factors. Firstly, political factors played a role. Specifically, the Civil Code of the Russian Soviet Federated Socialist Republic of 1922, the Principles of Civil Legislation of the Soviet Union and the Union Republics of 1961, and the New Civil Code of the Russian Soviet Federated Socialist Republic of 1964, which influenced the civil legislation at the early stages of China's reform and opening. These influences continued until the early 1990s. The civil legislation of the Soviet Union was also deeply influenced by the German model, which further led to the 'indirect' influence on China's legislation at its initial stages of reform and opening. Secondly, jurists who received their legal education before 1949 became more influential during the period of reform and opening, and had a great influence on the civil legislative works in the Chinese mainland; the legal education of these jurists had been heavily influenced by the study of German and Japanese laws. Thirdly, since China's reform and opening in the 1980s, the civil law theory in Taiwan of China began to exert its influence on the mainland. Some renowned Taiwan-based civil law scholars (Shi Shangkuan, Zheng Yubo, Wang Zejian, and others) had their civil law-themed books circulating in Mainland China, where they gained extensive influence. Yet still, the civil law theory in Taiwan of China was also influenced by the German model. China's civil legislation has therefore been influenced by the German model over a long period. Some scholars had noted that the adoption of the German-style's general part in the process of the Civil Code's codification might turn out problematic;[5] however, in general China's Civil Code codifiers had never seriously considered abandoning the 'General-Specific' legislative structure that is typical of the German style. Once it was decided that there must be a German counterpart's general part in the Civil Code, the main content of the General Principles of the Civil Law was referenced. In this way, it was almost natural to take the General Principles of the Civil Law as the basis for codifying the Civil Code's General Part.

Finally, an additional factor that played a role in the process of Civil Code's codification, is the respect for the guiding principle that the legislation that proved its success in civil legislation since 1978, should always be kept in place. Since its promulgation, the General Principles of the Civil Law have been highly praised as China's 'Declaration of Civil-law Rights'. This also explains why it was more than reasonable to maintain the structure and system of the General Principles of the Civil Law in the codification of the Civil Code's General Part.

3 Structural Arrangement and Possible Explanation of the General Part

With regard to its macro-structure, the Civil Code's General Part is composed of a total of ten chapters. Chapter I introduces the General Provisions, Chapter II and Chapter III describe Natural Persons and Legal Persons respectively, Chapter IV introduces Unincorporated Organizations, Chapter V and Chapter VI list Civil-law Rights and Civil Juristic Acts respectively, Chapter VII describes Agency, Chapter VIII introduces Civil Liability, Chapter IX refers to Limitation of Action, and Chapter X describes Counting Periods of Time. These ten chapters have 204 articles in total. Based on civil law scholars' generalization of all these contents of the General Part, the logic of the General Part's system structure can be explained from the following perspectives.

Firstly, the General Part is based on the notion of civil juristic relationship. The so-called civil juristic relationship refers to a specific type of social relationship, which is extracted from various types of social relationships and regulated by legislators based on certain standards. It is regulated by vesting corresponding persons of the civil law with a series of civil-law rights and duties. In the exercise of rights and performance of duties, the civil law

5 See Wei Zhenying, 'Which General Principles of the Civil Code Do We Need—Comparison with German Civil Code' (2016) 3 Northern Leg Sci 5–19 (魏振瀛, 我们需要什么样的民法总则—与德国民法比较，《北方法学》).

regulates social life. As for the nature and scope of social relationships regulated by the Civil Code, article 2 clearly stipulates that "[t]he civil law regulates personal and proprietary relationships among the persons of the civil law, namely, natural persons, legal persons, and unincorporated organizations that are equal in status". This article has demarcated the scope of social relationships regulated by the Civil Code. A juristic relationship is generally composed of the subject, content and object. The subject of a civil juristic relationship is persons of the civil law, which is reflected in Chapter II, III and IV of the Civil Code's General Part. These three chapters respectively stipulate three types of persons of the civil law (i.e. natural persons, legal persons and unincorporated organizations). The content of a civil juristic relationship mainly appears to be a series of civil-law rights and duties. The provisions in this regard are mainly shown in the Civil Code's Chapter V "Civil-law Rights", where a variety of civil-law rights are listed. Those provisions on juristic acts and agency in Chapter VI and VII can be regarded as 'dynamic' dimensions of a civil juristic relationship, that is, the provisions on civil juristic acts, namely targeting an important type of "juristic facts" that can lead to the creation, alteration, or termination of a civil juristic relationship. "Limitation" and "Period" are also provided for on juristic facts.

Secondly, there is a legal norm logic based on the so-called "Rights, Duties and Liabilities". This mainly explains why there is a unique chapter of "Civil Liability" in both the General Principles of the Civil Law and the Civil Code's General Part. According to this theory, any legal norm is a legal rule (vesting legal rights and imposing statutory obligations) by the legislator aimed at specific actors, who will be subject to legal liabilities if they violate the rule. The emphasis on "legal liability" is a prominent feature of many pieces of legislation in China. Structurally, many Chinese laws stipulate how the relevant actor shall act under certain circumstances, with the final chapter of the law typically dedicated to "legal liabilities". This typical structure has an impact on the General Principles of the Civil Law. Legislators at that time understood 'Civil Law' as a law like other ones and took it for granted that the Civil Law's last chapter should be 'Civil (Legal) Liability' for violating civil law provisions. After the General Principles of the Civil Law was formulated, some scholars tried to interpret such a structure theoretically, believing that Chinese civil law's basic system was made up of 'civil-law rights/civil-law duties/civil liability'.[6] However, such interpretation faced many difficulties. Provisions on civil

---

6 See Feng Jue, 'A Theoretical Reflection on the Positioning and Function of the Civil Liability System in China' (2022) 4 Tribune Pol Sci and L 72–86 (冯珏, 我国民事责任体系定位与功能之理论反思《政法论坛》).

liability in the General Principles of the Civil Law combined various claims with different natures and constituent elements, and therefore posed serious problems both in theory and practice. With the promulgation of the Contract Law, the Property Law and the Tort Liability Law, the provisions on civil liability in the General Principles of the Civil Law became meaningless. Nonetheless, the structure of the General Principles of the Civil Law was referenced totally to codify the Civil Code's General Part. For this reason, "Civil Liability" as an independent chapter was maintained as a structure arrangement in the Civil Code's General Part. Nevertheless, an in-depth analysis of this chapter reveals a lot of problems; for many, the presence of this chapter is a notable defect in the structure of the Civil Code's General Part.[7]

At its source, the reason why the General Principles of the Civil Law has this chapter is because, at that time, the legislators had not fully recognized that, as private law, the main characteristic of civil law is not to establish a series of mandatory rules of conduct for private actors. Therefore, differently from what happens for other laws with public law attributes, it is not appropriate to adopt the usual legislative mode of providing rules on 'Legal Liability' in the last chapter. Over four decades after the promulgation of the General Principles of the Civil Law, both theoretical research and judicial practice have proved that civil-law rights of different types have corresponding rules of legal claims. Different sorts of civil liabilities have unique functions and constituent elements, and it is meaningless to combine them together into one chapter.

Thirdly, the structure of the Civil Code's General Part, theoretically supported by Chinese mainstream civil scholars, is based on the so-called legislative technique of 'extracting the common factor'. In other words, the General Part is essential in the structure of the Civil Code, as it provides for common issues involved in specific books of the Civil Code all together to avoid repetition. This is the main reason for the Civil Code's 'General-Specific' structure. According to such a theory, the most core element of the Civil Code's General Part is the juristic act system. As the core of juristic acts, the system of expressions of intent is involved in the fields of real rights, rights *in personam*, marriage and family, and succession, and thus it is appropriate to cover it in the General Part. Similarly, the scope of civil law regulation, the basic principles, the legal sources, the civil actors, and the civil rights covered by the Civil Code, also deserve to be regulated in the General Part. In a sense, the Civil Code's General Part with juristic acts as its core, is the most notable feature of the

7 See Wei Zhenying, 'On the Civil Liability System in the Civil Code' (2001) Peking U L J 356 (魏振瀛，论民法典中的民事责任体系《中外法学》).

German Civil Code's structure. In this regard, China's Civil Code has indeed learned from the German one.

However, even in China, there was no general agreement as to whether the German-style highly abstract juristic act system was an appropriate legislative model to be followed. Critics believed that there were many differences among different types of juristic acts, such as between the juristic acts in the fields of property law and marriage law, between unilateral and bilateral juristic acts, as well as the acts of making resolutions in company law, and between the acts inter-vivos and mortis causa. Therefore, it was unfeasible to extract a common rule. To be more prudent, corresponding rules should be established for specific types of juristic acts. Unfortunately, such critical opinions failed to have any bearing on the legislation. The main reason is that, if the unified category of juristic acts was extracted from the General Part, the German-style general part would have little content, and thus could be replaced by the so-called preamble book. As such, the Civil Code would have to be significantly re-structured, yet most Chinese civil scholars were used to the German-style civil code's general part, and therefore did not support such re-structuring.[8]

So far, we have analyzed three models of theoretical interpretation of the structure of the Civil Code's General Part given by Chinese civil law scholars. These theories attempt to explain why there is currently such a Civil Code's General Provisions and why it contains said contents. But strictly speaking, the decisive factor which has bearing on the establishment and content coverage of it, is the 'path dependency' effect on the Civil Code's codification imposed by the legislative pattern formed before its codification. The codification of China's Civil Code is more, in nature, a 'restatement' ranging between code codification and a pure law compilation. At the outset, the codifiers of it always stressed 'continuity', namely to keep those contents that were deemed successful in the existing civil legislations. Some improvements were introduced only to the extent that they were strictly necessary and mainly at the level of specific rules. Such an idea of codifying the Civil Code inevitably led to the adoption of the overall structure of its blueprint – General Principles of the Civil Law in its General Part.

8 Xue Jun, 'General Principles of Civil Law: Background, Problems and Prospects' (2017) 3 ECUPL J 6–17 (薛军, 民法总则:背景、问题与展望《华东政法大学学报》).

4 Preliminary Analysis on Important Rules of the Chinese Civil Code's General Part

About specific system rules, the Chinese Civil Code's General Part is distinctive mainly in the following areas: the chapter on "General Provisions" (Section 4.1); the regulation of persons (Section 4.2), of civil law rights (Section 4.3) and of civil juristic acts (Section 4.4); the rules on agency (Section 4.5), civil liability (Section 4.6) and limitation of action (Section 4.7).

4.1 *The General Provisions*

Chapter I of the Civil Code's General Part describes the General Provisions.

Article 1 of the Civil Code stipulates the purpose of the legislation, and outlines two points: "carrying forward the core socialist values" and "in accordance with the Constitution of the People's Republic of China". There has been heated debate surrounding these two points. First, whether the core values and related expressions could be resorted to in the interpretation of the Civil Code's articles.[9] From an abstract perspective, the purpose of the legislation stipulated in article 1 of the Civil Code, can serve as an important basis for the interpretation of the legal rules contained within it. But since a series of basic principles have been provided for in Chapter I of the Civil Code's General Part, interpretation of law can be based on related basic principles, so as to achieve the same purpose. Excessive reliance on so called "core values" to interpret laws may lead to uncertainties. In judicial practice, a relatively stable precedent system has been formed for interpreting the law and filling gaps by relying on the basic principles of civil law, which is conducive to stability and predictability. From the perspective of comparative law, it also facilitates the exchange of legal knowledge and experience across legal fields.

To formulate the Civil Code "in accordance with the Constitution of the People's Republic of China" requires consideration of the debate over the relationship between civil law and the Constitution in civil law theory. A mainstream view of civil law scholars holds that, despite its own particularity, the Civil Code is still within the scope of legal order established by the Constitution and takes the Constitution as its basis of legitimacy.[10] In this regard, amongst

9 See Cui Jianyuan, 'Institutional Innovation and Historical Significance of China's "General Principles of Civil Law"' (2017) 3 J Comp L 180–192 (崔建远, 我国〈民法总则〉的制度创新及历史意义《比较法研究》).

10 See Ning Kaihui, 'The Constitutional Value of China's "Civil Code"' (2020) 4 J Jianghan U (Soc Sci Edition) 5–14 (宁凯惠, 我国〈民法典〉的宪法价值,《江汉大学学报（社会科学版）》).

the means of interpretation of civil law, there is a so-called method of 'constitutionality interpretation', which means interpretation of the civil law rules on the basis of the Constitution. However, given the lack of constitutional precedents in China, it is difficult to develop civil law by virtue of constitutional precedents in the Chinese context.

Article 2, in Chapter 1 of the Civil Code's General Part, stipulates "civil law's regulated objects", such as the spheres covered by the Civil Code. This is a legislative technique frequently adopted by Chinese legislators to create and distinguish between different legal sectors. As previously mentioned, the provision defines civil law's scope and its boundary with other laws stating that "[t]he civil law regulates personal and proprietary relationships among the persons of the civil law, namely, natural persons, legal persons, and unincorporated organizations that are equal in status". In China's practice, there is uncertainty in the understanding of the category of "persons that are equal in status"; the category turns often out to be problematic when the State acts as a party to the juristic relationship. The most typical example is a contract for the transfer of the right to use land for construction purposes, in which the state is the transferor, and the real estate developer is the other party of the contract. As a result, there are major disputes about whether this contract is a civil or administrative one, and which legal proceedings, civil or administrative litigation, should be applied in case of dispute. According to the mainstream view, although the State is an actor endowed with public power, when it enters into a contract as a person with equal status to the other party it is acting within the civil law's regulated objects, so that the aforesaid contract falls within the scope of civil matters.

Another highlight of Chapter 1 of the Civil Code's General Part is its list of a series of civil law's basic principles in articles 3–9. These principles include the protection of civil-law rights and interests (article 3), the principle of equality (article 4), the principle of voluntariness (article 5), the principle of fairness (article 6), the principle of good faith (article 7), the principle of public order and good morals (article 8) and the principle of conservation of resources and protection of the ecological environment (article 9). On a worldwide basis, it is very distinctive to provide so many principles at the beginning of the Civil Code. Yet such a practice has existed earlier in the General Principles of the Civil Law, which is also common in China's legislation. A problem underlying this list is that, despite its length, the principles of protection of civil-law rights and interests, equality, voluntariness and fairness are either included in other rules without having their separate connotations or absorbed into other principles. Out of so many principles, the ones that are really valued in both theory and practice are those of good faith and of public order and good morals.

As to legal sources, article 10 of the Civil Code's General Part stipulates that "[c]ivil disputes shall be resolved in accordance with law. Where the law does not specify, custom may be applied, provided that public order and good morals may not be offended". Any civil code's term concerning legal sources is eye-catching since it reflects whether the civil code's legal source system is closed or open. Compared with European civil codes, especially the German Civil Code, the Swiss Civil Code, and the Italian Civil Code, we have to admit that there is an obvious defect in this legal source clause of China's Civil Code. Law is the primary legal source, and custom can serve as a supplementary legal source when certain conditions are met. However, in practice, it is not uncommon for situations to arise in which there are neither legal provisions, nor corresponding customs. How shall a judge make decision in such a case? Many Chinese civil law scholars proposed the introduction of 'jurisprudence' as a further third-ranked supplementary legal source.[11] But legislators did not accept such a proposal. As a result the supplementary legal sources in China's Civil Code need to be established through interpretation. Given the provisions of a series of civil law's basic principles in Chapter I of the Civil Code's General Part, these principles can, when specific conditions are met, be applied in civil cases. This implies that if there is no explicit norm (i.e., no statutory or customary norm), a judge can apply the basic principles stipulated by the Civil Code to handle the case. However, in order to apply basic principles to concrete cases, the judge would still need some guidance in form of paths of argumentation and legal reasoning.

4.2 *Civil Law Persons*

Chapters II, III and IV of the Civil Code's General Part provides for persons of the civil law, respectively involving natural persons, legal persons, and unincorporated organizations. Compared with previous legislation, the Civil Code has made some important changes.

In the "Natural Persons" chapter, a noteworthy normative change is the adjustment of the age standard for natural persons having limited capacity for performing civil juristic acts. According to previous legislation, natural persons under the age of ten had no capacity for performing civil juristic acts, those aged between ten and eighteen had limited capacity, and those above eighteen years of age had full capacity. The Civil Code has changed the age from ten to

11 See Yi Jun, 'On "jurisprudence" as the source of civil law' (2022) 1 Modern Leg Sci 79–93 (易军, 论作为民法法源的"法理",《现代法学》).

eight years. The purpose of doing so seems to be expanding the space where minors can perform autonomous acts.

The Civil Code has also strengthened the protection of fetuses. Article 16 of the Civil Code stipulates that "[a] fetus is deemed as having the capacity for enjoying civil-law rights in estate succession, acceptance of gift, and other situations where protection of a fetus's interests is involved". The protection of fetuses was mainly limited to their succession rights in the previous legislation. Compared with previous provisions, this term expands the range of protection of their interests. However, there remains a dispute in the specific extent to which such a range is expanded.[12] For example, when it comes to issues such as compensation for housing demolition and relocation, whether a fetus is also presumed as a legal actor and enjoys corresponding rights and interests, is also an important issue. Considering the significant changes in China's population growth trend, a more relaxed legal interpretation that favors the interests of fetuses would clearly be more appropriate.

Some provisions on natural persons in the Civil Code try to respond to issues incurred by China's rapidly aging population. One example is the adult guardianship system stipulated in article 33 of the Civil Code that "[a]n adult with full capacity for performing civil juristic acts may, in anticipation of incapacity in the future, consult his close relatives, or other individuals or organizations willing to be his guardian, and appoint in writing a guardian for himself, who shall perform the duties of guardian when the adult loses all or part of the capacity for performing civil juristic acts". This provision secures that when an adult loses all or part of the capacity for performing acts, he can independently choose and appoint their guardian. With the arrival of the era of aging, a large elderly population who are unable to look after themselves is expected. The appointment of their guardians is quite critical. Given the long-term implementation of the one-child policy in China, the elderly's offspring may, if deemed as the elderly's only guardian, bear a heavy burden. In such a case, with the help of the adult guardianship system, the range of eligible guardians can be properly expanded, which is an achievement of great importance.

The Civil Code's provisions on legal persons are of little value in general. This is because, as for legal persons of the commercial nature, the most important norms are included in laws on commercial organizations, such as the Companies Law, while for juridical associations of the non-commercial

---

12 See Yang Guoqiang, 'On the Judicial Protection of the Rights and Interests of the Fetus – From the Perspective of the Fetus' Right to Claim Compensation for Damage' (2020) 19 Ind & Sci Tribune 31–33 (杨国强, 论胎儿权益的司法保护——以胎儿的损害赔偿请求权为视角,《产业与科技论坛》).

nature, there are many legal norms of administrative nature. In terms of the system, the most notable characteristic of the Civil Code's provisions on legal persons lies in abandoning the traditional division in civil law systems between juridical associations and consortium legal persons, and adopting a division between for-profit legal persons and non-profit legal persons instead. Such a division corresponds to China's dualistic administrative system. Specifically, for-profit legal persons are regulated following the model of commercial organizations; an overall encouraging attitude is taken towards these persons. By contrast, non-profit legal persons are subject to strict supervision, especially in their registration process, which must go through strict review and approval. It is worth mentioning that according to the second paragraph of article 92 of the Civil Code, a site legally established to hold religious activities may be registered as a legal person and attain the status of an endowed legal person. This provision has solved the long-lasting issue of religious sites' ambiguous legal status. Previously, there have been religious sites established as commercial companies to gain an independent legal status – a practice which was heavily criticised,[13] and thus should not happen again.

Special legal persons include State-organ legal persons as mainly referred to in previous legislation. Since the Chinese legislation does not explicitly recognize the division of public and private legal persons, it must adopt the concept of special legal persons to deal with such legal persons of a special nature. According to article 96 of the Civil Code, State-organ legal persons, rural economic collective legal persons, urban and rural cooperative economic organization legal persons, and primary-level self-governing organization legal persons are special types of legal persons. The range of legal persons included in the category of special legal persons is thus deeply varied. It is also worth mentioning that rural economic collective legal persons, and urban and rural cooperative economic organization legal persons have clear characteristics of cooperative legal persons.

4.3 *Civil Law Rights*

Chapter v of the Civil Code's General Part provides for civil-law rights. The main function of this chapter is to enumerate the major types of rights involved in civil law; thus, the chapter is full of legislative definitions of various civil-law rights. One of the Civil Code's key characteristics is to provide legislative definitions of some basic concepts in civil law. Considering the relationship

13 See Mo Jihong, 'On the legal status of religious organizations in China' (2009) 16 Jinling L Rev 36–46. (莫纪宏，论我国宗教组织的法律地位《金陵法律评论》).

between the General Part and the subsequent specific provisions, some of the provisions of Chapter V have incurred criticism. For example, the second paragraph of article 114 defines real rights, article 115 provides for the objects of real rights, article 116 sets the *numerus clausus* principle, and article 117 deals with the expropriation and requisition systems. Thus, it is difficult to find a convincing reason as to why these provisions are part of the real right system contained in the General Part, rather than in the book of Real Rights. In previous legislation, these provisions were also covered by the Property Law. The only explanation must be that, based on the rationale of building a systematic structure, irrelevant provisions were deliberately pieced together to justify the usefulness of setting one independent chapter on "Civil-Law Rights".

Of course, there are also some innovations in Chapter V that have triggered the research interest. One example is the reference to "data and online virtual assets" in article 127. Although the article vaguely stipulates that "[w]here there are laws particularly providing for the protection of data and online virtual assets, such provisions shall be followed", it is deemed to be the Civil Code's response to the development of the Internet information technology. Many discussions about the civil law's protection of data are based on this provision. Another of these much-discussed rules is article 132 on the prohibition of the abuse of rights: "[n]o person of the civil law shall abuse his civil-law rights and harm the interests of the state, the public interests, or the lawful rights and interests of others". The prohibition of abuse of rights is not taken as one of the civil law's basic principles, and as such it is not provided in Chapter I of the Civil Code's General Part. Instead, it is considered as a rule for exercising rights, and thus it is provided for in Chapter V on Civil-law Rights. Given that the issue of the reasonable boundaries for exercising certain civil law rights is getting increasingly prominent in some new types of rights, such a rule will inevitably have significant practical value.

4.4 *Civil Juristic Acts*

Chapter VI of the Civil Code's General Part describes civil juristic acts. As analyzed above, in the system of German-style civil code's general part, juristic acts are the fundamental legal instrument to materialize the private autonomy and are deemed to be the general part's core content. This model of interpretation is also accepted by most Chinese civil law scholars. Compared with the provisions on juristic acts in the General Principles of the Civil Law, Chapter VI of the Civil Code contains more contents in this regard. Likewise, the rules on the expression of intent are part of the new content within the aforementioned chapter. Due to the limited length of this paper, only a few issues which have been regarded as key concerns by the Chinese civil law academic community can be discussed.

In article 133 of the Civil Code, the definition of a civil juristic act has a major difference in comparison with that of the General Principles of the Civil Law: the 'legitimacy' is no longer taken as a feature of civil juristic acts. Such a change is of little importance in practice, but is deemed as an important development in the understanding of the nature of juristic acts. As a direct consequence, the Civil Code also defines invalid and revocable juristic acts as juristic acts, which, in the system of the General Principles of the Civil Law, are considered as civil (but not juristic) acts, due to their defects in legitimacy.

In the Civil Code's provisions on juristic acts, a variety of defects in the expression of intent are enumerated in detail, alongside the effects associated to them. These contents were originally a part of the Contract Law, and now are provided for in the Civil Code's General Part, thus becoming rules of general application. However, there is a problem: the rules in question are still assuming that the expression of intent occurs in contractual settings and need to be properly adjusted to be applied to non-contractual types of juristic acts, such as unilateral and multilateral juristic acts. Likewise, these rules mainly apply to the field of property law, but not entirely to the field of personal status law. Even in the field of property law, rules on juristic acts mainly apply to juristic acts concerning rights *in personam*, but often do not apply necessarily to those of the nature of real rights. The aforesaid several issues prominently show the adverse consequences of such an abstract legislative model in practice.

One of the Civil Code's provisions attracting great attention, is the rule stating that a civil juristic act in violation of the mandatory provisions of laws or offending public order or good morals is void. This is provided for in the first paragraph of article 153 of the Civil Code. Specifically, "[a] civil juristic act in violation of the mandatory provisions of laws or administrative regulations is void", unless such mandatory provisions do not lead to the invalidity of such a civil juristic act. The expression of this provision is perplexing at first glance. Such an expression suggests that, in Chinese theory and practice, mandatory provisions are further divided into regulatory ones and 'effectiveness' ones. Juristic acts (contracts mainly) are made void only when in violation of 'effectiveness' mandatory provisions; in other words, they are not void if only in violation of regulatory mandatory provisions. Understanding this context may help to understand the meaning of the first paragraph of article 153. Yet, there is a long-lasting problem that besets Chinese theory and practice – how to identify whether a certain mandatory provision is a regulatory one or an 'effectiveness' one. Despite the many theories formed in this respect, specific conclusions are still in dispute.

The second paragraph of article 153 of the Civil Code specifies what is meant by public order and good morals. At first, there was no major disagreement over this in practice. It is normally up to a judge, in accordance with mainstream public moral values, to identify whether relevant juristic acts offend public order and good morals. However, recently, China's Supreme Judicial Court has often resorted to the expression of public order and good morals to intervene on the effects of contracts that were deemed to be violating regulatory rules in the financial field. The reason why the second paragraph of article 153 is resorted to, is mainly because most financial regulatory norms are ministry level regulations rather than laws or administrative regulations, resulting in the first paragraph of article 153 of the Civil Code not being applicable to determine the invalidity of contracts. Such a new approach, while proving useful to solve some practical problems, has caused scholars' concern about whether it may give rise to significant uncertainty in judging the effectiveness of contracts.

4.5 *The Agency System*

Chapter VII of the Civil Code's General Part provides for the agency system. The Civil Code's provisions on agency basically confirm those contained in the Contract Law and General Principles of the Civil Law. Of course, there are also some normative changes. The provision in article 170 on an agent who fulfills his responsibilities is a new one, and has essentially absorbed the manager's authority theory in the commercial field. The second paragraph of article 170 provides that "[r]estrictions imposed by a legal person or an unincorporated organization on the scope of authority of a person who performs the responsibilities assigned by the legal person or unincorporated organization are not effective against a bona fide third person". This provision associates typical duties with the scope of presumed authority, increasing the certainty in legal communication.

In the agency system provided for by the Civil Code (strictly speaking, also including the former Contract Law), it is the provision on apparent authority that has caused the most concerns for scholars and incurred the largest number of issues in practice. Article 172 of the Civil Code provides that "[a]n act performed by a person without authority, beyond their authority, or after the authority is terminated is effective if the counterparty has reasons to believe that the said person has authority". The provision protects the reliance interest of the counterparty, yet neglects the interest of the said bona fide, non-negligent person. Hence, proper consideration should be given to the protection of the legitimate interests of bona fide persons when clarifying the meaning of the expression that "the counterparty has reasons to believe".

4.6 *Civil Liability*

Chapter VIII of the Civil Code's General Part concerns civil liability.

As set forth in the preceding text, this structural arrangement is based on the General Principles of the Civil Law. It makes sense if the General Principles of the Civil Law is regarded as a complete set of law, thus having the issue of legal liability in its last chapter. However, there is no real reason for keeping an independent chapter on the civil liability in the Civil Code's General Part. As a matter of fact, Chinese scholars almost turn a blind eye to this chapter. A careful examination of the specific provisions of this chapter will reveal that they either lack normative meaning or are more appropriate if provided elsewhere. Several valuable provisions would be more suitable in a chapter titled "The Exercise of Civil Rights".

4.7 *Limitation of Action*

Chapter IX of the Civil Code's General Part provides for limitation of action.

This chapter, in its macrostructure, largely repeats the relevant provisions already present in the General Principles of the Civil Law. Yet, the chapter also sensibly extends the duration of the limitation of action period, increasing it from two years to three years. This extension is reasonable, however in contrast, the causes that may lead to the interruption of the limitation of action have remained excessively broad. For example, when an obligee makes a performance request to the obligor, the request leads to the interruption of the limitation of action period. This may cause a de facto indefinite extension of the limitation period. To avoid such a case, the second paragraph of article 188 of the Civil Code stipulates that the longest limitation period is twenty years.

5 Brief Conclusions

The Chinese Civil Code's General Part is deeply influenced by the structure of its German counterpart. Such an influence can be explained due to many historical factors. The German civil code model has influenced China's civil law directly and indirectly over a long time. The Chinese Civil Code's General Part has used the structure of the General Principles of the Civil Law for reference, which is related to the fact that the Chinese Civil Code was codified mainly to reflect continuity and keep the existing legislative achievements that are deemed successful. The Civil Code's General Part has many noteworthy specific contents that reflect the response by legislators to emerging social issues (such as the aging trend) and new technological developments (especially information network technology[14]). The normative value of this part will be further expanded and confirmed by future judicial practice.

14 See Xue Jun, 'Research on Internet Tort Clauses of the Civil Code: Focusing on the Reconstruction of the Legal Interpretation Framework' (2020) 4 J Comp L 131–144 (薛军, 民法典网络侵权条款研究: 以法解释论框架的重构为中心,《比较法研究》).

CHAPTER 5

Comparative Perspectives on the General Part of the Chinese Civil Code

Pascal Pichonnaz

1 Introduction

In 1911, the Civil Code Draft of Qing (Da Qing Min Lü Cao An) was published. It has never been in use, but a complete Civil Code was enacted in 1929/1930 and was applied until 1949 when the People's Republic of China was founded. After a long process, after several independent laws, such as the Contract Law promulgated in 1999, the Property Law promulgated in 2007 and the Tort Liability Law enacted in 2009, the quest for a Civil Code seemed to fade away. Yet, a clear political endeavour moved towards a Civil Code in 2014; a Civil Code Drafting Group was set together and worked at high-speed, so that finally, on 28 May 2020, the Civil Code of the People's Republic of China (hereinafter: Chinese Civil Code or CCC) was promulgated; it came into effect on 1st January 2021.

Even if the process of codification was based on many comparative analyses, including large conferences with foreign experts,[1] the main structure of the CCC has largely been influenced by the German Civil Code, as German legal culture already constituted the principal source of inspiration for the above-mentioned specific laws, and provided a scholarly framework with which many Chinese professors and judges were familiar. For the history of this codification, I refer readers to the chapters by Ivan Cardillo and Xue Jun in this volume.[2] Yet, I had to mention these milestones, as they explain, among

1 I participated in two large comparative gatherings aimed at providing those comparative perspectives, one held at the University of Torino (Italy) on 15–16 February 2016 (see Pascal Pichonnaz, 'The Civil Codes of Switzerland from a Historical and Comparative Perspective: Some Reflections Based on the Swiss Experience', in Michele Graziadei and Lihong Zhang (eds), *The Making of the Civil Codes. A Twenty-First Century Perspective* (Springer 2023) 295–313), and another one ('Sino-European Conference on the New Chinese Civil Code') held at the University of Beijing (People's Republic of China) on 21–22 September 2019, where I presented a paper on the 'Liability for Artificial Intelligence – some thoughts'.

2 Ivan Cardillo, 'The Chinese Way to the Civil Code', and Xue Jun, 'General Part of the Civil Code of The People's Republic of China: Formulation, Structure and Features', both in this volume.

 | DOI:10.1163/9789004704428_006

other reasons, why the Chinese Civil Code cannot be considered as an entirely new product, but rather as a codification that is largely built on the many laws previously in force governing specific sectors. My aim in this paper is to highlight, in a comparative perspective, the elements of surprise and the questions that were triggered by the reading of the translated text of Book I of the Chinese Civil Code.

Contrary to some Civil Codes in Europe, such as the Swiss Civil Code (hereinafter: Swiss CC) or the French Civil Code (hereinafter: French CC), which both contain only a 'Preliminary Title' composed of ten and six provisions respectively, the Chinese Civil Code provides for a thorough general part (Book I) on 'General Provisions' composed of 204 provisions. This is similar to the German Civil Code, with its roughly 240 provisions (some have additional letters, and some have been abrogated since its enactment in 1900). It is also largely structured according to the previous 'General Principles of the Civil Law', composed of 156 articles, which were formulated in 1986.[3] As we will see, Book I, as a general part, may present some advantages, but it also opens up some risks in the application of the Code.

2 The Structure and What Is at Stake

The Chinese Civil Code is divided into seven books. Apart from Book 1 on 'General Provisions',[4] the other books are Book II on 'Property Rights', Book III on 'Contracts', Book IV on 'Personality Rights', Book V on 'Marriage and Family', Book VI on 'Inheritance', and Book VII on 'Tort Liability'. This structure is quite different from most civil codes in Europe, which to a larger or lesser extent have followed the traditional division inherited from the Roman Jurist Gaius (2nd century AD) in his *Institutiones* (160 AD) and elaborated during several centuries. This Roman-derived structure typically implies a first book on *personae* ('persons'), including guardianship and some aspects of marriage, a second book on *res* ('things'), including issues of ownership first, and then obligations (i.e., rights arising from contracts, delicts and further sources of obligations), and a third book dedicated to *actiones* ('actions'), dealing with all types of procedural aspects. The Chinese Civil Code provides for novelties. Not only does it contain a whole book dedicated to 'Personality Rights' (Book IV), but it

3 Xue Jun (n 2).

4 All translation of the Chinese Civil Code are taken from Lei Chen, Jiangqiu Ge, Jian He, Qiao Liu, Zhicheng Wu, Bingwan Xiong (eds), *The Civil Code of the People's Republic of China. English Translation* (Brill/Nijhoff 2021).

has also put apart provisions on 'Contracts' (Book III) and provisions on 'Tort Liability' (Book VII), where however one would think there might be good reasons to keep those books close to one another, especially as *Negotiorum Gestio* (unauthorized management) and *Unjustified Enrichment*, provided for by Part Three of Book III, are kept within the book on 'Contracts'. It will be interesting to see whether this structure will have an impact on the interpretation of the provisions on 'Basic Rules' and 'Damages' of 'Tort Liability' placed in Book VII. This is even more sensitive as Chapter 5 of Book I, dealing with 'Civil rights', provides specifically that "[w]here a civil right or interest is infringed, the victim has the right to claim against the tortfeasor to bear tort liability" (article 120 CCC). The provision obviously creates a link between Book I and Book VII that may reveal difficult to handle.

It is true, however, that this difficulty is not confined to tort law only. As a matter of fact, articles 119 to 122 Chinese Civil Code deal with all the sources of obligations, without mentioning them clearly, and reproduce therefore elements that appear again in the other books dedicated to those sources. Article 119 CCC provides that "[a] legally formed contract binds parties to it", which is close to article 1103 French Civil Code (former article 1134); yet, instead of being at the beginning of Book III on 'Contracts', this provision is placed in this General Part of Book I. One can therefore wonder whether this implies that one could give more significance to article 119 CCC rather than to some other provisions of Book III, dedicated to Contracts. Similarly, article 120 CCC is the general provision for tort, which is then dealt with in Book VII. Article 121 CCC deals with *negotiorum gestio* and the management of "another's business without a prior duty by operation of law or by consent, but for the purpose of avoiding loss suffered by such party", which is then dealt with in Book III. Finally, article 122 CCC is about unjustified enrichment, as the provision reads as follows: "Where a party is unjustifiably enriched without a legal basis at the expense of another, the aggrieved party has the right to claim for restitution of the enrichment acquired by the enrichee". Unjustified enrichment is however dealt with in detail in Book III. One wonders therefore whether it was really justified to have these four provisions together here, rather than at the beginning of the parts specifically dealing with them. This choice might be linked to the fact that the General Part has been influenced by the General Principles of the Civil Law of 1986, which were a segregated and self-referential legislation. Book I is, however, no more alone, but must be read in line with the rest of the Code. This being said, I will not cover here these sources of obligations, as they will be dealt with by other authors in their chapters on these specific books. I will also not deal with the further sources of civil rights mentioned at article 123–126 Chinese Civil Code, but will mainly focus on other aspects of Book I.

Book I entails 'General Provisions' and is structured around ten titles: '1. Fundamental Rules', '2. Natural Person', '3. Legal Person', '4. Unincorporated Organization', '5. Civil Right', '6. Civil Juridical Act', '7. Agency', '8. Civil Liability', '9. Limitation Period' and '10. Measurement of Time Periods'. The scope of my paper does not allow me to go in detail with all these titles. I will limit myself to some topics which have an overall importance, such as interpretation (Section 3), the notion of juridical act (Section 4), problems of false expression and misunderstanding (Section 5), followed by an analysis of some issues of agency (Section 6). Finally, I will briefly address the issue of the limitation period (Section 7). Many observations could be made about the notion of natural and legal persons, as well as of unincorporated organizations. For reasons of space, however, I will remain silent on such issues, even though some of these provisions may attract the attention of comparative scholars in the future. For instance, article 16 Chinese Civil Code provides for the protection of the interests of a fetus that goes beyond pure inheritance law aspects. Article 16 CCC states that the "fetus shall be seen as having the civil capacity to hold rights". It is unclear, however, how many days after the conception one has to consider the fertilized egg as a fetus, and whether the drafters of the Code would have made a difference between an embryo and a fetus, or whether this provision applies only to naturally or also to in-vitro fertilized fetus, to implanted or also to (still) freezed embryos. The recognition of the civil capacity to hold rights for a fetus in need for protection could be deployed broadly, at least of such provision would also cover embryos, as shown by a thorough analysis done for Swiss law.[5]

3 Interpretation and Gap-Filling of the Chinese Civil Code

Chapter 1 of Book I deals with 'Fundamental Rules'. Article 1 is about the aims and values of the Civil Code. Those values are expressed as follows "protecting the lawful rights and interests of civil subjects, governing civil relationships, maintaining the social and economic order, meeting the developmental requirements of socialism with Chinese characteristics, and upholding core socialist values". This provision is of great interest, as it shows that private law and a civil code are not pure dogmatic constructs, but rather entail values intended to be protected and promoted. Articles 6, 7, 8 and 9 CCC refer to

5 Valérie Savioz-Viaccoz, *L'embryon in vitro: Émergence d'un nouvel objet de droit. Qualification juridique et contrats* (Schulthess 2021).

further values such as the “principle of fairness”, the “principle of good faith”, the duty to “adhere to honesty and keep promises”, the duty not to violate “the law, offend public order or good morals” and to facilitate “the conservation of resources, as well as ecological and environmental protection”.

One may recall, for example, that the 2002 Brazilian Civil Code also entails a provision, at the beginning of its part dedicated to “contractual obligations”, underlining the social function of a contract,[6] as a response for a need for more social justice in contractual matters. This triggered courts to use this provision to limit or soften the mandatory force of contracts when important values were in jeopardy.[7] One wonders whether the expression of those values at the very start of the Chinese Civil Code may trigger similar effects.

The provisions about the aims and values of the Code should however be read together with article 10 CCC. Article 10 CCC sets the principles for “resolving civil disputes”, which is in a way the core of the application, and therefore the interpretation of the Code. Under article 10 CCC, “[c]ivil disputes shall be resolved in accordance *with the law*; or if the law remains silent, *custom* may apply, but not in a way contrary to public order and good morals” (emphasis added). This provision calls for at least two distinct remarks, one on the interpretation of statutory provisions (a), and the other on gap-filling techniques (b).

(*a*) In the CCC, there is no specific provision on statutory interpretation, whereas there are provisions on interpretation of expression of intent (article 142 CCC), of standard clauses (article 498 CCC), and of contracts concluded in several languages (article 466). I understand that article 10 CCC is the true provision on interpretation and gap-filling. The affirmation that a dispute must be resolved “in accordance with the law” triggers the question of how such law should be interpreted. It seems to me that the interpretation of any specific provision of the Chinese Civil Code will necessarily have to consider the values on which the Code is grounded, as expressed by articles 1, 6, 7, 8 and 9 CCC. These values are very general and could be source of uncertainties in the interpretation, but this is exactly the role of the interpreter; the judge must interpret a specific clause in light of the facts and the fundamental values of the Chinese Civil Code. Interpretation is never a mathematical process and needs a careful analysis of the possible solutions to identify the best option

---

6 Article 421 Brazilian Civil Code: “A liberdade de contratar será exercida em razão e nos limites da função social do contrato” (author’s translation: “The freedom to contract will be exercised in accordance with and within the limits of the social function of the contract”).

7 See on this point Ignacio Maria Poveda Velasco and Eduardo Tomasevicius Filho, *The 2002 Brazilian Civil Code*, in Michele Graziadei/ Lihong Zhang (eds) (n 1) 323–324.

in line with the underlining values of the Code. In case a provision leads to different possible interpretations, one would need to opt for the meaning that is compliant with the "core socialist values", the "principle of fairness" and the "principle of good faith", but also with the aim to conserve resources and to protect ecology and environment, as the latter values are also expressed by the drafters of the Chinese Civil Code. It is obvious that conflicting views or interests may force the judge to decide what matters more in the specific case, and given the cultural background. It remains to be seen, however, to what extent judges will opt for interpretations more favorable to principles such as 'protection of ecology and environment' than others, and how they will deal with conflicting values in specific cases.

(*b*) If the law is silent, "civil disputes" shall be resolved by reference to custom, as long as this is not contrary to public order and good morals. Obviously, the Chinese society might be based on a broader concept of custom and tradition as would be the case in Europe for example. Yet, article 10 CCC is silent about what has to be done when neither the statutory provision, nor custom gives an answer to a specific legal problem. There seems to be no *référé législatif*, which would ask a judge to request a specific answer from the legislator (such *référé législatif* was enacted in France by article 12 of the Statute of 16–24 August 1790, and then abrogated in 1804 by article 4 French Civil Code). There is no duty for a judge to decide by applying the rule it would create if it were a legislator, to recall article 1(2) Swiss Civil Code. The CCC seems to have rejected the idea of a judge-made law to fill-in gaps of the Code.[8] Instead, a judge could (and, in my opinion, should) at least be able to apply the general principles expressed in articles 1, 6, 7, 8 and 9 CCC to find an appropriate solution to resolve a civil dispute. By doing so, a judge will necessarily create some more specific rules based on these general principles. This does not mean, however, that such interpretation would necessarily be applicable to, or impose itself in further cases, as the Code seems to reject the idea of an open-system, in which the judge could explicitly fill-in gaps with judge-made law.[9]

Following modern approaches to interpretation, one could consider that any legal interpretation entails the creation of law.[10] Under this view, the boundaries between interpretation and creation of a judge-made law are

8 See, for the idea that the Chinese legislator rejected to introduce jurisprudence as a source of law, Xue Jun (n 2).

9 See on this the analysis by Xue Jun (n 2).

10 For a presentation, see among others Pascal Pichonnaz, 'Challenging Textual Interpretation in Multilingual Legal Systems' (2023) French Journal of Legal Policy (published in December 2023) vol 1, 1–12.

blurred. This is true for example when looking at the methodology applied by the Swiss Supreme Federal Court, expressed as a "pragmatic pluralism of methods". The Swiss Supreme Federal Court does not assign a pre-defined hierarchy between the various tools of interpretation: the text has no more weight than the aim or the systematic interpretation of a specific provision, and the overall approach is to get the most equitable result in view of the specific facts at hand. The Swiss Supreme Court has described its methodology in following terms: "[a] statute must first and foremost be interpreted on its own merits, i.e., according to its wording, meaning and purpose and the underlying evaluations on the basis of a teleological method of understanding. The interpretation of the law must be guided by the idea that it is not the wording alone that constitutes the norm, but only the law understood and concertized through the facts. What is required is the factually correct decision in the normative structure, oriented towards a satisfactory result of the *ratio legis*. In doing so, the Federal Tribunal follows a pragmatic pluralism of methods and refuses to subject the individual elements of interpretation to a hierarchical order of priority".[11] If judges would follow a similar approach in China, which they do not – as far as I understand –, they would indeed be able to create the appropriate solution for cases through 'interpretation' using such pragmatic plurality of methods.

4 The Civil Juridical Act and the Manifestation of Intent

Article 129 Chinese Civil Code provides that "[c]ivil rights may be acquired by virtue of civil juridical acts, factual acts, events provided by law, or other methods of acquisition provided for by law". Apart from events and other methods "provided by law", the Chinese Civil Code sees the source of civil rights either in a civil juridical act (*Rechtsgeschäft*) or in a factual act (*Realakt*).

Let us turn first to the notion of 'factual act'. The notion is not defined by the Chinese Civil Code, but one can find it also in article 231 CCC, dealing with the creation or extinction of a property right as a result of factual acts, "such as lawful construction or demolition of houses". Article 231 CCC states that, in such cases, "[the property right] shall become effective upon the completion of these factual acts".

Yet, as it is the case in German law, Swiss law and further legal systems influenced by the German dogmatic tradition, the central piece of the Chinese Civil

11 See for example DFT [Decision of the Swiss Federal Tribunal] 131/*2005* III 33 reason 2 (author's translation).

Code is the 'civil juridical act' (*Rechtsgeschäft, acte juridique, negozio giuridico*). Chapter 6 of Book I Chinese Civil Code is dedicated to this important notion.

Article 133 CCC begins with a definition: "[c]ivil juridical acts are acts carried out by civil subjects to create, alter, or discontinue civil legal relationships through manifestation of intent". What the provision does not explicitly say, however, is that the manifestation of intent directly creates the legal effect intended, i.e., without the need of a judiciary intervention or of any further requirement (unless provided specifically by the law). Despite the absence of this precision, this is certainly what is meant by the definition. Article 134 CCC then recalls the various types of civil juridical acts (bilateral, multilateral, or unilateral). Article 135 CCC provides that such juridical act may take the form of a writing, of a verbal communication, or of any other form; however, if a specific form is required by law or by an administrative regulation or is stipulated by the parties' agreement, such a formal requirement has to be respected. The provision does not state whether the form has a declaratory or a constitutive effect, but its formulation probably indicates that such juridical act can only become effective where the appropriate form has been respected. Article 136 CCC provides that "a juridical act becomes effective at the moment of formation, except as otherwise provided for by law or agreed by parties", which may mean that, if a specific form has been stipulated by the parties, the juridical act only becomes effective if such form has been complied with.

Some provisions lay down the requirements for the manifestation of intent to become effective. When the manifestation of intent is transmitted by instantaneous communication, the addressee needs to have knowledge of its content (article 137 CCC). The principle of reception seems to apply, but reference to knowledge may give the impression that there is more to it. When the communication is not instantaneous, the manifestation of intent becomes effective only "when it reaches the counterparty" (article 138 CCC). One would consider therefore that the principle of reception (and sphere of influence), as developed by most jurisdictions in Europe, would apply similarly here. Further, this provision indicates also how to deal with "data messages" which should be received by a particular system, considering that a communication through a data message "becomes effective at the moment when the data message enters such particular system". This is a tricky provision, as it does not distinguish between the situation in which the addressee has designated data messages as the system of communication and the situation in which he has not. In the first case, it is the reception of the message which makes the communication effective. By contrast, when the system has not been designated by the addressee, what matters is the effective or normative knowledge by the addressee ("knows or ought to know") of the arrival of the data message within the system. This adds therefore a layer to the principle of reception; the intent of the drafters of the CCC was probably to protect the addressee who might not have expected the use of data messages on a given system. This solution, however, creates some practical difficulties, as it may not always be easy to determine whether the addressee has designated a specific system to receive a data message. Courts will have to determine in particular whether it is sufficient that the designation is public, or whether it does need more specificity to consider that a specific system has been designated. For example, is a relationship between two people on LinkedIn sufficient to consider that any message sent by one of many thousands of 'contacts' to the addressee is effective at the time it enters the system? Or does the use of such data messages need a specific determination by the addressee in advance? Is an indication of Instagram or any other social media on a business card sufficient to consider that the addressee has designated the given system pursuant to article 138 CCC, or is something more expected? This remains to be seen.

In principle, silence is not a manifestation of intent pursuant to article 140(2) CCC, unless "provided by law, stipulated by parties' agreement, or compatible with customary trade practices among the parties". Thus, a letter of confirmation of an oral agreement will in principle not produce legal effects if it remains not contradicted or opposed by the addressee. To consider the addressee's silence as legally relevant, one would need to prove either that there are trade practices as to confirmation letters among the parties, or that good faith, as a general principle provided by law (see article 7 and above), justifies giving full legal effect to a confirmation letter that has not been contested by the other party. The latter is the position taken by the Swiss Supreme Court.

Another provision has triggered my attention. Under article 141 CCC, the withdrawal of a manifestation of intent is possible only where the notice of withdrawal reaches the addressee before or at the same time as the arrival of the prior manifestation of intent. This corresponds to the situation under Swiss law, where the withdrawal of an offer or an acceptance is effective under the same requirements as those provided in the CCC (see article 9 Swiss Code of Obligations, hereinafter Swiss CO). Does it mean therefore, as it is accepted under Swiss law, that once received by the addressee an offer cannot be withdrawn and therefore, if the addressee has accepted the offer within the given timeframe, the contract is necessarily concluded, even if in the meantime the author of the offer has concluded a contract for the same object with a third party? Article 475 CCC (in the general part of Book III) refers expressly to article 141, providing that "[a]n offer may be withdrawn. The withdrawal of the offer is governed by the provisions of article 141 of this Civil Code". One should, however, not mingle two concepts used by the Chinese Civil Code: withdrawal and revocation. Indeed, article 476 CCC provides that "[a]n offer may be revoked, except for in one of the following circumstances: (1) the offeror indicates a fixed time for acceptance or otherwise explicitly states that the offer is irrevocable; or (2) the offeree has reason to believe that the offer is irrevocable and has made reasonable preparation to perform the contract". In other words, once the offer has reached the addressee, before any declaration of withdrawal, the possibility to revoke an offer is very limited. In particular, an offer may be irrevocable even in the absence of an explicit declaration of irrevocability, provided that the addressee was allowed to infer from the circumstances that the offer was irrevocable, even if it was not intended so.

Finally, let us consider the principles of interpretation of manifestations of intent. Article 142(1) CCC provides as follows: "[a] manifestation of intent involving a counterparty shall be interpreted in light of the wording, relevant clauses, nature and purpose of the conduct, custom as well as the principle of good faith, in order to determine the meaning of such manifestation of intent".

Contrary to some legal systems in Europe, such as Swiss law (see article 18 Swiss CO), the manifestation of intent is not interpreted according to the real and common intent of the parties, but according to some objective factors, including the principle of good faith, which leads to the way the addressee could understand the manifestation of intent pursuant to the principle of trust and good faith. The factors mentioned by such provision raise, however, some concerns. First, does the expression "nature and purpose of conduct" refer to the conduct that is expected by the other party or does it refer to the behavior of the parties before or during the manifestation of intent? Many legal systems in Europe would consider that, where the manifestation of intent is interpreted objectively, only behaviors occurring before the manifestation of intent might be considered to interpret such manifestation. The English formulation, at least, is far from clear as to what is exactly meant by "nature and purpose of conduct".

Furthermore, one can wonder whether the list enumerates factors exhaustively. Could for example environmental interests that were set as fundamental principles of interpretation of the Code be used to interpret the parties' intent? Could precontractual documents and messages be used to this purpose? Furthermore, parties may have disguised their intent by using different wordings (they may have called 'sale' what in fact is a donation, or the other way around). In such cases, would the wording prevail, or can the conduct and "nature and purpose of the conduct" be relevant to interpret the parties' manifestation of will? Article 142(1) CCC does not seem to impose a strictly literal interpretation, as other factors may be considered, especially those linked to the underlying values of the Chinese Civil Code.

Article 142(2) CCC underlines however that, when a manifestation of intent does not involve a counterparty, such manifestation "shall not be rigidly interpreted in light of its wording, but shall instead be interpreted in light of the relevant clauses, nature and purpose of the conduct, custom, as well as the principle of good faith, in order to determine the genuine intent of the actor". For unilateral juridical acts, what matters is therefore the subjective intent of their author, rather than their objective meaning. This seems however to be in contradiction with article 476(2) CCC, in which the objective interpretation of the irrevocability of the offer prevails over any subjective intent not to have it irrevocable.

Finally, since article 142(2) CCC stresses that the wording should not be taken rigidly for unilateral manifestations of intent, one may wonder whether this mean that by contrast the wording is more important for bilateral manifestations of intent pursuant to article 142(1) CCC. When reading this article, one is thus left with more questions than answers. Yet, this is inevitable, no matter how hard a legislator tries to write down a complete and self-contained code. Indeed, as to the interpretation of manifestations of will, one can ask whether the principle of good faith allows to trump the literal meaning when the manifestation of intent involves a counterparty, or whether the principle of good faith can only be used in a restrictive way, obliging judges to stick to reading the mere wording of manifestations of intent. To illustrate, if I intend to make a loan of money, but the way I express myself creates in the addressee, pursuant to the principle of good faith (and to article 142(2) CCC), a reasonable expectation that this was a donation, would the donation prevail over my subjective intent as the author of the manifestation to make a loan?[12] Certainly, this will trigger interesting thoughts by judges in decisions to come.

5 False Expression and Misunderstanding

A juridical act produces the effect directly intended by the author's will. As a consequence, a manifestation of such will which is not truly intended (sham) is void, as put by article 146 CCC. If such sham intends to hide another juridical act (the hidden act), the latter act might be valid, depending on the "relevant legal provisions" (article 146(2) CCC). The hidden juridical act may for instance be valid when, in case of a bilateral juridical act, both parties have intended to perform such an act, and have complied with all the formal requirements for

12 For such a case in Swiss law, see DFT 144/*2018* III 93.

its validity. The contractual parties should however not be allowed to invoke the validity of the hidden juridical act vis-à-vis third parties, as this would be contrary to the principle of good faith. This is explicitly stated by article 18(2) of the Swiss Civil Code.

Article 147 CCC provides that "the mistaken actor has the power to *rescind* the civil juridical act done by *gross misunderstanding* via the People's Court or arbitral tribunal" (emphasis added). Contrary to article 146 CCC, when there is an intended manifestation of will, but the author of such manifestation of will commits a mistake in his manifestation, creating a gross misunderstanding, such manifestation is valid in principle, but it can be rescinded by a court. The rule clearly follows the German[13] and Swiss[14] traditions of granting the author of a mistake a remedy only in case of an 'essential mistake', understood as a the one resulting from a "gross misunderstanding", since rightly one has to look at the consequences of the misunderstanding (wrong contract, wrong amount, wrong person, etc.). Yet, the Chinese Civil Code does not follow the German and Swiss systems on two aspects. Firstly, article 147 CCC does not consider the manifestation of will as void, but only as voidable ("rescind"), whereas following the theory of will (*Willenstheorie*) both Swiss law[15] and German law[16] consider the manifestation of will as null and void from the start if one party raises the issue of mistake (*relative Nichtigkeit*). It is true, however, that pursuant to article 155 CCC, a "rescinded civil juridical act is not legally binding *ab initio*"; there is therefore a retroactive effect of the avoidance. Secondly, the Chinese Civil Code does not provide for a formative right (*Gestaltungsrecht*), which would by a qualified juridical act directly producing the effect of voiding the mistaken act. To impose the recourse to a judge or an arbitrator is not only cumbersome, but also strange, as the current tendency, as expressed by the newly revised Belgium Code,[17] is to allow the unilateral rescission of the manifestation of will. Moreover, having adopted the juridical act as the cornerstone of the code, the drafters of the CCC should coherently have allowed for a unilateral (formative) manifestation of will to rescind the contract. In case of fraud (articles 148–149 CCC) and coercion (article 150 CCC), the Chinese Civil Code provides for the same solution of allowing avoidance upon request to a court, whereas under the will theory the result of a fraudulent or coerced manifestation of will should be

---

13 § 119(1) German Civil Code.
14 Article 24(1), nos 1–3, Swiss CO.
15 Article 31 Swiss CO, and DFT 114/*1988* II 131 reason. 3b.
16 § 200 German CC.
17 Article 5.59(3) Belgium CC.

its voidness from the start, and such voidness should be raised by a mere manifestation of will (*formative right*).

Article 152 CCC sets the limitation period for such request for rescission. This calls for two remarks, one concerning the double period of limitation and the other regarding the very short period applicable to the case of gross misunderstanding.

Article 152 CCC provides for a double period of limitation. Firstly, there is an overall (absolute) limitation of five years "after occurrence of the civil juridical act" to exert the power of rescission set by article 152(2) CCC. The provision mentions that, once the period is closed, the power of rescission is extinguished, which might allude to the fact that such period of limitation cannot be interrupted or suspended, as it is a period of limitation set for the introduction of a request in front of a court. In other words, time does not affect the claim as such; it should be considered as *Verwirkung* and not *Verjährung*, as German lawyers would say. Secondly, article 152(1) CCC provides for a relative period of limitation, still affecting the power to request rescission, but with a starting point commencing at the time of effective or normative knowledge ("knows or ought to know") of the cause or rescission. In cases of duress, such a starting point would be when the duress comes to an end, whereas in cases of gross misunderstanding it would be when the actor has knowledge of the gross misunderstanding. However, the period of limitation is different between fraud and coercion, which are both subject to a limitation period of one year, and gross misunderstanding, which is subject to a limitation period of ninety days.

The tricky point with the absolute limitation period of five years is that, if the coercion lasts for more than five years, nothing can be done. This seems to run against the principle of good faith, and I would not be surprised if courts would consider that this limitation period of five years should not apply to coercion. For fraud, there may be situations where such limitation period may also become abusive, in particular when the party having committed fraud has done its best to avoid any claim for rescission by using fraudulent behavior.

As to the short period applicable in cases of gross misunderstanding, article 152(1) CCC provides that "in the case of gross misunderstanding, [the power of rescission is extinguished] where the party fails to exercise the power of rescission within ninety days from the date on which the party knows or ought to know of the cause of rescission". Especially as pursuant to article 199 CCC such period cannot be suspended or interrupted, a ninety days period seems a very short period to prepare a rescission request to be filed in court. Under Swiss law for example, where a mere declaration by the party in error is sufficient, that party has one year at its disposal. A short period is of course even more tricky when it is based on normative knowledge, as the effective knowledge may be shorter than what "ought to have been known", reducing even more any possibility to rescind the civil juridical act. It would have probably been better to fix the starting point of the period in question by the moment of effective knowledge, as this would have been more protective of the rights of the person in error. The abuse of rights would still be applicable in cases where there is gross negligence in not discovering the gross misunderstanding.

6 Agency

Rules on agency cover traditional issues in this area, distinguishing between agency conferred by mandate or agreement, and agency conferred by a statutory provision (article 163(1) CCC). For an agent to bind a principal, one needs such an agent to carry out a civil juridical act (1) in the name of the principal and (2) with the authority given to it by such principal (article 162 CCC and article 170 CCC). A civil juridical act carried out by an agent acting with oneself or acting simultaneously as agent of another principal (double agency) is void, as article 168 Chinese Civil Code mentions that such an agent "shall not carry out" such acts, unless duly authorized. Violation of the prohibition triggers voidness of the civil juridical act pursuant to article 153 CCC.

As to the naming of the principal, the Chinese Civil Code is apparently silent on the consequences of the failure to name the principal. Some legal systems, such as the Swiss one (article 32(2) in fine Swiss CO[18]), provide for a valid effect if it did not matter for the counterparty with whom the contract was made or if the counterparty could deduce *bona fide* from the circumstances that the agent was acting as an agent for a principal. The text is also silent about whether it is possible to act for a principal that remains to be named or whose name is not yet disclosed, but will be in due course. One would not see why such agency relationship would not be valid, as long as the counterparty receives knowledge of the name of the principal when it wants to act. This is also the solution adopted by soft law texts such as the Principles of European Contract Law (hereinafter PECL) and the Draft Common Frame of Reference (hereinafter DCFR).[19]

As to the conferring of authority, article 165 CCC states the formal requirements needed when the conferring of authority is done in writing. This means, *a contrario*, that these requirements are not necessarily to be followed if the authority is conferred orally or by implied conduct. Strangely the conferring

18 See also DFT 117/*1991* II 387 reason 2.

19 See article 3:203 PECL and article II – 6:108 DCFR; see also Pierre Tercier and Pascal Pichonnaz, *Le droit des obligations* (6th edn, Schulthess 2019) para 429.

of authority shall then be very specific, as it shall "expressly state the agent's name or business name, subject-matter of the agency, scope of authority, and duration, and shall be executed under signature or seal of the principal". One can understand that it would be optimal to have all these information, but one wonders what the consequence of absence of all these requirements is, where, for example, the name of the principal might be determined based on the circumstances, or the subject-matter of the agency may be interpreted out of the facts of the case. It might be difficult to believe that this would trigger an absence of power, when in fact a conferral of power does not necessarily need be given in writing, and could or should also be deduced from an oral statement or even implied from the conduct of the principal. That would at least be the logical consequence of article 140(1) CCC Code, which provides that a civil juridical act can be made expressly or implicitly. The conferral of authority is a civil juridical act; therefore, one would expect that it would be possible to do it by an implicit manifestation of will, or even by a mix of an explicit (or even written) manifestation of will and an implicit one.

Article 171(1) CCC provides that "[a]n act of agency carried out by someone despite the fact that the actor has no power of agency, that the actor acts beyond the power of agency, or that the actor's power of agency has been extinguished, does not bind the principal without the principal's ratification". The absence of powers of agency does not necessarily lead to the fact that the principal is not bound by the act of the agent.

If the agent can be considered as having acted for the principal, the principal will be bound, despite the absence of powers (or more restricted powers or the previous extinction of those powers), in the following alternative situations:

(a) *ratification.* When the principal ratifies the civil juridical act by the agent, this works as a retrospective conferral of powers of agency that produces the effect of a valid act of agency;
(b) *apparent conferral of powers.* Despite the seemingly restrictive approach of article 171(1) CCC, a civil juridical act performed without any powers of agency may nevertheless bind the principal "as long as the counterparty has good reason to believe that the actor has power of agency" (article 172 CCC). These "good reason to believe" are based on a good faith analysis of the principal's behavior and the circumstances of the case. Thus, if the principal knows about the agent's activity on his behalf and does not react, there might be "good reasons" for the counterparty to believe that powers of agency have been conferred (*Duldungsvollmacht*). Or the principal may act in such a way that the counterpart is in good faith allowed to believe

that the agent has powers of agency (*Anscheinsvollmacht*).[20] 1) *absence of knowledge about the extinction of powers.* Pursuant to article 174 CCC, "an act of agency carried out by an agent remains valid even after the death of the principal", which would normally trigger extinction of the powers of agency (article 173(4) CCC), if "(1) the agent has no knowledge and ought not to have knowledge of the principal's death". Further, ratification by the successors, acting in the benefit of the principal's successors or an express provision in the conferral of powers that the agency will continue beyond the principal's death (note that there is no express requirement to comply with the formalities of a will), will also maintain or justify the power of agency to such agent. This is traditional (good) doctrine, presented from the point of view of the agent. It remains to determine whether the solution should be different if the agent was unaware of the principal's death, but the counterparty knew about it. Should one consider that, in such a case, the counterparty has a duty to inform the agent, or should one consider that there would be an abuse of rights (pursuant to article 132 CCC) for the counterparty to invoke (and benefit) from article 174 CCC, when it knew about the death of the principal? This will certainly have to be decided by courts. Under Swiss law, the fact that the counterparty had knowledge of the extinction of powers would for example prohibit that party from invoking the continuation of power under article 37(2) Swiss CO.[21]

If there is no conferral of the power of agency and there are no circumstances justifying a party's reliance on an apparent conferral, article 171(3) CCC gives that party the right to claim from the pseudo-agent "to perform obligations or to compensate any damage suffered, the amount of which shall not exceed the benefit which such counterparty would have gained had the act of agency been ratified". In a system based on the theory of will, it is surprising that the counterparty of a pseudo-agent may ask him to perform the obligation himself, as the pseudo-agent may well have had no intention to carry out the civil juridical act by himself, and he has acted by naming the principal (despite having no power of agency), which underlines his intent not to be personally bound by such civil juridical act. Dogmatically, it is therefore difficult to structure the

20 Tercier and Pichonnaz (n 19) para 479–480.

21 Tercier and Pichonnaz (n 19) para 487.

relationship in such a way as to create a legal relationship between the counterparty and the pseudo-agent. This is also why damages should normally be limited to the loss accrued on the counterparty because of his reliance on the validity of the civil juridical act with the principal (i.e., the so-called compensation of the negative interest). Some systems, as does Swiss law, provide for more extensive damages, if this is 'equitable' under the circumstances, underlining that the reason for such extended right of compensation is not based on a legal ground but on equity.[22] In absence of any explanation, it is difficult to understand why the drafters of the Chinese Civil Code considered that the counterparty is allowed to obtain the full benefit of the invalid civil juridical act (i.e., the so-called compensation of the positive interest).

7 Limitation Period

Chapter 9 of Book I deals with the limitation period in twelve provisions. It would go beyond the scope of this chapter to deal with all of them. This section will discuss three issues only: the duration of the limitation period, its starting point, and whether or not it can be suspended or interrupted once it starts running.

As to the duration and the beginning of the limitation period, the Chinese Civil Code provides for two default periods, which pursuant to article 197 CCC cannot be modified by agreement.

The general rule for duration is set forth by article 188(1) CCC, according to which "[t]he limitation period for a claim brought before the People's Court for the protection of civil rights is three years, except as otherwise provided by law". The default limitation period is in line with German Law;[23] by contrast, article 2224 French Civil Code sets a default limitation period of five years, and the default rule of Swiss law sets a ten-year limitation period.[24] It is true, however, that the three years period mentioned in article 188(1) CCC is in line with soft principles, such as article 14.201 PECL and article 10.2(1) UNIDROIT Principles on International Commercial Contract (hereinafter UPICC[25]). Despite the wording of article 188 CCC, such limitation period would and should apply also before other courts than the People's Court, if the Chinese Civil Code is

22 Tercier and Pichonnaz (n 19) para 466.

23 §195 German Civil Code.

24 Article 127 Swiss CO.

25 The rule provided for a three years limitation period already since 2004, and was confirmed in the 2016 edition.

applicable, be it an arbitration court (as expressly stated by article 198 CCC) or a foreign court. As a matter of fact, the limitation period is a provision of substantive law, and therefore should apply whichever court has jurisdiction to hear the civil dispute.

As to the beginning of such limitation period, article 188(2) CCC provides that "the limitation period begins to run from the date when the right-holder knows or ought to know of the infringement of his or her right and the identity of the duty-bearer, except as otherwise provided for by law". So, not only effective knowledge, such as under Swiss law,[26] but also normative knowledge triggers the running of the limitation period, such as in German law[27] and French law,[28] as well as soft principles.[29] This creates however some uncertainties as to when exactly such normative knowledge intervenes. The situation is particularly difficult, as the running of the limitation period starts the following day of the day when a party "ought to know" about the infringement. Often, such day is fixed later by a judge; this creates a retroactive effect and unsettles the whole discussion. By having the start of the running at the end of the year in which the triggering event occurred,[30] instead of the following day as in Chinese law, German law has partly removed the difficulties linked to the normative knowledge.

Article 188(2), 2nd sentence, of the Chinese Civil Code then sets a second period of limitation, with an absolute starting date: "The People's Court shall not protect the right after the expiration of twenty years from the date on which the infringement of such right occurred; but, under exceptional circumstances, the People's Court may decide to extend the limitation period upon application of the right-holder". In other words, there is an absolute period of limitation of twenty years from the infringement. Such period could exceptionally be extended when requested. One could think for instance of asbestos-related cases, for which the duration of latency of the illness may be between 15 to 50 years. In such cases, therefore, it would make sense to extend the twenty years limitation period. One could also think of the consequences of an earthquake, when such earthquake reveals defects in a construction that was supposed to reduce or avoid damages in case of earthquake. In such a case, some countries, including Turkey, have extended the limitation period to allow victims to complain about defects in construction.

---

26 Article 60(1) Swiss CO; article 128a Swiss CO.
27 § 199(1)(2) German Civil Code.
28 Article 2224 French Civil Code.
29 Article 14:301 PECL; article 10.2(1) UPICC.
30 § 199(1)1 German Civil Code.

The starting of the limitation period in case of instalments (article 189 CCC) or for persons without or with limited civil capacity (article 190 CCC), and the specific provision for victims of sexual assault (article 191 CCC), do not raise too many concerns.

Mandatory provisions which cannot be modified by agreement, present some intriguing loopholes as to the suspension (article 194 CCC) and the interruption ('reset') (article 195 CCC) of the limitation period.

As regards article 194 CCC, force majeure, the death or loss of power of agency for a statutory agent, the absence of determination of a successor or an administrator or a situation of control between creditor and debtor ("the right-holder is controlled by the duty-bearer or other persons") may cause some difficulties of interpretation, but these can be easily solved. One however is left to wonder what meaning should be assigned to the catch-all provision conveyed by article 194(1) no (5) CCC, under which "other obstacles causing the right-holder to be unable to exercise his or her claim-right" are a cause of suspension. Does the fact that there is no arbitral or jurisdiction of the People's Court justify suspension? Probably not, as the obstacle may be overcome by filing a claim in a foreign country. Does the absence of effective knowledge justify a suspension? Probably not, if the party ought to know about the circumstance, as many provisions expressly refer to such a normative knowledge; the absolute limitation period has been introduced exactly to put an end to situations in which the absence of knowledge (effective and normative) implied that the limitation period could not run. It would, therefore, not be possible to invoke the absence of knowledge to suspend the absolute period of limitation, as this would contradict the very purpose of article 188(1) CCC. The absence of occurrence of a damage linked to asbestos or similar cases of late and latent damages may trigger a suspension, even of the absolute limitation period, but article 188(2) *in fine* CCC seems already to deal with that.

Given the mandatory nature of the provision on limitation (article 198 CCC), there would be no possibility for parties to agree on any different ground for suspension of the limitation period. In particular, the question arises whether negotiations between the parties would justify a suspension of the lapsing of the limitation period. There is no specific provision for that issue, which is expressly regulated in many other legal systems.[31] For a party negotiating with another or being in a mediation process, it would not make sense to file a claim for preserving its rights. The absence of any suspension process in case of negotiations is certainly a gap that should be filled. Potentially, one could

31 § 203 German Civil Code; article 2238 French Civil Code; article 136, no 8, Swiss CO.

therefore argue that negotiations or a mediation process represent an 'obstacle' provided for by article 194(1), no (5), CCC, as no one should be forced to jeopardize the negotiation or mediation by filing a claim during such process.

Interestingly, the suspension may trigger an extension of the limitation period, as the latter cannot expire less than six months after the date on which the obstacle causing the suspension has ceased to exist (article 194(2) CCC).

As to the interruption, there is nothing very special provided for by article 195 CCC. A claim for performance, an agreement to perform, the commencement of an action or an application for arbitration will reset the limitation period. As to "other circumstances with the same effect as bringing an action or applying for arbitration" provided by article 195(4) CCC, one could envisage, for instance, a request for seizure to guarantee a claim.

A final comment as to the limitation period: A court cannot raise the defense of the expiry of limitation period on its own initiative (*ex officio*) (article 193 CCC). This is the correct view, but also triggers the following question. Why would then all provisions on limitation period be mandatory as expressed by article 197(1) CCC? If the Chinese legislator has recognized the autonomy of will of the debtor, by leaving it to him or her to raise or renounce to raise the defense of the limitation period, once it has expired, why would the autonomy of will not also be available at least to extend such period of limitation by mutual agreement, or unilateral decision of the debtor? This is significant as the fundamental values on which the Chinese Civil Code is based include the respect for the free will (article 5 CCC) and principle of fairness (article 6 CCC).

8 Conclusion

It is time to conclude, despite that there would be many more points to raise in relation with Book I of the CCC. My comments do not mean that this codification of Chinese civil law is not welcome or has not dealt with the most important points of civil law. It shows only that a code can never be considered as a closed normative text. It is always a work in progress, which needs to be further shaped by judges when confronted with real-world cases, that will necessarily trigger new views, ideas, and solutions. Interpretation and gap-filling are at the core of judges' work to give shape and consistency to any codification.

My aim was to pick a few provisions that may give rise to interpretive difficulties, showing why and how judges may promote some of the basic values on which the Chinese Civil Code is based. It will certainly be interesting to come back on this in a couple of years from now, to discover how judges have created solutions for the various issues I have listed in my text.

Acknowledgements

I thank my assistant, MLaw A Lopes Vilar de Ouro, PhD candidate at the University of Fribourg (Switzerland), for his valuable help in revising my draft.

CHAPTER 6

Reshaping Chinese Real Right Law through the New Chinese Civil Code

朱晓喆 *Zhu Xiaozhe*

1 Setting the Context

The enactment of the Civil Code of the People's Republic of China (hereinafter the Civil Code) was one of the major milestones in China's history of law, exerting a profound and proactive influence on the state, society, and individuals. The Civil Code has comprehensively and systematically revised and codified the existing civil laws that had been formulated in different eras. Considering the demands and practices of the new era, the Civil Code formulated state-of-the-art legal norms suited for the new situations and legal issues arising from recent civil and commercial activities. Different from the French Code Civil of 1804 (originally comprising three books) and the German Civil Code of 1900 (comprised of five books), the Chinese Civil Code was innovatively structured into seven books, respectively: General Part, Real Rights, Contracts, Personality Rights, Marriage and Family, Succession and Tort Liability. The Second Book on Real Rights of the Civil Code (hereinafter the Book on Real Rights) stipulates three categories of real rights: (1) ownership (state, collective, and private ownership), (2) usufruct (including the right to use land for construction purposes, the right to contractual management of land, the right to use a home site, the right of habitation, and easements), and (3) security interests (including mortgage, pledge, and lien). Instead of expounding the various real rights, this chapter draws an overall depiction of China's real rights system, and dissects Chinese real right law from three perspectives, i.e., comparative law and localization, the creation and consolidation of China's property system with Chinese characteristics, and the optimization of the business environment and as reform of the regime of secured transactions. The chapter also aims to provide some normative perspectives and observations on Chinese real right law.

 | DOI:10.1163/9789004704428_007

2 China's Real Rights Legal System

2.1 *Legislative Background of the Book on Real Rights*

The expired Real Right Law stipulated four systems of relationships with assets: ownership, usufruct, security interests, and possession. Each system was then detailed by a set of specific regulations on state property ownership, ownership of a building's units, right to contractual management of rural land, right to use land for construction of residential units, and so on and so forth. The Real Right Law contributed to safeguarding the basic economic system of the state, maintaining the socialist market economic order, clarifying property ownership, wielding the functions of real rights, and protecting the holders' property.[1]

However, with the social and economic growth of the state, the original Real Right Law became insufficient to meet the demands of the new era. Thus, the CPC Central Committee proposed "improving the modern regime of property rights, [and] advancing the legislation of property rights protection". It also declared "adhering to equal protection, comprehensive protection, law-based protection, joint participation, and pursuit of both temporary and permanent solutions".[2] Under the guidelines of these and other major policies, the drafters of the Book on Real Rights, sticking to China's legal practice, revised and codified the existing real right law based on domestic legal scholarship and state-of-the-art worldwide legislation. They coordinated both the requirement to consolidate the reform and the demand to respond to the current needs of society. As a result, the Book on Real Rights has further improved China's property legal system.

2.2 *The Relationships among the Book on Real Rights, the Book on General Provisions, and Other Books*

The Civil Code is an organic whole comprised of the Book on the General Part and other Books. Among them, the Book on the General Part summarizes the general principles and notions underlying the Code by extracting common rules from each Book. Hence, the understanding and application of the Book on Real Rights, as well as the other books, requires a combined interpretation

1 Zhang Mingqi, 'The Compilation of Specific Parts of the Civil Code' (2020) 3 China Legal Science 9 (张鸣起, 民法典分编的编纂,《中国法学》).

2 See 'Opinions of the Central Committee of the Communist Party of China and the State Council on Improving the Property Rights Protection System and Protecting Property Rights According to the Law', November 4, 2016, 28 (Zhongfa) (中共中央国务院关于完善产权保护制度依法保护产权的意见中发).

of the Book on the General Part. In addition, the Book on Real Rights is closely correlated and cross-applicable to other Books, as the following will show.

First is the relationship between the Book on Real Rights and the Book on the General Part. The legislation of the Civil Code took the so-called 'two steps' strategy: the General Part of the Civil Law was promulgated in 2017, while the other Books were formulated later. Thus, the draft of the Book on Real Rights had to comply with the general rules established in General Part. For instance, articles 114 to 117 in Chapter V on "Civil Rights" of the Book on the General Part provide for the concept of real rights, the objects of real rights, *numerus clausus*, and the principles of expropriation and requisition of immovables and movables. Chapter VI on "Civil Juristic Acts" stipulates the general rules regarding private transactions, which governs the relevant real rights rules in the Book on Real Rights, such as transfer of ownership, usufruct, and security interests. Another example is the claims to which limitation of action do not apply under article 196 of the Book on the General Part, which include cessation of the infringement, removal of the nuisance, elimination of the danger, and restitution of immovables or registered movables property. Even though these types of claim based on real rights are specified in articles 235 and 236 of the Book on Real Rights, they are also bound by article 196 of the Book on the General Part.

Second is the relationship between the Book on Real Rights and the Book on Contracts. The contractual relationships set in the Book on Contracts, such as sales, gifts, and exchanges, serve as one of the main tools leading to the creation, alterations, and assignment of real rights. Likewise, contracts on the right to contractual management of land, easement contracts, and security contracts are all regulated in the Book on Real Rights. According to article 467 of the Book on Contracts, the General Part of this Book governing contracting, validity, modification, termination, and breach of contract shall be applied *mutatis mutandis*.

Third is the relationship between the Book on Real Rights and the Book on Succession. The right of succession is most closely associated with real rights, and can be considered as an extension of the latter in succession relationships.[3] According to the Book on Succession, the main distributions of inheritance are intestate succession, testate succession, testamentary gift, legacy-support agreement, and escheat. Among these distributions, the issue where

3 Fang Shaokun, 'On the Legislative Coordination of Succession Section and Real right Section of Civil Code' (2019) 5 Jurist 74–86 (房绍坤，论民法典继承编与物权编的立法协调，《法学家》).

successors become holders of inheritance involves the alteration of real rights, the modification of which is governed by article 230 of the Book on Real Rights.

Lastly, the Book on Real Rights correlates and overlaps with the Book on Marriage and Family. The Book on Marriage and Family adjusts marital relationships and marital property relations, with the latter relating to the ownership and changes of real rights. In academic circles, scholars disagree over the question of whether marital property relations should be governed directly by rules from the Book on Real Rights or by other provisions. For example, the Book on Real Rights specifies the principle of change of real rights as "contract + registration or delivery public notice". However, if marital property agreements (such as gift, property division agreement, or contractual property system) adopt the aforementioned form of change of real rights, a couple will have difficulties continuing their property transmutation, with the potential of hampering their relationship. Some scholars have proposed a rule of 'separate tests'.[4] Likewise, a contract under the contractual property system will be valid for the couple when they reach an agreement; however, a *bona fide* third party is protected against such claims thereof. This proposal has been widely acknowledged in judicial practice.

As such, each book of the Civil Code regulates its own legal field. However, when tackling legal disputes related to real rights, it is necessary to start from a systematic perspective, by identifying the relevant rules from the Book on the General Part and other Books, and by applying them together in a complementary manner, so as to adapt them to the complex and ever-changing property relations in social life.

2.3 *The Relationship between the Book on Real Rights and Special Laws*

Starting from its length, the Book on Real Rights in the Civil Code only contains about two hundred articles, which are too few to cover all of the issues related to real rights. Likewise, apart from the Book on Real Rights, the current Chinese legal framework keeps plenty rules and regulations concerning real rights. First, from the perspective of the state's economic system and the fundamental rights of citizens, the Constitution of the People's Republic of China prescribes the socialist public ownership of the means of production, the non-public sectors of the economy, private property of citizens, and other issues, which determines the structure of the Book on Real Rights and other civil legislation. In addition, the existing legal system also keeps many special

4 Pei Hua, 'Conflict and Harmony between the Marital Property System and General Property Law Rules' (2017) 4 Chinese Journal of Law 12 (裴桦, 夫妻财产制与财产法规则的冲突与协调,《法学研究》).

laws involving real rights, such as the Land Management Law, Real Estate Administration Law, Rural Land Contracting Law, Maritime Law, and Civil Aviation Law. The Book on Real Rights adopts, complements, and coordinates the rules from these special laws. For instance, on the issue of rural land for agricultural operation, in 2003, the National People's Congress enacted the Law of the People's Republic of China on Rural Land Contracting to regulate this area comprehensively. The expired Real Right Law and the new Book on Real Rights, in accordance with the fixed legal structure, merely added regulations that touched on civil relations. Another example is the legislation on natural resources. Forest Law, Grassland Law, Water Law, Fisheries Law, Wild Animal Conservation Law, and other laws establish special legal rules in this field. These special laws take priority over the related rules specified in the Book on Real Rights.

3 The Book on Real Rights: Mixed-Reception and Local Integration

The Book on Real Rights in the Civil Code systematically summarizes the academic research and judicial experiences on real rights during the past decades, and absorbs the rules contained both in the original General Part of the Civil Law and in the Real Right Law. Accordingly, through codification, the Book on Real Rights has confirmed, consolidated, and developed the judicial achievements since the reform and opening up of China. On this basis, the drafters also adopted and adapted state-of-the-art legislation from different countries and formulated a system of Real Right Law with Chinese characteristics, suited for the demands of modern economic markets.

3.1 *Diverse Rules Designed for Changes of Real Rights*

Different from the Civil Codes of other countries, that typically adopt a unitary approach to changes of real rights, the new Chinese Civil Code designed diverse rules based on the distinctive contents and characteristics of real rights.

In conformity with the legislative practices of various countries, the Civil Code adopts the principle of public notice on changes of real rights, under which any change in immovable rights become valid upon registration, while changes in movable rights become valid upon delivery (articles 209 and 224). Conversely, articles 209 and 224 add that this happens "unless otherwise provided by law", thus retaining a connection to rules providing for exceptions in changes of title on real rights. In the Civil Code, there are mainly two situations that qualify these exceptions. First, as to the right to contractual management of rural land (article 335), easement (article 374), special movables like a vessel, aircraft, motor vehicle (article 225), and chattel mortgage (article 403), the principle of registration confrontation governs, whereby registration is not required for the transfer of the real right, but an unregistered title cannot be used as a defence against a *bona fide* third party. Second, changes of titles on real rights are recognized as legally valid without public notice if they are related to state-owned natural resources (article 209(2)) or due to administrative decisions, judicial rulings, succession, or de facto acts as prescribed by articles 229–231.

3.2 *The Relationship between Right of Real Claim and Tort Liability*

Articles 235 and 236 of the Civil Code identify restitution of property, removal of the nuisance, and elimination of the danger as the main remedies for right holders to protect their real rights. However, article 1167 of the Book on Tort Liability provides that "[w]here a tortious act endangers another person's personal or property safety, the infringed person has the right to request the tortfeasor to bear tort liability such as cessation of the infringement, removal of the nuisance, or elimination of the danger". Therefore, a regulatory overlap between the real right-based claim and tort liability could emerge as a legal pitfall.

To some extent, the regulatory overlap results from the collisions among different legal philosophies when adopting doctrines from various legal systems. The legal mindset for real rights claims originated from the German legal system, while independent civil liability was established by the original General Part of the Civil Law, which was deeply influenced by the socialist legal system. During the codification of the Civil Code, there was a heated controversy on how to coordinate the conflict between these two legal views. Based on the available legislative materials, there were three main positions on the issue: the first one argued that civil liability should completely replace the claim for protecting an absolute right, defining all violations of civil obligations as "civil liabilities" (tort liabilities);[5] the second one insisted that tort liability is a form of debt for compensating damages, which should be strictly distinguished from real actions through legislation;[6] the third one proposed

5 Wie Zhenying, *Research on the Separation between Civil Liability and Debt* (Peking University Press 2013) 3 (魏振瀛, 民事责任与债分离研究).

6 Cui Jianyuan, 'Choice and Basis for a Model of Protection of Real Rights' (2005) 1 Jilin University Social Science Journal 116–129 (崔建远, 物权救济模式的选择及其依据,《吉林大学社会科学学报》); Wang Hongliang, 'The Right to Claim the Return of the Original: The Right to Claim Back the Object or the Way to Tort Liability' (2014) 1 Jurist 91 (王洪亮, 原物返还请求权: 物上请求权抑或侵权责任方式,《法学家》).

a juxtaposition of both claims for protecting absolute rights and tort liability. For example, Professor Hu Zhu believed that remedies for tort liability should not be limited to compensation, but should also encompass preventive claim rights, restitution of property based on strict liability, and others. Under such a view, tort liability could cover all kinds of civil rights and interests.[7] The Civil Code adopts this third view in dealing with the relationship between real claim rights and tort liability. For this reason, in Chinese civil law, there is an overlap of regulation between claim rights and tort liability regarding the protections of real rights. According to article 186 of the Civil Code, where there is regulatory overlap in civil lawsuits, the aggrieved party is entitled to choose the applicable legal rules.

3.3 *The Unitary Application of Bona Fide Acquisition in Movable and Immovable Property*

In continental legal systems, the rule on *bona fide* acquisition, the origin of which dates back to a principle of early Germanic law, i.e., '*Hand Muss Hand Wahren*' (meaning "the owner of a movable property who has entrusted it to another person can only demand its return from him and not from the third party"), normally only applies to movable property. The principle obstructs the owner's right to recover goods, thus playing an essential role in safeguarding the interests of *bona fide* purchasers and the safety of transactions. Since the conception of the Real Right Law, China has extended the application of *bona fide* acquisition from movable property to immovable property. However, according to the traditions of the continental legal system, immovable property rights must be registered. A party is entitled to reliance protection as long as he completes the transaction as required by the register of immovable property, leaving the rule of *bona fide* acquisition redundant. During the legislative process of the Real Right Law, Professor Huixing Liang proposed to adopt German legislation stipulating that movable and immovable property are strictly differentiated in the way that the former follows the principle of *bona fide* acquisition, while the latter follows the effect of the register of immovable property. Professor Liming Wang, in line with the dual principle, added that special provisions should be given to '*bona fide* acquisition of immovable property'. This compromise solution was absorbed by the Real Right Law, which laid down the

7 Zhu Hu, 'Independence and Aggregation of Real Rights Claims' (2013) 6 Global L Rev 29 (朱虎, 物权请求权的独立与合并,《环球法律评论》).

premise of the register of immovables, and extended the principle of *bona fide* acquisition to immovables.[8]

Judicial practice reveals that applying *bona fide* acquisition to immovables corresponds with the realities and needs of China. Prior to the enactment of the Real Right Law, the registration system in China was less developed. There was a myriad of situations where the real owners of the immovable property did not correspond with the registered owners. This happened, for instance, because of mistakes in registration by the registry, registration under another name, false impersonation, reversal or invalidity of registration arising from changes of real rights, and failure to register due to de jure changes of real rights. Considering the relatively weak public awareness of registration, if Chinese law, like German law, afforded the register absolute effect, the rule would be exceedingly harsh on the real owners. The Civil Code has also recognized the success achieved by the applications of *bona fide* acquisition to immovables. It maintains the legislative solution of the Real Right Law and adopts a unitary doctrine of *bona fide* acquisition in both movable and immovable property, as prescribed in article 311.

3.4 *Reconstructing the Regime of Chattel Guarantee (Secured Transactions)*

The chattel guarantee regime of the Civil Code follows the doctrine of functionalism, which is a significant reform of civil legislation (the issue will be discussed more in detail in Section 5). From a functionalist point of view, the law of chattel guarantee blurs the distinctions between mortgage, pledge, retention of ownership, and other forms. As long as the chattel guarantee forms assume the functions of securing an interest, the guarantee will be governed by a generic unitary regime that prescribes creation, confrontation, priority, and enforcement of security interest.[9] This legislative framework is borrowed from Article 9 on "Secured Transactions" of the Uniform Commercial Code (UCC) of the United States. Article 9 of the UCC pioneered a uniform legal framework and terminology for chattel guarantees, recognized the diverse forms of secured transactions in commercial markets, and greatly influenced the law of security interests around the world.

8 Zhu Guangxin, 'Limits of the Rule of Bona Fide Purchase in Real Estate' (2009) 4 Chinese J L 41 (朱广新, 不动产适用善意取得制度的限度, 《法学研究》).

9 Ji Hailong, 'Civil Code – The Systematic Development of the Movable Property and Related Security Rights' (2021) 1 Jurist 41 (纪海龙, <民法典>动产与权利担保制度的体系展开, 《法学家》).

In order to merge the doctrine of functionalism into the Chinese chattel guarantee, the Civil Code set out several new rules. For instance, the Civil Code integrates the registration confrontation of floating charge into the general registration confrontation of chattel guarantee, specifying that floating charge is merely a form of chattel mortgage (article 396); it unifies the creation, confrontation and other aspects of retention of ownership with the provisions of chattel mortgage (article 641); it enunciates the priority among conflicting security interests in the same collateral (article 414). Based on the rules above, a relatively complete system of security right sequence rule is constructed by combining the order of payments between mortgage and pledge on the same collateral (article 415), the superiority of purchase price security interest (article 416), and the priority of possessory lien (article 456). In addition, the Civil Code deleted the provisions on the specific registries for security interests in the Real Right Law, thus eradicating the negative impact of decentralized registries on the establishment of a uniform registration system. The People's Bank of China issued 'Measures for Unified Registration of Movable Property and Rights Guarantee', achieving the unification of an online registration system of chattel and right guarantee.

In brief, the Book on Real Rights retains the characteristics of the socialist legal system, absorbs several doctrines from the continental legal system and American legal system, observes and respects the social realities of China, and develops a real rights legal system suited for the Chinese market economy.

4 The Consolidation and Innovation of the Book on Real Rights on the Property System

The Book on Real Rights of the Civil Code is the basic regulation for adjusting various property relations, and is the most significant and commonly-used basic norm that governs the ownership of property, as well as changes of property. In order to fully execute the policy of "Improving the System of Protecting Property Rights According to Law" raised by the CPC Central Committee,[10] the Book on Real Rights delineates a series of property rights through various specific rules, realizing a significant institutional innovation.

10 See《中共中央、国务院关于完善产权保护制度依法保护产权的意见》(n 2).

4.1 *The Trichotomy of State, Collective, and Private Ownership with Chinese Characteristics*

The Civil Code inherits the trichotomy of ownership from the expired Real Right Law. It divides the subjects of ownership into three categories, i.e., state ownership, collective ownership, and private ownership.

State ownership embodies China's long-term adherence and development of the socialist system with Chinese characteristics. With respect to state ownership, article 246(1) of the Book on Real Rights confirms the legal qualification of the state as a subject of rights in civil law, and article 246(2) further specifies the way the state may exercise its ownership. Articles 247 to 259 enumerate the scope of state ownership, the representative bodies of the state ownership, their responsibilities and legal liabilities. Theoretically, the significance of the legal provisions above is to exclude bodies other than the state from acquiring property ownership with specific characteristics, especially to inhibit certain privileged powers or hostile groups towards a sovereign country.[11]

According to the provisions of the Civil Code, natural resources belong to the state. However, to fully develop the socialist market economy, the Civil Code encourages, supports, and protects collective or private exploration, exploitation, development, or other economic activities on natural resources. Through the real rights system of the Civil Code, strengthening the flexible utilization of natural resources is an inevitable requirement for promoting a healthy economy and upgrading the industrial structure. It is also a necessary measure to exploit resources efficiently, allocate resources reasonably, and boost the creation of social wealth.

The collectively owned system is a core component of socialist public ownership provided in China's Constitution. According to the Civil Code, collective ownership is a form of the collectively owned system. In recent years, the CPC Central Committee has adhered to collective ownership of farmers and promoted the reform of the collective economic system of villages. Some reform policies point out that "collective ownership of rural land, rural household contracting right, and the right to management of land, the so-called 'separation of three rights' shall be carried out"[12]. "To improve the 'separation of

11 Xie Hongfei, 'The State in the Civil Code' (2022) 5 L Rev 17 (谢鸿飞, <民法典>中的国家《法学评论》).

12 See 'Several Opinions of the Central Committee of the Communist Party of China and the State Council on Deeply Promoting Agricultural Supply-Side Structural Reform and Accelerating the Cultivation of New Momentum for Agricultural and Rural Development' (2017) Zhongfa 1 (中共中央、国务院关于深入推进农业供给侧结构性改革加快培育农业农村发展新动能的若干意见, 中发).

three rights' of contractual rural land, the right to management of land should receive equal protection while safeguarding collective ownership of rural land and rural household contracting right".[13] In order to bolster up the collective economy of villages, to realize the efficient use of collective ownership, and to help farmers, the Civil Code sets out systematic rules on the collective property system and guards the implementation of the preceding policies. Concerning the collective ownership of villages, article 260 of the Civil Code specifies the scope of collectively-owned property. Article 261 stipulates that the property of a farmer collective is collectively owned by the members of the collective, and sets out the necessary statutory procedures to exercise rights. Article 262 defines the subjects of collective ownership. With respect to collective ownership organization, the second sentence of article 264 adds a new right to be informed, namely, "[m]embers of the collective have the right to retrieve and make copies of the relevant materials". Besides, article 265(2) provides the circumstances under which the decisions made by a rural collective economic organization or a villagers' committee may be revoked, with the aim of protecting the lawful rights and interests of members of the collective, and warding off infringements committed by the collective organization through decisions.

Private ownership is the most common form of rights. The Civil Code, without imposing too many special rules, only stipulates the scope, legal protections, and investment rights of private ownership in articles 266–268. The provisions, which further develop and confirm private ownership and its protections, manifest the principle of the Constitution that private property may not be encroached upon.

In terms of the relationship among state, collective and private ownership, article 207 establishes the doctrine of real rights for equal protection, meaning that there is no superiority among the three types of ownership. Since the reform and opening up, a prominent characteristic of China's property system has been its focus on protecting private ownership. The codification of the Book on Real Rights of the Civil Code has strengthened this trend. The root of this change may be that the policymakers have realized that a modern state should take property protection as a premise of its political ethics. This change plays a vital role in the development of the socialist market economy with Chinese characteristics, the preservation of property rights of civil entities, and the enhancement of citizens' fulfillment and happiness.

---

13 See 'Opinions of the Central Committee of the Communist Party of China and the State Council on the Implementation of the Rural Revitalization Strategy' (January 2, 2018) Zhongfa 1 (中共中央、国务院关于实施乡村振兴战略的意见, 中发).

4.2 *Further Reform on Rural Land Rights: The Right to Management of Land*

Since 1978, China has carried out a reform of the rural land system and granted farmers rights to contractual management of agricultural land through a household contract system. Consequently, the motivation for farmers to produce has risen, and thus the state's agriculture has rapidly developed. In 2003, the Rural Land Contracting Law consolidated the achievement through legislation. However, within this legal framework, the land contractual management rights granted through household contracts, were limited in various ways when the rights circulated in markets (especially because of the prohibition on collateralized finance). These rules also obstructed the diverse utilization of land. In recent years, the Chinese government has initiated reform pilots to carry out the 'separation of three rights' in some areas and to segregate the right to management of land from land contractual management rights, releasing the values and vitalities of rural land. Thus, considering the success of these pilots, the legislature amended the Rural Land Contracting Law in 2018 with specific provisions empowering right holders to lease their rights through subcontracting, to contribute it as shares, and to transfer the right to manage land to others. The Law also allowed farmers to use the right to management of land of the contracted land to secure financing from financial institutions. All these measures have further confirmed and consolidated the achievements of the reform.

The Civil Code thus absorbs the amended rules from the Rural Land Contracting Law. Article 339 provides that "[a] person with the right to contractual management of land may decide on his own to transfer the right to management of land to others by leasing, contributing it as shares, or other means in accordance with law". Article 340 provides that "[w]ithin the time limit as agreed in the contract, the person with the right to management of land is entitled to possess the rural land, to carry out agricultural production and operation on his own, and to benefit therefrom". Articles 341 and 342 respectively stipulate the registration of the right to management of land and transfer of the rights by means including leasing, contributing it as shares, or mortgaging. Meanwhile, the Civil Code deleted article 184 of the Real Right Law that prohibited the mortgage of agricultural land (article 399), responding to the need to include the right to management of land in the market after the 'separation of three rights'. The provisions above have implemented collective ownership, stabilized rural household contracting, and further liberalized the right to management of land.

4.3 *The Transfer Limitations of the Right to Use a House Site and a Probe on the Reform*

In China, rural homesteads are guaranteed house sites provided to farmers through collective land, wherein distribution, utilization, and transfers are more restrictive. Articles 362–365 of the Civil Code formulate the right to use a house site, leaving detailed legal regulations in the Land Management Law.

Farmers are entitled to use rural homesteads, but they must adhere to the principle of 'one family, one house, prescribed area'. Likewise, as to the inheritance and assignment of the homestead, the subjects are limited to the members of the collective economic organization. In other words, one who is not a member of the collective economic organization shall not inherit or purchase the right to use a house site.

The purpose of the aforementioned restrictions is to safeguard farmers' habitation and property, to prevent farmers from losing their homesteads, and to protect them from being reduced to destitution or homelessness. However, it is important to note that the above restrictions may have adverse impacts contrary to the legislative intent. Moreover, housing is an essential asset of a modern family, and farmers may need to convey unnecessary estates to resolve their financing difficulties. Faced with the noncommercial, nonmarketable, and noncapital rural homestead, farmers of the state are unable to turn them into massive wealth, and suffer from the loss of their property rights. Thus, local governments considered the conflicts between the supply and demand of homesteads. They clung to the premise that homesteads provided a basic social protection to the villages and tried to enlarge the number of actors having the right to use homesteads (the 'open system theory').[14] Some scholars proposed the establishment of a "compensatory opt-out mechanism for homesteads" and "mortgage loan for homesteads".[15] Generally, the majority view holds that, since the right to use a house site is free of charge, its transfer should be strictly limited.[16]

This paper argues that the reform of the right to use a house site should first follow the doctrines in the Civil Code that endows homesteads with social protection and essential functions. Therefore, the market characteristics of all

14 Ding Yufeng, 'The Normative Logic of Homestead Circulation' (2022) 4 Xuehai 148–149 (丁宇峰, 宅基地流转的规范逻辑 《学海》).

15 Chen Meiqiu et al., 'China's Rural Homestead System Reform: Logic and Path' (2022) 7 China Land Science 27 (陈美球等, 中国农村宅基地制度改革：逻辑与路径《中国土地科学》).

16 Liang Huixing and Chen Huabin, *Property Law* (Law Press 2020) 294 (梁慧星、陈华彬, 物权法).

homesteads must be built on the premise that the homesteads are first meant to ensure that farmers have 'a house for one family' and 'a house to live in'. On this basis, the next objective should be revitalizing the economic attribute and market value of homesteads. Besides, local governments ought to play a dynamic role in this respect by considering the real situations and demands of local villages, and formulating operable regulations to help farmers transfer their homesteads.

4.4 *The Establishment of the Right of Habitation and Its Diversified Applications*

The right of habitation originated from *servitutes personarum* in ancient Roman law[17] and was inherited by the Civil Code of France and Germany in modern times. At the time of the drafting of the Real Right Law in 2005, there was a fierce debate on whether to adopt the right of habitation. Since the original Real Right Law did not respond to this question, the debate has continued during the drafting of the Civil Code.[18] Considering the increasing conflicts of urban residence and the necessity of the right to habitation, the legislators eventually incorporated it into the Civil Code in a dedicated chapter. Theoretically, adopting this legal right has both formal and substantive significance. As such, the Civil Code creates an entirely new usufructuary right in the principle of *numerus clausus*; in terms of substance, the right of habitation has improved and increased the right to use and benefit from the property by civil entities. The content of this chapter can be briefly described as follows.

Article 366 of the Civil Code stipulates that "a person with the right of habitation is entitled to the right to usufruct of possessing and using another person's dwelling as agreed in the contract, so as to meet his needs of habitation". Meanwhile, article 371 allows the parties to create a right of habitation through testamentary acts. Regardless, according to article 368, the right of habitation is only valid upon immovable registration.

---

17 Zhou Nang, *Principles of Roman Law* (The Commercial Press 2001, vol 1) 406–407 (周枏,罗马法原论).

18 Among the opponents, see Liang Huixing, 'Several Issues Concerning the Draft Parts of the Civil Code' (2019) 4 Research on Rule of Law 3–16 (梁慧星, 关于民法典分则草案的若干问题 《法治研究》); Chen Huabin, 'Study on the Legislation of the Property Rights of China's Civil Code' (2017) 5 Tribune of Political Science and Law 38 (陈华彬, 我国民法典物权编立法研究 《政法论坛》). Among those in favor, see Cui Jianyuan, 'Study on the Legislation of Real Rights Book in the Civil Law' (2017) 2 China Legal Science 51–52 (崔建远, 民法分则物权编立法研究,《中国法学》); Ma Xinyan, 'Residence Right Legislation and Inheritance System Innovation' (2018) 2 Tsingshua L 164–178 (马新彦, 居住权立法与继承编的制度创新 《清华法学》).

As for the content of habitation rights, a person with the right of habitation is entitled, in principle, to possess and use the dwelling where they reside, and shall not transfer and inherit it. However, article 369 also provides that "the dwelling in which a right of habitation is created may not be let on lease, unless otherwise agreed by the parties", meaning that, if parties voluntarily reach an agreement, the person with a right of habitation may rent out the dwelling. Therefore, unlike the civil law tradition that the right of habitation is limited to residential use, the right of habitation in Chinese Civil Law may also assume a function of commercial use.

5 Optimization of the Business Environment and the Functionalist Reform of the Chattel Guarantee Regime

5.1 *Background of the Functionalist Reform of the Chattel Guarantee Regime*

As an essential indicator of the investment climate of the world economy, the Doing Business Report issued by the World Bank, has had a significant impact on the security rights regulated in the Book on Real Rights, especially on the innovation of the chattel guarantee regime.[19] The guiding doctrine of functionalism runs through the reform of the chattel guarantee in the Civil Code. The legislative mode of functionalism originated from American law of chattel guarantee, gradually influencing European and international civil and commercial legislations. The functionalist approach advocated by the UCC and the UNCITRAL Model Law on Secured Transactions proposes the integration of various security interests with security functions, and the establishment of unified rules for their creation, confrontation, publication, priority, and enforcement.

Another context of China's reform of chattel guarantee is long-term numerous implicit guarantees in economic activities and judicial practice, such as retention of title and transferring guarantee. As these implicit guarantees are elusive by nature, their legal effects remain unclear and unable to be publicized through the register, causing great uncertainty to the parties. Given the

---

19 Ji Hailong, 'China's Law on Secured Transactions on Movable Property under the Background of the World Bank's Doing Business Survey' (2020) 2 Law Science Magazine 34–35 (纪海龙, 世行营商环境调查背景下的中国动产担保交易法, 《法学杂志》); Gao Shengping, 'Interpretation of the Priority Rules for Security Rights in Movable Assets in the Civil Code' (2020) 3 Tinsghua L 94 (高圣平, 民法典动产担保权优先顺位规则的解释论 《清华法学》).

situation, the Civil Code establishes a unified registration system for chattel guarantees, clarifying the situations of registration validity (e.g., pledge of rights) and registration confrontation (e.g., chattel mortgage, retention of title, financial lease, factoring). This new mechanism vitalizes various atypical methods of secured transactions, which are now included in the unified public notice system of chattel guarantee.

5.2 *Key Points on the Reform of the Chattel Guarantee Regime*

Firstly, the scope of security contracts expands. The purpose of the reform is to maximize the means of chattel guarantee, because narrow and solidified statutory guarantee methods will restrict social financing and inhibit the market economy growth. In terms of the type and scope of security contracts, compared with article 172(1) of the Real Right Law, the Civil Code adds a provision in article 388(1): "Security contracts include mortgage contracts, pledge contracts, and other contracts with a function of security". This rule is to "expand the scope of security contracts and clarify the security functions of atypical security contracts such as financial leasing, factoring, and retention of title".[20] Although transferring guarantees are not enumerated, the stipulation of "other contracts with a function of security" opens a door for integrating transferring guarantees into the chattel guarantee regime in the Civil Code.[21]

Secondly, retention of title, as a type of sales contract in the Book on Contracts, is also bound by the rules of chattel guarantee. For example, regarding the creation and confrontation of retention of title, on the basis of article 134 of the Law of Contracts, article 641 of the Civil Code adds a new rule: "The ownership of the subject matter retained by a seller, without being registered, shall not be asserted against a *bona fide* third" (article 641(2)). Therefore, "registration confrontation" is adopted by the Civil Code in this guarantee method. For the effect of retention of title, article 642 adds that "[t]he seller may negotiate with the buyer to take back the subject matter. Where such negotiation fails, the procedures for enforcement of security interests may be applied mutatis mutandis" (article 642(2)). This provision effectively unifies the rules

---

20 On May 22, 2020, at the third session of the 13th National People's Congress, Wang Chen, vice chairman of the Standing Committee of the National People's Congress, issued the 'Explanations on the Civil Code of the People's Republic of China (Draft)' ('关于《中华人民共和国民法典（草案）》的说明').

21 Zhu Xiaozhe and Ma Qiang, 'Legal Structure and Effectiveness of Movable Property Assignment Guarantee from the Perspective of Optimizing the Business Environment' (2021) 2 Social Sciences in Yunnan 2 (朱晓喆、马强, 优化营商环境视野下动产让与担保的法律构造及效力,《云南社会科学》).

between retention of title and chattel mortgage in the enforcement process. Thus, it is evident that the retention of title has a strong attribute of security interests.

Thirdly, although financial leasing and factoring are regulated as contracts by the Book on Contracts in the Civil Code, they are designed according to the structure of security interests. For example, article 745 of the Civil Code adds a rule of registration confrontation for financial leases. Article 768 stipulates that, where a creditor of an account receivable concludes multiple factoring contracts with different factors, the priority shall be determined by order of registration and notification.

Finally, the Civil Code recognizes the possible combination of chattel mortgage with floating charge. Article 403 of the Civil Code merges article 188 and article 189(1) of the Real Right Law, by which registration confrontation of floating charge is included in that of general chattel mortgage. Therefore, it is clear via legislation that floating charge is merely a special form of chattel mortgage. Compared with general chattel mortgage, floating charge is unique only because it can cover future acquired property. As for other aspects, floating charge is consistent with general chattel mortgage in terms of creation, confrontation, priority, and enforcement of security interests. Theoretically, it is believed to be a reference to the "American floating lien".[22]

Thus, optimizing the business environment as an important national policy, has an essential impact on the reform of the regime of chattel guarantees in the Civil Code. The reform has responded to the growing financing needs of market entities, promoted the improvement of China's credit trading market, and integrated China's secured transactions system with international standards.

6 Conclusion

Taking the original Real Right Law as a model, the drafters constructed the Book on Real Rights by systematically sorting out China's local legal resources and absorbing advanced foreign legislative experiences. The Book on Real Rights of the Civil Code further consolidated the achievements of the property rights reform brought about by the development of the Chinese market economy in the past forty years, upon which the Book on Real Rights created new legal frameworks. Under the socio-economic background of optimizing

22 Ji Hailong and Zhang Yutao, 'The 'Ordinary Business Buyer's Rules' in the Property Rights Book (Draft) of the Civil Code' (2019) 5 Social Sciences in Yunnan 106 (纪海龙、张玉涛, <民法典>物权编（草案）中的"正常经营买受人规则",《云南社会科学》).

the business environment and responding to social demands, the Civil Code has initially completed the reform of the chattel guarantee regime characterized by modern functionalism. Numerous theoretical disputes have arisen in compiling the Book on Real Rights, and will continue after the Civil Code has come into force. These disputes await clarification and specification in future theoretical research, prospective judicial application, and social practice. In general, the Book on Real Rights of the Civil Code has reshaped China's real rights legal system and has constituted a milestone in constructing China's rule of law.

CHAPTER 7

The New Chinese Civil Code: Outer Perspectives. A View from Comparative Property Law

Sjef van Erp

1 Paradigm Changes in Property Law

Today's world is faced with numerous fundamental global changes. Among them are the rapid hybridisation of society and climate change.[1] Both are having a direct impact on how we look at the world around us, how subjects use the objects around them, how persons deal with their patrimony. Property law deals with the legal relationships between a subject and a considerable and relevant number of other subjects regarding an object. In traditional Civil Law phraseology, property law deals with 'rights against the world' (rights '*erga omnes*') or so-called absolute rights, to distinguish these from relative rights which arise from contract, tort and unjust enrichment. Remarkably enough, the Civil Law tradition gathers the latter three sources of rights around the 'law of obligations', thus focussing more on the duty than on the right. This is different when looking at absolute rights, where the focus is on the right, not on the duties which rest on others resulting from the holder of an absolute right being entitled to (positively) do with the object as the holder decides and as a consequence (negatively) compel all others to accept this as the holder can exclude all others from its use. Absolute rights create their own sphere of sovereignty. Or, to put it differently, where in the law of obligations the right is the mirror image of the duty, in the law of property the duty is the mirror image of the right. In both approaches it will be obvious that there can be neither a right without a duty, nor a duty without a right. In this paradigm, if taken to its very limits, the idea that the right holders themselves may have duties being a constituent part of their rights is absent. It will be obvious that such a strict approach is untenable from a societal viewpoint. So also in the Civil Law tradition a typical definition of a right of ownership includes limitations resulting from the fact that we all live in a society together with others and

1 See my valedictory address at Maastricht University: Sjef van Erp, *All good things come to an end, but access remains* (Wolf Legal Publishers 2021).

 | DOI:10.1163/9789004704428_008

have to take into account both the position of our neighbours and must accept that public interests might prevail over our private interests. A typical Civil Law definition of ownership, for example, therefore reads: "Ownership is the most comprehensive property right that a person, the 'owner', can have to (in) a thing", immediately followed by: "The owner is free to use the thing to the exclusion of everyone else, provided that he respects the rights and entitlements of others to the thing and observes the restrictions based on rules of written and unwritten law".[2] Also, in many other Civil Law jurisdictions the so-called 'social function' of ownership has been stressed.[3] Ownership should be used such that a person's own freedom does not limit another's freedom in a way unacceptable in society and it must be used such that it also promotes the general interest ('common good'). Furthermore, in the Civil Law tradition the possibility that a property right may not be absolute in the sense of *erga omnes*, but relative in the sense of functioning against some third parties but not against others is considered as a violation of the fundamental *summa divisio* between relative and absolute rights. This is different in the Common Law tradition where strict dogmatic distinctions are, generally speaking, absent and consequently the distinction in various types of rights is less rigorous. This is, in part, the outcome of legal history, but also the result of a difference in legal mentality compared with the Civil Law. In the Common Law traditions the construction of property rights still is founded on the theory of feudalism with its split ownership to which later equitable rights as an extra level were added. As is well-known this resulted in the institution of the trust. Although immediately after the codification movement on the continent of Europe Civil Law jurisdictions rejected the trust as too much reviving old memories to the pre-existing feudal system, nowadays Civil Law systems more and more accept 'trust-like' institutions, such as the '*Treuhand*' in German law and the '*fiducie*' in French law. Accepting the relativity of property rights thus seems to go hand in hand with a growing awareness of property rights as also having a social function, not only in theory but also in practice.[4] The paradigm change we, therefore, see is that the absolute nature of ownership is seen as a relict from

2 Article 5:1 (1) and (2) Netherlands Civil Code.

3 Agustin Parise, *Ownership Paradigms in American Civil Law Jurisdictions: Manifestations of the Shifts in the Legislation of Louisiana, Chile, and Argentina (16th-20th Centuries)* (Brill Nijhoff 2017) 185 ff.

4 See Martin Löhnig, 'The "Social Function of Property" in German Law', in Paul Babie and Jessica Viven-Wilksch (eds), *Léon Duguit and the Social Obligation Norm of Property. A Translation and Global Exploration* (Springer Nature 2019) 111, and Bram Akkermans, 'Sustainable Ownership – new obligations towards achieving a sustainable society' (2021) 10 Eur Property L J 277.

the past and that all relations, also property relations, can only be relative even though relative can also mean against a group or entity of persons. Ownership is no longer a '*droit inviolable et sacré*', an inviolable and sacred right, as defined in the French *Déclaration des droits de l'homme et du citoyen* of 1789.[5] It was, foremost, an idea in the minds of the '*citoyen*', the well-established land owner, but it does not fit in today's world which is drastically different from what is was in the 19th century. Ownership is a right belonging to, above all, '*l'homme*', in this context now also to be understood as mankind or society.

In light of our hybridisation of society (resulting in a mixed world of 'real' and 'virtual' objects, in which the essence of objects may be data and data can be copied, thus creating several identical versions of one object) and the importance we today give to the law as facilitating, promoting and, if necessary, compelling measures to combat climate change and take care of sustainability, a classical Civil Law dogmatic approach might not only be counterproductive, but even dangerous. It risks that the law looses sight of far reaching developments in the world around us and by loosing sight might result in legal approaches which are perhaps outright counterproductive by working against sustainability solutions or bringing for example consumers in a position where the use of modern digital technologies takes away their rights to protection as the inherently weaker party. If owners can decline to take sustainability measures (such as installing solar panels, isolating homes, reducing carbon dioxide (CO_2) and nitrogen (N) emissions) arguing that their ownership right is 'inviolable and sacred', this ignores the interest of the *bonum commune*, the common good.[6] When businesses can argue that their algorithms are pre-programmed

---

5 Déclaration des Droits de l'Homme et du Citoyen de 1789. Article 17 reads:"*La propriété étant un droit inviolable et sacré, nul ne peut en être privé, si ce n'est lorsque la nécessité publique, légalement constatée, l'exige évidemment, et sous la condition d'une juste et préalable indemnité*" ("Since the right to Property is inviolable and sacred, no one may be deprived thereof, unless public necessity, legally ascertained, obviously requires it, and just and prior indemnity has been paid"). See also article 2: "*Le but de toute association politique est la conservation des droits naturels et imprescriptibles de l'homme. Ces droits sont la liberté, la propriété, la sûreté, et la résistance à l'oppression*" ("The aim of every political association is the preservation of the natural and imprescriptible rights of Man. These rights are Liberty, Property, Safety and Resistance to Oppression"). The original French version is available at <https://www.conseil-constitutionnel.fr/le-bloc-de-constitutionnalite/declaration-des-droits-de-l-homme-et-du-citoyen-de-1789> (accessed January 15, 2023); its English translation is available at <https://www.conseil-constitutionnel.fr/sites/default/files/as/root/bank_mm/anglais/cst2.pdf> (accessed January 15, 2023).

6 On the idea of the '*bonum commune*', see Kurt Seelmann, 'Bonum Commune – An Outline' (2004) 6 Eur J L Ref 289. Cf, on the role of communitarian values in Chinese property law, Lei Chen, 'Private Property with Chinese Characteristics: a Critical Analysis of the Chinese Law

in such a way that consumer rights, for example to a cooling off period, are no longer possible because the transaction is final (think of a smart contract running on a blockchain) so returning a bought object is no longer possible, then weaker parties in society are again unprotected on the basis of 19th century formalistic arguments that contracts and property transactions are concluded on the basis of mutual '*liberté*' (freedom) and '*égalité*' (equality), and hence are to be binding, forgetting that the third rallying cry of the French Revolution also was '*fraternité*', to be translated as solidarity. In a society citizens should take care of one another and take economic inequality in account, as they also should take care of future generations.

Of course, traditional definitions of the most complete property right in Civil Law: ownership, do contain a reference to the rights of others, that ownership must not cause damage to others and that ownership brings with it a social responsibility, but these are not the main focus. At the heart of property rights still is the notion of freedom and the right to exclude. In the present debates regarding how the law can contribute to combatting climate change and how the law should respond to our world being in large part more digital than 'real', we do see, however, a change in focus from looking at the rights which property law confers on holders of a property entitlement towards looking at duties. In other words we see a paradigm change. The focus is becoming how property rights should be used in such a way that, for example ownership, contributes to measures limiting the impact of how our economy and life style influence climate change and how any entitlement rights to data should be used in such a way that in as far as data can be traced back to persons such data should be used only in a very limited and careful way. It is interesting to note that such a paradigm change can also be seen in the new Chinese Civil Code, although its starting point is that ownership in the Civil Law sense and meaning of the word does not really exist, given the primary and leading role of the state.[7] It could be argued that ownership is changing from a traditional absolute right of one subject against all, or at least a considerable and relevant

on Property of 2007' (2010) 18 Eur Rev Priv L 983, 995 ff, and Hao Jiang, 'The Making of a Civil Code in China: Promises and Perils of a New Civil Law' (2021) Tul L Rev 777, 810 ff.

7 Cf in this respect article 9 of the Chinese Civil Code: "When conducting a civil activity, a person of the Civil Law shall act in a manner that facilitates conservation of resources and protection of the ecological environment", and also article 127: "Where there are laws particularly providing for the protection of data and online virtual assets, such provisions shall be followed". Cf Tiantian Zhai and Yen-Chiang Chang, 'The Contribution of China's Civil Law to Sustainable Development: Progress and Prospects' (2019) 11 Sustainability 294, and Igor Szpotakowski, 'The New Chinese Civil Code and Its Contribution to Sustainable Development' (2020) Transformacje Prawa Prywatnego 233.

group of, others to a right which in itself contains an implicit duty to take care of the interests of others who else might suffer the negative consequences of a traditional view on property rights.[8]

Given this paradigm change, it is extremely interesting to study one of the most recent Civil Codes, the Civil Code of China to look for signs of the paradigmatic change described above.

But before I will do this, my approach will be somewhat more of a technical nature, although in property law legal technique and policy decisions may go hand in hand. The attribution and distribution of wealth has always been of a highly political and socio-economic nature, but the legal-technical expression of the choices based upon such considerations seems to follow certain distinct paths which surface in Civil Law, Common Law and mixed legal systems. At the centre of this technical expression are three prominent tenets and I will hold the new Chinese provisions, first of all, against the light of these three leading property law principles: *numerus clausus*, transparency and hierarchy.

Numerus clausus has both a substantive and a procedural aspect. From a substantive viewpoint the *numerus clausus* principle implies that the number and content of property entitlements are limited and strictly regulated by mandatory law, leaving hardly any freedom for the parties to shape their property relations. To put it differently: the principle demarcates property law from the law of obligations. Hidden behind its substance is something also extremely fundamental, which was only realised relatively late: a closed list of the subjects who can hold property rights, and consequently the subjects against whom property rights may be invoked, and a closed list of the objects of property rights. Historically, subjects are natural and legal persons, such as corporations, foundations and associations, but could an autonomously functioning computer system, driven by Artificial Intelligence, also be qualified as a 'legal person' and consequently a subject of legal relations vis-à-vis other subjects? Could data be a legal object, that not only is given a special status in public law (privacy protection), but also in private law (for example when it comes to forced execution of a debtor's assets in a case of insolvency)? Legal objects are at the core of a subject's patrimony, its shadow consisting of economically speaking valuable assets in the world around that subject. But not only are legal objects and legal subjects closely connected, the same applies to legal relations the nature and content of which vary based on the subject and object concerned, as each relation depends for its existence and content

8 Cf. Sjef van Erp, 'Covid-19 apps, Corona vaccination apps and data "ownership"' (2022) 8 China-EU L J 45.

on the subject that is a party to the relation and the object involved. This can be clearly when looking at the Chinese Civil Code in its article 206: “The State upholds and improves the fundamental socialist economic systems, such as the ownership system under which diverse forms of ownership co-develop with public ownership as the mainstay, the distribution system under which multiple forms of distribution co-exist with distribution according to work as the mainstay, as well as the system of socialist market economy”. Of course, this definition is the result of ideological and political policy choices, but it does show clearly that property rights are the outcome of a triangle of subjects, objects and rights. *Numerus clausus* also has a procedural aspect, as it is a matter for mandatory law to lay down how property rights can be created, transferred and how they terminate. The procedural aspect implies a particular view on sovereignty: only a state can create and enforce property rights and within the state a primary role is given to the legislature, while the judiciary may create property rights as well but to a very limited degree.[9] Transparency implies that a property right, given its strong nature, must be visible to the subjects against whom the right may be invoked (for example through registration). Today, given our heavily digitalised society, we are more aware of the fact that such visibility should not be unlimited and must be balanced by a person's right to privacy. Finally, property law is characterised by hierarchy. Unlike in the law of obligations, where rights are equal unless they are made unequal by a specific provision or arrangement, in property law because of their '*erga omnes*' nature rights may come into fierce conflict with one another. Therefore, such conflicts need to be (ex post) resolved, but preferably (ex ante) avoided and hence rules must exist that make clear which right has priority over another right. In today's world we now see more clearly that these hierarchical conflicts may not only arise 'inside' property law, but also from the 'outside' because of the growing weight and priority that is now given to fundamental human rights also in private relationships.

In the following paragraph I will more particularly look at the various new Chinese property law provisions from the perspective of the three leading principles of *numerus clausus*, transparency and hierarchy, and the perspective of who can be a legal subject, what can be a legal object and which legal relations may exist between these subjects regarding an object.

9 Cf Sjef van Erp, 'Ownership of Data. The Numerus Clausus of Legal Objects' (2017) 6 Brigham-Kanner Property Rights Conference J 235.

2 An Overview of Property Law Provisions

The major provisions on property law are to be found in Book Two of the Chinese Civil Code.[10] Its technical structure resembles very much that of any Civil Code in a Western economy, except that the ideological background, and consequently the political and socio-economic choices, are fundamentally different. This is clearly expressed in Book Two, on real rights, Part One, general provisions, Chapter I, general rules, article 206, stating that the "State upholds and improves the fundamental socialist economic systems", to which is added that the "State implements a socialist market economy and protects the equal legal status and development rights of all market participants".[11] The following article then makes clear that, next to, what a Civil Lawyer would call, the state's '*dominium eminens*' (eminent domain as the supreme expression of its sovereignty) also other legal subjects may be entitled to protection of property rights, as the "real rights of the State, collectives, private individuals, and the

---

10 For more background reading, see Jonas Alsen, 'An Introduction to Chinese Property Law' (1996) 20 Ml J Int'l L 1; Lei Chen, 'The New Chinese Property Code: A Giant Step Forward?' (2007) 11(2) Electron J Comp L (now Eur J Comp L & Gov; articles in the Electron J Comp L are no longer electronically available, but are on file with the author); Xiaomin Chen, 'Chinese Property Law (Rights in rem) in the Civilian Tradition' (2009) 16 Trans Stud Rev 421; Quinglan Long, 'Reinterpreting Chinese Property Law' (2009) 19 So Cal Interdisc L J 55; Yuanshi Bu, 'Security Rights in Property in Chinese Law: The Unattainable Goal of Constructing a Coherent Legal System?' (2010) 18 Eur Rev Priv L 1005; Chen (n 6); Lei Chen, '100 Years of Chinese Property Law. Looking Back and Thinking Forward', in Lei Chen and C.H. (Remco) van Rhee (eds), *Towards a Chinese Civil Code. Comparative and Historical Perspectives* (Martinus Nijhoff Publishers 2012) 87; Weiguo Wang, 'Restructuring Modern Property Law on a Theoretical Basis', *ibid*, 109; Shitong Qiao, 'The Evolution of Chinese Property Law. Stick by Stick?', in Yongjian Zhang, Wei Shen, Wenyu Wang (eds), *Private law in China and Taiwan: legal and economic analyses* (Cambridge University Press, 2017) 182; Jiang (n 6).

11 See also article 12 of the Chinese Constitution: "The state shall protect socialist public property. It is prohibited for any organization or individual to seize or damage state or collective property by any means". At the same time the Chinese constitution also protects private property in its article 13, which reads: "The state shall protect the right of citizens to own and inherit private property in accordance with the provisions of law. The state may, in order to meet the demands of the public interest and in accordance with the provisions of law, expropriate or requisition citizens' private property and furnish compensation". These two articles find their more general expression from a private law perspective in article 1 Chinese Civil Code: "This Law is formulated in accordance with the Constitution of the People's Republic of China for the purposes of protecting the lawful rights and interests of the persons of the Civil Law, regulating civil-law relations, maintaining social and economic order, meet the needs for developing socialism with Chinese characteristics, and carrying forward the core socialist values".

other right holders are equally protected by law and free from infringement by any organization or individual". What follows is a rather extensive and detailed set of mandatory rules on property rights, apparently aimed, so it seems, at minimising the role of the judiciary in extending or limiting any of the rules, given their in essence ideological and political nature.

The basic structure of the property law part is as follows. After Part One, dealing with general provisions, Part Two on ownership rights follows. The latter part is aimed at attributing and distributing objects to and over subjects, thus articulating a crucial element of the *numerus clausus* principle, following which the law not only limits number and content of property rights, but also who can be a legal subject and what can be a legal object.

Regarding the acceptance of legal subjects as those who can be entitled to property rights or against whom a property right can be invoked, the answer is not to be found in Book Two, but in Book One of the Chinese Civil Code. According to Book One, Chinese law recognises as legal subjects natural and legal persons, the latter category consisting of for profit, non-profit, and special legal persons, next to unincorporated organizations. According to article 58, a "legal person shall be established in accordance with law", implying that the role of courts here is extremely limited and that accepting new forms of legal personhood, as indicated earlier regarding autonomously functioning and AI-driven computer systems, is not to be expected soon, if at all. This means that a Decentralised Autonomous Organisation (better known by its abbreviation: DAO), a smart contract-based algorithmic system that is running as if it were a traditional legal person but without human intervention (except, of course, in the stage of its programming), is unlikely to be recognised as an independent legal person with its own separate patrimony containing proprietary rights.

Regarding the (closed) list of legal objects, these can be found in Part Two of Book Two. It contains first of all a full list of objects which can only belong to (be in the ownership of) the State. Besides what can be a legal object and to which subject a legal object belongs, Part Two also provides rules on ownership by collectives and, finally, individuals. Part Three of Book Two has rights on usufructs (to which also easements belong) and Part Four is about security interests in property. Remarkably enough the property law rules are concluded by provisions on possession (articles 458 ff), but these seem to be more part of the law on damages and unjustified enrichment than property law. Possession does not appear to be connected with rules on prescription, either directly resulting in acquisition of a proprietary right or through a proprietary claim being barred by limitation, thus resulting in de facto acceptance of someone else's right.[12] Possession obviously is a matter of fact, not of law.

Given that categories of legal subjects are dealt with in Book One, let me in what follows more specifically concentrate on what, according to the Chinese Civil Code, can be a legal object and which property rights among legal subjects might exist concerning such a legal object. In this respect the code is far more explicit than, generally speaking, Western Civil Codes, but at the same also rather conservative. The various provisions reflect the 'classical' socialist (Marxist) ideas of who can control which assets and what such power over a legal object implies. The Civil Code calls this power 'ownership', but immediately gives this concept a differentiating connotation depending on the nature of the object and the category of subject claiming such right. That latter approach is, as such, although in its origins more classical socialist, at the same time rather innovative, because it allows a diversification of approaches to what control means. This is particularly important regarding data, more particular digital assets. However, remarkably enough, digital assets are hard to find in the code. A relevant provision can be found in article 127 ("Where there are laws particularly providing for the protection of data and online virtual assets, such provisions shall be followed") and perhaps also in article 1225 on medical records, although the latter article does not deal specifically with e-records. Furthermore, article 1034 states that "A natural person's personal information is protected by law", but this seems to be – although it is a provision within the Civil Code – more an aspect of public law rights to privacy and protection of personal information than attributing private law control over data and data clusters such as virtual assets.[13]

---

12 Articles 188 ff providing rules on limitation of action, seem to confirm this. See in particular article 196, which states: "The limitation period does not apply to the following rights to claim: […] (2) a claim for return of property of a person who has a real right in an immovable or a registered movable property". It seems to imply that possession may not create any proprietary right, even though the period of possession might be considerable.

13 Article 1034 defines 'personal information' as follows: "Personal information is the information recorded electronically or in other ways that can be used, by itself or in combination with other information, to identify a natural person, including the name, date of birth, identification number, biometric information, residential address, telephone number, email address, health information, whereabouts, and the like, of the person". This resembles article 4 (1) of Regulation (EU) 2016/679 of the European Parliament and of the Council of 27 April 2016 on the protection of natural persons with regard to the processing of personal data and on the free movement of such data, and repealing Directive 95/46/EC (General Data Protection Regulation). See in this respect also the E-Commerce law of China which is about dealings in commodities (goods?) and services, but which does not provide clarity as to what 'commodities' are (E-Commerce Law of the People's

First, then, a description of what 'ownership' means. Again, the terminology sounds somewhat confusing for a Civil Lawyer, as it has a (too) familiar echo. Article 240 states that an owner is entitled to possess, use, benefit from, and dispose of his own immovable or movable property in accordance with law, and, as is added by article 241, is entitled to create a right to usufruct and a security interest on his own immovable or movable property. However, a usufructuary or security interest holder, when exercising their rights, shall not harm the rights and interests of the owner. In case of state ownership of immovable or movable property, no organization or individual may acquire ownership of it (article 242). State ownership means (article 246) that where "a property is provided by law to be owned by the State, the property belongs to the State, namely, to the whole people". We already see how the content of the right is qualified by the subject having the right and the object concerned. We will also see this later on when analysing collective ownership and private (individual) ownership.

Following the general rules on ownership the Civil Code continues to describe the objects of state ownership, collective ownership and private ownership, thus at the same time delineating the ambit of such right and who can be right holder (subject). The list of objects which can only be owned by the state is rather lengthy. What is interesting to note is that the list is positive, not negative. It is not stated that all means of production belong to the people, followed by exceptions such as for consumer goods, but it is stated explicitly in articles 247 ff which specific objects can only be state owned. The list contains such objects as mineral deposits, waters, sea areas, uninhabited islands, urban land, natural resources, such as forests, mountain ridges, grasslands, unreclaimed lands, and mudflats, other than those provided by law to be collectively-owned, wild animal and plant resources that are provided by law to be owned by the state, radio-frequency spectrum resources, cultural relics, assets for national defense and, finally, infrastructures such as railways, roads, electric power facilities, telecommunication facilities, as well as oil and gas pipelines that are provided by law to be owned by the State. Articles 260 and 261 provide a list of collectively-owned immovable and movable property, such as by farmer collectives. Article 266 defines the object of private (individual) ownership, which is then followed in article 268 by adding enterprises (companies) to the categories of subjects which may own property. Here we can see how Chinese private law is becoming a mixture of socialist idealism,

Republic of China, adopted at the Fifth Session of the Standing Committee of the 13th National People's Congress on August 31, 2018). Cf Wang (n 10) 141 ff.

characterised by a centralised (and collectivised) economic system, and a more decentralised open market approach where individuals and companies can be independent legal actors. Article 266 stating that a "private individual has the right to own his lawful income, houses, articles for daily use, production tools, raw materials, as well as other immovable and movable property" would also be acceptable in a more conservative, strictly socialist, legal system, but the acceptance of for profit legal persons as legal subjects shows how socialist legal thinking further developed in China allowing non-state actors to deal with means of production.[14]

The Civil Code then continues with ownership of building units (condominium ownership) as a special legal object. This is followed by rules on adjacent relationships (which seem to resemble neighbour law). Finally, the Code recognises co-ownership in two forms: co-ownership by shares (ownership is divided over share holders) and joint co-ownership (no shares exist).[15] In the case of co-ownership a share may be transferred, which means that the legal object is (a share in) the immovable or movable property concerned, the ownership being limited by its shared nature. However, the other owners have a right of pre-emption (article 305).

Chapter IX concerns special provisions on the acquisition of ownership. One provision should attract particular attention because of its rather unexpected impact on immovable property transfers. Article 311 states that where "a person with no right to dispose of an immovable or movable property transfers it to another person, the owner has the right to recover it; unless otherwise provided by law, the transferee acquires the ownership of the immovable or movable property under the following circumstances: (1) the transferee is in good faith at the time when the immovable or movable property is transferred to him; (2) the transfer is made at a reasonable price; and (3) the transferred immovable or movable property has been registered as required by law, or has been delivered to the transferee where registration is not required". The conditions mentioned for protection of a third party in good faith are well known in legal systems which protect such third parties in case a person a non domino transfers a movable, as, for example can be seen in French law: "*En fait de meubles, la possession vaut titre*" (in case of movables, possession equals title).[16] Of

14 Article 269 repeats that for profit legal persons are to be treated as legal actors, in the same way as private individuals: "A for-profit legal person has the right to possess, use, benefit from, and dispose of its immovable and movable property in accordance with laws, administrative regulations, and its articles of association".

15 Articles 298 and 299 Chinese Civil Code.

16 See article 2276 French Civil Code: "*En fait de meubles, la possession vaut titre*" ("In the case of movables, possession is equivalent to title").

course, article 311 gives the original owner a damages claim against the seller, but nowhere is there an exception in case the good is stolen.[17] In case a thing has been lost (so not: stolen, and this can only apply to movables) article 312 has extensive rules on the right to return the thing or claiming damages against the fraudulent seller. Remarkably enough, the third party protection approach which is laid down in article 311 is likewise followed regarding immovable property, although an extra condition then is that registration must have taken place. The latter raises the question whether this provision protects indeed buyers in good faith of immovable property or provides a fundamental rule on the effect of registration of legal acts in a registry, in this case the land registry. If the latter is what is intended the solution somewhat resembles the Torrens system of land registration under which the signature of the land registrar transfers ownership, irrespective of any fraudulently agreed sale, albeit that under the Chinese Civil Code the purchaser must also be in good faith and have acquired the property for value. That would resemble more what in English property law is often referred to as the protection of 'equity's darling'.[18] Article 311 furthermore explicitly states that these provisions will also be applied mutatis mutandis where a party acquires, in good faith, a real right other than ownership. So article 311 really has been formulated as a leading principle of Chinese property law: third party protection mixes with justified reliance on a registry.

After the Chinese Civil Code dealt with ownership rights as such, Parts Three and Four deal with usufruct and security rights respectively. Usufruct is being defined as (article 323) "the right to possess, use, and benefit from the immovable or movable property owned by another person in accordance with law".

17 Article 2276 French Civil Code does make an exception in case the movable has been lost or stolen: "*Néanmoins, celui qui a perdu ou auquel il a été volé une chose peut la revendiquer pendant trois ans à compter du jour de la perte ou du vol, contre celui dans les mains duquel il la trouve; sauf à celui-ci son recours contre celui duquel il la tient*" ("Nevertheless, a person who has lost a thing or from whom it has been stolen may claim it for a period of three years from the date of the loss or theft against the person in whose hands it was found; except for the latter's recourse against the person from whom it was held").

18 'Equity's darling' is a buyer, who, having purchased a legal estate in good faith and for value without notice of any equitable interests, is considered to be entitled to the property at common law. See the analysis by Frederic William Maitland in his famous series of lectures on Frederic W. Maitland, *Equity also The Forms of Action at Common Law: Two Courses of Lectures* (Cambridge University Press 1910); for a brief reference in his lectures to the maxim 'possession vaut titre', see id at 142. Cf, for an analysis of 'equity's darling' as an idea, a concept and its underlying policies, Aruna Nair and Irit Samet, What Can 'Equity's Darling' Tell Us about Equity?, in Dennis Klimchuk, Irit Samet, Henry E. Smith (eds), *Philosophical Foundations of the Law of Equity* (Oxford University Press 2020) 264.

So it is not a different type of ownership (otherwise it would have been dealt with in the previous parts), but a property right less than ownership. If ownership can be qualified as the primary property right, because it gives its holder the most extensive power over an object, usufruct is a secondary property right, since it does confer control over an object towards others but less than an owner would have had. Part of the law on usufruct is the right to contractual management of land, the right to use land for construction purposes, the right to use a house site, the right of habitation and, finally, easements. Analysing and reconsidering these provisions, it is quite interesting to see how 'real rights' are seemingly perceived under Chinese Civil Law. In fact 'real rights' can never be 'real' in the traditional Western approach to real rights. All means of production are owned by the state, implying that, whoever claims whatever right against others and even when such rights are attributed and distributed by the state, it is that very same state which ultimately decides about their creation, content, transfer and extinguishment. Legal certainty, so characteristic of property law systems, is not to be found in the state securing that an individual will have its right fully safeguarded, but by the state always having ultimate control. Therefore, at the end of the day, a 'real right' (as the right of usufruct) can be no more than a personal (i.e. contractual) right, even when that right is given a certain amount of stability and durability by for example making it a right for a particular period, which can be extended, and a right that is transferable and can be made the object of a security right. In its essence the right is personal and only binds the state in as far as the state continues accepting or tolerating it. From that perspective it cannot come as a surprise that also easements are seen as a particular form of usufruct (see article 372 ff). At the same time, we should not forget that the creation, content, transfer and extinguishment of real rights in a Western legal system are, ignoring the ideological divergence and looking at it from a strictly functional viewpoint, not that different. When in a Western legal system a real right is created, such as a right of usufruct, its foundation is a contract to establish such a right, after which following the principles of *numerus clausus*, transparency and hierarchy a strict procedure has to be followed to transform it from a personal to a real right, and only in as far as the right fits within the list and prescribed content of real rights. To give an example: a permission to drive over one's land is, in and of itself, a contract creating a personal right, which may become a real right by laying it down in a deed, which upon registration in a land registry, creates a servitude. A real right can, hence, also from a Western legal perspective be defined as a personal right with *erga omnes* third party effect, if, and only if, certain strict and mandatory conditions were fulfilled. What we, in other words, see is that although the dogmatic structure of the right of usufruct's fundamental nature under Chinese law is a personal right with third party effect, it is not effectively different from a real right in a Western legal system. The starting points certainly differ. A Western legal system will consider, for example, a right of habitation to be a real right (a specific type of usufruct) and thus give that right third party effect which a contract would not immediately provide. The Chinese Civil Code considers it a personal right, but with a strong third party effect. Nevertheless, the practical outcome does not have to be very different: the holder of the right is protected against third parties which are bound by the original right as laid down in the initial agreement. The main difference is the ideological setting of the real right, which makes it possible under Chinese Civil Law that the state can act as the 'brooding omnipresence in the sky', whereas in a Western legal system the state will be perceived as facilitating real rights as part of a broader legal system without the need to ultimately control them.[19]

Again we see that, for a lawyer from a Western legal system, well-known terms are being used, but again with a context that is strongly dependent on the ideological framework underlying the Chinese Civil Code. The contractual rights mentioned here are set up as use rights with a limited duration and, although they are contractual in nature, they are tradable and registered rights. An important question, of course, is what happens after the right lapses. An answer can be found in article 359: "The right to use a lot of land for construction of residential buildings is automatically renewed upon expiration of the term". However, this does not seem to be unconditional (very much like in case of a renewal of a right of emphyteusis in a Western legal system the owner would want to renegotiate any monetary compensation for extending the right). Unsurprisingly, the next sentence of article 359 reads: "The payment, reduction, or exemption of the renewal fees shall be dealt with in accordance with the provisions of laws and administrative regulations". Another problem is what happens with ownership of the buildings on the land, because article 359 only regulates what happens with the surface under any buildings. Article 359 also gives provisions for that situation, but limited to non-residential buildings: "The renewal of the right to use a lot of land for construction of buildings other than residences, upon expiration of the term, shall be dealt with in accordance with the provisions of the laws. The ownership of the buildings and other immovable property on such lot of land shall be determined in accordance with the agreement, or, where there is no agreement or the agreement is unclear, in accordance with the provisions of laws and administrative

19 Cf, on law as a 'brooding omnipresence in the sky', William P. LaPiana, 'Swift v. Tyson and the Brooding Omnipresence in the Sky: An Investigation of the Idea of Law in Antebellum America' (1986) 20 Suffolk U L Rev 771.

regulations". It all looks somewhat uncertain and even slightly unpredictable. Legal certainty will depend on further implementing and enabling legal rules.

Security interests are defined in article 386 as having "priority to be paid from the collateral in accordance with law, unless otherwise provided by law". To security rights belong mortgages (including a mortgage for floating claims), pledges and liens. Article 388 provides the basic requirements for a security arrangement. First of all, a security contract is needed, which includes mortgage contracts, pledge contracts, and other contracts with a function of security. The latter is quite interesting as it seems to imply that the list of security rights is not closed. Article 388 then continues: "A security contract is a contract secondary to the principal contract with the principal claims and obligations. Where the principal contract is void, the security contract is also void, unless otherwise provided by law". The latter means that Chinese law made a choice for an accessory type of security right, which is confirmed in article 393(1) stating that a security interest is extinguished, among others, when the claim under the principal contract is extinguished.[20] Following the general provisions, more specific provisions follow, first, on mortgage. Property which can be mortgaged is described both positively (only certain specifically enumerated assets can be mortgaged, such as buildings attached to the land) and negatively (certain assets may not be mortgaged, such as land ownership).[21] Here, again, we see the impact of ideology on law. Land is and remains under the sole control of the state given its dominium eminens. Land ownership does not necessarily mean that also constructions (buildings) on the land are owned by the same legal subject (and vice versa). These two are separate, in line with classical socialist law, to prevent the accumulation of too much capital in the hands of one individual legal subject if that person is not the state. The principle, as developed eloquently by the Glossators, that "*Cuius est solum, eius est usque ad coelum et ad inferos*" ("His alone is his, even to heaven and hell") does not apply here. Given the outer limits of security rights, the Civil Code provides more technical rules. A mortgage on immovable property needs to be registered to be valid (article 402), a mortgage on movable property comes into existence when the mortgage contract enters into effect, without registration (article 403). The first reflects a transfer system of property rights, the second a consensual system. The latter requires third party protection of those who are in good faith and those who paid a reasonable price and acquired the mortgaged property in the ordinary course of business, and this is precisely what

20 Cf. Sjef van Erp, 'Surety Agreements and the Principle of Accessority – Personal Security in the Light of a European Property Law Principle' (2005) 13 Eur Rev Priv L 309.

21 Articles 395 and 399.

articles 403 and 404 offers them. Article 414 lays down the '*prior in tempore, potior in iure*' rule: an older property right has priority over a younger property right, but the transparency principle demands that a registered right has priority over a non-registered right, the publicity of which is more unclear due to its dependence on possession which, of course, is absent when the security is non-possessory.[22] It is important to note that article 407 makes it impossible to transfer a mortgage separately from the underlying claim or be used as security for another claim. Where a claim is transferred, so article 407 continues, the mortgage securing the claim shall be transferred concomitantly with it, unless otherwise provided by law or agreed by the parties. The possibility under German law to register a mortgage the existence of which is independent from the underlying loan agreement seems thus to be discarded.[23] After having provided rules for the object of a mortgage right and the contents of that right, the Chinese Civil Code gives specific rules on claims the payment of which may arise at a future moment. Such claims can also be secured by a mortgage ('maximum mortgage for floating claims' under articles 420 ff).

Pledge is, unlike mortgage, a possessory security right (article 425). As with mortgages a contract is needed to create the pledge, the object can be movable property and rights. The pledge is created by either delivery of the pledged property by the pledgor (article 429) or registration (for example proprietary rights in intellectual property and accounts receivable, articles 444 and 445).

Finally, the security part deals with liens, which create a right of retention. Article 447 gives the following definition: "Where a debtor fails to perform his obligation due, the creditor may retain the debtor's movable property which is already in the lawful possession of the creditor and has priority to be paid from the movable property". Article 448 limits the possibility of liens as security by adding that movable property retained under a lien by the creditor shall be in the same legal relationship as the underlying claim, unless the lienholder and the debtor are both enterprises. The right of lien is lost when the lienholder loses possession or accepts another form of security (article 456).

---

22 Article 414 reads as follows: "Where a property is mortgaged to two or more creditors, the proceeds obtained from auction or sale of the mortgaged property shall be applied in accordance with the following provisions: (1) where the mortgages have all been registered, the order of payment is based on the priority in time of registration; (2) a registered mortgage has priority over an unregistered mortgage to be paid; and (3) where none of the mortgages are registered, payment shall be made on a pro rata basis against the claims. The preceding paragraph shall be applied mutatis mutandis with regard to the priority order of payment for other security interests that are registrable".

23 Cf van Erp (n 20) 309, 316 ff.

3 Final Remarks – Brief Evaluation

The Chinese Civil Code shows that Chinese property law is becoming a mixed legal system. The terminology used is frequently rather typical of the Civil Law tradition. Yet, a first word of caution is appropriate here as the translation that was available to me is in English, and the English language and English law are intimately connected, making it hard to correctly transpose Civil Law terminology. So we are confronted with a double linguistic barrier: the translation from Chinese to a Western language and, within the group Western languages, the translation of Civil Law concepts in English. A second word of caution should be mentioned regarding the political and intellectual framework that surrounds the code. China has a political system which is socialist, resulting in certain crucial pre-legal views, the most important of which is that the state owns, in the sense of controls, attributes and distributes, all means of production. Legal persons and private individuals only have freedom to do so within explicit limits set by the law, which is not seen as expressing the interests and the will of a ruling class (as, according to Marxism, is the case in a capitalist society) but the expression of an economy rooted in socialism embodied by the state. This explains why a mortgage cannot rest on land ownership, but only on the building as such.

The structure of the code seems to be inspired by German law, although it could also have been the Netherlands Civil Code which in certain respects is more German than the German Civil Code. The Netherlands Civil Code is based on a clear and strict subject, object and relations triangle. Books 1 and 2 deal with natural and legal persons respectively, its general part in Book 3 provides an overview of all patrimonial rights, followed by books on the law of obligations and on property law. In any case, the structure of the code is highly dogmatic and will demand extensive further elaboration by court rulings, administrative decisions and legal scholarship. No doubt, enacting and enabling legislation next to other forms of rule making will prove to be unavoidable.

The property law part is, as such, highly consistent, clear in its structure and content, but needs understanding of socialist legal thinking to fully grasp the impact of, for example, such contractual rights as a contractual right to land management, which because of its content and third party effect resembles a real right without being a real right in the sense which that term has in a Western legal system.

What is clearly missing from the Chinese Civil Code are the private law (particularly property law) aspects of data. The Code does have extensive provisions on personality rights and data protection, but does not cover such questions as rights to digital assets and the possibility to create a security right in such assets. One can understand the hesitation of the legislator, as this is an area still very much in development and from a regulatory viewpoint it might not be wise to regulate private law aspects of, for example, crypto-assets, but at the same time these are developments which are going on and leaving them unregulated might prove to me more risk full than not acting. It seems regrettable that the Code does not even offer an opening here towards how to deal with digital assets, but this may still come later.

CHAPTER 8

An Introduction to the Book on Contracts of the Civil Code of the PRC

韩世远 *Han Shiyuan*

1 Introduction

Compared to the Italian Civil Code with six parts, the Civil Code of the People's Republic of China (hereinafter referred to as the 'Civil Code') consists of seven parts. This is because the Chinese Civil Code takes as its basis the five books that are typical of the *Pandekten* system (enshrined for instance in the German Civil Code (BGB) and in the Japanese Civil Code), to which the Chinese Civil Code adds a Book on Personality Rights and a Book on Tort Liability. By contrast, the Italian Civil Code has changed and developed on the basis of a system based on the *Institutiones* of Justinian. The content of Book Four on 'Obligations' of the Italian Civil Code is divided into two books in the Chinese Civil Code, namely Book Three on Contracts and Book Seven on Tort Liability. This paper intends to interpret Book Three of the Chinese Civil Code with particular reference to Book Four of the Italian Civil Code.

Book Four of the Italian Civil Code is composed of nine chapters: Obligations in General, Contracts in General, Specific Contracts, Unilateral Promises, Negotiable Instruments, Management of Affairs of Another, Payment of What Is Not Due, Unjust Enrichment, Unlawful Acts. The Book on Contracts of the Chinese Civil Code, by contrast, is divided into three parts (General Provisions, Nominate Contracts, and Quasi-Contracts) and does not cover the entire law of obligations. In particular, the Book on Contracts does not deal with tort liability, while it basically covers all the other parts of law of obligations. The main characteristics of the Book on Contracts are as follows. First, the Book abandons the paradigm of a book of general provisions of obligations that is typical of any *Pandekten* system. Second, it adopts the legislative style of combining civil and commercial codes, and therefore stipulates commercial contracts in the Civil Code. Third, the Book provides some new types of contracts as nominate contracts. Fourth, it introduces the concept of quasi-contracts, which cover *negotiorum gestio* and unjust enrichment.

The compilation of the Chinese Civil Code has both integrated the existing civil legislation and absorbed mature judicial experience; as a result, the

 | DOI:10.1163/9789004704428_009

reference to comparative law becomes an important factor that cannot be ignored.

2 A Pragmatic Model: A Book on Contracts instead of General Provisions on Obligations

The Chinese Civil Code does not adopt the *Pandekten* style general provisions of obligation. However, this does not mean it gives up the concept of law of obligations. In the Chinese Civil Code, the norms of law of obligations are scattered among the different books.

First, the Chinese Civil Code clearly defines the concept of rights *in personam* and its causes (article 118(2), Chapter V on 'Civil-law Rights' in Book One), including contracts, tortious acts, *negotiorum gestio*, unjust enrichment, and other stipulations of law. Thus, it can be seen that, although there is no form for law of obligations in the Civil Code, the organizational structure of norms of law of obligations is not disorderly, but rather there are traces to follow.

Second, although obligations can arise from various kinds of causes, there is no doubt that contracts and torts acts are the two most common and important causes in practice. China takes a pragmatic path in terms of choosing how to organize norms of law of obligations. Prior to the era of the Civil Code, China formulated Contract Law (1999) and Tort Liability Law (2009), therefore realizing legislations on the major parts of law of obligations. After entering the era of the Civil Code and creating Contracts and Tort Liability as two Books of the Civil Code respectively, the legislator also stipulates *negotiorum gestio* and unjust enrichment as quasi-contracts in the Book on Contracts, grasping the majority without overlooking the minority of law of obligations. Finally, the aim of the legislator is to have relevant rules for all kinds of obligations. Depending on the causes of obligations in mind, some special provisions can be applied directly, while some can be applied *mutatis mutandis*. It is true that having general provisions on the law of obligations is a mature model for regulating the law of obligations with a long history, but, from a comparative perspective, this is not the only model. The basic idea of the general provisions of law of obligations is from the perspective of a single obligation relationship, which aims to extract the common factors from the obligation relationships arising from different causes, gather the corresponding common norms, and achieve a norm-number-reduction purpose. To achieve a similar norm-function, people can also choose contractual relationship as their main target in laws available in the Book on Contracts, and subsidiarily regulate non-contractual obligations with the same law by either a direct application or a *mutatis mutandis* application. After all, 'all roads lead to Rome'. Of course, different codification models require different ways of law-application, and therefore affect the relevant legal education and theoretical composition.[1]

Third, why not a Book on general provisions of obligation in the Chinese Civil Code? Some scholars hold that this is not to deny its value in the civil law system, but rather out of consideration for legislative technology. Since 1986, China has successively promulgated a series of specific regulations such as the General Principles of the Civil Law, the Contract Law, the Property Law, and the Tort Liability Law. It would have been a time-consuming and arduous task to integrate them in order to formulate a Book Law of Obligations (especially the general provisions of obligation).[2] Some other scholars believe that abolishing the general provisions of law of obligation and allowing Contracts and Tort Liability to be independent of the whole structure of law of obligations, are the result of the rebellion against the model of Soviet-Russian Civil Code by the drafters of Chinese civil law in the 1960s. They hold that once an independent tort liability law is formulated, the law of obligations will disintegrate because its essence is to "extract the common factors" in contracts and tort liability which are deemed as two unrelated things.[3] The author believes that, since the restoration of the legal system construction in the 1980s in China, the one-step goal of civil law legislation has been abandoned, and a step-by-step path of pragmatism has been adopted. Thus, it has gradually made Chinese legal practitioners accustomed to the idea that the Contract Law and the Tort Liability Law are independent of each other. Therefore, insisting on the integration of the norms of law of obligations and extraction of common factors, will inversely make legal practitioners unaccustomed.

The following text will focus on a description and analysis of the characteristics of the Book on Contracts in the Civil Code and the new additions or changes compared with the original Contract Law.

1 Han Shiyuan, *Contract Law* (Higher Education Press 2022) 7–8 (韩世远, 合同法学, 高等教育出版社).

2 Wang Zejian, 'Characteristics of Chinese Civil Law and Its Interpretation for Application' (2020) 1 Journal of Law Application 9 (王泽鉴, 中国民法的特色及解释适用,《法律适用》).

3 Xu Guodong, 'The Domestic Legislative History and Comparative Law Basis Explaining Why the Civil Code Did Not Adopt the General Principles of Law of Obligations' (2020) 6 Research on Rule of Law 137–138 (徐国栋,《民法典》不采用债法总则的本国立法史和比较法依据,《法治研究》).

3 Adjustment and Supplement of Chapter I on 'General Rules'

3.1 *Guidelines on the Application of Law*

There are three main guidelines on the application of the general rules on contract law that deserve to be recalled. As we are about to see, the rules contained in Chapter I of the Book on Contracts may also apply to the so-called acts-in-person-law (meaning acts concerning personal relationships), to obligations arising (not from contract, but) according to the law, and to nominate contracts.

Article 464 of the Civil Code slightly adjusts the wording of article 2 of the original Contract Law. In particular, article 464(2) of the Civil Code supplements the application of laws relating to personal relationships such as marriage, adoption, and guardianship by providing that, when laws relating to such personal relationships are absent, "the provisions of this Book may be applied *mutatis mutandis* according to the nature of such an agreement". In other words, the Book on Contracts regulates the so-called acts-in-property-law, but, where there is no specific provision for the acts-in-person-law, the provisions of the Book on Contracts, especially those in the General Provisions of the Book, can be applied *mutatis mutandis*. For example, whether a divorce agreement is formed may be determined by a reference to the rules of contract conclusion in the Book on Contracts.

Article 468 of the *Civil Code* provides that "[f]or a creditor-debtor relation not arising from a contract, the provisions of laws relating to such relations shall be applied; in the absence of such provisions, the relevant provisions of the General Provisions of this Book shall be applied, unless they are not applicable due to the nature of the creditor-debtor relation", which guides its application as to obligations arising according to law. A few examples are *negotiorum gestio*, unjust enrichment, and tortious acts. It is particularly noteworthy that, the word used is "apply", but not "apply *mutatis mutandis*" in the latter part of this article. This indicates that the articles of General Provisions of the Book on Contracts are not limited to the contractual obligations but also applicable to statutory obligations, thus making the articles serve as the general provisions of the law of obligations. In other words, "the General Provisions of the Book on Contracts functions as a Book on general provisions of obligation".[4] For example, Chapter V of the Book on Contracts is entitled 'Preservation of Contract' merely for structural reasons of keeping continuity

---

4 Huang Wei (ed), *Interpretation of the Book on Contracts of the Civil Code of the People's Republic of China* (Beijing:Law Press China 2020), 1028 (黄薇, 中华人民共和国民法典合同编释义：法律出版社).

with other chapters in names, but its essence is the preservation of claims, and the rules in Chapter V "are general rules of the law of obligations, but not confined to contracts".[5]

Article 467(1) of the Chinese Civil Code maintains the basic contents of Article 124 of the original Contract Law, with adjustments only in wording, thus guiding how the provisions related to nominate contracts can be applied directly, *mutatis mutandis*, or analogously.

3.2 *Promotion and Adjustment of Fundamental Principles in the Layer Structure of the Code*

The fundamental principles of the contract law stipulated in the original Contract Law, including the principle of equality (article 3), the principle of voluntariness (article 4), the principle of fairness (article 5), the principle of good faith (article 6), and the rule of law, public order and good morals (article 7), have been moved to Chapter I ('General Provisions') of Book I on the 'General Part' of the Civil Code (articles 4 to 8), and upgraded as basic principles of civil law. Article 465 of the Civil Code, which is adjusted from article 8 of the original Contract Law, is retained, but the original paragraph 1 becomes paragraph 2, stating that "[a] contract formed in accordance with law is legally binding only on the parties to the contract, unless otherwise provided by law". By adding the word "only" and removing the original expression ("The parties shall perform their respective obligations pursuant to the terms of the contract, and shall not arbitrarily modify or rescind the contract"), the principle of privity of contract is defined.

4 Conclusion of Contracts

In the course of drafting Chapter II on 'Conclusion of Contracts' (articles 9 to 43) of the original Contract Law, the United Nations Convention on Contracts for the International Sale of Goods (CISG) was a key reference. The Unidroit's Principles of International Commercial Contracts (PICC) were also taken into consideration. Chapter II of the Book on Contracts of the Civil Code (articles 469 to 501) maintains Chapter II of the original Contract Law in general, although with several supplements and adjustments. Among the most important modifications, it is worth mentioning those concerning (1) the moment in which offer and acceptance become effective, (2) standard clauses,

5 Huang Wei (n 4) 165.

(3) preliminary contracts, (4) reward advertising, and (5) the liability for *culpa in contrahendo* and for breach of confidentiality duties.

(1) The original Contract Law adopted the arrival principle to determine the effectiveness of the expression of intent, such as an offer or an acceptance (articles 16 and 26), while the Civil Code promotes relevant rules into the general rules for the effectiveness of expression of intent (article 137), and elaborates them further (Article 137(1) provides that "an expression of intent made through real-time communication" shall be effective when the other party "is aware of" its contents; in addition, article 137(2) elaborates the expression of intention in the form of electronic data message).

(2) As for standard clauses, there are special provisions from articles 39 to 41 in the original Contract Law. Although article 39(1) stipulates the user's duties to arouse attention and give necessary explanations, it does not specify the legal consequences of violation of such duties. The Supreme People's Court (the SPC) responded to this issue in its 'Judicial Interpretation II of the Contract Law', article 9 of which stipulates that if the standard clause provider's violation of such a duty "causes the other party to be unaware of the clauses that exempt or restrict the clause provider's liability, the people's court shall support the other party's claim for revocation of such a standard clause". This practice is very unique from a comparative perspective and has drawn criticism from scholars. A new provision is added to article 496(2) of the Civil Code, which stipulates that "[w]here the party providing the standard clause fails to perform the aforementioned duty of arousing attention or giving explanations, thus resulting in the other party's failure to pay attention to or understand the clause concerning its major interests and concerns, the other party may claim that such clause does not become part of the contract". The expression "does not become part of the contract" means that the standard clause is not included in the contract. In other words, unlike the SPC's Judicial Interpretation, the legislator does not include the standard clauses and therefore make them invalid by means of revocation. Instead, the legislator pays attention to the systematic position of the relevant legal rule (i.e. it is in the Chapter on the 'Conclusion of Contracts', rather than the Chapter on the 'Effect of Contracts'), defining the problem as to whether a standard clause should be included in the contract. This practice brings order out of chaos and thus deserves appreciation.

(3) After absorbing a judicial interpretation rule (article 2 of the SPC's 'Judicial Interpretation on Sales Contracts'), the Civil Code specially

regulates preliminary contract and stipulates the legal consequences of breaching such a contract in article 495. This is not stipulated in the original Contract Law. Compared with the provisions under article 1987 of the Italian Civil Code, the provisions in China's legislation are more principled. However, the connotation of "liability for breach of the preliminary contract" still needs further interpretation.

(4) Although reward advertising is sometimes used in real life, there is no specific provision for it in the original Contract Law. Regarding the nature of reward advertising, there is theoretical divergence in China, insofar as reward advertising may be considered as either a unilateral act or as a contract. The latter understanding is usually adopted in judicial practice (article 3 of the SPC's 'Judicial Interpretation II of the Contract Law' regulates reward advertising). After drawing on judicial experience, the Civil Code regulates in article 499 that, "[w]here a rewarder making an announcement promises to pay a reward to anyone who has completed a particular act, the person who has completed the act may request the rewarder to pay the reward". Although there is only one singular article here, it is still worth appreciating it as 'a breakthrough from nothing' in China's legislation.

After the promulgation of the Civil Code, there are still debates on the nature of reward advertising. However, from the systematic position of this article, it seems more acceptable to interpret it according to the contract theory. Of course, this leaves open some theoretical problems concerning how to deal with rewards claimed by persons who were not aware of the advertising or by persons who have limited capacity for such an act.

(5) Drawing lessons from the PICC and the Principles of European Contract Law (PECL), the original Contract Law stipulated liability for *culpa in contrahendo* and breach of confidentiality duties in articles 42 and 43. Articles 500 and 501 of the Civil Code further improve the provisions of the confidentiality duty while taking the provisions above as a basis. Application of article 43 in the original Contract Law is a little bit perplexing in practice, since this article only involves "trade secrets" obtained in the course of concluding a contract. However, the meaning of "trade secrets" is strictly interpreted without including other confidential information in a case such as a non-businessman. Therefore, article 501 in the Civil Code adds "other confidential information", along with "trade secrets", which are equivalent to "confidential information" in Article 2.1.16 of PICC and Article 2:302 of PECL.

5 Validity of a Contract

Chapter III ('Validity of a Contract') of the Book on Contracts of the Civil Code places particular emphasis on the effectiveness of contracts.

Compared with Chapter III ('Validity of the Contract') of the original Contract Law, the provisions in Chapter III of the Book on Contracts of the Civil Code have been adjusted significantly. The rules on invalidation and revocability of contract have been upgraded to Book I on the General Provisions of the Code, as invalidation and revocability of civil juristic acts. As a result, the concurrent possible effect of judicial modification of a revocable contract, as provided in article 54 of the original Contract Law, has been deleted in the Civil Code. The appropriateness of this deletion is however debatable. For example, on the occasion of a deposit, the bank staff entered an extra '0' into the computer due to a wrong operation. According to the original Contract Law, a court could have corrected the mistake and modified the contract as the parties intended, without any need to rescind the whole transaction (the deposit contract). This is no longer possible. Yet the illustration makes it clear that, under some circumstances, modifying the contract does solve the problems better than invalidity or recovation.

There are only seven articles (articles 502 to 508) in Chapter III of the Book on Contracts of the Civil Code. These rules provide for the entry into force of contracts and other issues related to the effectiveness of contracts, such as obligations to apply for statutory or administrative approval (article 502), the presumption of ratification by the principal as to contracts concluded by an unauthorized agent (article 503), the effects of contracts concluded by an *ultra vires* representative (article 504), the validity of contracts which go beyond one party's scope of business (article 505), the invalidity of broad exemption clauses (article 506), the autonomy of dispute resolution clauses (article 507) and a general guidance rule about the applicability of the General Provisions contained in Book I (article 508).

6 Performance of Contracts

Chapter IV ('Performance of Contracts') of the Book on Contracts of the Civil Code is derived from Chapter IV with the same title in the original Contract Law, but with some adjustments. Compared with Italian law, the provisions are roughly equivalent to Title I ('Obligations in General'), Title II ('Contracts in General'), and Title VII ('Payment of What Is Not Due') in Book Four on 'Obligations' in the Italian Civil Code. Some provisions of Chinese law have been influenced by the international instruments like the UNIDROIT PICC; this is particularly the case for rules on earlier performance (article 530; PICC article 6.1.5), partial performance (article 531; PICC article 6.1.3) and change of circumstances (article 533; PICC articles 6.2.1 to 6.2.3). Such rules also exist in the Italian Civil Code, such as article 1181 (partial performance), article 1185 (pendency of the time limit), articles 1256 to 1259 (supervening impossibility of performance for cause not imputable to the debtor), and articles 1467 to 1469 (excessive onerousness) of the Italian Civil Code.

The first distinct modification brought by Chapter IV ('Performance of Contacts') of the Book on Contracts of the Civil Code, compared with the original Contract Law, is that the preservation of rights *in personam* serves as one independent chapter (that is, Chapter V on 'Preservation of Contracts'). Another notable change is the elaboration on the general provisions of the law of obligations, which include pecuniary obligations (article 514), multiple-objects obligations (articles 515 to 516), several obligations (article 517), joint obligations (articles 518 to 521), obligation performed by a third-party (article 524), and so on and so forth. Additionally, the rule on change of circumstances has been supplemented by new criteria that have largely absorbed previous judicial interpretations.

7 Preservation of Contracts

Chapter V on 'Preservation of Contracts' of Book Three of the Civil Code, as a new independent chapter, stipulates the creditor's right of subrogation and the creditor's right of revocation. The regulation about these two rights or capacities as a creditor, which consists of only three articles (articles 73 to 75) in the original Contract Law, is now expanded into eight articles (articles 535 to 542). This part of Chinese law may have been more influenced by Japanese law (articles 423 to 423–7, 424 to 424–9, 425 to 425–4 and 426 of the Japanese Civil Code) and French law (articles 1341–1 and 1341–2 of the French *Code civil*), whilst the creditor's right of revocation originated from *actio Pauliana* in Roman law. Such Roman genes are reflected in modern Italian law too (articles 2900 to 2904 of the Italian Civil Code).

8 Modification and Assignment of Contracts

Chapter VI ('Modification and Assignment of Contracts', articles 543 to 556), which modifies Chapter V of the original Contract Law (article 77 to 90), roughly corresponds to articles 1260 to 1276 (on assignment of claims) of the Italian Civil Code. The number of provisions has remained, but the content has been changed.

Since the General Provisions of the Book on Contract provides both general rules of contract and general rules of obligation, the wording of provisions has been adjusted specifically, so that such general principles, like the assignment of claims (rights) and transfer of obligations, are applicable to but not limited to a case of contract. As such, they are also applicable to rights and obligations arising from other sources. For this purpose, from the Contract Law to the Civil Code, the wording has been adjusted in many places. For example, "rights under a contract" and "rights" are changed to "claims" (article 551(1), article 553(1), article 547(1)), "the nature of the contract" to "the virtue of the claim's nature" (article 545(1), subparagraph 1), and "obligations under a contract" to "obligation". So, in the absence of special provisions, the related provisions in the General Principles of the Book on Contract (article 468 of the Civil Code) shall be applied to modifications and assignments of creditor-debtor positions not arising out from a contract.

Likewise, as a new provision in article 545(2) makes it clear, an agreement prohibiting the assignment of claims is valid. Accordingly, pecuniary claims and non-pecuniary claims are distinguished. In the case of assignment of a pecuniary claim, the agreement prohibiting assignment may not be enforced against a *bona fide* third party, while, in the case of assignment of non-pecuniary claims, the same agreement may not be asserted against a third party, no matter whether that party is *bona fide* or not. The provisions in Chinese law use PICC (article 9.1.9), PECL (article 11:301(1)), the General Rules for International Factoring (GRIF) (article 6(1)) and the UNIDROIT Convention on International Factoring (article 9) for reference, which embody the latest trend of legislation in this regard.[6]

Thirdly, article 552 of the Civil Code is added to clarify the joining of obligation by a third party; in this case, the original debtor and the new debtor are jointly and severally liable. Article 84 of the original Contract law (now article 551(1) of the Civil Code) stipulated the transfer of obligations, and under that law the interpretation of transfer of "part of its obligation" was a controversial issue. Article 552 has now put an end to the controversy, and embodies a progress in Chinese law.

6 Huang Wei (n 4) 191.

9 Termination of Rights and Obligations under a Contract

Chapter VII ('Termination of Rights and Obligations under a Contract') of the Book on Contracts of the Civil Code (articles 557 to 576), which has been modified from Chapter VI of the original Contract Law, roughly corresponds with articles 1210 to 1214 (deposit), articles 1236 to 1255 (remission of debt, set-off, merger), and articles 1453 to 1462 (dissolution for non-performance) of the Italian Civil Code. The number of provisions in this part has increased by four, as well as undergoing substantive changes in the content.

9.1 *An Intentional Distinction between the Narrow Sense and Broad Sense of Obligation Relationships*

Under the title of 'Termination of Rights and Obligations under a Contract', article 91 of the original Contract Law covered both the ways to extinguish obligations (performance, set-off, deposit, exemption, and merger) and the way to terminate a contract (rescission), without making any distinction between them. Now a significant change of the Civil Code is that article 557 separates the contents of the original article 91 of the Contract Law into two paragraphs. Article 557(1) deals with how to extinguish obligations (namely performance, set-off, deposit, exemption, and merger, etc.), while article 557(2) refers to the ways for terminating contracts, stipulating that "[t]he relationship of rights and obligations under a contract is terminated upon rescission of the contract".

9.2 *Supplementary Provisions on Imputation of Payments*

There are no rules on imputation of payments in the original Contract Law, and the gap was filled by referring to the comparative study of foreign laws. In 2009, articles 20 and 21 of the SPC's 'Judicial Interpretation II of the Contract Law' supplemented rules on imputation of payments, effectively filling the legal loophole. Articles 560 and 561 of the Civil Code absorb the judicial interpretation rules above. Among them, article 560 provides for the discharge of multiple obligations; article 561 provides for the imputation of payments first to expenses, then interests, and finally the principal obligation.

9.3 *Post-Contractual Obligations and Their Expansion*

Article 92 of the original Contract Law provided for post-contractual obligations. Article 558 of the Civil Code has been amended and expanded on this basis, and the main novelties are the following ones.

Firstly, the original expression "after the termination of the rights and obligations under a contract" has been modified to "after the parties' claims and obligations are terminated". As proposed in the legislative process, this amendment stipulates that these obligations may arise not only in contractual cases, but also in cases of statutory obligations. The legislator adhered to this suggestion and made the relevant amendment. Therefore, in accordance with this article, obligations of rendering assistance and keeping confidentiality may also arise in cases of statutory obligations (e.g., obligations arising out of *negotiorum gestio* or other sources).[7] In this way, the application of post-contractual obligations has been expanded to statutory obligations.

Secondly, the obligation of recycling used articles, as a post-contractual obligation, has been introduced in the Civil Code. In order to implement the Green Principle (article 9), the legislator added the obligation of recycling used articles in article 558. Additionally, article 625 further specifies the obligation of recycling used articles in the context of sales contracts. Such an obligation considers the need of recycling of packages. The obligation of recycling used articles reflects the expansion of the content of post-contractual obligations.

Neither article 92 of the original Contract Law nor article 558 of the Civil Code provides specifically for the legal consequences of a breach of post-contractual obligations. Article 22 of the SPC's 'Judicial Interpretation II of the Contract Law' provided that, where a party violates the obligations and causes losses to the other party, the other party can request compensation for its actual losses. Now, this judicial interpretation is invalid and a new judicial interpretation is being drafted, which will likely have similar provisions regarding legal consequences. Of course, as to the liability for breach of a post-contractual obligation, it is still to be clarified whether this liability is based upon fault liability or not.

9.4 *The Amendments and Improvements of Rules on Rescission of Contract*

General rules on rescission of contract are provided in articles 93 to 98 in the original Contract Law. Their main features were as follows:

- there was no distinction in the legislation between contracts to be performed at one time and long-term contracts (continuing contract); the *Contract Law* provided for unified rules, collectively referred to as 'rescission' of contract;
- the 'fundamental breach of contract' standard was adopted as to rescission because of a breach;
- there was no requirement of fault of the breaching party as to the other party's right of rescission;

7 Huang Wei (n 4) 216.

- *force majeure* was acknowledged as a reason for the right of rescission;
- rescission of the contract in the context of anticipatory breach was acknowledged.

Although the rescission rules in the original Contract Law had many merits and deserve recognition, problems have still occurred in practice. One of the main problems affected the rules on rescission of long-term contracts, that were not sufficient.

In light of this situation, the Civil Code has substantially improved the rules on rescission as originally provided in the Contract Law. More in particular, the main improvements brought by the Civil Code concern clarifications concerning (1) the reasons entitling to rescission, (2) the duration of the period of limitation for asking rescission, (3) the ways to exercise the right to rescission and (4) the effects of rescission.

(1) Article 563(2) of the Civil Code now provides that, "[f]or a contract under which the debtor is required to continuously perform an obligation for an indefinite period of time, the parties to the contract may rescind the contract at any time, provided that the other party shall be notified reasonably in advance". This provision supplemented a special rule focusing on rescission of the long-term contract lasting for an indefinite period of time. There is still no special rule in this part (Chapter VII of the Book on Contracts) for the rescission of a long-term contract lasting for a definite period of time. Therefore, whether a three-year-long house rental agreement can be rescinded when one party has a special *encheson,* is still an issue without a clear rule. Article 580(2) of the Civil Code is a new rule on the so-called 'judicial termination', apparently provides a possible solution to this issue. However, the scope of application of article 580(2) is limited to cases of non-pecuniary obligations, and therefore the provision is useless for a party, like a tenant, whose main obligation is pecuniary.

(2) As for the extinguishing period (Ausschlussfrist) of the right of rescission, article 95 of the original Contract Law only stipulated that limitation can be provided for by laws or by agreement of the parties, and clarified that the legal consequence of its expiration is the vanishment of right; it did not specify, however, how long the general extinguishing period of the right of rescission was. Article 564(2) of the Civil Code has clarified the issue by providing that, "if the party with the right to rescission has not exercised the right within one year after it knows or should have known the causes for rescission", such a right is extinguished.

(3) As to the manners of exercising of a right of rescission, article 96(1) of the original Contract Law provided as a general rule that a party could

rescind a contract by notification to the other party, and that the contract should be dissolved when the notice reached the other party; if the other party had an objection, that party could apply to a people's court or an arbitration institution to determine the validity of the dissolution of the contract. Comparing with the above rule, there are three improvements in article 565 of the Civil Code. Firstly, article 565 clarifies that the notification of rescission of a contract can include a period of grace, stating that the contract is to be automatically rescinded if the debtor fails to perform his obligation within a specified period of time. Secondly, the article provides clearly for the timing of rescission of the contracts when the rescission is requested by directly filing a lawsuit or applying for arbitration; in such cases, the contract is rescinded when a duplicated copy of the complaint or the application letter for arbitration is served on the other party (article 565(2)). Thirdly, where the other party objects to the rescission of the contract, article 96(1) of the original Contract Law acknowledges that it can file for a declaratory judgement (or apply for arbitration), while article 565(1) clarifies that "either party" may request the people's court or an arbitration institution to determine the validity of the rescission.

(4) Compared with article 97 of the original Contract Law, which provided for the general effects of the rescission of a contract, article 566 of the Civil Code adds two new paragraphs to the old rule. Article 566(2) is a further specification of the rule enshrined in article 566(1) (which also corresponds to article 97 of the original Contract Law) that the parties "have the right to request for compensation for the losses". Article 566(2) clarifies that "[w]here a contract is rescinded due to a default, the party with the right to rescind the contract may request the breaching party to bear default liability", which may include damages for breach. Of course, where the parties agree on either liquidated damages or earnest money, these agreements should be followed first.

Article 566(3) provides for the security provider's obligation where the principal contract is rescinded. It states that, "after the principal contract is rescinded, a security provider shall still be obligated to secure the debtor's liability, unless otherwise agreed in the security contract".

9.5 *Improvement of the Escrow Rules*

With regard to escrow, article 571 of the Civil Code is a new provision, which has two separate paragraphs referring to two different issues: the formation time of an escrow and its effects.

The original Contract Law did not provide a clear rule on which time an escrow is formed, leaving it to scholars for interpretation. Now, article 571(1) of the Civil Code absorbs the rule embraced by the SPC in its judicial interpretation and stipulates that the escrow is established when the subject matter or the proceeds obtained from auction or sale of the subject matter is delivered to the escrow agency in accordance with law. It can be seen that the nature of escrow is better understood as a contract for custody performed to a third party. As a contract for custody, it should follow the basic orientation of *contractus re*, meaning that its formation should be consistent with the formation of custody contracts (article 890 of the Civil Code).

With regard to effects of an escrow, two opposite rationales, namely the 'condition precedent theory' and the 'condition subsequent theory', have been traditionally proposed to determine them. Under the original Contract Law, it remained unclear which one had been adopted, and this issue was left to scholars for further interpretation. Now article 571(2) of the Civil Code clearly states that, "[w]here a subject matter or its proceeds has been placed in escrow, the debtor is deemed to have delivered the subject matter to such extent". The provision deems that, after the formation of an escrow, the debtor is discharged from his obligation, no matter whether the creditor is satisfied from the subject matter or its proceeds placed in escrow. Therefore, it may be said that the Civil Code has adopted the 'condition subsequent theory'.

10 Liabilities for Breach

Chapter VIII ('Liability for breach of contract') of the Book on Contracts of the Civil Code includes articles 577 to 594, which are a revised and reorganized version of Chapter VII of the original Contract Law (articles 107 to 122). Two new articles provide for substitute performance (article 581) and the delay in acceptance by the creditor (article 589).

10.1 *Characteristics of the Chapter on Liabilities for Breach in the Original Contract Law*

The Chapter on Liabilities for Breach of Contract in the original Contract Law was mainly drafted with reference to the CISG, PICC and PECL. At that time, it was said that the most characteristic feature of Chinese contract law was the internationalization of its rules on liability for breach.[8] Under the influence of

8 Wang Zejian (n 2).

these international conventions and model laws, the main features of Chinese law on contractual liability are as follows.

Both the Contract Law and the Chinese Civil Code adopt a unified concept of breach of contract, without making any distinction among the types of non-performance, such as impossibility, delay and incomplete performance (positive infringement of creditor's rights). Where a party fails to perform its contractual obligations or the performance does not conform to the agreement, that party shall bear liability in the form of continuing to perform, taking remedial measures, or paying damages (article 107 of the original Contract Law; article 577 of the Civil Code).

Further, in the Contract Law as well as in the Chinese Civil Code, the fault of the debtor is not necessary for the liability (especially for damages) to arise. A party who breaches a contract due to a third party's reason shall bear liability for breach to the other party in accordance with the law (article 121(1) of the original Contract Law; article 593(1) of the Civil Code). Where a party is unable to perform the contract due to *force majeure*, that party shall be exempt from liability in part or in whole in light of the impact of the *force majeure*, except as otherwise provided by law (article 117(1) of the original Contract Law; article 590(1) of the Civil Code).

A further feature shared by both the Contract Law and the Chinese Civil Code is that the liability for defects in the sale of goods is integrated within the general concept of liability for breach. Where a subject matter delivered by the seller fails to meet the quality requirements, the buyer may request the seller to assume liability for breach of contract pursuant to the general rules on breach of contract (article 155 of the original Contract Law; article 617 of the Civil Code).

The above-mentioned features were present in the original Contract Law and have been preserved in the Civil Code. In addition, the Civil Code has also made a number of new amendments and additions to the old rules. The most important ones are described below.

10.2 *A Claim for Judicial Termination in Cases of Non-performance of Non-pecuniary Obligations*

Article 580(2) of the Civil Code is a totally new paragraph added on the basis of article 110 of the original Contract Law. This new provision is unique and without any precedent in comparative legislation.

As regard to specific performance, the Civil Code maintains the basic structure of the Contract Law, distinguishing between specific performance of pecuniary obligations (article 579) and specific performance of non-pecuniary obligations (article 580). The choice is to a considerable extent affected by the

PICC (articles 7.3.1 and 7.3.2). Although this liability is qualified as a kind of liability for breach, it is shown by articles 579 and 580 that what is actually at stake is a right to obtain performance after a breach. The significance of distinguishing pecuniary from non-pecuniary obligations is that, while there is no 'exception' provision to the right to claim performance for pecuniary obligations, there is one exception inasmuch as non-pecuniary obligations are concerned.

The 'exception' provision of article 580(1) of the Civil Code is generally in line with article 7.2.2 of the PICC, except for the omission of subparagraph (c) of the PICC, (according to which a claim for performance is excluded when "the party entitled to demand performance may reasonably obtain performance from another source" – the so-called replacement transaction). According to article 580(1), "[w]here a party fails to perform a non-pecuniary obligation or his performance does not conform to the agreement, the other party may request for such performance unless (1) the performance is impossible either de jure or de facto, (2) the object of the obligation is not suitable for a compulsory performance or the expenses for the performance are too high; or (3) the creditor fails to request for performance within a reasonable period of time".

On the basis of the above-mentioned 'exception' provision, article 580(2) provides for the right of the parties (especially the breaching party) to request judicial termination whenever one of the above mentioned situations exist. Namely, according to article 580(2), "[w]here one of the situations specified in the preceding paragraph exists so that the purpose of the contract cannot be achieved, the people's court or an arbitration institution may terminate the contractual relationship of rights and obligations upon request of either party, without any prejudice to the assumption of the liability for breach". Given its novelty and uniqueness, there exist many divergent theoretical interpretations as to its meaning. It is still unknown how this paragraph will be applied in practice.

10.3 *A Replacement Performance by a Third Person*

Article 581 of the Civil Code stipulates that, "[w]here a party fails to perform the obligation or the performance does not conform to the agreement, if the obligation may not be enforced by virtue of its nature, the other party may request such party to bear the expenses of a substitute performance by a third person".

10.4 *Damages*

Inasmuch as damages are concerned, the main novelties concern the introduction of a right to compensation for mental distress caused by a breach of contract, the modification of the rule of punitive damages in case of breach, and the adoption of new rules on comparative negligence.

Article 996 of the Civil Code stipulates that, where the personality rights of a party are harmed by the other party's breach of contract and the injured party thus suffers severe mental distress, if the injured party elects to request the other party to bear liability based on breach of contract, his right to claim for compensation for mental distress is not affected. Although this article is located in the first chapter ('General Rules') of the Book on Personality Rights of the Civil Code, it also applies to liability for breach. Prior to this, the legislative and judicial interpretations adopted a conservative position on whether compensation for mental distress caused by the breach of contract was allowed. Presently, it is commendable for legislators to make such breakthrough stipulations with reference to the new developments in comparative laws, cases and theories.

As to punitive damages, article 113 of the original Contract Law, as a referential provision, stipulates that, under an occasion when a merchant engages in any fraudulent activity while supplying goods or services to a consumer, the merchant shall bear the liability of damages in accordance with the Law of the People's Republic of China on Protection of Consumer Rights, which means punitive damages. The text of article 113 of the original Contract Law now corresponds to article 584 of the Civil Code, but article 113(2) has been deleted. Does the deletion mean that there are no more punitive damages in a case of breach of contract? The answer should be no. According to article 179(2) of Chapter VIII ('Civil Liability') in Book One on the General Part of the Civil Code, where punitive damages are available as provided by law, such provisions shall be followed. The Civil Code affirms that punitive damages are to be deemed as a special form of civil liability. It is then worth asking if the punitive damages are recognized in the Civil Code as a liability for tort, for breach of contract, or both. From the location of article 113 in the original Contract Law, the legislators have apparently considered the punitive damages provided for in the Law on Protection of Consumer Rights as a special kind of damages for breach of contract. Therefore, although article 584 of the Civil Code no longer retains the referential provision of article 113(2) of the original Contract Law, this is not a reason to deny the possibility of a punitive damages award based on a breach. The availability of punitive damages in Chinese law is a major point of divergence with European laws, which are generally reluctant to accept them. Against the European context, Italy seems to be more tolerant and open to the possibility of allowing punitive damages awards.

Finally, the Civil Code adds new rules on contributory negligence. Under the original Contract Law, the rule of contributory negligence was stated in the occasion of regulating compensation for *culpa in contrahendo*. According to article 58 of the original Contract Law, where both parties were at fault, the parties shall bear their respective liability accordingly after a contract was invalidated or revoked. The Contract Law did not mention contributory negligence while discussing compensation for breach of contract. Article 592(2) of the Civil Code clearly introduces contributory negligence in the field of contracts by stipulating that, "[w]here one party's default causes losses to the other party, and the other party's fault contributes to such losses, the amount of compensation may be reduced correspondingly".

10.5 *A New Integration of Rules of Earnest Money*

Earnest money is usually interpreted as a precaution against breach (earnest money against breach) under Chinese law. Earnest money was originally stipulated as a kind of security for creditor's right under the original Guarantee Law (articles 89 to 91). It is juxtaposed with a personal security (guarantee) and a real security (mortgage, pledge, lien), and is considered as a pecuniary security. Italian civil law distinguishes between confirming earnest (article 1385) and earnest as compensation for withdrawal (article 1386), which is different from the earnest money available under Chinese law. There were two provisions related to earnest money in the original Contract Law. Article 115 of the original Contract Law repeated the content of article 89 of the original Guarantee Law, while article 116 was a further stipulation, allowing the non-defaulting party to choose to apply for either liquidated damages, or earnest money in case of breach by the other party where the parties have agreed on both of them. In addition, the SPC's former 'Judicial interpretation on the application of the Guarantee Law' also had stipulations on earnest money. However, with the entry into force of the Civil Code, the original Guarantee Law and other laws have been abolished, and the rules related to earnest money have been integrated into the Chapter on 'Liability for breach' (articles 586 to 588) in the Book on Contracts.

Compared with the original law provisions, the main novelties introduced by the Civil Code are as follows.

It is now clearly stipulated that an earnest money contract is formed upon actual delivery of the earnest money (the last part of article 586(1)), correcting the stipulation in article 90 of the original Guarantee Law which stated that an earnest money contract is effective upon actual delivery of the earnest money, thus indicating that the earnest money contract is a *contractus re*.

Article 91 of the original Guarantee Law stipulated that the amount of the earnest money "shall not exceed 20% of the value of object of the principal contract", but it was not clear how to deal with the excess. On this basis, article 586(2) of the Civil Code now provides the same rule but also adds that "any excessive amount does not have the effect of earnest money. Where the amount of the earnest money actually delivered is more or less than the agreed amount, the agreed amount of the earnest money is deemed to have been changed".

The Civil Code also amends the punitive rule about earnest money, adding that the punitive rule shall be applied only when the breach is a fundamental one, resulting in "the purpose of the contract cannot be achieved" (article 587 of the Civil Code).

Finally, the Civil Code absorbs the contents of article 28 of the original SPC's 'Interpretation of the SPC on Issues Concerning the Application of Law for the Trial of Cases of Disputes over Sales Contract', taking earnest money as the minimum damages, and treating it as a general remedy that can be agreed upon all kinds of contracts. Article 588(2) stipulates in this regard that, "[w]here the amount of the earnest money is insufficient to compensate the losses caused by one party's default, the other party may request compensation for the losses in excess of the amount of the earnest money".

10.6 *A Newly Added Article on 'Delay in Acceptance by the Creditor'*

With regard to the legal consequences of the delay in the acceptance of performance by the creditor, there have always existed theoretical divergences; for example one theory defines the creditor's delay as a form of special legal responsibility, while another one insists in qualifying it as a form of liability for non-performance. The Italian Civil Code deals with the creditor's delay under article 1206 of the Chapter on 'Performance of Obligations', but not in the Chapter on 'Non-Performance of Obligations' (article 1218 and following); the choice should be taken into account when considering the above mentioned theoretical divergences.

The chapter on liabilities for breach of contract in the original Contract Law did not mention the delay in accepting performance. By contrast, the Civil Code is not hindered by such theoretical divergences. It adopts a pragmatic approach and responds positively to the needs of the practice, setting up two paragraphs in article 589 to provide for the legal effects of delay in accepting performance. According to article 589(1), "[w]here a debtor performs the obligation in accordance with the agreement, and the creditor refuses to accept the performance without just cause, the debtor may request the creditor to compensate for any additional expenses". Article 589(2) further adds that "[t]he debtor does not need to pay interests for the period of delay in acceptance by the creditor".

11 Nominate Contracts

11.1 *A Summary of the Amendments to Nominate Contracts*

Chapters 9 to 23 of the original Contract Law stipulated fifteen types of nominate contracts: sales contracts; contracts for supply and consumption of electricity, water, gas, or heat; gift contracts; loan contracts; lease contracts; contracts for financing lease; contracts for construction project; transport contracts; technology contracts; contracts for custody of property; warehousing contracts; entrustment contracts; brokerage contracts and intermediary contracts.

On this basis, the Civil Code has integrated the rules on the above types of contracts and further added a regulation for four additional contracts, namely: suretyship contracts (integrated from the guarantee contract as covered by the original Guarantee Law), factoring contracts (newly added), contracts for property management service (taken from the Property Management Regulations and its judicial interpretations) and partnership contracts (newly added). In addition, the name of the 'intermediation contract' covered by the original Contract Law has been changed into 'intermediary contract'.

11.2 *Sales Contracts: Changes as to the Right of Disposal and Unauthorized Disposal*

Article 132(1) of the original Contract Law provides that: "[t]he seller shall own the targeted matter for sale or have the right of disposal". Legislators have realized that the subject matter of a sales contract may be an existing object or an object which will become existing in the future. They insisted on making it a precondition stating that at the time of delivery the seller shall own the targeted matter for sale or have the right of disposal, otherwise the rule for disposal without power shall be applied.[9] This refers to article 51 of the original Contract Law, which provided that "[w]here a person without the right of disposal disposes of another's property, upon ratification by the obligee or if the person without the right of disposal obtains the right of disposal after making the contract, the contract shall be effective".

Now, looking at the Civil Code again, article 132(1) of the original Contract Law has been deleted and replaced by article 597(1) of the Civil Code. This provision stipulates that, "[i]f the ownership of a subject matter is unable to be transferred due to the fact that the seller fails to obtain the right of disposal

9 Hu Kangsheng (ed), *Interpretation of the Contract Law of the People's Republic of China* (Law Press China 1999) 206–207 (胡康生, 中华人民共和国合同法释义, 法律出版社).

thereof, the buyer may rescind the contract and request the seller to bear liability for the breach". Accordingly, article 51 of the original Contract Law was deleted.

Prior to the above-mentioned legislative change, there were already indications in the same direction in a SPC's judicial interpretation. Article 3 of the 'Judicial Interpretation on Sales Contracts' in 2012 stipulated that, "[w]here one party claims that a contract is void on the ground that the seller had no ownership or right of disposal of the subject matter at the time of the contract being concluded, the people's court shall not support such a claim". "Where the ownership of the subject matter cannot be transferred because the seller failed to acquire the ownership or right of disposal, and the buyer requests the seller to assume liability for breach of contract or requests rescission of the contract and claims compensation for losses, the people's court shall support such claims". The above-mentioned judicial interpretation followed a route that "in accordance with the principle that all contracts are subject to the provisions of the Contract Law, and changes of real rights are subject to the provisions of the Property Law. In a sales case, the sales contract is the basis for a change of real rights, and the transfer of ownership is the result of such a change. That the seller has no ownership or right of disposal of the subject matter at the time of concluding contract does not affect the validity of the sales contract, which serves only as the ground for such transfer of ownership. However, whether the transfer of ownership can be generated or not, depends on whether the seller can obtain ownership or right of disposal afterward, so the change in real rights is subject to a status of pending validity".[10]

From the above, the following points were clarified: (1) the existence of the right of disposal and the corresponding legal consequences are not determined at the time of the formation of contract, but at the time of delivery; (2) there is a clear distinction between rights *in personam* and real rights, whereby contracts are subject to the provisions of the Contract Law, and changes in real rights are subject to the provisions of the Property Law; (3) what is affected by a disposal without power is only the change of real rights, and the so-called 'pending validity' does not affect the sales contract, which shall be effective *ab initio*. The basic conclusion is that whether the seller has the right to dispose of the subject matter is an issue regarding the change in real rights, and does not render a sales contract invalid. Article 597(1) of the Civil Code is merely a codification of the above-mentioned SPC's judicial interpretations.

---

10 No. 2 Civil Division of the SPC (最高人民法院民事审判第二庭), *Understanding and Application of the SPC's Judicial Interpretation on Sales Contracts* (People's Court Press 2012) 69 (最高人民法院关于买卖合同司法解释理解与适用).

12 Quasi-Contracts

Unlike the civil codes in the *Pandekten* style, a new feature of the Civil Code is the inclusion of the sub-part on 'Quasi-Contracts' in the Book on Contracts. The emergence of the separate part of 'quasi-contracts' is a flexible measure under the occasion of no general provisions of law of obligations, for the purpose of making an arrangement for the two kinds of obligations, i.e. *negotiorum gestio* and unjust enrichment.

In Roman law, a 'quasi-contract' was a cause of obligations, which was equivalent to *ex contractu*, *ex delicto*, and *quasi ex delicto*. Gaius divided obligations into two categories: *ex contractu* and *ex delicto*. "Obligations arise from contracts, from *ex delicto,* or from any other causes prescribed by law".[11] With respect to obligations which occur "for other causes prescribed by law", Justinian added two additional categories in its Institutiones; on the basis on the extent of their similarities with the first two categories, these additional categories were called obligations arising out *quasi ex contractu* or *quasi ex delicto.*[12]

As mentioned above, the legislators of the Civil Code included in the General Provisions of Contract of the Civil Code both general provisions of contract and general provisions of obligation, treating the latter much more in line with China's legislative, judicial and legal education traditions. From a comparative law perspective, a country that has no separate general rules on the rights *in personam* may learn from the experience of treating *negotiorum gestio* and unjust enrichment as quasi-contracts in civil law traditions similarly lacking general rules (such as France) and in common law traditions; this would confirm that it is more appropriate to regulate *negotiorum gestio* and unjust enrichment in the Book on Contracts as quasi-contracts.[13] Before the Civil Code, 'quasi-contracts' were very rare in China's legislations and legal theory. The introduction of this concept in the process of compiling the Civil Code has been to a large extent accidental.

---

11 Gaius, *Digesta*, 44, 7, 1 pr., in Sandro Schipani (ed), *Contractual Obligations and Quasi-Contractual Obligations* (Chinese trans. by Ding Mei (丁玫), China University of Political Science & Law Press 1998) 3 (桑德罗·斯契巴尼, 契约之债与准契约之债).

12 Barry Nicholas, *An Introduction to Roman Law* (Chinese trans. by Huang Feng (黄风), Law Press China 2021) 190 (巴里·尼古拉斯, 罗马法概论).

13 Huang (n 4) 1028–1029.

13 Conclusions

It is one of the remarkable characteristics of Chinese law that the Civil Code has no book on the general provisions of obligations. This approach, which is different from the German *Pandekten* system, appeared as early as 2002 in the Civil Law of the People's Republic of China (Draft). The late Japanese Professor Zentaro Kitagawa described it as "a shift from the Pandekten system to a more pragmatic approach" that was made "to advocate the solution of problems in the corresponding practical context".[14] Professor Kitagawa's generalization is still correct for today's Chinese Civil Code.

Of course, in order to understand the current Chinese Civil Code, the history of Chinese law should not be ignored. Before the founding of the People's Republic of China, the modernization of Chinese law was done, to some extent, by learning from Western legal system through Japan. Nearly eighty per cent of the civil law of the Republic of China was borrowed from German law and Swiss law, and the other part was inspired by Japanese law and other countries' laws. After the founding of New China, China began to learn from the Soviet Union; Later, Sino-Soviet relations fell through, and, coupled with the Cultural Revolution, there were few achievements in the construction of a civil law system in the thirty years that followed. Since the 1980s, China has begun to resume the construction of a legal system, actively opening to other countries, and connecting with the world. The objects of study have become more and more diverse, including the civil law system, common law system, international conventions, and model laws. In China, such a pluralistic 'mixed reception' of law will inevitably require a corresponding 'integrated interpretation' of the doctrines in the future, rather than a simple 'doctrine reception' borrowing from one country. As such, it could be asserted that much remains to be done in the future for Chinese lawyers and scholars.

Acknowledgements

The author would like to express thanks to Ms. Sun Lan, Ms. Bao Rongrong and Ms. Zhao Xun for their kind help.

14 Zentaro Kitagawa, 'Development of Comparative Law in East Asia', in Mathias Reimann and Reinhard Zimmermann (eds), *The Oxford Handbook of Comparative Law* (Chinese trans. by Han Shiyuan (韩世远), Peking University Press 2019) 259 (北川善太郎, 比较法在东亚的发展, 牛津比较法手册).

CHAPTER 9

Comparative Perspectives on the Book on Contracts

Umberto Celli Jr and Ligia Espolaor Veronese

1 Introduction

The challenge of this Chapter is to bring an outer and comparative analysis of the rules provided in Book Three of the Chinese Civil Code (CCC), which is, by far, the largest of the CCC's Books. With more than 500 articles, Book Three would entail an entire project solely dedicated thereto. The Book is divided into two Parts, where Part One provides for the general provisions and Part Two the rules on typical contracts.

Given the extension of the Book Three, the option made was to focus on Part One, which sets the tone for the entire treatment granted to contracts under Chinese Law and whose rules, to a great extent, are reflected in the specific provisions of Part Two. Therefore, the Chapter will go through the main Chapters of Part One, bringing the comparative highlights related to, first, the general rules (1), followed by the detailed provisions regarding the conclusion of the contract (2), effect and performance of the contract (3), termination and default liability (4), closing with some final remarks. Due to the few provisions and smaller room for comparative contributions (especially by virtue of the general alignment with national systems and international harmonization initiatives), this Chapter will leave aside Chapters V and VI of Part One, which address rules of subrogation (aiming at the preservation of contracts) and modification/assignment of contracts (articles 535 to 556).

The idea is to discuss some innovations, differences and/or impacts of these rules compared to general rules on contract law. This means that not all the provisions of Book Three will be discussed.

The bases for comparison are the most successful and recognized rules on international contract law, such as those of the Unidroit Principles of International Commercial Contracts (PICC – 2016 Edition) and the United Nations Convention on Contracts for the International Sales of Goods (CISG).[1]

---

1 Jing Leng and Wei Shen, 'The evolution of Contract Law in China: Convergence in Law but Divergence in Enforcement?' in John O. Haley (ed), *Comparative Contract Law* (Edward Elgar 2017) 330–331 and 357; Shiyuan Han, 'A snapshot of Chinese Contract Law from an historical and comparative perspective', in Lei Chen and C.H. Remco Rhee (eds), *Towards a Chinese Civil*

 | DOI:10.1163/9789004704428_010

It is known that these initiatives strongly inspired the CCC and this Chapter purports to show how the former's final provisions reflect, differ or even detail the international provisions in order to fit into Chinese commercial reality. Moreover, given the nationality of the authors, comparison to Brazilian contract law (from civil law tradition) will also appear with the purpose of showing the modern character of Chinese rules and how they can inspire other civil law legislations.

2 General Rules

Overall, one main feature that marks the CCC rules are their comprehensiveness and detail compared to other national systems and international harmonization initiatives. Originally, the Chinese law has a strong influence of the German law and there have been issued subsequent sets of rules on civil relationships since the 1949 Chinese Revolution in an attempt to codify the country's civil law, such as the General Principles of Civil Law of 1986, the Contract Law of 1999 and the General Rules (or Provisions) of Civil Law of 2017.[2]

The successive and hard legislative work on defining civil law rules, coupled with the country's interest in being integrated into (and taking the lead of) the international trade, allowed Chinese legislators go beyond and be able to build what can be considered the most updated and complete set of provisions when compared to other civil codes and harmonization initiatives. The influenced may have become the influencer.

One example of this innovative completeness is article 464 of the CCC which brings a definition of contract, an absent provision in the PICC, CISG as well as in other civil legislations, such as the Brazilian one. According to the article, a contract 'is an agreement on the establishment, modification, or termination of a civil juristic relationship between persons of the civil law'. The provision goes beyond in clarifying that the definition (as well as the rules set forth in Book Three) does not directly apply to contracts marriage, adoption, guardianship, or the like, but rather residually.

Code: Comparative and Historical Perspectives (Nijhoff 2012) 239; Mimi Zou, *Chinese Contract Law and the 2020 Civil Code* (LexisNexis 2020) 10; Knut B. Pissler, 'Chinese Law, Influence of European Private Law', in Jürgen Basedow et alii (eds), *The Max Planck Encyclopedia of European Private Law*, vol I (OUP 2012) 184.

2 For details on Chinese legal background on civil law, Luigi Moccia, 'The idea of "law" in China: an overview', in Lukasz Golota et alii (eds), *Perspectives on Chinese Business and Law* (Intersentia 2018) 59–94; Zou (n 1) 1; Han (n 1); Pissler (n 1) 183.

While general national laws begin straight towards to the rules on interpretation and general principles applicable to contracts, the legislators of the CCC took a preliminary step to define the contract's objective (establishment, modification, or termination of a civil juristic relationship) and subjective (between persons of the civil law) aspects.

The definition is aligned with the notion of contract discussed in the literature of other countries, such as in Brazil.[3] Perhaps because it is a common sense, other systems preferred not to have a fixed definition of contracts and, in this case, the CCC provision facilitates the literature and jurisdictional work. On the other hand, authors are generally worried with excessive detail and specific rules, which may limit the freedom that characterizes the contractual relationships.[4]

Another interesting provision contained in the first Chapter is article 466, which provides for a different rule on the interpretation of contracts drafted in different languages. While the PICC stipulates the prevalence of the 'original draft' in case of discrepance (pursuant to article 4.7), the CCC privileges the internal aspects of the contract and the principle of good faith[5] by stating that interpretation 'shall be made in accordance with the related clauses, nature, and purpose of the contract, and the principle of good faith, and the like'.

Additionally, the provision refers to the interpretation standards of article 142 of the CCC which, in its turn, shows another innovation of the Code when treating the 'expression of intent' not made to an specific person. In this case, the consideration of the used terms and sentences of an expression of intent is relativized if compared to expressions made to a specific person.[6]

Finally, noteworthy is article 467 of the CCC, which provides for the mandatory application of Chinese Law (and, hence, the CCC) in international contracts related to exploration and exploitation of natural resources that are to be performed within the Chinese territory. The provision limits the principle of 'voluntariness', one of the pillars of Chinese civil law[7] and, with respect to

---

3 According to Orlando Gomes, the contract is "a legal instrument for the constitution, transmission and extinction of rights": Orlando Gomes, *Contratos* (new edition by Antônio Junqueira de Azevedo and Francisco P. de Crescenzo Marino, 26th ed., Forense 2008) 5.

4 William Jones, 'Sources of Chinese Obligation Law', in Haley (ed) (n 1) 305.

5 Good faith is one of the pillars of Chinese civil law, pursuant to article 7 of the CCC.

6 Article 142(2) CCC: "Where an expression of intent is not made to any specific person, the true intent of the person performing a civil juristic act shall not be interpreted solely on the words and sentences used, but along with the relevant terms, the nature and purpose of the civil juristic act, custom, and the principle of good faith".

7 Pursuant to article 5 of CCC: "When conducting a civil activity, a person of the civil law shall, in compliance with the principle of voluntariness, create, alter, or terminate a civil juristic relationship according to his own will".

contract, similar to the widely applicable principle of freedom/autonomy of the parties.

The limitation of the parties to freely choose the applicable law to contracts is not an exclusivity of China though. Under Brazilian Introductory Law (Decree Law No 4,657/1942, as amended), article 9 states that the place of the obligation's constitution determines the applicable law and, in cases of contracts, the applicable law shall be the law of the proposing party's domicile. Such limitation was the focus of heated debate among scholars in Brazil and claims for law reform.[8] However, given the state protectionist character, which may be the same in case of China with respect to its natural resources, the discussion remains unsolved.

3 Conclusion of the Contract

Chapter 2 of the Book Three, Part One, comprises the rules on formation of contracts and, as the entire CCC, the provisions stand out in comparison with other national law and international initiatives due to their comprehensiveness, detail and, to some extent, contradictory nature.

As previously mentioned, this Chapter purports to discuss the CCC provisions that instigate comparisons from an outsider perspective. The issue of formation of contracts is one of the longest of the Book, entailing some interesting questions to be herein posed for reflection.

The Chapter begins with article 469 which is aligned with international harmonization initiatives and other national systems of civil law in establishing the freedom of form (writing, orally or in other forms) and defines 'writing' such as the PICC (reproduced in 'tangible form' – article 1.11). The provision goes beyond in qualifying electronic contracting as contract in 'writing', also in accordance with the Official Comments of the PICC, but absent in many national systems such as the Brazilian case, whose Civil Code does not provide for any rule on electronic contracting.

In fact, the CCC innovated in customizing all the provisions related to formation of contracts to the electronic sphere, which is even more complete and updated than the last edition of the PICC.[9] On the other hand, some of the CCC provisions are very unique and may imply some limitation on the proposed freedom, specially when observed from an outer perspective.

8 Beat Walter Rechsteiner, *Direito Internacional Privado. Teoria e Prática* (15th ed., Saraiva 2012) 161.

9 See articles 474 and 482, for example.

For instance, article 470 contains some 'general clauses' for a contract (and, therefore, to be contained in an offer) which are even more detailed than article 14 of the CISG.[10] Although such 'clauses' are not posed as mandatory, but rather options to the parties, it is still unclear if a party may claim the inexistence of a contract in case it fails to contain one of them. In such a case, instead of strengthening, the provision limits the parties' freedom to contract and, maybe due to this reason, the drafters of the CISG and the PICC (as well as most national laws) preferred to issue more open rules.

Another particular provision of the CCC that operates as a contradiction and limitation of the freedom of contract is article 494 which concerns State purchase in case of emergency (including pandemic prevention). Absent in international initiatives, but not unfamiliar to national systems, the provision states that a party 'shall' conclude the contract with a 'reasonable offer in a timely manner'. Moreover, the provision states that a party with the obligation of acceptance 'shall not reject' a reasonable offer.

As commented in literature, the provision was a reaction to the emergency situation faced with the COVID-19 pandemic.[11] However, similar provisions are generally set forth in specific administrative laws drafted to regulate State contracting (such as the case of Law 14.133/2021 in Brazil which regulates contracts in general with the Public Administration) and not in civil codes, which purports to regulate private relationships.

As regards the rules on revocation of the offer, a controversial issue under Brazilian law, the CCC article 476 opted for the objective and subjective criteria of the PICC, i.e., the offer is irrevocable when expressly so provides or where the offeree has reasons to believe that it is irrevocable. In Brazil, the lack of clarity in legislation (article 427 of the Brazilian Civil Code solely states that the offer 'binds' the offeror) created different understanding on the possibility of offer revocation.

On one side, some authors defend that the 'binding' effect of the offer is equivalent to 'irrevocability',[12] while others – the prevailing and most adequate opinion – defend that, although binding, the offer may be revoked until the conclusion of the contract and, in this case, the offeror shall indemnify the

10 Which provides for minimum requirements of quantity and price of the goods.

11 See, in this regard, Zou (n 1) Ch 3.

12 Francisco Cavalcante Pontes de Miranda, *Tratado de Direito Privado. Parte Geral. Bens. Fatos Jurídicos*, tomo II (new edition by Ovídio Rocha Barros Sandoval, Revista dos Tribunais 2012) 511; Iacyr de Aguilar Vieira, *L'applicabilité et l'impact de la Convention des Nations Unies sur les contrats de vente internationale de marchandises au Brésil* (Strasbourg Presses Universitaires 2010) 340.

offeree for any damage suffered due to the revocation.[13] The binding effect of an offer has another meaning, i.e. that the offeror shall conclude a final contract, if accepted, in the same terms and conditions of the offer.

The prevailing opinion in Brazil is aligned not only with article 476, but also article 472 (2) of the CCC (binding effect of the offer). The detail and clarity of the CCC would be able to solve many academic and practical discussions in Brazil.

As regards detail and clarity, article 477 of the CCC innovates in differing the 'timing' of revocation in case of 'real-time communication' – which is not common in national systems – and, as in other provisions of the Chapter, refers to the 'knowledge' of the offeree or, when parties are absent, to the 'reception theory' for concluding contracts.

In this context, interesting to note that the CCC does not provide for a fixed rule for the conclusion of the contracts, such as the CISG and the PICC that privilege the 'reception theory' (the acceptance must 'reach' the offeror – articles 18 and 2.1.6, respectively). Differently, the CCC provides for the 'cognition theory' in cases of real-time communication (articles 483 and 484 combined with article 137, and 477) by stating that the contract is formed when the offeror is aware of the acceptance's content.[14] In any other forms of communication, including electronic contracting, the rules lead to the 'reception theory' by stating that the acceptance must 'reach' the offeror or the 'enters the server' of the offeror (similar to CISG and the PICC).

However, the CCC also contains specific rules in cases of contracts in writing agreements or letters pursuant to articles 490 and 491, which deviates from the reception or cognition theories. According to these rules, the contracts/letters must be signed, but exception is made when, failing the signature or stamp, the parties perform and accept the principal obligation and/or, in case of electronic contract, when the party submits the order.

---

13 Haroldo Malheiros Duclerc Verçosa, *Contratos Mercantis e a Teoria Geral dos Contratos: O Código Civil de 2002 e a Crise do Contrato* (Quartier Latin 2010) 315; Caio Mário da Silva Pereira, *Instituições de Direito Civil: Contratos. Declaração Unilateral de Vontade. Responsabilidade Civil* vol III (11th ed., Forense 2004) 43; Silvio de Salvo Venosa, *Direito Civil. Teoria Geral das Obrigações e Teoria Geral dos Contratos* vol II (5th ed., Atlas 2005) 547.

14 Article 483 provides that the contract is concluded when the acceptance becomes effective and article 484 refers to article 137 in order to rule the effectiveness of the acceptance. Article 137, in its turn, states that an express of intention is effective from the time the person to whom the intent is expressed is aware of its content (in cases of real-time communication).

The Brazilian Civil Code, on the other hand, differs from the CCC (and other international initiatives) by providing for the 'dispatch theory' (pursuant to article 434, the contract is formed when the acceptance is dispatched). Nevertheless, there are so many exceptions to this general rule that may lead to the reception theory, such as that of article 433, which states that the withdrawal of acceptance occurs when such withdrawal 'reaches' the offeror before the acceptance.[15]

In any case, the completeness of the CCC rules is very important in order to avoid disputes regarding the time of the conclusion of the contract, which may happen in other countries such as Brazil. For instance, when there are exchanges of effective offer and acceptance, but the contract is not 'signed' by the parties and a dispute begins, doubts arise as to whether the contract was effectively concluded or not and, hence, if there are already duties, rights and even the start of limitation periods. In this case, which is more common than expected, the CCC provides for a clear rule that interpreter shall assess the engagement of the parties in requiring 'signature' of a contract or, alternatively, to the performance by the parties. The Brazilian law, however, does not contain specific parameter and provides for acceptance by conduct if the nature of the contract or the offeror dispenses express acceptance.[16]

The same happens with the rules on standard terms, electronic contracting and liability of the parties during this phase of formation of the contracts. The CCC provides for definitive rules on these issues (articles 496–498 and 500–501, for instance) which is an innovation compared to other national laws, such as the Brazilian one, facilitating the job of judges, arbitrators and literature.

Lastly, a comparative analysis between the CCC and the Brazilian Civil Code on the place of the conclusion of the contract is the example that, in many cases, different rules may lead to the same result.[17] While the CCC states that the contract is concluded where the 'acceptance becomes effective' (article 492),

---

15 For a more detailed analysis on the formation of contracts under Brazilian Law, see Alberto do Amaral Junior, Umberto Celli Junior and Lígia Espolaor Veronese, 'A Formação dos Contratos após a CISG entrar em vigor no Brasil. Uma análise prática aos operadores do Direito', in Ingeborg Schwenzer, Cesar A. Guimarães Pereira and Leandro Tripodi (eds), *A CISG e o Brasil* (Marcial Pons 2014) 206.

16 Pursuant to article 432 of the Brazilian Civil Code: "If the juristic act is one of those in which express acceptance is not customary, or if the proponent has dispensed with it, the contract shall be considered concluded, if the refusal does not arrive in time" (authors' translation).

17 In alignment with the functional comparative method of Konrad Zweigert and Hein Kötz: see Konrad Zweigert and Hein Kötz, *An Introduction to Comparative Law* (Tony Weir transl, 3rd edn, OUP 1998) 34–40.

under the Brazilian Civil Code the contract is concluded 'where it is proposed' (article 435). Although different, both rules direct the conclusion to the offeror' place, since it is where the contract is 'proposed' and where the acceptance is effective, by 'reaching' the offeror or where he/she is 'aware of its content'.

4 Effect and Performance of the Contract

Chapter III of Book Three provides for a few rules on effect of the contract which are very aligned with comparative and harmonization initiatives, related to rules on authority to conclude and cases where additional procedure is necessary to give enforceability to a contract.

Interesting, however, is the rule set forth in article 506 related to clauses exempting liability. These types of clauses are very common in contracts and, as such, national systems and international initiatives discuss their permission and, more importantly, the circumstances where these clauses must not be applied. Under the PICC, the drafters prefer to establish an open rule which refers to 'gross unfairness', having regard to the purpose of the contract (article 7.1.6). The Official Comments of the PICC illustrate the cases of 'evident imbalance' and 'gross negligence'.

Article 506 of the CCC goes on the same path by specifying the circumstances of 'physical injury' and intentional harm or gross negligence in causing losses to the other party. The existence of specific rules on such regard is very relevant for comparison purposes, especially for their influence on countries that lack 'black letter rules' and rely on literature and case law. Under Brazilian law, the absence of a specific provision on these widely used clauses led the literature to develop instances where such clauses are not applicable, such as the *dolo* (intentional behaviour), gross negligence, personal integrity, violation of public order and when such limitation would imply a 'waiver' for the debtor in performing the contract (the breach is more advantageous than the performance).[18]

Another noteworthy provision of this chapter is article 507 which expresses the preservation of the validity of the dispute resolution clause even if the contract is deemed void, revoked, terminated or unenforceable (a rule that

18 Antônio Junqueira de Azevedo, 'Cláusula cruzada de não indenizar (cross-waiver of liability), ou cláusula de não indenizar com eficácia para ambos os contratantes-renúncia ao direito de indenização-promessa de fato de terceiro-estipulação em favor de terceiro' (2001) Revista dos Tribunais – Obrigações e contratos: contratos: formação e regime 561–569.

is reiterated in article 567 in Chapter VII of the CCC[19]). The provision goes beyond the open articles 3.2.13 and 3.2.14 of the PICC which provide for the limitation of avoidance to specific clauses when such clauses can be segregated from the contract, and the Official Comments refer to the dispute resolution clause as one example.[20] Brazilian Civil Code follows the open treatment on partial avoidance (article 184), but there is specific provision on the autonomous nature of dispute resolution clause in the Brazilian Arbitration Law (in this case, limited to the arbitration clause).[21]

In contrast to Chapter III, Chapter IV of Book Three comprises a very long and detailed set of rules on the performance of the contract, specifying parameters on price, quantity, time, place and quality on performance, including the particularities of electronic contracting. Most of them are aligned with (and more complete than) the PICC and even the CISG, with contributing role to other national systems that require some modernization of rules.

Innovatively, the CCC searched for the adequacy of the contract rules to one of its primary principles: environment conservation and protection established in article 9 of the CCC. Pursuant to this principle, the parties shall act "in a manner that facilitates conservation of resources and protection of the ecological environment".[22] Article 509 applies this principle in what concerns contracting relationship, by stating that parties shall 'avoid wasting the resources, polluting the environment, or damaging the ecology in the course of performance of the contract'.

Absent in the CISG or the PICC, the duty to protect the environment is common in many national systems, but provided for in specific laws and administrative regulations and, when important to some contracts, the parties expressly contract the observation of such duties (with clauses for the supply of environmental licenses, for examples). Therefore, similarly to what was seen above in the case of State contracting, the CCC uniquely merges the environmental concern into contract law, subjecting all parties to observe this special

---

19 Article 567 of the CCC: "Termination of the relationship of rights and obligations under a contract does not affect the validity of the contract clauses regarding settlement and liquidation".

20 UNIDROIT, *UNIDROIT Principles of International Commercial Contracts* (2016), at <https://www.unidroit.org/english/principles/contracts/principles2016/principles2016-e.pdf> (accessed January 20, 2023) 117.

21 Article 8 of Law 9,307/1996: "The arbitration clause is autonomous in relation to the contract it is inserted, and the nullity of the latter does not necessarily imply the nullity of the former" (authors' translation).

22 In this regard, see Zou (n 1) 38; Yuanshi Bu, *Chinese Civil Code. The General Part* (Beck 2019) 21.

duty. This is another provision with an important contribution for other systems and even for international initiatives on a very relevant matter.

Article 513 also calls the attention in protecting the parties in case of delayed performance when government-set or government-guided pricing applies. While Brazilian law solely provides that the parties are free to establish official prices valid for a day and place (article 486 of the Brazilian Civil Code), the CCC specifies what happens if a performance does not occur as expected, giving prevalence to the price at the time of delivery if the price falls or keep the original price if it rises.

The contribution of such a rule to protect the parties in case of governmental pricing is noteworthy to many civil law countries, since this circumstance falls 'under the risk' of the contracting parties and a revision of price would entail the application of revisional legal rules, which normally requires hard threshold to be met. For instance, article 317 of the Brazilian Civil Code allows the parties to adjust contract prices, but it is not automatic and subjects the affected party to the judicial proof of disproportion and non-foreseeability.[23]

In most countries or even international harmonization initiatives, the possibility of changing price falls under the rules of changing circumstances, which apply to any other change, such as the rules on hardship. The CCC distinguishes the treatment dispensed to governmental pricing (protecting the parties of a contract) from other circumstances, which fall under the hardship provision of article 533.

Article 533 was one of the most important innovations of the CCC in comparison to former Chinese contract laws (the GRCL or the Contract Law) and has its roots in one of the Peoples Court's Interpretations on Contract Law.[24] Moreover, the provision is strongly influenced and aligned with articles 6.2.1–6.2.3 of the PICC, by stating a first step of renegotiation attempt in case of

---

23 Article 317 of the Brazilian Civil Code: "When, for unforeseeable reasons, a manifest disproportion arises between the value of the service due and the value at the time of its execution, the judge may correct it, at the request of the party, so as to ensure, as far as possible, the real value of the service" (authors' translation).

24 Interpretation on Certain Questions Concerning the Application of Contract Law, article 26 of Interpretation n. 2 of 2009: "Where any significant change in the objective environment has taken place after the formation of a contract which could not have been foreseen by the relevant parties at the time of entering into the contract, and does not belong to any commercial risk occasioned by any force majeure cause, rendering the continual performance of the contract manifestly unfair to the relevant party or rendering it impossible to realise the goal of the contract, the People's Court shall confirm whether the contract shall be varied or dissolved in accordance with the principle of justice taking into account the actual circumstance, where a relevant party petitions a People's Court to vary or dissolve the contract".

hardship and subsequent resort to court in case of failure to negotiate. Similar to the PICC and different from Brazilian law, the CCC provision (*i*) seeks to avoid litigation in cases of hardship, while in Brazil this is a judicial measure (unless expressly set forth in the contract) and (*ii*) privileges the revision of the contract instead of termination, while the Brazilian black letter rule only discusses termination (article 478 of the Brazilian Civil Code – however, literature and case law accept the application of hardship for revision of contracts[25]).

Finally, article 534 brings another sign of the Chinese 'controlling' aspect by creating a stronger degree of liability in cases of contracts that "endangers the State's interests and public interests, the market regulatory authority and other relevant administrative authorities". Another uncommon provision when compared to international initiatives and, as regards national systems, it approximates to the rules of objective liability (regardless of fault) in cases of parties engaging in dangerous activities, such as article 927, sole paragraph, of Brazilian Civil Code.[26]

5 Termination and Default Liability

As mentioned in the introduction, Chapters of Book Three – Chapters V and VI – will not be addressed in this Chapter.

Moving to Chapter VII, it discusses the termination of contracts and begins by expressly indicating the possible grounds for termination, which are related to issues of 'performance' or exemption to perform, such as offset, payment in escrow, confusion (the same person has the debt and credit) and agreement of the parties (article 557). All of the circumstances are very aligned with other national and international systems.

An interesting provision of this Chapter is article 558 which expressly recognizes the duty to observe good faith in case of termination of the contract. The provision reinforces the primary principle of good faith present in article 7

25 See Francisco Paulo de Crescenzo Marino, *Revisão Contratual: Onerosidade Excessiva e Modificação Contratual Equitativa* (Almedina 2020). See also Statement 176 of Civil Law Journey: "In attention to the principle of contract preservation, article 478 of the Civil Code od 2002 shall conduct, whenever possible, to the judicial revision of the contracts and not to the termination" (authors' translation).

26 Article 927, sole paragraph, of Brazilian Civil Code: "There will be an obligation to pay damage, regardless of fault, in the cases specified by law, or when the activity normally performed by the author of the damage implies, by its nature, risk to the rights of others" (authors' translation).

of the CCC and innovates by expressly applying the principle when a contract is terminated.

In the PICC, the good faith is provided in an open manner, applicable to 'international trade' (article 1.7(1)) which implies its application throughout the entire contractual relationship (conclusion, performance and termination). In Brazil, on the other hand, there is only express legislation on good faith in the phases of conclusion and performance of the contract (Article 422 of the Brazilian Civil Code[27]), while the termination phase has been recognized by the development of literature.[28]

Similar to other systems, the CCC establishes that the parties may agree on the termination of the contract and defines specific circumstances for its termination (Article 562 clearly privileges the autonomy of the parties). However, article 563 specifies some circumstances where the parties may rescind the contract, such as force majeure, anticipatory breach, breach of contract even after the grant of additional time, loss of the purpose of the contract after the breach and other circumstances provided by law. Moreover, article 564 provides for a limitation period for the extinguishment of the rescission right (one year or reasonable time), and article 565 states that rescission may be made through notice to the other party or, in case of resistance, through court decision (and the parties are free to go directly to court in order to request rescission).

Such provisions reflect the strong influence of the PICC and the CISG on the CCC. By allowing a party to directly rescind a contract due to 'delayed performance after additional time' and 'loss of contract's purpose' after breach, the CCC follows the recognition of termination due to breach after the grant of supplementary time, as well as due to 'fundamental breach' or 'fundamental non-performance' (present in the PICC articles 7.1.4 and 7.3.1 and in the CISG articles 24, 49 (a) and (b) and 64 (a) and (b)).

The recognition of these power of the party to directly declare the termination of the contract (known as a 'self-help remedy') places China in perfect harmony and integrated into international trade rules, as well as civil law

27 Article 422 of the Brazilian Civil Code: "The contracting parties are obliged to observe the principles of probity and good faith, both in the conclusion of the contract and in its performance" (authors' translation).

28 Legal experts have approved the Statements 25 and 170 of the Civil Law Journeys: "Article 422 of the Civil Code does not prevent the judge from applying the principle of good faith in the pre-contractual and post-contractual phases"; "Objective good faith must be observed by the parties at the preliminary negotiation stage and after the execution of the contract, when such requirement arises from the nature of the contract" (authors' translation).

countries with modernized legislations, such as Germany.[29] In Brazil, despite the reform of the Civil Code in 2002, the system still refrains from accepting the autonomy of the party in rescinding the contract, much less to define specific instances for the exercise of such autonomy.

Pursuant to the Brazilian Civil Code – and in the opposite direction of international initiatives and modern civil law jurisdictions –, if the cause of termination is not expressly established by the parties beforehand in the contract, the interested party shall resort to court/arbitration to have a contract terminated (pursuant to article 474[30]). Moreover, literature and case law developed the understanding that only an 'absolute breach' entails the termination of the contract and the concept of this type of breach,[31] although not provided by law, is very aligned with fundamental breach of the CISG and the PICC, since it refers to the loss of interest and purpose to preserve the contract (similar to the black letter rules of the CCC article 563 (4)).

The mandatory resort to court for the termination of the contract is now mitigated in Brazil after the country's adhesion to the CISG (with the promulgation of Decree Law 8,327/2014). However, for contracts other than international sales of goods, the Civil Code provision (and the need for a court-supervised decision) still prevails, but not without some criticism.[32]

The difference in the compared systems (Chinese and Brazilian) leads to practical impacts. While in Brazil the parties must wait for a court decision to consider the contract terminated, in China, the parties might be discharged by the mere notification or, even when resorting to court, the decision operates retroactively to the date of the termination notice (article 565 of the CCC),

---

29 For instance, § 324 of the German *Bürgerliches Gesetzbuch*: "*Verletzt der Schuldner bei einem gegenseitigen Vertrag eine Pflicht nach § 241 Abs. 2, so kann der Gläubiger zurücktreten, wenn ihm ein Festhalten am Vertrag nicht mehr zuzumuten ist*" (If the debtor breaches an obligation under section 241(2) in a mutual contract, the creditor may rescind the contract if it can no longer reasonably be expected to adhere to the contract – authors' translation).

30 Article 474 of the Brazilian Civil Code: "The express termination clause operates automatically; the tacit one depends on judicial interpellation" (authors' translation).

31 Ruy Rosado de Aguiar Junior, 'A extinção dos Contratos', in Wanderlei Fernandes (ed), *Contratos Empresariais: Fundamentos e Princípios dos Contratos Empresariais* (2nd ed., Saraiva 2012) 503–505.

32 Antonio Junqueira de Azevedo, 'Insuficiências, deficiências e desatualização do projeto de Código Civil na questão da boa-fé objetiva nos contratos' (2000) 1 Revista Trimestral de Direito Civil 3–12. For ananalysis of the judicial requirement for termination of contracts in Brazil compared to the CISG, see Lígia Espolaor Veronese, *A Convenção de Viena e seus Reflexos no Direito Contratual Brasileiro* (Almedina 2019) Part II, Ch 2 pt 4 (passim).

which is a legal direction much more aligned with the dynamism of the international trade.

The remaining rules of Chapter VII detail the effects of termination and other circumstances of termination, such as the confusion, deposit in escrow and agreement between the parties, which do not raise discussions from an outer perspective.

Finally, the last Chapter of Part One sets forth rules on default liability. The first provisions are those generally adopted on the liability for damages, compensation, taking remedial measures, interests and remuneration, the limitation of compensation to the foreseeable damages (article 584), as well as the instances where a creditor cannot request for the specific performance of the contract after a breach (article 580).

Comparative attention should be given, however, to the rules established in articles 585 onwards, which deal with the liquidated amounts to couple with breaching situations. Article 585 provides for the possibility of the parties to 'pre-liquidate' damages by stipulating a certain amount to be owed by the debtor in case of breach, which can be increased or diminished by the court/ arbitral tribunal in accordance with the concrete incurred damages.

Such a provision deviates from Brazilian law and even the PICC by granting more power to judges/arbitrators to change the amount agreed by the parties. In Brazil, similar to the PICC, it is recognized the possibility of reasonable reduction of the contract fixed amount when it becomes excessive compared to the breach and/or to the damages incurred (article 7.4.13 (2) of the PICC and article 413 of the Brazilian Civil Code[33]).

Aiming at protecting the parties, the CCC rule represents a higher degree of court interference in the relationship and risks attributed between the parties, which, from an outer perspective, may be detrimental to the contractual relationship and its binding effect, since the agreed provision on liquidated damages might be innocuous.

Articles 586 and 587 also provide for rules that limit the freedom of the parties and deviate from Brazilian contract law. The provisions state that the parties may agree on 'earnest money', which is a deposit made by one party to ensure performance. The institute is very similar to the 'arras' provided for in

---

33 Article 7.4.13 (2) of the PICC: "However, notwithstanding any agreement to the contrary the specified sum may be reduced to a reasonable amount where it is grossly excessive in relation to the harm resulting from the non-performance and to the other circumstances". Under Article 413 of the Brazilian Civil Code, "The penalty must be reduced equitably by the judge if the main obligation has been partially fulfilled, or if the amount of the penalty is manifestly excessive, taking into account the nature and purpose of the business" (authors' translation).

articles 417–420 of the Brazilian Civil Code and, in case of breach, the aggrieved party may retain the deposited amount, while in case of performance, the amount may be kept or refunded by the receiving party. However, while the Brazilian law does not provide for any limitation on the 'arras' (the CISG and the PICC either), the CCC establishes that its amount shall not exceed 20% of the principal obligation (article 586), which, again, entails a more controlling character on the relationship of the parties, especially considering that the party can opt between the liquidated damages or the 'earnest money' in case of breach (article 588).

In other words, the provisions of the CCC on default liability and liquidation of damages move away from the modern and vanguard shown in the previous Chapters and follows a different path that may be detrimental to the autonomy of the parties to contract, by allowing strong external interference in private relationships.

Also noteworthy is the rule contained in article 591 of the CCC which goes beyond the general treatment of the so called 'duty to mitigate the loss'. Such a duty is one of the most contributing provisions of the CISG (article 77) and the PICC (article 7.4.8) to Brazilian system – despite the absence of an express provision in legislation, literature and case law have been relying on the CISG to apply the duty to Brazilian concrete cases.[34]

The CCC completes and reinforces this duty by establishing that 'no compensation' shall be claimed by the aggrieved party in case he/she fails to take the appropriate measures to prevent damages, and not the mere reduction of the claimed compensation (as provided by article 77 of the CISG). Therefore, the CCC increases the burden on the affected party, which cannot stay inert in face of a breach, but rather act actively to mitigate harm.

6 Final Remarks

This Chapter intended to analyse certain provisions of Book Three of the CCC from an outer perspective. Given the extension of Book Three (the longest of the entire Code), the authors opted to concentrate the analysis in its first part, which provides for rules applicable to all types of obligations and contracts, instead of assessing specific contracts.

34 For an analysis of the contribution of the CISG and the duty to mitigate the loss to Brazilian case law, see Lígia Espolaor Veronese, 'A Contribuição da CISG para o Direito Contratual Brasileiro: Uma Análise Jurisprudencial', in Gustavo Kulesza and Rodrigo Moreira (eds), *Direito Contratual e Convenção de Viena* (CISG) (Almedina 2021) 61–88.

The purpose was to highlight some rules that entail comparative discussions with international harmonization initiatives (such as the PICC and the CISG) and the Brazilian system.

The choice of these comparative instruments was important to demonstrate how the CCC (*i*) is aligned with internationally accepted rules; (*ii*) was able to go beyond other systems in terms of completeness and actuality and (*iii*) can contribute to other national systems by establishing specific rules instead of open provisions that generally leads to disputes.

However, while specificity and completeness may help parties to avoid conflicts, such elements have the effect of limiting parties' freedom and autonomy to contract, which is paradoxically one of the primary principles of Chinese civil law (article 5). The present Chapter showed that some provisions of the CCC work as limitation and interference in parties' relationship, such as those related to State contracting and default liability, circumstances which the parties are not free to discuss price and even the extension of parties pre-liquidated liability.

As mentioned throughout the Chapter, the CCC system can be considered an influenced system that now may have become the influencer. Nevertheless, caution should be taken in order to not endanger one of the most important principles of contract law with the purpose of avoiding conflicts. Freedom will necessarily entail liability and, to some extent, conflicts. The challenge to all systems is to achieve a balance between these opposite goals, and this is not different in China.

CHAPTER 10

Ambitious Goals for the Book on Personality Rights of the Chinese Civil Code

张家勇 *Zhang Jiayong*

1 Introduction

An independent Book on Personality Rights is considered to be one of the greatest innovations of the Chinese civil code.[1] To some extent, the quality of the Book on Personality Rights reflects the quality of the entire Civil Code, since this book has been the most concerned and debated one amongst all of the books of the code. Does this independent book provide "a Chinese experience on, and a Chinese approach to, the protection of personality rights that are inspiring to all other countries",[2] or is it "too overestimated, whether from the perspective of innovation of theory or from the perspective of its impact"?[3] This chapter aims to evaluate the experiences and lessons that can be learned from the compilation of the Book on Personality Rights by elaborating on the following three aspects in particular: the legislative goals for the compilation of the independent Book on Personality Rights, its specific content, and its main limitations.

2 Legislative Goals for an Independent Book on Personality Rights

'Whether to have an independent Book on Personality Rights' and 'if the answer is affirmative, how to do it', are two distinct yet closely related questions. To a greater extent, the answer to the latter question forms the basis for

1 Another innovation is the adoption of functionalism in security rights in movable things. Although the independent Book on Tort Liability can be said to be another innovation in terms of legislation, as it is based upon the Chinese Torts Law promulgated before the Civil Code, it is not an innovation in the compilation of the Civil Code.

2 Wang Liming, 'Highlight and Innovation of the Part of Improvement Rights in the Civil Code' (2020) 4 China Leg Sci 5–6 (王利明, 民法典人格权编的亮点与创新,《中国法学》).

3 Su Yongqin, 'Evaluation and Prospects of the Civil Code in Mainland China from a Codicological Perspective' (2020) 1 Xiamen U L Rev 24 (苏永钦, 从法典学的角度评价和展望中国大陆的民法典,《厦门大学法律评论》).

 | DOI:10.1163/9789004704428_011

evaluating the appropriateness of the answer to the former, while answering the former question is a precondition for the necessity of answering the latter. Since the objective of this article is to evaluate how the book has been made, it is not redundant to review the arguments for and against the necessity and desirability of an independent book on personality rights.[4]

It should be mentioned that in spite of the different points of views expressed on the matter by Chinese scholars, there is consensus on the following: the protection of personality rights in Chinese Civil Code should be strengthened in the 21st century, so as to respond to the challenges presented by new technologies and new situations. Due to this consensus, scholars differ mainly in the specific approaches to achieve such a goal. In other words, they have different views about how to highlight the importance of personality rights, how to improve current provisions, how to coordinate the civil code with the existing provisions, and how to guide judges in rendering judgments.

2.1 *Highlighting the Values Underlying Personality Rights*

The proponents for an independent Book on Personality Rights believe that it is the paramount aim of a legal system to uphold the personality and dignity of people. As such, in the new era of substantial improvements in material living standards, it raises expectations for personality rights and dignity, which highlights the humanistic spirit of the contemporary era and the belief that those values should be upheld.[5] In contrast, the opposing views express that personality rights are mainly civil rights belonging to natural persons, which means that placing these rights in the Book on General Provisions is more suitable for the purpose of highlighting their importance.

As such, if an arrangement in terms of statutory layout and style is available to highlight the significance of the values that the legislators mostly cherish, then such an arrangement should be employed.[6] The Chinese General Principles of Civil Law, by juxtaposing personality with other civil rights such as ownership, obligation claims (*choses in action*) and intellectual properties, already set a precedent by which the arrangement of these rights are used to highlight certain rights over others; the same precedent is now followed by the independent Book on Personality Rights of the Civil Code. Concurring

4 It should be noted that even if we assume that the Book on Personality should be independent, it does not follow that the specific provisions in the independent Book are satisfactory.

5 See Wang Liming, 'Reasons for Personality Rights to Be a Separate Part' (2017) 6 L Rev 1–5 (王利明, 论人格权独立成编的理由,《法学评论》).

6 See Geng Lin, 'Personality Rights and Its Legislative Techniques' (2017) 6 Oriental L 106 (耿林, 人格权及其立法技术,《东方法学》).

on the necessity to protect personality rights, those opposing the idea of an autonomous book do not deny the opportunity of highlighting the importance of personality rights. Rather, they are concerned about the following: while it is true that one of the objectives of the Chinese civil code is to highlight the importance of personality rights, obviously it is also true that the substantial implication of any technical choice should be considered. If having an independent Book on Personality Rights results in incoherence and inefficiency, the aforementioned function of such an arrangement would be undermined or even totally fail. Likewise, given the fact that the protection of personality and dignity is already stipulated by the Constitution Law, one should not rely too heavily on the Civil Code and its layout to highlight the rights.

2.2 *Improving the Provisions on Personality Rights*

The proponents of an independent Book on Personality Rights believe that, with the development of technology and society, the protection of personality rights has become increasingly challenging. The traditional oversimplified legal provisions regarding personality rights, if they remain, are doomed to fail in this mission.[7] Thus, after WWII, many countries saw an uptick in their personality rights-related legislation.[8] For the proponents, the traditional approach of treating personality rights as only having a defensive function is insufficient for its realization, as personality rights also attribute positive privileges, either material or spiritual, that can be exercised by their holders in a positive manner. According to this view, *usus*, *fructus* and *abusus* are prerogatives of personality rights, and the right of correction and reply, the right to ask for a preliminary injunction, and the right to delete, modify or supplement data are all reflections of the positive prerogatives of personality rights.[9] By delineating the positive dimensions of these rights, civil law rules can better accomplish their missions of guiding behaviors of people and prevention of infringements.[10] In contrast, for the opponents, personality rights are formed spontaneously and endogenously from society, and thus are self-evident.[11]

---

7 See Wang (n 5) 4.

8 See Shi Jiayou, 'Historical Evolution and Trend of Personality Rights Legislation' (2018) 4 J CUPL 159 (石佳友，人格权立法的历史演进及其趋势，《中国政法大学学报》).

9 Wang Liming, 'The Nature of Personality Rights: From Negative Defense to Positive Utilization' (2018) 4 Peking U L J 849 (王利明，人格权的属性:从消极防御到积极利用，《中外法学》).

10 Wang Liming 'On the Positive Confirmation of Personality Right – The Relationship of Personality Right Law and Tort Liability Law' (2016) 2 The Jurist 8 (王利明，人格权的积极确权模式探讨—兼论人格权法与侵权法之关系，《法学家》).

11 Su (n 3) 24.

With its open-ended content, personality rights can only be described instead of defined, with the legal provisions of personality rights or their categories having nothing to do with their enjoyment by their holders, since personality rights are *a priori*. As the main function of personality rights is to defend their right holders against infringements (instead of providing right holders with *usus*, *fructus* and *abusus*), personality rights are defensive in nature. Therefore, it is not worth it to delineate the positive dimension of personality rights.[12]

Generally speaking, the more complete a legal provision about a specific right is, the better protected it becomes. As is agreed by both sides, since personality rights are open-ended, it is impossible to provide rules for all personality rights; it is only possible to provide rules for a part of them. Rules on personality rights generally fall within one of the following two types: the rules delineating the content of personality rights from a positive dimension and the rules preventing their infringement from a negative dimension. Rules providing the right to determine, to modify or to transfer one's name, the right to transfer one's image, and the licence to its use, fall within the former category, whereas the prohibition of the purchase and sale of organ trade, and the prohibition of a specific infringement of one's personality fall within the latter category. The higher the need to delineate the content of the personality rights, the more reasonable the presence of an independent book on personality rights would be. In other words, the need to delineate the content of personality rights in a positive way is an argument supporting the independence of the personality rights.

2.3 *Making a Systematized Civil Law*

The proponents of an independent book on personality rights believe that every specific personality right is distinguishable from the personality *per se* of a person because, in spite of the closeness of the two concepts, the former focuses on the interests associated with the latter.[13] Thus, personality rights have a status similar to that of proprietary rights and do not have to be provided in the general provisions of the civil code.

12 Liang Huixing, 'Major Controversies in the Compilation of Civil Code – Comment on Two Volumes on the Personality Rights Drafted by Legislative Affairs Commission of NPC Standing Committee' (2018) 3 J Gansu U Pol Sci and L 10 (梁慧星, 民法典编纂中的重大争论——兼评全国人大常委会法工委两个民法典人格权编草案, 《甘肃政法学院学报》).

13 Han Qiang, 'The Legal Dimension of Confirming and Constructing the Personality Right' (2015) 3 China Leg Sci (2015) 3: 141–142 (韩强, 人格权确认与构造的法律依据《中国法学》).

In addition, it is noted that the very notion of personality rights has already evolved from a negative dimension (whereby these rights were affirmed only inasmuch as they were protected against infringement) to a positive dimension (whereby these rights are also attribute specific prerogatives). Thus, to have the Book on Tort Liability provide all rules regarding personality rights would harm the coherence of the legal system. By contrast, an independent Book on Personality Rights providing the categories and content of the personality rights, the duties one has to bear vis-a-vis right holders, the rules for exercising and using the rights, the rules restricting them and the rules for their special protections, would not only clarify the respective scope of application of personality laws and tort laws, but would also provide a basis for the enforcement of administrative (rather than civil law) remedies.[14] Likewise, the law of torts can do little about emerging phenomena such as 'the positive use of personality rights' and 'the commercialization of personality rights'.[15]

In this regard, those who are against the idea of an autonomous book on personality rights, indicate that the protection of personality rights has traditionally been done by resorting to the law of torts, and therefore the development of personality rights is tantamount to the development of the law of torts (dealing with personality rights).[16] The personality rights of a natural person would only become salient when they are infringed upon; delineating the content of personality rights in positive terms would hinder their development rather than promote them.[17] Furthermore, according to this view, allowing the transfer and commercialization of personality rights would bring about serious problems, both of legal and ethical nature, rendering the legislation in conflict with basic humanitarian values.[18] Likewise, when it comes to compensation for mental distress due to a breach of contract and the licensed use of personal identity, the underlying legal issues are actually typical contract law issues, thus it would derange the coherence of the civil code if these aspects were to be regulated by rules on personality rights.

---

14 Wang Liming, 'The Distinction and Articulation between the Book of the Personality Rights and That of Tort Liability in the Chinese Civil Code' (2018) 2 J Comp L 4–8 (王利明, 论人格权编与侵权责任编的区分与衔接《比较法研究》).

15 Wang (n 9) 858 ff.

16 Liang (n 12) 10–12.

17 Sun Xianzhong, 'Research on Establishing Scientific Thinking of Civil Law System' (2022) 1 Sci L J Northwest U Pol Sci & L 39 (孙宪忠, 民法体系化科学思维的问题研究, 《法律科学：西北政法大学学报》).

18 Sun Xianzhong, 'Thoughts on Codification of Specific Provisions of Civil Code of the PRC' (2019) 5 ECUPL J 100 (孙宪忠, 当前我国民法典分则编纂的几点思考《华东政法大学学报》).

2.4 *Improving Adjudicative Guiding Effects*

Both the proponents and opponents agree that the law of torts is indispensable in the protection of personality rights and that the protection of personality rights should be improved. However, they disagree on whether an independent book of personality is the sole method to achieving this goal. The proponents of such a book contend that the fact that someone owes duties to the holders of personality rights is the very *raison d'être* for the tortuous liability based upon the infringement of personality rights.[19] As such, having a book delineating the content and scope of personality rights can reduce uncertainty and can offer a basis for guiding and limiting the discretion of judges.[20] In contrast, the opponents believe that the role now entrusted to the Book on Personality Rights could have been better performed by the newly independent Book on Tort Liability, whose independence creates an opportunity for expanding remedies available to victims of infringements of personality rights.[21] In addition, the experience gained in the judicial practice of the protection of personality rights in China proved the impotence of any positive specification of personality rights, as the plethora of incomplete articles (*unvollständige Rechtssätze*) in this regard would hinder judges in rendering sound judgement rather than help them.[22]

Considering all the above, we can see that its trivial to question whether an independent book on personality rights is the best way to highlight the importance of the rights. The lynchpin of a successful independent book on personality rights lies in whether the provisions in this book are able to identify each and every specific personality right and personality interest, specifying their contents and effects, and strengthening the remedies protecting them.[23] Therefore, it is the quality of each specific rule and principle in the personality book that is pivotal for the success of the independence of the book.

---

19 Zhu Hu, 'What Makes Personality Rights Civil Rights?' (2021) 5 L Rev 60 (朱虎, 人格权何以成为民事权利？《法学评论》).

20 Wang (n 10) 8–9.

21 Yin Tian, 'Technical Barriers of the Personality Right as an Independent Part' (2016) 1 J Pol Sci & L 57 (尹田, 论人格权独立成编的技术障碍《政法论丛》).

22 Liang (n 12) 11–12, 17–18.

23 See Wang (n 2) 6.

3 Content of the Book on Personality Rights

The Book on Personality Rights is located after the Book on Real Rights and the Book on Contracts, and before the Book on Marriage and Family, the Book on Inheritance and the Book on Tort Liability. The Book on Personality Rights comprises six chapters and fifty-one articles, which are more than those of the Book on Inheritance (forty-five articles), yet less than those of the Book on Marriage and Family, and the Book on Tort Liability (ninety-five articles). Apart from one general provision on personality rights, the Book on Personality Rights alongside the framework set out in the Book on general provisions (articles 109–111), stipulates eight specific personality rights and one interest in personal information.[24] In addition, in providing that "natural persons are entitled to other interests in personality derived from liberty and dignity" (article 990(2)), the Book on Personality Rights remains open to other types of personality interests.

The specific personality rights that are covered by the Book are stipulated in different chapters and arranged in an order reflecting their relations. They differ in their content, in the obligations that the concerned obligees have to bear, in the behaviors considered as infringements and in the remedies available to the injured party once that specific personality right is infringed. Considering this perspective, the most important contents and special features of the Book on Personality Rights are the following: the delineation of specific personality rights (Section 3.1), the creation of duties corresponding to personality rights (Section 3.2), the prohibition of infringing personality rights (Section 3.3) and the remedies provided in case an infringement occurs (Section 3.4).

3.1 *The Delineation of Specific Personality Rights*

In spite of the fact that the Civil Code applies to legal relations concerning the enjoyment and the protection of personality rights, the very concept of 'personality rights' is not clearly defined. Rather, the boundary of personality rights is set by an enumeration of different types of specific personality rights, while

24 Some argue that the interest of personal information is also a right, and that freedom of movement (article 1011) and credit (article 1011) are also independent type of rights. Thus, there are at least twelve types of rights stipulated in the Book on Personality Rights. See Wang (n 2). However, it is clear from a legislative point of view that freedom of movement and credit has been incorporated in the corporal right and the right of reputation (article 1003, sentence 2; article 1024(2)), which means the aforementioned view is purely academic in nature. Besides, the provisions regarding the protection of personality rights can be applied *mutatis mutandis* to the protection of a natural person's relation-based rights such as a right arising from a marital and familial relationship (article 1001).

other non-enumerated personality interests can be protected based upon the open-ended category of 'liberty and dignity'. The enumerated specific personality rights, such as the right of life, the right of corporal integrity, the right to health, the right of reputation, the right of honor, right to privacy and the interests on personal information, are generally all delineated in the same simple manner ('A natural person is entitled to XX rights'), without any specification of the special prerogatives associated with the relevant right. Exceptions are made for the so-called 'symbolic personality rights', whose content is often delineated in detail: "[a] natural person enjoys the right to name, and is entitled to determine, use, change, or allow others to use his name in accordance with law" (article 1012); "[a] legal person or an unincorporated organization enjoys the right to entity name, and is entitled to decide, use, change, transfer, or allow others to use its entity name in accordance with law" (article 1013) and "[a] natural person enjoys the right to likeness, and is entitled to make, use, publicize, or authorize others to use his image in accordance with law" (article 1018(1)).

Other situations where the detailed content of specific personality rights is specified are the following.

- A person with full capacity for performing civil juristic acts has the right to make a voluntary decision in accordance with law to donate his cells, tissues, organs, and remains, in writing or through a will (article 1006). Likewise, in the event of a clinical trial, the participants in the trial or their guardians have the right to consent in writing (article 1008).
- A natural person has the right to choose his or her own surname (article 1015).
- A civil law subject may check its own credit report in accordance with law (article 1029).
- A natural person's name, entity name, likeness, or the like, of a subject of the civil law may be used by others upon authorization (article 993). Where the parties have expressly agreed on the term of authorized use of the image, the person holding the right to likeness over the image may terminate the contract authorizing such use provided that there is a just cause (article 1022(2)).
- Where an awarded honorary title of a civil law person should have been recorded, the person may request that it be so recorded; where the honorary title is not correctly recorded, that person can ask it to be correctly recorded (article 1031(2)).
- Natural persons have the right to retrieve or make copies of their personal information from the information processors; where incorrect

information is found, natural persons have the right to raise an objection and to request correction or deletion in a timely manner (article 1037).

3.2 *The Creation of Relative Duties Correlative to Personality Rights*

Personality rights (as absolute rights) generally do not impose any positive duties on a specific person to be realized or protected. However, exceptions exist where a duty-bearer does bear the duty to act. For example, where a natural person's right to life, right to corporeal integrity, or right to health is infringed upon or is otherwise in peril, the organization or individual who is legally obliged to aid shall promptly provide rescue (article 1005). Where a clinical trial is needed for developing new drugs and medical devices, or developing new prevention and treatment methods, the participants in the trial or their guardians shall be informed of the details including the purposes, methods, and the possible risks of the trial, and their written consent must be obtained (article 1008(1)). State organs, enterprises, schools, and other organizations shall take reasonable precautions to prevent and stop sexual harassment (article 1010(2)). A person whose act (such as reporting news or supervising public opinions or the like for public interest purposes) may adversely affect others' reputation, shall fulfill the obligation to reasonably verify the information (articles 1025–1026). The processing of personal information shall be compliant with the principles of lawfulness, justification, and proportionality, shall not be excessively processed and shall satisfy the conditions prescribed by law (article 1035); furthermore, the information processor shall also ensure the security of the personal information collected and stored (article 1038). State organs and chartered institutions assuming administrative functions as well as their staff shall keep confidential the privacy and the personal information of natural persons known to them during the performance of their responsibilities (article 1039).

3.3 *The Prohibition of Infringing Personality Rights*

In stipulating that no organization or individual may infringe upon personality rights (article 992), the Civil Code lays down a general prohibition of infringement upon personality rights. Such prohibition is reiterated in provisions concerning the right of life, the right of corporal integrity, the right to health and the like, as general prohibitions of the infringement upon the aforementioned rights (articles 1002–1004).

In addition to the abstract prohibitions aforementioned, the civil code also specifies prohibitions of specific acts infringing upon specific personality rights. For example, the following is prohibited: to sexually harass others through oral words, written language, images, physical acts, or the like (article 1010(1)); to deprive or restrict the freedom of movement of others by illegal detention or the like measures, or illegally searching the body of others (article 1011); to infringe upon other's rights to name or rights to entity name by means such as interference, misappropriation, impersonation, or the like (article 1014); to infringe upon other's rights to likeness by vilifying or defacing the image thereof, or through other ways such as falsifying other's image by utilizing information technology, or using or publicizing the said image by ways such as publishing, duplicating, distributing, leasing, or exhibiting thereof (article 1019); to infringe upon other's right to reputation via insults, defamation, or the like (article 1024(1)); to unlawfully deprive others of their honorary titles or defame or degrade the honors thereof (article 1031(1)); to infringe upon the other's right to privacy by prying into, intruding upon, disclosing, or publicizing other's private matters (article 1032(1)) and private sphere without the consent of the right holder (article 1033). The prohibition of these acts as provided in the civil code delineate the content of personality rights in their negative dimension, and serve as criteria for determining whether an act constitutes or not an infringement upon a personality right.

In contrast with the aforementioned prohibitions, the civil code also outlines the fair use principle as an exception thereto: when it comes to news reporting, supervision of public opinions, or the like, for public interests, the name, entity name, likeness, personal information, and the like, of a civil law person may be reasonably used (article 999). If the requirements of purpose and objects are met, i.e., if the purpose of the fair use is a public interest and its objects are limited to the name, image, personal information, privacy and the like, excluding material personality elements such as life, corporal integrity and health,[25] the elements concerned can be used without the consent of the right holder. By contrast, if the actor who uses these elements exceeds the appropriate limits and thus infringes upon others' personality rights, that actor would still incur liability.

3.4 *The Remedies in Case of Infringement upon Personality Rights*

A person whose personality rights are infringed upon has the right to get remedies in accordance with provisions of the Civil Code and other laws (article 995, sentence 1). The remedies provided in the Book on Personality Rights can be roughly divided into two categories: contractual remedies and tortious remedies.

---

25 Wang (n 2) 11.

3.4.1 Compensation for Mental Distress as a Result of Breach of Contract

The Book on Personality Rights does not provide a legal basis (*Anspruchsgrundlagen*) for claims for infringement of personality rights due to breach of contract. Therefore, a claim for compensation for the damage caused should be based upon the general provisions as outlined in the Book on Contracts (articles 577 and 584). It has been debated both in theory and in practice whether the aggrieved right holder has the right to claim compensation for mental distress in this case.[26] As a response, the Civil Code made it clear that the aggrieved right holder does have such a right (article 996). It should be noted that this article is not a general provision regarding mental distress damages, but rather it applies only to situations where severe mental distress has been caused by a breach of contract infringing upon personality rights. In cases where no infringement upon personality rights is involved, whether such a claim can be raised or not, remains an issue to be solved by the Book on Contracts; the question is yet to be answered unanimously.

The Civil Code provides that where, owing to an actor's intentional or grossly negligent act, an object of personal significance of a natural person is infringed upon, which causes serious mental distress to the person, the infringed person has the right to claim compensation thereof (article 1183(2)). Therefore, if the aforementioned object is infringed due to a breach of contract, it is also debatable whether the article 996 is applicable in such a case.

3.4.2 Special Provisions for the Protection of Tortious Infringement of Personality Rights

The legal basis for claim for tortious infringements upon personality rights exists in the Book on Personality Rights, in the Book on Tort Liability, and in the provisions regarding tortious liability in other laws. The most important provisions in the Book on Personality Rights are those relating to: (a) the range of claims for the protection of personality rights; (b) the possibility to ask for an injunction against the infringement; (c) the existence of substantial judicial discretion in awarding remedies for infringement of non-material personality rights; (d) and other original miscellaneous provisions.

(a) Some contend that, since personality rights are *erga omnes*, they are equipped with a defensive basis for claims similar to that associated

26 For a detail elaboration on this question, see Zhang Jiayong, *Research on Modes of Regulation in the Overlapping Field Between Contract Law and Tort Law* (Peking University Press 2016) 268 ff (张家勇, 合同法与侵权法中间领域调整模式研究).

with real rights, which means that claims of stopping the infringement, removing the nuisance, eliminating the danger, and the like, can all be raised in the context of personality rights (article 995, sentence 2).[27] However, this contention is wrong, as the general legal basis for such claims is found in the Book on Tort Liability (article 1167) rather than in the Book on Personality Rights. In the Book on Personality Rights, the only basis for claims is provided by the articles on the right to raise an objection to, and to request the correction or deletion of, an inaccurate evaluation or inappropriate record (articles 1028, 1029, 1038). The aforementioned basis for claims does not hinge on the illegality of the infringement, nor on the existence of fault on the part of the tortfeasor or on the existence of damage suffered by the victim. In contrast, claims for "eliminating the adverse effects, rehabilitating the reputation of the victim, or extending apologies" are claims for compensation of damage, and thus require the existence of fault on the part of the tortfeasor (article 1165(1)).[28] In the Book on General Provisions, only claims for "stopping the infringement, removing the nuisance, eliminating the danger" are provided as not subject to the limitation period (article 196, subparagraph 1). The Book on Personality Rights extends the list to include also claims for "eliminating the adverse effects, rehabilitating the reputation of the victim, or extending apologies" (article 995, sentence 2). This provision is noteworthy, as it emphasizes the fact that remedies for the infringement of spiritual personality rights are in fact homogeneous to the rights themselves. Nevertheless, given the meagre number of provisions in this regard, it would be an exaggeration to say that the Book on Personality Rights has established its unique approach to the protection of personality rights.

(b) Prior to the enactment of the Civil Code, Chinese courts tentatively granted injunctions for protecting personality rights in several cases, such as that of 'the letters of Qianzhongshu'.[29] In addition, the Law Against Domestic Violence includes in its text an order similar to

27 Wang Liming, 'The Legislative Highlights, Speciality and Application of the Book of Personality of Chinese Civil Code' (2020) 17 J L Application 16 (王利明, <民法典>人格权编的立法亮点、特色与适用,《法律适用》).

28 Wu Xiangxiang, 'The Norms System of Personality Rights in Civil Code from the Perspective of Legal Bases of Claims' (2021) 4 Social Sciences in Chinese Higher Education Institutions 129 (吴香香, 请求权基础视角下《民法典》人格权的规范体系,《中国高校社会科学》).

29 See Beijing's Second Intermediate People's Court (2013) Er Zhong Bao Zi No. 9727.

this injunction. Injunctions are crucial for solving the issue where judicial protection only typically intervenes after a personality right is infringed upon. In order to avoid infringements, the injunction is now included in the newly enacted Chinese Civil Code, and can be found among the remedies available to the right holder (article 997).

The requirements for ordering an injunction are: an act infringing upon a personality right is imminent or in progress, where such an act is illegal, and it is necessary to thwart such an act so as to prevent irreparable damage. The goals the injunction aims to achieve are similar to those pursued by the defensive claims of stopping the infringement, removing the nuisance, eliminating the danger, although the purpose of the two sets of remedies are not identical.[30] At best, the injunction can be said to be a specific approach to stop the infringement, remove the nuisance and eliminate the danger.[31] As the injunction seeks to prevent infringement "imminent" or "in progress", its effects are obviously temporary and disconnected from the issue of the ultimate liability to be borne by the tortfeasor.[32] Due to its temporary nature, the injunction is impotent to render the case involved a *res judicata*.[33] This is why, in the 'Provisions on the Causes of Action of Civil Cases' issued by the Supreme People's Court, the level-2 cause of action 'Cases filed for an application for the injunction against the infringement upon the right of personality' is categorized as a sub-type of the level-1 cause of Action 'Cases Subject to Non-litigation Procedures'. Likewise, due to its temporal nature, the injunction is also limited in period and scope according to the principle of proportionality, and is available

30 Cheng Xiao, 'On the Injunction in Personality Rights Protection in Civil Code of China' (2021) 3 J Comp L 140 (程啸，论我国民法典中的人格权禁令制度，《比较法研究》).

31 Wu Yingzi, 'The Principle of the Construction of Civil Injunction Procedure' (2022) 2 China Leg Sci 84 (吴英姿，民事禁令程序构建原理，《中国法学》).

32 See Leading Small Group for the work of the implementation of the Civil Code of the Supreme People's Court [hereinafter Leading Small Group], *The understanding and Application of the Book of Personality Rights of Chinese Civil Code* (People's Court Press 2020) 90. For the opposite view, see Zhu Hu, 'Procedural Realization of Injunctions against Infringement of Personality Rights' (2022) 1 Mod L Sci 174–175 (朱虎，人格权侵害禁令的程序实现，《现代法学》).

33 Wang (n 31). For the opposite view, see Bi Xiaoxiao, 'A Study on the Injunctive Relief for Personality Rights Infringement' (2022) 3 Oriental L 173 (毕潇潇，人格权侵害禁令研究，《东方法学》).

only for the protection of personality rights.[34] For example, Article 30 of the Law Against Domestic Violence provides that 'a personal safety protective order' shall be valid for not more than six months, commencing from the date when it is granted. Before the personal safety protective order expires, the people's court may, upon application, cancel, modify or extend the order. Whether this provision can be applied by analogy in a context involving an injunction against infringement upon personality rights is not yet clear. The injunction can be applied and granted before or after a trial; where after a final judgment is rendered, the injunction automatically ceases to be effective.[35] Unlike preservative measures in litigation, the applicant of an injunction does not have to provide security.[36] But he or she should bear the liability for any damage that may arise out from his or her wrongful application.

(c) Material personality rights such as the right of life, the right of corporal integrity, the right to health, are clear in their content and scope, and absolute in their effects: their infringement is directly presumed to be illegal. Thus, symbolic personality rights, such as the right to name and the right to image, and spiritual personality rights, such as the right to privacy and the right of reputation, collectively referred to as non-material personality rights, are comparatively fuzzy in their content and scope. The protection of these rights often is in conflict with other justified interests, such as news publication, public opinion, literary and artistic creation, and expression of one's opinion. Therefore, it is not appropriate to directly presume the illegality of an act that infringes upon such rights. Whether an infringement is illegal or not should be determined by the judge, taking into consideration the relevance of the justified interests involved.[37] Therefore, by adopting 'the theory of dynamical system', the Civil Code requires the judge to consider "the occupations of the actor and the injured person, the scope of impact of the act, the degree of fault, as well as the factors such as the purposes, methods, and consequences of the act" in dealing with cases involving non-material personality rights (article 998).

34 Huang Wei (黄薇) (ed), *The Interpretations of the Book of Personality Rights of Chinese Civil Code* (Law Press China 2020) 41 (《中华人民共和国民法典人格权编释义》).

35 Leading Small Group (n 32) 90.

36 Zhu (n 32) 174–175; see also Leading Small Group (n 32) 98.

37 Wu (n 28) 148.

This approach should have been replicated in the Book on Tort Liability as well,[38] yet the legislators did not mention it, thus making it a unique principle in the Book on Personality Rights.

(d) On the top of the aforementioned provisions, the Book also contain other provisions with special features: the indirect protection of the personality interests of deceased persons (article 994), the ways of remedying to violations by "eliminating the adverse effects, rehabilitating the reputation of the victim, or extending apologies" (article 1000(2)), and the protection of the voice of natural persons (article 1023(2)).

4 Limitations of the Book on Personality Rights

It is undeniable that the independent Book of Personality Rights is the most noticeable feature of the Chinese Civil Code. However, apart from several highlights that may hardly be qualified as 'innovations', it should overall be concluded that the legislators have not yet achieved their goals of making a code with 'scientific rules, rigorous structure, reasonable norms, and consistent contents'.

4.1 *The Goal of Highlighting the Values Underlying Personality Rights*

The values underlying the personality rights are highlighted by the fact that personality rights have their own independent book. Juxtaposing the Book on Personality Rights along with the Book on Real Rights, the Book on Contracts and the like, is of great significance in its declarative and guiding function, and thus contributes to the promotion of personal and social awareness of the importance of personality interests, the establishment of a society based on the rule of law and the focus on the protection of personal dignity.[39]

However, this achievement should not be overestimated. As mentioned above, the same could have been achieved by simply including the provisions of personality rights in the Book on General Provisions. In addition, the Book on General Provisions was compiled before the content of the other books was determined, and when the following books were drafted it was no longer possible to greatly alter the content and the structure of the Book on General Provisions. Therefore, the delineation of personality rights

38 See *Principles of European Tort Law*, Article 4:102.

39 Wang Zejian, 'The Speciality of Chinese Civil Law and its Interpretation and Application' (2020) 13 J L Application 13 (王泽鉴中国民法的特色及解释适用《法律适用》).

was unable to enter into the Book on General Provisions and accordingly an independent Book on Personality Rights was needed. Likewise, even if one accepts that the highlighting function would be better achieved by an independent book, it would have been better for the relevant book to be put right after the Book on General Provisions and before the other Books. In reality, the Book on Personality Rights is placed after the Book on Real Rights and the Book on Contracts, which indicates an attitude that attaches more importance to things rather than to persons, and thus results in a drawback in the layout of the Civil Code.[40] Thus, the reasons why the order was arranged in this way when it could have been done in a more reasonable manner, remain a mystery.

4.2 *Lack of a Sufficient Delineation of Personality Rights*

It is argued that personality rights can be better delineated in an independent book, and therefore this is the greatest advantage expected from the autonomous regulation of personality rights. However, the achievement of this goal is unsatisfactory. It is true that some provisions, such as the donation of human organs and the clinic testing on humans, the licensed use of symbolic elements of personality, the personality interests of the deceased and the protection of the voice of natural persons, have clear and specific content that could have not been provided elsewhere. Likewise, the percentage of these provisions in the entire Book on Personality Rights is too small, compared to other not-so-useful provisions. Some provisions almost copy *verbatim* the provisions regarding personality rights in the Book on General Provisions, with article 990 reiterating articles 109 and 110, and articles 991 and 1002–1004 reiterating article 3, which seems ironically an application of the internet meme that 'important things should be repeated three times'. Conversely, the provisions that delineate specific rights are either too abstract, or express clichés such as the safety and dignity of life deserving protection, mental and physical health deserving protection, corporal integrity and freedom of movement deserving protection, a natural person having the right to create and publicize his or her image. Are these declarations truly necessary? In situations where a person is in peril, "the organization or individual who is legally obliged to aid shall promptly extend rescue" (article 1005). For example, if the organization or individual is already under the duty to intervene, why is it necessary to write down an article providing the same obligation? If the credit of a person can be incorporated into his

40 Xu Guodong, 'The Books of the Civil Code Should Be Sorted by the Order of Humanism' (2020) 3 Popular Tribune 10–11 (徐国栋，民法典各编应以人文主义方向排序《群言》).

reputation (article 1024(2)), why are their right of honor (article 1031) unable to be similarly incorporated? It is provided that the holder of an honorary title has the right to request a record and the correction of his honorary title (article 1031(2)), yet it is not provided who shall bear the corresponding obligation, which means that it remains unclear how the right holder can exercise their right. Likewise, it is debatable whether it is appropriate to incorporate the freedom of movement within the notion of the right to corporal integrity (article 1003, sentence 2).

4.3 *Not a So Systematized Civil Law*

It is true that the delineation of the content of personality rights is necessary, just as it is in the context of real rights and of contractual rights. However, unlike in the case of real rights (especially limited real rights) where both the internal and external relations are important, the internal relation (i.e., how to exercise the interests involved in a positive way) is not so important in the case of personality rights. While in the case of intellectual property rights legislation is needed to delineate in detail the content and scope of such rights and to publicize them, this need is much less urgent in the case of personality rights. When it comes to material personality rights, their scope is by nature clear without the need of legislative delineation; when it comes to symbolic and spiritual personality rights, whose scope is often blurred, legislative delineation is indeed needed, but unfortunately such delineation can only provide abstract criteria. Thus, the judges are responsible for finding concrete ways to implement these abstract criteria in their judgments. Personality rights are also unlike contractual rights. Provisions about contractual rights tend to focus on the acquisition and realization thereof, with the only such provision in the Book on Personality Rights being the licensed use of symbolic personality rights. Therefore, the real linchpin of the Book on Personality Rights lies in the provisions regarding the scope of the liberty of an actor whose act has a potential to infringe upon a personality right, and the remedies the right holder may resort to when such an infringement does occur. More than half of all the provisions of the book address this. Since provisions regarding prohibition of infringements and remedies are important for tortious liability, it would have been obviously better to incorporate them in the Book on Tort Liability. However, a guiding principle for the compilation of the Civil Code was to maintain the structure of the Chinese Tort Law when brought into force, and under this principle it was difficult to incorporate various new provisions regarding personality rights in the Book on Tort Liability. Thus, it partially explains the reason for the existence of an independent Book on Personality Rights.

In assembling nearly all provisions in one Book, the Book on Personality Rights not only redundantly reiterates provisions that already exist in the Book on General Provisions, but also contains many provisions that should have been incorporated in other books. For instance, the rules on compensation for mental distress due to a breach of contract and on the contract of licensed use of symbolic elements of personality should have been incorporated in the Book on Contracts; the rule on judicial discretion in non-material personality rights and the attribution of liability should have been incorporated in the Book on Tort Liability. The Book on Personality Rights even goes so far as to incorporate provisions belonging to public laws (for example, articles 1005, 1009, 1031, 1039). Being such a smorgasbord of provisions, the book undermines the structural coherence of the entire Civil Code.

4.4 *Insufficient Adjudicative Guiding Effects*

In spite of the fact that the Book on Personality Rights fares relatively poorly in terms of the previously mentioned goals, if it could improve the judicial application of the Civil Code, it would be safe to say that it is worthy of its independence. The following provisions can be used as arguments in this regard: the prohibition of waiving or transferring personality rights (article 992), the enumeration of various kinds of acts constituting infringement upon personality rights (for example, articles 1010(1), 1014, 1019, 1027–1028, 1031(1), 1033, 1038), the reasonable use of certain rights and exemptions from liability (articles 998, 1026), the non-applicability of the limitation periods (article 995, sentence 2), and the compensation for emotional distress based upon torts or contractual breach (article 996).

However, the independent Book on Personality Rights with all the aforementioned provisions, complicates the application of the relevant rules rather than simplifying it, and as such triggers an extra degree of difficulty in the coordination between the Civil Code and other laws.

The former problem is mainly reflected in the plethora of incomplete articles (*unvollständige Rechtssätze*) which divide a single rule among the Book on Contracts, the Book on Tort Liability and the Book on Personality Rights, and force readers to shuttle back and forth between different books of the Civil Code. The latter problem is manifest in the incoherence between the provisions regarding personal information in the Book on Personality Rights and in the Law on the Protection of Personal Information. Whether based upon the principle of *lex specialis derogat legi generali*, or that of *lex posterior derogat legi priori*, it is always the Law on the Protection of Personal Information that should prevail. Therefore, the provisions in the Civil Code, except for "the provisions on the right to privacy, or, in the absence of which, the provisions on the protection of personal information, shall be applied to the private personal information" (article 1034(2)), are all to be superseded by provisions of the Law on the Protection of Personal Information. In other words, the provisions in the Civil Code regarding personal information are inapplicable.

In conclusion, the Book on Personality Rights in the Civil Code, having barely achieved its goal of highlighting the values underlying personality rights, is not fully unsatisfactory in terms of its substantive functions, which are by far more important in the context of the compilation of the Civil Code. Thus, to say that the independent Book on Personality Rights is a great success may be an overestimation. After all, what makes a good legislation is the extent of accomplishment of the goals set instead of the setting of the goals *per se*.

CHAPTER 11

Comparative Perspectives on the Book on Personality Rights

Ken Oliphant

1 Chapter Outline

This chapter seeks to place the provisions of Book Four of the Chinese Civil Code (hereinafter CCC), dealing with personality rights, into comparative perspective. It contrasts the systematic and comprehensive treatment of personality rights in the CCC with the piecemeal and haphazard development of personality rights protection in other countries. Following a comparative introduction, it focuses on the following specific features of the CCC provisions: the general approach taken, including allocation of these provisions to a separate book of the CCC, independent from the law of tort (Book Seven CCC); the definition and scope of 'personality rights' in the CCC; their means of protection; and the remedies provided for infringement.

2 Comparative Introduction

An extensive comparative literature already charts the development of a law of personality rights across jurisdictions.[1] From their early days, all legal systems have treated the protection of rights and interests in the *physical* person as fundamental, especially by providing tort remedies for personal injury and death. But the protection of *immaterial* aspects of personality has been less consistent and indeed has proved highly variable over time. Though in the civil law it dates back at least to the *actio iniuriarum* of Roman law,[2] the early modern European codifications mostly abstained from explicit acknowledgement

1 See in particular Christian von Bar, *The Common European Law of Torts*, vol 2 (OUP 2000) paras 46–118; Gert Brüggemeier, Aurelia Colombi Ciacchi, Patrick O'Callaghan (eds), *Personality Rights in European Tort Law* (CUP 2010); Ken Oliphant, Zhang Pinghua, Chen Lei (eds), *The Legal Protection of Personality Rights: Chinese and European Perspectives* (Brill Nijhoff 2018).

2 Reinhard Zimmermann, *The Law of Obligations: Roman Foundations of the Civilian Tradition* (OUP 1996) ch 31.

 | DOI:10.1163/9789004704428_012

of such rights, which came to be recognized by a variety of indirect routes. Two pathways may be regarded as paradigmatic for the civil law of delict, the French and the German.[3]

2.1 *French Law*

Notwithstanding the lack of any explicit basis in the *Code civil* (hereinafter CC), the *Rachel* case of 1858 demonstrated the potential for judicial protection of immaterial personality rights in French law.[4] Over time courts were able to extend that protection by exploiting the broad conception of 'damage' for which tortious liability was provided under art 1382 CC (now art 1240).[5] The right to respect for private life (art 9 CC) and the inviolability of human dignity (art 16 CC) were later written into the *Code civil*, but there remains no discreet and comprehensive statement of the personality rights afforded by French law, which are still in some instances to be inferred from the heads of damage that generate civil liability. Further, the scope of protection under the Code is restricted by the Press Act 1881[6] which displaces the application of the *Code civil* in cases involving infringements of the right to honour (*droit à l'honneur*) by the media, leaving the victim to seek compensation through the criminal process for the new offences of *diffamation* and *injure* that the Act introduced.[7]

2.2 *German Law*

As is well known, the German codification of 1900 (*Bürgerliches Gesetzbuch*, BGB) premised its general liability for fault (§ 823 I BGB) not on the mere causation of damage with negligence or intent, but also on the violation of one of a set of specified rights or interests, namely life, body, health, freedom, property, or 'other right' (*sonstiges Recht*). Non-material rights in the person were not expressly included in the list, reflecting a general acceptance at the

3 See in particular Gert Brüggemeier, 'Protection of personality rights in the law of delict/torts in Europe: mapping out paradigms', in Brüggemeier, Colombi Ciacchi, O'Callaghan (eds) (n 1) 7–8 and 10–25; Eva Ondreasova, 'Personality Rights in Different European Legal Systems: Privacy, Dignity, Honour and Reputation', in Oliphant, Zhang, Chen (eds) (n 1) paras 3–22.

4 Tribunal Civil de la Seine (Trib civ Seine), 16 June 1858, Recueil Dalloz (D) 1858, 3, 62 (images of famous actress on her deathbed).

5 John Bell, Sophie Boyron, Simon Whittaker, *Principles of French Law* (2nd edn, OUP 2008) 376–380; Jonas Knetsch, *Tort Law in France* (Wolters Kluwer 2021) paras 118–122. As to the right to respect for private life in particular, see Roger Nerson, 'La protection de la vie privée en droit positif francais' (1971) 23 Revue internationale de droit comparé 737.

6 *Loi* of 29 July 1881.

7 Bell, Boyron, Whittaker (n 5) 377–378; Knetsch (n 5) para 121.

time of enactment that interferences with honour, reputation and other such immaterial interests should not be vindicated through an action for damages.[8] At first, the protection afforded to human personality developed gradually and in piecemeal fashion, with reference to the right to the use of one's name under § 12 BGB, as well as through the distinct tortious liabilities for violation of a protective statutory norm (§ 823 II BGB in conjunction with the criminal liabilities for insult, malicious gossip and defamation under § 185 ff of the Criminal Code) and intentional harm *contra bonos mores* (§ 826 BGB). This was supplemented through targeted legislative interventions in specific areas, notably § 22 of the Act on Artistic Creations (*Kunsturhebergesetz*) which prohibits the publication of a person's picture without their consent (subject to defined exceptions).[9]

The decisive step in the German development of a law of personality rights came after World War II, reflecting a determination to prevent a repetition of the horrors of Nazism through a commitment to the basic rights recognized in the German Constitution (*Grundgesetz*, GG) of 1949. Article 1 GG recognised the inviolability of human dignity and art 2 the right to free development of personality. Relying on these provisions, the Federal Supreme Court in 1954 affirmed the existence of a general personality right (*allgemeines Persönlichkeitsrecht*) falling within the 'or other right' clause of § 823 I BGB,[10] and soon after confirmed the necessity of compensating even (or perhaps especially) the non-pecuniary losses consequent on the right's violation.[11] Consequently, the German courts have proceeded to recognize and compensate the violation of a large set of specific rights within the scope of the general right, including the appropriation of a person's likeness, the release of medical records, keeping intimate pictures of an ex-partner, 'stalking', sending unsolicited advertisements, the unauthorised opening of sealed mail and the imitation of the voice of a recently deceased actor for the purposes of advertising.[12]

The German approach proved influential internationally, for example in Austria. In fact, art 16 of the Austrian General Civil Code of 1812 (*Allgemeines Bürgerliches Gesetzbuch*, ABGB) already expressly affirmed the innate rights

---

8 Zimmermann (n 2) 1090–1092; Basil S. Markesinis, John Bell, André Janssen, *Markesinis's German Law of Torts* (5th edn, Hart 2019) 43.

9 Franz Wieacker, *A History of Private Law in Europe* (trans Tony Weir, OUP 1996) 410; Markesinis, Bell, Janssen (n 8) 43 and 45.

10 BGHZ 13, 334 ff (*Schacht*), 25 May 1954.

11 BGHZ 26, 349 ff (*Herrenreiter*), 14 February 1958. See further Zimmermann (n 2) 1092–1094; Markesinis, Bell, Janssen (n 8) 43–49.

12 Markesinis, Bell, Janssen (n 8) 45–46.

arising from the nature of human personality and apparent from reason, but it was only relatively late that the Austrian courts recognized the centrality of this provision, the Supreme Court waiting till 1978 to use it to establish a general personality right.[13]

2.3 *The Common Law*

The historical pattern evident from the preceding overview, beginning with the provision of tort remedies for injury to the physical person, followed by the gradual extension of protection to immaterial aspects of personality, is also evident in the common law. Trespass to the person, consisting of the distinct torts of assault, battery and false imprisonment, developed in the early common law to provide a remedy for specified forms of direct interference with the person.[14] Significantly, trespass is actionable without proof of damage so the trespass torts have long served to protect some aspects of human dignity, bodily integrity, personal autonomy and liberty. A slap in the face, an unwanted kiss and a medical procedure undertaken without knowledge of its nature might all give rise to liability in battery (the wrongful application of force to another person without their consent). Wrongful arrest or detention would be false imprisonment (though not merely the partial obstruction of a person's liberty of movement). With the rise of the distinct common law liability for negligence, the trespass torts came to be limited to the *intentional* interference with the person,[15] and ceded to negligence their former role in respect of accidental personal injury, but they still play an important role in the modern law in the protection of civil liberties and patient autonomy in healthcare provision.

Another longstanding common law cause of action of relevance here is defamation, which protects reputation, though not dignity or self-esteem as such – in notable distinction from civilian traditions.[16] English common law also continues to reject any general liability for invasion of privacy.[17] However,

---

13 Ondreasova (n 3) paras 1–2, 42 and 59–60; Ernst Karner, 'Human Rights and the Protection of Personality Rights in Europe: Comparative Reflections', in Oliphant, Zhang, Chen (eds) (n 1) paras 1, 9 and 17–19.

14 See generally David Ibbetson, *A Historical Introduction to the Law of Obligations* (OUP 1999) 39–43; J.H. Baker, *An Introduction to English Legal History* (5th edn, OUP 2019) 67–68; Donal Nolan and Ken Oliphant, *Lunney & Oliphant's Tort Law: Text and Materials* (7th edn, OUP 2023) ch 2.

15 *Letang v Cooper* [1965] QB 232; Nolan and Oliphant (n 14) 44–46.

16 Zimmermann (n 2) 1076.

17 *Kaye v Robertson* [1991] FSR 62; *Wainwright v Home Office* [2004] 2 AC 406.

the recently created tort of misuse of private information serves significantly to narrow that gap in protection.[18]

The English history contrasts with that in the United States where a famous and highly influential law journal article of 1890[19] persuaded state courts across the country to recognize a right to privacy and the entitlement to compensatory damages in tort for its infringement.[20] This development was reflected in the concluding volume of the Restatement of Torts issued by the American Law Institute in 1939 in furtherance of its project of identifying the underlying general principles of the common law.[21] In another celebrated journal contribution Prosser, the original author of the second Restatement of Torts, sought to systematize the law's protection of privacy with reference to four distinct interests[22] and this schematic duly found its way into the new Restatement on its completion in 1977.[23] The four situations covered are: (1) intrusion upon seclusion; (2) appropriation of name or likeness; (3) publicity given to private life; and (4) publicity placing a person in a false light. Of these, only the first and third relate to privacy in a classical sense and the grouping together of such disparate cases underlines the umbrella nature of this provision and the functional equivalence of 'privacy' in the United States with 'personality' in civil law jurisdictions as an overarching category with disparate content.

2.4 *Recent Codifications*

It is the most recent civil codes that provide the closest precursors for the Chinese approach inasmuch as they reflect the general modern recognition of the importance of personality rights and the specific challenges posed to them in contemporary society. Book Four CCC may be seen as following but expanding on the models provided by the Civil Code of Quebec of 1991 and the Brazilian Civil Code of 2002. The former specifies in its opening provisions:

> Every person is the holder of personality rights, such as the right to life, the right to the inviolability and integrity of his person, and the right

---

18 *Campbell v MGN Ltd* [2004] 2 AC 457.

19 Samuel D. Warren and Louis D. Brandeis, 'The Right to Privacy' (1890) 4 Harv L Rev 193.

20 William L. Prosser, 'Privacy' (1960) 48 Calif L Rev 383, 383–388; Joseph A. Page, 'American tort law and the right to privacy', in Brüggemeier, Colombi Ciacchi, O'Callaghan (eds) (n 1) 38–53.

21 American Law Institute, Restatement of Torts (1939) § 867.

22 Prosser (n 20) 389.

23 American Law Institute, Restatement of Torts 2d (1977) § 652A–E. By this time Prosser had died and been replaced as Reporter by John W. Wade: see further John W. Wade, 'Second Restatement of Torts Completed' (1979) 65 American Bar Association Journal 366.

> to the respect of his name, reputation and privacy. These rights are inalienable.[24]

There then follows a title section on 'Certain Personality Rights',[25] consisting of 50 articles that provide for (amongst other things) the integrity of the person[26] and respect for reputation and privacy.[27] Similarly, the Brazilian Civil Code commences with a Book on Persons that has eleven articles in its Chapter on Personality Rights[28] including provision for the inviolability of the private life of a natural person.[29]

3 Book Four of the CCC in Comparative Context: General Approach

The historical and comparative survey above testifies to both the piecemeal and haphazard development of protection for personality rights across legal systems and its common direction of travel towards the increasing recognition and protection of the immaterial aspects of personality. Many contemporary civil codes now give explicit recognition to personality rights, whether by express general statement[30] or with reference to the unlawfulness of their violation[31] or the availability of compensation for such violation.[32] At supranational level, the European Convention on Human Rights (ECHR) provides a means of recourse for the infringement of rights that are not adequately protected in national law and the decisions of the European Court of Human Rights (ECtHR) have been a driving force in promoting the greater protection of personality rights generally.[33] The European harmonization projects reflect the international convergence that has ensued. The Principles of European Tort Law include life, bodily or mental integrity, human dignity and liberty in

24 art 3 CC (Quebec).
25 Book 1 Title 2: Certain Personality Rights.
26 art 10 CC (Quebec).
27 arts 35–41 CC (Quebec).
28 Book I Title I Ch 2: Personality Rights.
29 art 21 CC (Brazil).
30 Eg art 23 CC (Poland); art 70 CC (Portugal). These and other cited provisions are extracted in English translation in Ernst Karner, Ken Oliphant, Barbara C. Steininger (eds), *European Tort Law: Basic Texts* (2nd edn, Sramek 2018).
31 Eg arts 1045(4) and 1046 Law of Obligations Act (Estonia).
32 Eg arts 1098 and 1100 Civil Obligations Act (Croatia); art 134 Law of Obligations Act (Estonia); art 3-6 Law of Damages Act (Norway) (infringement of the right to private life); art 49 Code of Obligations (Switzerland); art 58 Code of Obligations (Turkey).
33 Ondreasova (n 3) paras 26–31; Karner (n 13) paras 23–27.

their set of protected interests and specify that they enjoy the most extensive protection of all.[34] The Draft Common Frame of Reference provides that loss to a natural person that results from the infringement of their right to respect for dignity, liberty, privacy or (subject to national law) reputation is legally relevant damage.[35]

3.1 *A Separate Book*

The authors of the CCC sought to reflect this growing international consensus about the importance of personality rights and to effect their comprehensive, systematic regulation.[36] They aimed in particular to extend the types of personality right given protection in Chinese law, detail the scope and content of such rights, introduce rules about how personality rights may be exercised (including commercial use), provide means for reconciling countervailing rights, and detail the obligations that personality rights impose on the action of other persons.[37] An ulterior ambition was to produce a 21st Century Code for a digital age,[38] recognizing the specific challenges that new technologies pose for personality rights.[39]

The decision to dedicate a separate book of the CCC to the topic of personality rights has been called '[p]erhaps, the biggest structural innovation in the code'.[40] It reflects a schematic approach whereby 'lawful rights' are categorized as 'personal', 'proprietary' or 'other' (art 3 CCC), with personal rights listed first

---

34 art 2:102(2) PETL.

35 art VI–2:203 DCFR.

36 Wang Liming, 'On the Reasons for the Separate Compilation of the Law of Personality Rights', in Wang Liming and Shi Jiayou (eds), *Chinese Law of Personality Rights I: Theory and Practice* (Routledge 2022) 6–9; Yang Lixin, 'The Innovative Development of Personality Right Legislation through the Law of Personality Rights in China's Civil Code', in Wang Liming and Shi Jiayou (eds), *Chinese Law of Personality Rights II: Codification Experience* (Routledge 2022) 39–40.

37 Wang, 'Separate Compilation' (n 36) 11–13.

38 Wang Liming, 'Discussion on the Positive Rights Confirmation Mode of Personality Rights', in Wang and Shi (eds), *Personality Rights I* (n 36) 28–30.

39 Wang Jia, 'The Right to Privacy in the Internet Age: The Chinese Perspective', in Oliphant, Zhang, Chen (eds) (n 1); Liming Wang and Bingwan Xiong, 'Personality Rights in China's New Civil Code: A Response to Increasing Awareness of Rights in an Era of Evolving Technology' (2021) 47 Modern China 703; Hao Jiang, 'Chinese tort law: tradition, transplants and some difficulties', in Mauro Bussani and Anthony J. Sebok (eds), *Comparative Tort Law: Global Perspectives* (2nd edn, Elgar 2021) 397; Ken Oliphant, Zhang Pinghua, Chen Lei, 'Introduction', in Oliphant, Zhang, Chen (eds) (n 1) para 17. For a European perspective, see Laura Emilia Weissel, 'Personality Rights and the Internet in Europe', in Oliphant, Zhang, Chen (eds) (n 1).

40 Jiang (n 39) 424.

to underline their importance.[41] The CCC thus assigns a prominence to personality rights that is not to be found in the codifications of the 19th and early 20th centuries, while also giving them a foundation that is independent of the law of tort.

3.2 *Independence from Tort*

Historically, both civilian and common law legal systems adopted tort law as their primary mechanism to protect personality rights, both material and immaterial. They recognized liability for infringement of such rights well in advance of any sustained effort to catalogue those rights and define their extent. The existence of the right was implicit in the imposition of liability. The focus was on providing a remedy for violation rather than on any positive conception of the right.[42] The CCC, by contrast, recognizes that rights are in a sense logically prior to liabilities and have a legal significance that transcends the tort liabilities arising from their infringement.[43]

One implication of this is the availability of various forms of specific relief, distinct from the award of damages, that promote and protect the safe enjoyment of personality rights. The most prominent example is the injunction.[44] On one level, injunctions are remedies in tort law. The court orders the tortfeasor, or a person whom it considers is likely to commit a tort, to desist from acting or continuing to act in such a way as to violate the right. But injunctions need not be tied to the requirements of tortious liability. The positive conception of personality rights evident in the CCC enables the assertion of the right even in contexts where there has been no violation and is no threat thereof. This aligns with the approach taken in many other legal orders, where codes or other core provisions of civil law expressly recognize a right to request the termination of an infringement independently of liability in tort.[45]

A positive conception of personality rights also makes more transparent the inalienable character[46] of personality rights and the absolute prohibition against their waiver, transfer or inheritance (art 992), notwithstanding the provision for civil liability for the benefit of the close relatives of a deceased

---

41 Wang, 'Separate Compilation' (n 36) 13.

42 See Section 2 above.

43 Wang, 'Positive Rights' (n 38) 34–36.

44 For comparative analysis of injunctions in general, see Willem van Boom, 'Comparative Notes on Injunction and Wrongful Risk-Taking' (2010) 17 Maastricht Journal of European and Comparative Law 10.

45 See eg art 12 CC (Brazil); art 1048 Civil Obligations Act (Croatia); art 28a ZGB (Switzerland).

46 For a comparative perspective, see Ondreasova (n 3) para 1.

whose personality has been harmed (art 993). Additionally it provides clarity about the extension of personality rights to legal persons: they have the right to 'entity name' (art 1013), reputation (art 1024) and honour (art 1031) but not likeness or privacy, which are limited to natural persons (arts 1018, 1032).

Another perceived advantage is to facilitate regulation of the use of personality rights, especially in the commercial context; enabling the commercial use of personality rights through licensing is seen as a means of promoting the development of China's data industry.[47] Preventing *misuse* is a related aim, evident in the prohibition of the purchase or sale of human cells, tissues, organs, or remains (art 1007).[48]

4 Definition and Scope of Personality Rights

4.1 *Definition of 'Personality Rights' (Open System)*

In the comparative literature two alternative approaches have been identified in defining the meaning of 'personality rights': the listing of a 'bundle' of specific rights and the recognition of a single, overarching personality right from which other more specific rights are derived.[49] The latter is famously the approach of German law, by way of the judicial recognition of a 'general personality right' (*allgemeines Persönlichkeitsrecht*) as an 'other right' within the meaning of § 823 I BGB.[50] The former is apt to describe the rather unstructured protection of personality rights in most other civilian codes, as well as in the common law.

De lege ferenda each approach has its pros and cons.[51] A singular general personality right allows the courts freedom to adapt the law to changing social conditions, recognizing new aspects of personality as requiring protection as the need becomes apparent. But it is the judiciary that is left to flesh out the content of the right, raising questions about the ability of judges to balance the opposing interests involved and the legitimacy of their so doing. The contrary approach of listing different aspects of personality as protected by law

47 Wang Liming, 'Major Highlights and Innovations in the Separate Law of Personality Rights', in Wang and Shi (eds), *Personality Rights II* (n 36) 10.

48 See further Wang, 'Positive Rights' (n 38) 27, highlighting concern at the possible creation of human clones.

49 von Bar (n 1) para 81; Ondreasova (n 3) paras 41–47; Karner (n 13) paras 8–12.

50 As to the *allgemeines Persönlichkeitsrecht*, see Cees van Dam, *European Tort Law* (2nd edn 2013) para 706-2. A similar approach is taken in the laws of Greece, Italy and Portugal: von Bar (n 1) para 81. *Aliter*, notably in the Scandinavian legal systems: ibid.

51 Oliphant, Zhang, Chen (n 39) para 6.

provides greater clarity as to which aspects of personality are in fact protected, and how, but inevitably leaves gaps. There is a risk of 'fossilising' the recognized set of rights notwithstanding changing social attitudes.[52] Additionally, the listed rights may be understood as standing on a level footing, obscuring significant differences in terms of their relative importance.

The CCC seeks a middle course that avoids these potential pitfalls by providing a non-exhaustive definition of 'personality rights' that commences with a catalogue of examples, and then makes a catch-all reference to 'other' personality rights and interests. Article 990 provides:

> Personality rights are the rights enjoyed by persons of the civil law, such as the right to life, the right to corporeal integrity, the right to health, the right to name, the right to trade name, the right to likeness, the right to reputation, the right to honor, the right to privacy, and the like.
>
> In addition to the personality rights provided in the preceding paragraph, a natural person enjoys other personality rights and interests arising from personal liberty and human dignity.

The approach of non-exhaustive definition ('open system') allows new personality rights to be admitted over the course of time.[53] Personal liberty and human dignity are the 'general' rights from which other, specific rights may be derived.[54] Their foundational status is further evidenced by their presentation in Book One CCC (General Part) separately from and in advance of the statement of other personal rights. There we read first that "[t]he personal liberty and dignity of a natural person is protected by law" (art 109),[55] before being given a statement of the other rights that a natural person enjoys: life, corporeal integrity, health, name and likeness, reputation, honour, privacy, etc (art 110).

4.2 *Particular Personality Rights*

All legal systems recognize that personality rights extend to the physical aspects adumbrated for German law at the start of § 823 I BGB: life, body, health and freedom. In the French *Code civil* the rights are inherent in reflected form in the notion of 'damage' in respect of which liability arises under art 1240 and other provisions. This implied recognition of material personality rights

52 Ibid.
53 Wang, 'Separate Compilation' (n 36) 9.
54 Wang, 'Highlights' (n 47) 8.
55 Art 109 CC.

through tortious liability is also seen in the common law, especially through the torts of trespass to the person (assault, battery and false imprisonment) and negligence.[56]

Historically, there have been greater differences in respect of the immaterial aspects of personality, but these are being eroded with the passage of time. The immaterial personality rights set out in Book Four of the CCC broadly correspond with the significant area of common ground[57] across legal systems in the protection of name, likeness, dignity, honour, reputation and privacy, which we now consider in turn.

4.2.1 Name and Likeness

Book Four CCC contains detailed provisions on both the right to name (ch III) and the right to likeness (ch IV), including protection against impersonation (art 1014) and the falsification of images (art 1019). There are circumstances, however, in which another's image can be used without their consent without infringing their right to likeness, for example in news reporting or the use of publicly available images for private study, art appreciation or scientific research (art 1020).

The right to a name is widely recognized in civilian jurisdictions and found expressly in many civil codes, with provision for liability in respect of damage caused by its unauthorized used by another.[58] By contrast, it is somewhat unfamiliar in common law systems, where anyone is in principle allowed to call themselves by any name they wish to use and liability is mostly limited to 'passing off' for commercial gain and other fraudulent misrepresentations.[59]

There is a similar contrast between civil law and common law in respect of the use of another person's likeness. This is not generally tortious at common law, though depending on the precise circumstances it could be passing off,[60] defamation,[61] misuse of private information[62] or perhaps some other

56 See Section 2 above.

57 von Bar (n 1) para 46; Brüggemeier, Colombi Ciacchi, O'Callaghan, 'A common core of personality protection', in Brüggemeier, Colombi Ciacchi, O'Callaghan (eds) (n 1) 576–77; Ondreasova (n 3) para 2.

58 See eg art 23 ABGB (Austria); arts 16–19 CC (Brazil); para 12 BGB (Germany); arts 55–56 CC (Quebec); art 29 ZGB (Switzerland). For discussion, see von Bar (n 1) paras 83–85.

59 Ibid para 84. In exceptional circumstances, the use of another's name might also be defamation.

60 *Irvine v Talksport Ltd* [2003] 2 All ER 881 (fake endorsement of radio station by famous F1 driver).

61 *Tolley v Fry* [1931] AC 333 (another case of fake endorsement, but liability turned on the implied defamatory imputation that the claimant, a well-known amateur golfer, had accepted money in breach of his amateur status).

62 *Campbell v MGN Ltd* [2004] 2 AC 457 (photograph accompanying newspaper exposé).

tort.[63] In the United States the 'false light' tort might come into play, though only if the portrayal is highly offensive.[64] This falls some way short of the protection offered by civilian legal systems where the right to control use of one's image has been recognized since the 19th century.[65] It is with the latter systems that Book Four CCC is aligned.

4.2.2 Reputation and Honour

Chapter V of Book Four addresses rights to reputation and rights to honour, the latter including protection against deprivation of an honorary title and defaming or degrading such title (art 1031).

The protection provided is commensurate with that to be found in European civilian systems,[66] with a history that can be traced back to the *actio iniuriarum* of Roman law.[67] Admittedly, the action fell out of favour in pre-unification Germany, reflecting a general hostility to the compensation of non-pecuniary losses, and neither reputation nor honour were included in the list of protected rights in § 823 I BGB.[68] It was only through the recognition of a general personality right as an 'other right' that claims for injury to reputation and honour, and the associated non-pecuniary losses, came to be allowed under that provision.[69] In French law, by way of contrast, harm to reputation or honour in principle counts as 'damage' within the meaning of art 1240 CC (former art 1382). However, as indicated above,[70] the Press Act 1881 displaces the application of the *Code civil* to infringements of the right to honour (*droit à l'honneur*) by the media.[71] The Act created two criminal offences, *diffamation* and *injure*, each

---

63 See eg *Kaye v Robertson* [1991] FSR 62 (malicious falsehood, but dependent on the false assertion that the publication of the claimant's photograph was with his consent).

64 Restatement of Torts 2d (1977) § 652E. It has been suggested that, given the various restrictions on its scope, the future of the false-light privacy tort in the US may be in doubt: Page (n 20) 68–69.

65 See, for France, Trib civ Seine, 16 June 1858, Recueil Dalloz (D) 1858, 3, 62 (*affaire Rachel*); for Germany, Law relating to copyright in works of fine art and photography (*Kunsturheberrechtsgesetz*) of 9 January 1907. For discussion, see von Bar (n 1) paras 94–95; Ondreasova (n 3) paras 66–69.

66 See von Bar (n 1) paras 88–91; Ondreasova (n 3) paras 48–57.

67 Zimmermann (n 2) ch 31. Indeed, the *actio iniuriarum* remains alive and well in South Africa even today, albeit in modified form: ibid 1078–85.

68 Zimmermann (n 2) 1085–1092.

69 Zimmermann (n 2) 1092–1094; Markesinis, Bell, Janssen (n 8) 49 (applicable even postmortem).

70 Text at n 6 above.

71 Bell, Boyron, Whittaker (n 5) 377–378; Knetsch (n 5) para 121.

contingent on proof of malice or bad faith, and that requirement also came to be applied to actions for damages, simple *faute* being insufficient to establish liability. Following a landmark decision of the *Cour de cassation* in 2005, the application of the *Code civil* has now been wholly excluded in such cases and the victim therefore left to seek damages through the criminal process, negotiating the additional procedural protections there afforded to the defendant.[72]

The common law protects reputation through the action for defamation, embracing the parallel torts of libel and slander, the former for publications in permanent form, the latter for transient publications, eg the spoken word (unless recorded, broadcast, etc).[73] 'Publication' here is conceived broadly to include any communication of a defamatory meaning to another person, including a defamatory meaning to be inferred from pictures or gestures. In its classic formulation, the test of whether a communication is defamatory is: 'would the words tend to lower the plaintiff in the estimation of right-thinking members of society generally?'[74] Older texts refer to exposing another to hatred, ridicule or contempt, but the focus of the modern tort is on falsehoods projected as truth, so it does not to extend to transparently untrue representations designed to make their target a figure of fun,[75] limiting the extent to which defamation can be seen as protecting honour and dignity as interests distinct from reputation.

4.2.3 Privacy

The international trend towards the recognition of privacy as a fundamental personality right was led by the United States, where a new privacy tort developed from the late 19th century and is currently enshrined in the Restatement (Second) of Torts.[76] The right to respect of private life is now also given express recognition in many national codifications[77] as well as in art 8 of the European Convention of Human Rights. This has been incorporated in English law through the Human Rights Act 1998 though the English courts continue to resist the recognition of a general tort of invasion of privacy.[78] However, the art 8 Convention right emboldened them to develop equitable principles of

72 Bell, Boyron, Whittaker (n 5) 378.

73 See generally Nolan and Oliphant (n 14) ch 12.

74 *Sim v Stretch* [1936] 2 All ER 1237, 1242 (Lord Atkin).

75 See especially *Charleston v News Group Newspapers Ltd* [1995] 2 AC 65 (transposition of TV stars' faces onto porn stars' bodies in picture accompanying front-page newspaper report on 'sordid' computer game).

76 Text at nn 19–23 above.

77 See eg art 1328a ABGB (Austria); art 21 CC (Brazil); art 9 CC (France).

78 *Wainwright v Home Office* [2004] 2 AC 406.

confidentiality to fashion a new tort of misuse of private information, which covers at least some of the same ground.[79] So there is broad international consensus that people have a right to keep their private lives private and should have a remedy in the event of violation.

In China, the right to privacy was not listed amongst the personality rights specified in the General Principles of Civil Law of 1986 but it came to be included among the 'civil rights and interests' whose infringement gave rise to liability under the (now repealed) Tort Liability Law of 2010 (art 2).[80] Chapter VI of Book Four CCC builds further on this protection. By art 1032,

> A natural person enjoys the right to privacy. No organization or individual may infringe upon the other's right to privacy by prying into, intruding upon, disclosing, or publicizing other's private matters.
>
> Privacy is the undisturbed private life of a natural person and his private space, private activities, and private information that he does not want to be known to others.

In view of the inherent vagueness of the term, art 1033 proceeds to give a set of illustrative examples of how privacy may be infringed, many of them no doubt familiar in other legal systems, including making (unwanted) phone calls, entering into, photographing or peeping into private spaces (eg a residence or hotel room), photographing or peeping at the private parts of another person's body, and eavesdropping on, photographing or peeping at private activities. A final catch-all ('infringing upon another person's privacy through other means') will allow Chinese courts to protect aspects of privacy not covered by the specific examples, but seems to leave a lot to judicial discretion.

Also expressly included amongst the examples in art 1033 is processing another person's *private* information, which entails a rather subtle distinction with the provisions that follow relating to the protection of *personal* information (art 1034 ff). These latter mostly concern the various obligations placed on the processor of personal information and the circumstances in which they may be liable for their breach. 'Processing' itself is defined widely to include 'the collection, storage, use, refinement, transmission, provision, disclosure, and the like, of the personal information' (art 1035). There are clear parallels here with the European General Data Protection Regulation,[81] though the CCC

---

79 *Campbell v MGN Ltd* [2004] 2 AC 457.

80 Wang (n 39) paras 14–15.

81 Regulation (EU) 2016/679 of the European Parliament and of the Council of 27 April 2016 on the protection of natural persons with regard to the processing of personal data

provisions are at a much higher level of generality. The detail is filled in by the Protection of Personal Information Law (PPIL) of 2021. It is unclear whether the corresponding provisions of the CCC are now effectively superseded by those of the PPIL or continue to have some residual relevance.

4.2.4 Gaps

The CCC's open-system approach to personality rights envisages that new examples may be added over time. So it is instructive to ask what is currently missing, having regard to rights that are already recognized in other legal systems or discussed in the academic literature. These include rights aiming at social inclusion and public participation, such as the rights to freedom of thought, conscience and religion,[82] freedom of expression[83] and freedom of assembly and association,[84] which are not just rights of a political nature but also merit protection in schools, universities, workplaces and other contexts. The right to self-determination[85] is also absent from the CCC, insofar as it extends beyond the right to corporeal integrity (art 1003). Though tort liability for medical malpractice can arise from a failure to gain the patient's informed consent (art 1219 CCC), it is not clear whether injury to autonomy as such satisfies the requirement for resulting damage. Finally, it may also fall to be considered whether a general right to personal identity should be recognized, including the right to authentic representation in public.[86] That could potentially include the right to determine one's official designation of sex or gender, as is already provided in some civil codes today.[87] It will be interesting to see how such questions are resolved by the Chinese courts in due course.

5 Means of Protection

It is recognized in the comparative literature that rights of personality are of diverse and varied character and it would be impossible to have uniform rules

---

and on the free movement of such data, and repealing Directive 95/46/EC (General Data Protection Regulation).

82 art 9 ECHR.

83 art 10 ECHR.

84 art 11 ECHR.

85 Brüggemeier, Colombi Ciacchi, O'Callaghan (n 57) 574–75; Ondreasova (n 3) para 74.

86 von Bar (n 1) para 85; Brüggemeier, Colombi Ciacchi, O'Callaghan (n 57) 573–74; Ondreasova (n 3) para 72–73.

87 See eg art 71 ff CC (Quebec); art 30b CC (Switzerland).

covering them all.[88] They are not all worthy of the same degree of protection and, at least insofar as the immaterial aspects of personality are concerned, they must be balanced against countervailing rights and interests. The rights to life, health and bodily security may be regarded as absolute rights, given the highest degree of protection. The rights to name, likeness, reputation, honour, privacy, etc, are qualified rights that have to be weighed against opposing interests such as freedom of expression and the freedom of the press. That balancing process is fundamental in determining whether a violation of an immaterial personality right has occurred.[89] The need to balance competing rights and interests in this context is now widely recognized in national laws[90] and in the jurisprudence of the European Court of Human Rights.[91]

The distinction between absolute and qualified personality rights is implicitly accepted in Book Four CCC, where art 998 prescribes that, in determining liability for infringing a personality right other than that to life, health or corporeal integrity, 'consideration shall be given to the occupations of the actor and the injured person, the scope of impact of the act, the degree of fault, as well as the factors such as the purposes, methods, and consequence of the act'. Public figures may be expected to tolerate greater exposure of their affairs than persons generally.[92] The need for balance also underpins the 'reasonable use' privilege in art 999, which negates civil liability for infringing a person's name, likeness, personal information, etc, except where the use causes 'unreasonable harm'. The privilege extends to persons 'engaged in news reporting, supervision of public opinions, or the like, for public interests'.[93] Further detail of the privilege is provided in respect of the right to likeness (art 1020) and right to reputation (art 1025). Article 1020 sets out a series of illustrative examples of reasonable use of another person's likeness, including use for the purposes of study, teaching or research, or news reporting. Article 1025 protects news reports, etc, from liability for injury to reputation save in case of fabrication

88 Barbara C. Steininger, 'The Protection of Personality Rights in Comparative Perspective: Basic Questions', in Oliphant, Zhang, Chen (n 1) paras 5–7; Karner (n 13) paras 13–14.

89 Oliphant, Zhang, Chen (n 39) para 7; Wang, 'Positive Rights' (n 38) 35.

90 Steininger (n 88) para 5; Knetsch (n 5) para 119.

91 See especially *von Hannover v Germany*, no 59320/00, 24 June 2004 (ECtHR).

92 Shi Jiayou, 'Pragmatic Combination of Conservation and Innovation: Comments on the *Law of Personality Rights in the Civil Law of the People's Republic of China (Draft)*', in Wang and Shi (eds), *Personality Rights II* (n 36) 130.

93 Public opinion supervision refers to public scrutiny of government officials through the media. See further Anne S.Y. Cheung, 'Public opinion supervision: a case study of media freedom in China' (2007) 20 Columbia J Asian L 357.

or distortion, the use of insulting words or breach of the obligation of verification provided in art 1026. The approach is reminiscent of that taken by English defamation law to publications on matters of public interest,[94] though retaining the test of 'responsible journalism' and the listing of relevant factors that English law has now dropped.[95]

Interestingly there is no express elaboration of the reasonable use privilege in respect of the right to privacy in Ch VI of Book Four CCC. Nor does the general provision on reasonable use (art 999) itself refer to the right to privacy; it speaks only of use of 'name, entity name, likeness, personal information, and the like'. Presumably privacy is caught by the catch-all 'and the like' and so the reasonable use privilege may apply to (for example) the disclosure of private information in news reports. It is certainly accepted amongst Chinese scholars that the right to privacy must be balanced against the freedom of the press.[96] However, the open-textured language makes it hard to predict how the balance will be struck in particular situations and again leaves much to judicial discretion.

6 Remedies for Infringement of Personality Rights

In the comparative literature it is recognized that a range of diverse remedies are required for the protection of personality rights, including damages for harm resulting from infringement, injunctions to stop infringement and to restore the status quo ante, and restitution of unjustly acquired gains.[97] Where civil liability arises under the CCC (art 995), no fewer than eleven 'main forms' are prescribed (art 179), performing all the functions that one might expect. We shall consider first damages, then injunctions and other forms of specific relief.

6.1 *Damages*

Historically, it has been the law of tort that has provided the principal private law mechanism for protecting personality rights. However, in some legal systems initial attempts to impose liability met with resistance founded on the objection that money cannot truly make good a non-pecuniary loss, with obvious ramifications for the legal protection of immaterial personality rights as

94 Defamation Act 2013 (UK) s 4.

95 See further Nolan and Oliphant (n 14) 755–60.

96 Wang, 'Positive Right' (n 38) 35.

97 See generally Monika Hinteregger, 'The Protection of Personality Rights in Private Law: Remedies', in Oliphant, Zhang, Chen (eds) (n 1).

their infringement may well cause no physical harm or provable economic prejudice to the victim. In German law, for example, non-pecuniary damages can be awarded only in cases specified by law, which include injury to the body, health and freedom (§ 253 BGB).[98] Following judicial recognition of the general personality right derived from the German Constitution, it came to be accepted that the right's effective protection required the availability of non-pecuniary damages in the event of its infringement.[99] It is now recognized across legal orders that the violation of personality rights requires the availability of damages for non-pecuniary loss.[100] Here, the CCC is perhaps a bit more restrictive than the international consensus inasmuch as it allows damages in tort (art 1183) or for breach of contract (art 996) only for *serious* or *severe* mental distress. Whether damages might be available for loss of reputation, honour or privacy in itself is not specified.

6.2 *Injunctions and Other Forms of Specific Relief*

The importance of injunctions and other forms of specific relief is underlined by the statement of 'the main forms of civil liability' in the General Part (Book One) of the CCC. The very first items in this list are cessation of the infringement, removal of the nuisance and elimination of the danger; compensation for losses is included only much further down (art 179). This accords with the importance attached to these remedies in the comparative literature, where they are identified as the remedies that best serve the interests of the victim by preventing altogether the infringement or bringing it to an end.[101] Injunctions and related remedies may also be available as a direct means of protecting a threatened right even where there is no proven fault and hence no tort liability in damages.[102] This too seems to be inherent in the CCC's allocation of a separate book to personality rights and consequently their independence from tort liability.

The wide range of forms of relief available under the CCC gives the courts desirable flexibility in crafting a remedy appropriate to the particular personality right in question. In the case of defamation, for example, the offending

98 See further Hinteregger (n 97) paras 11–12.

99 Text at n 11 above. By contrast, the Austrian General Civil Code of 1812 already recognized that 'full satisfaction' in respect of wrongful imprisonment or insult demanded the expunction of the offence suffered by the victim: arts 1329 and 1320 ABGB, read with art 1323; Karner (n 13) paras 29–30.

100 Karner (n 13) para 29 f.

101 See eg Steininger (n 88) para 10.

102 Hinteregger (n 97) paras 20–24; text at nn 44–45 above.

publisher may be required not just to apologize but to take suitable steps to rehabilitate the victim's reputation (art 178(10), (11)). Where the infringement is via the internet, the victim may request the network provider to delete offending material or block or disconnect other uses if necessary to prevent continuation (art 1195).

7 Conclusion

Book Four CCC is a notable landmark in the recognition and protection of personality rights internationally. Its systematic and comprehensive treatment of the topic contrasts favourably with the piecemeal and ad hoc outcomes of the frequently haphazard process of historical development in other countries. Its provisions reflect advanced international understanding of the importance of personality rights and the challenges posed to them by modern social and technological developments, as well as the opportunities waiting to be exploited. It consolidates existing legal norms while also leaving scope for the recognition of new personality rights in the future, derived from the fundamental concepts of personal liberty and human dignity. How the courts manage that process of further development in the coming years, and how they conduct the crucial exercise of balancing countervailing rights and interests, notably the right to freedom of expression, is going to be fascinating to observe.

CHAPTER 12

Formation of the Book of Marriage and Family of Chinese Civil Code, from a Historical Perspective: A Mixture of More Endogenous Resources and Less Elements Transplanted from Other Civil Law Countries

徐涤宇 *Xu Diyu*

1 Introduction

Unlike other books of the Chinese Civil Code, the Book on Marriage and Family does not seem like the product of legal transplantation. Traces of influence of the laws of major civil law countries, such as BGB (German Civil Code), Code Civil (French Civil Code) or ZGB (Swiss Civil Code), are hardly found. In other words, among all the books of the Civil Code, the Book on Marriage and Family has the most prominent local characteristic. This phenomenon actually exists in other countries as well, for example, the BGB hardly adopted anything from Roman Law in terms of family law.[1] Likewise, the draft of Japanese Civil Code in the Meiji Restoration, drafted by the French legal scholars Gustave Boissonade, did not include family law.[2] Family law was once considered as purely local knowledge, where legal transplantation and comparative study was impossible and unnecessary, as "influence of political motives, moral attitudes, and traditional customs over the legal regime of the family makes it (the family law) inevitably local".[3] However, nowadays this perspective is no longer firmly held; family law has become a subject of comparative law studies[4] and the barriers to legal transplantation are constantly disappearing.[5] The global

1 See Jan Schröder, 'The Sources of Modern German Private Law: Roman Law, German Law and Natural Law' (Xu Lan transl), in Mi Jian (ed), *Sino-German Legal Academic Papers. Volume 1* (Law Press China 2003) 40 (扬·施罗德, 现代德国私法的渊源：罗马法、"德国法"、自然法，许兰译，载米健主编：中德法学学术论文集（第一辑），法律出版社).

2 See Fujiko Isono, 'The Evolution of Modern Family Law in Japan' (1988) 2 Int J L & Family 186.

3 Maria Rosaria Marella, 'Critical Family Law' (2011) 19 J Gender, Soc Pol'y & L 727.

4 See Fernanda G. Nicola, 'Family Law Exceptionalism in Comparative Law' (2010) 58 Am J Comp L 778.

5 See Otto Kahn-Freund, 'On Uses and Misuses of Comparative Law' (1974) 37 Mod L Rev 13.

 | DOI:10.1163/9789004704428_013

industrialization has lessened the impact of political motivations, moral attitudes and traditional customs on the family.[6] Ideologically speaking, under the influence of international treaties like the Convention on the Rights of the Child and Convention on the Elimination of All Forms of Discrimination Against Women, the family laws of various countries have seen a pattern of convergent evolution. However, due to the fact that the family law has never been the product of rational construction, but that of the facts of life, we can still see differences in the family laws of various countries reflecting their differences in political motivations, moral attitudes and traditional customs. Comparing the Chinese Civil Code with the civil codes of typical civil law countries, the difference in the family laws remains rather salient, which is hard to explain from the perspective of both legislation techniques and choices of inspiring models. In fact, the superficial similarity of family laws of civil law countries lies in their common use of many roman law terminologies. Yet this set of common terminologies actually hides different local knowledge.

The Book on Marriage and Family Law, aside from its reintegration into the Civil Code, has largely maintained its continuity with the former separate Marriage Law and Adoption Law, thus the new Book has adopted the majority of the layout and the content of the latter two slip laws. In response to social changes, there are indeed some changes in the Civil Code compared to previous laws, but such changes are by no means significant. Therefore, in order to understand how the current Book on Marriage and Family is formed, it is necessary to hark back to its origin, as the current law did not come from nowhere, family law included. Hence, this chapter aims to elaborate from a historical perspective of the formation of the Book on Marriage and Family of the Chinese Civil Code.

2 Interrupted Transplantation and Family Law Revolution

2.1 *Interaction of Legal Transplantation and Local Experience before the Founding of PRC*

During the late Qing dynasty, China for the first time engaged in the compilation of modern family law. However, the Book on Family in the draft Civil Code of the Great Qing (Da Qing Min Lu Cao An) was not so modern in that its substantive content remained the same as traditional Chinese laws, with

6 See William J. Goode, *World Revolution and Family Patterns* (The Free Press of Glencoe 1963) 366–380.

only its style and layout westernized. In fact, The Qing Government appointed two Japanese legal scholars, Kotaro Shida and Yoshimasa Matsuoka, as the advisors for the compilation of the civil code. Yet, the scope of their work did not include the Book on Family and the Book on Inheritance. The two books were drafted by two local institutions: The Institute of Law (Xiu Ding Fa Lu Guan) and the Institute of Rites (Li Xue Guan). This means that the Draft Civil Code of the Great Qing was split in both spirit and substantive content.[7] This split carried over to the era of the Republic of China, where the various drafts of the Book on Family of the Civil Code of ROC vacillated between familism and individualism.[8] One thing is certain: family law became more receptive to legal transplantation. For example, the 1928 draft Book on Family of the Civil Code, "in adopting the advantages of both civil law countries and common law countries and imitating the recent innovations developed by Soviet Russia and Switzerland",[9] it established three principles: "recognizing the gender equality, promoting the health of the nation, and encouraging mutual aid among relatives while eliminating their dependency".[10] However, the 1930 draft Book on Family of the Civil Code stipulated that "having adopted modern European legal thought, especially the idea of independent personality and gender equality, [yet] as still influenced by traditional thought, did not entirely remove familism and Masculism".[11] In other words, although China was receptive to the legal transplantation from other civil law countries, as the society was being caught in a limbo between corporatism and individualism, the legal transplantation and endogenous tradition were always in a strained relation, and legislators were confronted with the task of choosing between 'substantive transplantation' and 'formal transplantation'. In the early period of this era, under the guide of the idea of "Chinese learning as substance, Western learning for application" (Zhong Xue Wei Ti, Xi Xue Wei Yong), there were

7 See Yu Yuhe and Zheng Xiaohui, 'The Draft of Civil Code of Great Qing', in He Qinhua (ed), *The Transplantation and Localization of Law* (Commercial Press 2014, revised edn) 311 (于语和、郑晓辉, <大清民律草案>——外来法与本土法混合的产物，载何勤华主编, 法的移植与法的本土化（修订本），商务印书馆); Su Yanying, 'The Integration of Chinese Traditional Culture and Modern Civil Law Culture – Interpretation of Law Culture in the Civil Code' (2020) 6 J Pol Sci & L 123 (苏艳英, 中华传统文化与现代民法文化的整合——民法典的法文化解读, 《政法论丛》).

8 See Shi Shangkuan, *On Family Law* (CUPL Press 2000) 6 (史尚宽, 亲属法论，中国政法大学出版社).

9 Xie Zhenmin, *Legislative History of the Republic of China. Volume 2* (Henan People's Press 2016) 906–907 (谢振民, 中华民国立法史（下），河南人民出版社).

10 Ibid.

11 Dai Yanhui, Dai Dongxiogn, Dai Yuru, *Family Law* (Self Publisher 2010) 12, 14 (戴炎辉、戴东雄、戴瑀如, 亲属法，作者自版).

more formal transplantation than substantive transplantation, thus mainly adopting terminologies of other civil law countries in a superficial way. In the latter period of this era, substantive transplantation prevailed, as the legislation started tilting more towards individualism. This history demonstrates the interaction between local resources and transplanted foreign laws in the evolution of the Chinese family law. "Legal transplantation is a multilateral and dynamic process, where foreign laws, in transforming local resources, are in fact also being transformed by the local resources, whereas the local resources, in interpreting and transforming foreign laws, are actually reinterpreting and constructing itself".[12]

2.2 *Revolution in the 1950 Marriage Law*

Being the first statute enacted after the founding of PRC, the 1950 Marriage Law is of considerable importance. Chairman Mao is known to have said: "the Marriage Law is a fundamental law relating to the interests of all men and women, second only in importance to the Constitution itself". Family revolution is the first step for social revolution. The 1950 Marriage Law established the framework of Chinese family law and laid the foundation for the current Book on Marriage and Family of Chinese Civil Code.

During the legislative process of the 1950 statute, the legislators consulted "various documents regarding urban and rural marriage, the marriage laws of Jiangxi soviet area and other liberated areas, and the marriage laws of Soviet Union and New democratic countries in eastern Europe".[13] In fact, this statute was more a product of the then national conditions than a transplantation from the Soviet Union.[14] "At that time, the small group in charge of drafting consulted mainly the 'Chinese Soviet Republic Marriage Ordinance' issued by the government of the Chinese Soviet Republic on 1st December 1931", which established principles of "abolishing the feudal arranged marriage and money marriage and implementing the freedom of marriage, the monogamy and the gender equality".[15] These principles constituted the internal values of the 1950

---

12 Na Heya and Huang Jungeng, 'Transplant of "Family Council" System in Modern China' (2020) 6 His Res 200 (娜鹤雅，黄骏庚, 近代"亲属会议"制度移植,《历史研究》).

13 Deng Yingchao, 'Report on the Marriage Law of PRC', in All-China Women's Federation (ed), *Analects of Cai Chang, Deng Ying Chao and Kang Keqing on the Liberation of Women* (People's Press 1988) 170 (《关于中华人民共和国婚姻法的报告》，载中华妇女联合会编：蔡畅邓颖超康克清妇女解放问题文选，人民出版社).

14 Deng (n 13) 171.

15 Huang Chuanhui, 'The Birth of the First Marriage Law of New China' (2007) 3 The People's Congress of China 52 (黄传会, 新中国第一部婚姻法的诞生（上）,《中国人大》).

Marriage Law. Taking the social reality into consideration, it was provided that some specific issues, such as marriage between cousins, were to be dealt with according to customs (article 5 of the 1950 Marriage Law).

With very few articles, the 1950 Marriage Law was nonetheless revolutionary.

Likewise, when confronted with the prevailing infringement upon freedom of marriage, like arranged marriage and money marriage, the statute highlighted the importance of such a freedom. Article 1 of this statute abolished arranged marriage and established the freedom of marriage. Article 2 prohibited any infringement upon the freedom of marriage of widowed women. Article 3 stipulated that those getting married should do it voluntarily, and that no spouse or third party could interfere with such a voluntariness. Article 17 established the freedom to divorce; with the exception of a mandatory meditation process, no substantive condition was required for a spouse to meet in order to be granted a divorce. The freedom to divorce was a controversial issue in the legislative process. However, in order to liberate women and break the chains imposed by the old society, this freedom was eventually established.[16]

As such, this statute emphasized the equality and independence of personality, abolished the old regime that overlooked the rights of women and children, highlighted gender equality and the protection of the legitimate rights of women and children. In Chapter 3 on "rights and duties of the spouses", article 7 provided for the equality of the spouses in the family; article 9 provided for the freedom of the spouses to choose occupations, work and participation in social activities; article 11 provided for the right of the spouses to continue to use their names. These provisions did not directly concern marriage, but rather reiterated the principle of equality between the spouses. In Chapter 4 on "relations between parents and children", article 13 provided that a parent shall not abandon or abuse their children and vice versa; article 14 provided that children born within or out of wedlock, enjoy the same rights and no one shall discriminate the latter. Article 16 provided that step children shall not be abused or discriminated. At that time, these provisions were ideologically more advanced than most countries.

In addition, taking into consideration the social reality that women were usually disadvantaged, the statute provided special protection for women. For example, article 18 stipulated that when the wife was pregnant and within one year after delivery, the husband had no right to apply for divorce. The law also tilted towards the wife with regard to the partition of marital property and debts.

16 See Huang Chuanhui, *Marriage in China* (The Writers Publishing House 2009) 37–43 (黄传会, 天下婚姻, 作家出版社).

According to article 23, at divorce, the premarital property of the wife belonged to her and the other property of the family had to be partitioned according to the agreement between the spouses; if the spouses failed to reach an agreement, the people's court was to adjudicate on how to partition property on the basis of factors like the status quo of the property of the family, the interests of the wife and the children, and the principle of favoring the development of production. If, after the partition, the wife and the children were left with enough money for their living and education expenses, the husband could be relieved from the obligation of providing money for such expenses. According to article 24, debts incurred for the life of both spouses shall be paid with the property acquired by the spouses when living together; if such property did not exist or was insufficient to pay the debts, then the debts were to be paid by the husband. By contrast, debts incurred on oneself were to be paid by each spouse separately. These provisions had positive implications, as in both the social and economic perspective, women were considerably more disadvantaged than men.

The 1950 Marriage law was not only revolutionary in its text (unlike the Book on Family of the ROC Civil Code, which has its influence limited only to urban areas), but also brought about a revolution of marriage in society. After the enactment of the 1950 Marriage Law, "the Party Center and the State Council issued a series of documents, the People's daily published several editorials, and campaigns to propaganda and implement the Marriage Law in the country were launched on a large scale in the country".[17] In spite of some problems, the accomplishment of those campaigns is noteworthy, as the enlightenment of cadres and citizens revolutionized their perception of marriage. Infringements upon the freedom of marriage, arranged marriages and money marriages saw a drastic decrease, and the status of women in the family improved accordingly.[18]

---

17 Zhang Xipo, *Legislative History of Chinese Marriage Law* (People's Press 2004) 207–208 (张希坡, 中国婚姻立法史,人民出版社).

18 See Liu Jingfan, 'The Summarizing Report of Central Committee for Observing the Marriage Law on the Implementation of the Marriage Law' (2010) 3 Literature of Chinese Communist Party 19–22 (刘景范, 中央观测婚姻法运动委员会关于贯彻婚姻法运动的总结报告, 《党的文献》); Ma Ji, 'Discourse on the Implementation of the Marriage Law in the early days of New China' (2010) 4 Jiangxi Soc Sci 146–150 (马冀, 新中国成立初期贯彻婚姻法运动论述, 《江西社会科学》); Li Honghe, 'Social Problems Cropping Up in the Implementation of the Marriage Law in Henan Province in the Early Days of New China and Their Solution' (2009) 7 CPC History Stud 96–103; Yang Liping, 'The Implementation of the Marriage Law in Shanghai in the early days of New China' (2006) 1 CPC His Stud 110–114 (杨丽萍, 新中国成立初期上海贯彻婚姻法运动, 《中共党史研究》); Bai Ruonan, *On the Implementation of the Marriage Law in the Early Days of New China – with a Focus on Shannxi* (doctoral thesis) (Shannxi Normal University

When it comes to the relation between the legal transplantation from abroad and the inheritance of local resources, the 1950 Marriage Law terminated the process of legal transplantation from other civil law countries. Although this statute was to some extent influenced by the family law of Soviet Union, it was mainly a product of local experience of socialist legislation.[19] This can be seen in the very name of the statute, which did not take the usual titles used by its Soviet and Eastern European counterparts, but continued to use the name of 'marriage law' that saw its origin in the period of 'Revolutionary base area'.[20] In addition, "the style and layout of the law is the product of the experience of the Revolutionary base area and the reforms of marriage custom carried out there, reflecting local characteristics and an independent style".[21]

3 'Reform and Opening Up' of Marriage Law

3.1 *Returning to the Right Way: The 1980 Marriage Law*

Due to the abstractness of the 1950 Marriage Law, the statute was somewhat impotent in regulating affairs arising within families. Accordingly, prior to the enactment of the 1980 Marriage Law, institutions like the Central People's Government and the Supreme People's Court made decisions on a case-by-case basis in several instances about marriage and family disputes, and issued a series of ordinances for regulating general issues in this regard. These non-binding documents were the main sources used to regulate the relations of marriage and family.[22] In this period, the legal regulation of marriage and

---

2018) (白若楠, 新中国成立初期贯彻婚姻法运动研究——以陕西省为中心, 陕西师范大学2018年博士学位论文); Zhang Hai, *The Propaganda and Implementation of the Marriage Law in the Early Days of New China* (doctoral thesis) (Party School of the CPC Central Committee 2017) (张海, 新中国成立初期湖南省宣传贯彻婚姻法运动研究, 中共中央党校2017年博士学位论文).

19 See Chen Shaoyu, 'Report to the Seventh Session of the Central People's Political and Legal Committee on the Drafting Process of and Reasons for the "Marriage Law of the People's Republic of China" at the Legislative Affairs Commission of the Central People's Government', on April 14, 1950 (陈绍禹1950年4月14日在中央人民政府法制委员会向中央人民政法委员会第七次会议所作《关于<中华人民共和国婚姻法>起草经过和起草理由的报告》).

20 See Li Xiuqing, 'On the Development of New Chinese Marriage Law and the Influence of Mode of Late Soviet Union' (2002) 4 Sci L (J Northwest U Pol Sci and L) 82 (李秀清, 新中国婚姻法的成长与苏联模式的影响, 《法律科学.西北政法学院学报》).

21 Wang Geya, 'Marriage Reform in China under the influence of Foreign Laws' (2007) 5 J Comp L 79 (王歌雅, 域外法影响下的中国婚姻法改革, 《比较法研究》).

22 Xipo (n 17) 214–228.

family relations withered, whereas the political intervention intensified. Both the freedom to marry and the freedom to divorce were fairly restrained. This was particularly clear with regard to divorce, considering that the principal criteria for determining whether or not to grant a divorce were political ones. Thus, the main reasons for divorce at the time, were political disagreement between the spouses.[23]

After the 'reform and opening-up', the common perception of marriage began to change. With the new and old ideologies struggling, the 1980 Marriage law came into being. "This law embodies the end of the era of politicization of the family relations and the beginning of the extinction of the traditional family model, propelled by the market economy".[24] After a long debate, this law eventually made 'loss of affection' the criterion for granting a divorce, thus reiterating the principle of freedom of marriage and shunning divorce criteria from the political realm back into the legal realm, and the control of the parties involved. According to the legislators, "it is inappropriate to use law to maintain an already-broken relation, which would only agonize the parties, or even escalate the tension to the point of homicide, which is to the detriment of the society, the family and the parties".[25]

In addition, some significant revisions were made for adapting to social changes. These revisions included but were not limited to: the modification of the conditions for marriage and the increasing of the legal marriage age to "22 years old for men and 20 years old for women", which manifested the national policy of the encouragement of 'late marriage and late childbearing'. Likewise, the law included a 'family planning policy' and stipulated the obligations associated thereto. In addition, the law extended the prohibited degree of kinship to incorporate all lineal relatives by blood and collateral relatives by blood up to the third degree of kinship. Thus, it established the regime of post-marital community property and modified the provisions for paying common debts. The law also intervened on the provisions of "husband and wife becoming the family member of each other", on the surname of children, on the supporting obligations among grand-parents and grandchildren, and on

23 See Ji Peng, 'The History of Chinese Divorce for the 60 Years' (2011) 18 National Humanity His 24 (纪彭, 60年来中国人的离婚故事,《文史参考》).

24 Qin Yan and Li Yajuan, 'Marriage Law and the Changes of Marriage and Family in 1980s' (2003) 3 Contemp China His Stud 118 (秦燕, 李亚娟, 20世纪80年代的婚姻法律与婚姻家庭变迁,《当代中国史研究》).

25 Wu Xinyu, 'Explanation on the Marriage Law of the People's Republic of China (Draft Amendment)' at the third session of the Fifth National People's Congress on September 2, 1980 (武新宇1980年9月2日在第五届全国人民代表大会第三次会议上所作《关于<中华人民共和国婚姻法(修改草案)>的说明》).

the supporting obligations among siblings. All these modifications reflected changes of attitude in the society.

The 1980 Marriage Law came from a revision of the 1950 Marriage law, based upon "the experience gained and problems arising from the evolution of social life and judicial practice in the 30 years".[26] Unlike its counterpart in 1950, the 1980 Marriage law was influenced not only by socialist countries like Soviet Union, but also by some Western European countries and other developed countries.[27] The most significant implication of this statute is the fact that it took the regulation of family relations back under legal control. The drawback of the statute is its oversimplification and its abstractness, which provided insufficient adjudicative norms on the basis of which judges can render judgments. The Supreme People's Court later issued a series of judicial interpretations to supplement the statute. These judicial interpretations "took into consideration the social development after 'the reform and opening-up', drew on the experience in the judicial practice, and tapped into some successful experience of foreign legislation and judicial practice of marriage and family law".[28]

3.2 *Independence of the Adoption Law and the Completeness of the System of Family and Marriage Law*

Both the 1950 and 1980 Marriage Law mentioned the relation between adoptive parents and adopted children, but the relevant provision in both statutes consisted of only one article, and were overly simple and abstract. Accordingly, the Supreme People's Court, the Ministry of Justice, and the Ministry of Civil Affairs issued a series of documents regarding adoption. Among them, in 1984, the 'Opinions on Several Issues Concerning the Implementation of Several Policies of Civil Law' issued by the Supreme People's Court made detailed provisions on adoption with 7 articles. However, "these provisions [were] all fragmented and not generally binding".[29]

---

26 Xipo (n 17) 229.

27 Xinyu (n 25).

28 Jiang Yue, *Family Law in 20th Century: from Tradition to Modernization* (China Social Science Press 2015) 348 (蒋月, 20世纪婚姻家庭法: 从传统到现代化, 中国社会科学出版社).

29 Jin Jian, 'Explanation on the Adoption Law of the People's Republic of China (Draft)' made by the Ministry of Justice at the 20th meeting of the Standing Committee of the Seventh National People's Congress on June 21, 1991 (金鉴1991年6月21日在第七届全国人民代表大会常务委员会第二十次会议上所作司法部《关于<中华人民共和国收养法（草案）>的说明》); Gu Angran, 'Report of the National People's Congress Law Committee on Amendments to the Marriage Law of the People's Republic of China (Draft)' at the 19th meeting of the Standing Committee of the Ninth National People's Congress on December 22, 2000 (顾昂然2000年12月22日在第九届全国人民代表大

As the entire Chinese civil law system was fragmented at that time, the 1991 Adoption Law, which was presented in the form of a slip law, provided insufficient protection to the legitimate interests of the parties to adoptive relations; this was done in order to regulate the adoption chaos in the society. The statute was divided into six chapters, namely general provisions, establishment of adoptive relationship, validity of adoption, termination of adoptive relationship, legal responsibility and supplementary provisions. The legislative style of this statute was in huge contrast with the Marriage Law. Although adoption is only one of the legal facts in the formation of the parent-child relationship, the number of articles in the Adoption Law reached a total of thirty-four, while the number of articles in the Marriage Law at that time was only thirty-seven. This contrast in legislative style has continued into the Civil Code era.

In 1998, in view of some problems occurred in the implementation of the Adoption Law, the Standing Committee of the National People's Congress revised it. Since the conditions for adoption were too strict, resulting in a large number of de facto adoptions, they were somewhat relaxed. This included relaxing the conditions for the adoption of children in social welfare institutions whose biological parents cannot be found, lowering the minimum age limit for adopters, and conditionally allowing the adoption of children over the age of fourteen. In response to the problem of non-uniformity of adoption procedures, it was clarified that all adoptions shall be uniformly registered by the civil affairs department. Thus, the provisions on foreign-related adoption were improved.[30] The compilation and revision of the adoption law were mainly based on local experience, but to some extent were also influenced by the legislation of other countries.[31]

3.3 *An Expedient Revision in the Transition Period: The Revision of the Marriage Law in 2001*

After the Marriage Law was enacted in 1980, the 'reform and opening up' continued to advance, and the market economy developed vigorously. The marriage and family *per se* and people's perception thereof underwent great

会常务委员会第十九次会议上所作《全国人大法律委员会关于<中华人民共和国婚姻法修正案（草案）>修改情况的汇报》).

30 Doje Cering, 'Explanation on the Adoption Law of the People's Republic of China (Revised Draft)' at the Fourth Session of the Standing Committee of the Ninth National People's Congress on August 24, 1998 (多吉才让1998年8月24日在第九届全国人民代表大会常务委员会第四次会议上所作《关于<中华人民共和国收养法(修订草案)>的说明》).

31 Doje (n 30).

changes. Accordingly, as new problems emerged in social life, a revision of the Marriage Law was conducted in 2001, and several changes were introduced.

Firstly, bigamy and domestic violence were added as legal grounds for divorce and for claiming damages. Secondly, in adapting to social developments, the conditions for marriage were revised, and as a result marriage registration became mandatory, and new provisions on the invalidity and revocation of marriage were added. Thirdly, as the economy developed and individual and family property increased significantly, provisions on community and individual property, and the contractual ways to determine its status, were refined. Likewise, in summarizing the experience learned from judicial practice, new grounds for divorce were added, such as the fact that, "when a military personnel is at great fault, [their] consent is not needed for the divorce". In addition, provisions on the obligations of children to visit their parents were added. As such, adopting the provisions in relevant judicial interpretations, it was clarified that the spouse who intentionally infringes upon the other spouse's rights or interests in the community property may receive less or no property upon the partition of the community property. Thus, provisions on divorce compensation were added. In response to the problem of the infringement upon the rights and interests of the elderly, provisions on the obligations of grandchildren to support their grandparents were added, and it was emphasized that children should respect their parents' freedom of remarriage, with their obligations to support their parents subsisting regardless of the status of their parents' marital relationship.[32]

Likewise, when the Marriage Law was revised, the compilation of the Civil Code had already started, and as a result the revision was considered expedient.[33] In other words, the revision only dealt with prominent problems that were in urgent need to be dealt with. "The [systematism] and completeness of marriage law will be seen to in the compilation of the Civil Code".[34] At this time, while the influence of Soviet law further waned, scholars were calling for a return of the marriage and family law to the tradition of (European) civil law systems. Therefore, on top of collating local resources, the legislators also

32 Hu Kangsheng, 'Explanation on the 'Amendment to the Marriage Law of the People's Republic of China (Draft)' at the 18th meeting of the Standing Committee of the Ninth National People's Congress on October 23, 2000 (胡康生在2000年10月23日在第九届全国人民代表大会常务委员会第十八次会议上所作《关于<中华人民共和国婚姻法修正案(草案)>的说明》).

33 See Wu Changzhen and Xia Yinlan, 'My View on the Part of Marriage and Family in the Civil Code' (2003) 1 Tribune Pol Sci & L 30 (巫昌祯, 夏吟兰,〈民法典·婚姻家庭编〉之我见,《政法论坛》).

34 Xipo (n 17) 246.

referred to laws and other materials from the United States, Germany, Japan, Philippine, Switzerland, Russia, United Kingdom, France, and the like.[35] However, in spite of the reference to materials of so many countries, the 2001 revision was not entirely a transplantation. For instance, in the regulation of damages in case of divorce, the revision was influenced by foreign laws (such as that of France),[36] but in addition determined the provisions for conditions for granting damages on the basis of the situation in China.

4 Social Changes and the Reintegration of Family Law into the System of Civil Law

4.1 *Reintegration of Family Law into Civil Law*

As aforementioned, ever since the 'reform and the opening up', the countries whose law Chinese family law emulated and took as models changed dramatically. The overall tendency was to depart from Soviet influence and to return to the tradition of Western European civil law systems, although it is true that this tendency emerged in family law at a slower pace than in property law. Academically, the departure from Soviet influence was demonstrated in the fact that many scholars called for a reintegration of family law into the system of civil law. Soviet legal scholars were generally of the opinion that family law was a branch of law independent from civil law.[37] Those who followed Soviet theories still maintain this stance today, believing that both family law and civil law are branches of private law, yet the latter does not include the former.[38] This stance has been accepted by some countries even after the dissolution of the Soviet Union and the drastic changes in Eastern Europe. As a matter of positive law, countries like Russia, Ukraine, Vietnam, Kazakhstan, Armenia, Belarus, Azerbaijan, Turkmenistan, Tajikistan, still juxtapose family law with civil law. In contrast, Hungary, Romania, Lithuania and other former

35 See Wang Shengming and Sun Lihai, 'Selected Collection of Legislative Documents for the Marriage Law of People's Republic of China' (Law Press 2001) 363–423 (王胜明、孙礼海, <中华人民共和国婚姻法>修改立法资料选, 法律出版社).

36 See Hu Kangsheng (ed), *Interpretation of the Marriage Law of the People's Republic of China* (Law Press China 2001) 181–182 (胡康生主编, 中华人民共和国婚姻法释义, 法律出版社).

37 See Wu Changzhen and Xia Yinlan, *Marriage and Family Law* (CUPL Press 2016) 43 (巫昌祯、夏吟兰主编, 婚姻家庭法学, 中国政法大学出版社).

38 See Evgueny A. Sukhanov (ed), *Russian Civil Law. Volume 1* (Huang Daoxiu transl) (CUPL Press 2011) 22–24 (〔俄〕E.A. 苏哈诺夫主编, 俄罗斯民法（第1册）, 黄道秀译, 中国政法大学出版社).

socialist countries or former Soviet republics have incorporated family law into their civil codes in the process of re-codification. This reform in positive law actually indicates a general change in the approach to family law. For instance, in Hungary, after the 1990s, although it is still believed that marriage and family law is to some extent unique, it is no longer considered as an independent branch of law.[39] Accepting the reintegration of family law into the civil law system actually embodies a substantial break from Soviet legal theory and legislative model.

When the Marriage Law was enacted in 1950, China was influenced by Soviet legal theories and legislative models. The 1954 draft Civil Code excluded the family law from its scope of regulation. Similarly, the 1962 draft Civil Code, although it did not follow the Soviet Russian Civil Code in its layout and style, was also only a property code, excluding family law. Even after the 'reform and opening up', the 1979 draft Civil Code, with its innovations such as setting up a book to stipulate the 'right to intellectual achievement', still excluded family law due to the influence of the Soviet Union. Yet, unlike the previous two drafts, the 1979 draft mentioned explicitly that it regulated "identity relations",[40] which generally consist of family relations and marriage relations. In 1986, the legislators realized that, since "the economic reform had just begun and there is little experience, it is immature to compile a complete civil code";[41] instead, it was more feasible to make simpler 'General Principles of Civil Law' that tapped on "the experience gained in recent years from making slip laws, carrying out economic reform and opening up, and trying civil and economic cases; and the folk customs of handling civil relations", and that covered only the "common issues in civil affairs".[42] The 1986 General Principle of Civil Affairs, in its Chapter 5 on 'Civil Rights', Section 4 on 'Personality Rights', specifically stipulated provisions on 'Marriage and Family Rights' (article 104). This shows that the influence of Soviet family law in China began to wane.

39 See Orsolya Szeibert, 'Marriage and Cohabitation in the New Hungarian Civil Code – Answering the New Challenges', in Attila Menyhárd and Emőd Veress (eds), *New Civil Codes in Hungary and Romania* (Springer 2017) 174.

40 For the relevant drafts, see He Qinhua, Li Xiuqing, Chen Yizhu, *Overview of the drafts of civil codes of New China* (Peking University Press 2017, revised edn) (何勤华、李秀清、陈颐主编, 新中国民法典草案总览(增订本), 北京大学出版社).

41 Wang Hanbin, 'Explanation on the General Principles of the Civil Law of the People's Republic of China (Draft)' at the Fourth Session of the Sixth National People's Congress on April 2, 1986 (王汉斌1986年4月2日在第六届全国人民代表大会第四次会议上所作《关于<中华人民共和国民法通则（草案）>的说明》).

42 Ibid.

By the late 1980s, "scholars of marriage and family law finally realized the problem of treating marriage and family law as an independent branch of law, and the reasonableness of modern family laws in the West, and abandoned the idea of excluding family law from the civil law system".[43] By the time the compilation of Civil Code restarted in 1998, the reintegration of family law into the Civil Code had become a consensus among scholars and was accepted by the legislators.[44] Various scholarly drafts all included family law, as did the 2002 legislative draft. However, "as the guiding principle of this draft was 'to collate existent laws', which is especially true in terms of adoption law",[45] and since it was somewhat urgent to publicize the draft, most provisions of the Marriage Law and Adoption Law remained unchanged, as the legislators planned to leave the work of modification and revisions to latter sessions of review.[46] Due to the fact that the draft was filled with problems and highly debatable, the said latter sessions never started. The Book on Real Rights and the Book on Torts of this draft were separately enacted as slip laws of Real Rights Law and Torts Law.

In 2015, when the compilation of the current Civil Code began, the integration of family law into the civil law system had become unquestionable. This meant a complete discard of the Soviet model of juxtaposing family law and civil law. Compared with the 2002 draft, the layout of this Civil Code is far more reasonable in its treatment of marriage and family law, as it no longer makes an independent Book on Adoption, but rather reintegrates adoption into the Book on Marriage and Family. However, restrained by the principle of 'keeping the laws as they are', the provisions of the Book on Marriage have not undergone any major overhaul, which means it is still less comprehensive than other books of the Civil Code. The Book on Marriage and Family is even less comprehensive than the adoption law that was integrated into it:[47] because of

---

43 Ma Yinan, 'The Legal Science of Marriage and Family in the 20th Century in China' (1998) 2 Peking U L J 91 (马忆男, 二十世纪之中国婚姻家庭法学, 《中外法学》).

44 See Xia Yinlan, 'The Relative Independence of Marriage and Family Law in Civil Code System' (2014) 4 Leg Forum 7 (夏吟兰, 论婚姻家庭法在民法典体系中的相对独立性, 《法学论坛》).

45 Sun Xianzhong, 'The Systematicity and Scientificity of the Legislation of Our Country' (2012) 6 Tsinghua U L J 57 (孙宪忠, 我国民法立法的体系化与科学化问题, 《清华法学》).

46 Wang Shengming, 'The Route that a Country with Legality Must Go – Several Questions in Compiling the Civil Code of People's Republic of China (Draft)' (2003) 1 Tribune Pol Sci & L 27 (王胜明, 法治国家的必由之路——编纂〈中华人民共和国民法(草案)〉的几个问题, 《政法论坛》).

47 See Xu Diyu, 'Reconstitution of Marriage and Family Law in the Civil Code: Concept and Details' (2019) 1 China L Rev 113–115 (徐涤宇, 婚姻家庭法的入典再造: 理念与细节, 《中国法律评论》).

the large quantities of provisions contained in the 1991 Adoption Law, adoption has become a separate chapter within the Book on Marriage and Family, which logically speaking makes it especially incoherent. In order to achieve internal coherence and consistency, as well as solve the problem of insufficient provisions in the Book on Marriage and Family, two *mutatis mutandis* articles are provided in the Book on Contract and the Book on Personality Rights (articles 464(2) and 1001). The former makes the provisions of the Book on Contract applicable to conventions on identity relations; the latter makes provisions for the protection of personality rights in the Book on Personality Rights applicable to the protection of rights arising from identity relations.

4.2 *Substantive Modification Based upon Social Changes*

Although the legislators, in maintaining the abstract style since the 1950 Marriage Law, have added few new provisions into the Book on Marriage and Family, they have made some modifications to adapt to social developments.[48]

In the Chapter on General Provisions, an important provision of the Constitution is reiterated: marriage and family are under the protection of the state (article 1041(1) of the Civil Code). In the same Chapter, new provisions are added to protect the legitimate interests of disabled persons in the family (article 1041(3)) and to promote family well-being, with article 1043 now stating that "families shall establish good family values, promote family virtues, and enhance family civility" and of that "[h]usband and wife shall be loyal to each other, respect each other, and care for each other". The addition of these general principles has intensified the function of the Book on Marriage and Family as a behavior norm, indicating that the Civil Code pursues "a mixture of rule of law and rule of virtue"[49] and has core socialist values as its guiding principles. Given the demographic situation of China and the revision of the family planning policy, the provision for family planning as a principle is deleted, and the provisions regarding adoption are revised accordingly. Further, while

48 For the major content and reasons for the modifications, see Yang Minglun, 'Major Provisions and Innovations of the Book of Marriage and Family' (2020) 15 The People's Congress of China 35–37 (杨明仑, 民法典婚姻家庭编的主要制度与创新, 《中国人大》); Long Yifei, 'Innovation and Application of Marriage and Family of the Civil Code' (2020) 21 People's Procuratorial Semimonthly18–21 (龙翼飞, 民法典婚姻家庭编的制度创新与适用, 《人民检察》); Wang Chen, 'Explanation on the 'Civil Code of the People's Republic of China (Draft)' at the third session of the 13th National People's Congress on May 22, 2020 (王晨在2020年5月22日在第十三届全国人民代表大会第三次会议上所作《关于<中华人民共和国民法典（草案）>的说明》).

49 Xia Yinlan, 'Innovation and Development in the Part of Marriage and Family' (2020) 4 China Leg Sci 72.

maintaining the definition of "close relatives" provided in the 'Opinions of the Supreme People's Court on Several Issues concerning the Implementation of the General Principles of the Civil Law of the People's Republic of China (For Trial Implementation)', the concepts of "relatives" and "family members" are distinguished (article 1045).

In the Chapter on Getting Married, in response to changes in the social perception, and in order to protect the freedom of marriage, the grounds for annulling and revoking a marriage are modified as follows: "suffering from a medical condition which makes it, medically speaking, inappropriate to marry" is eliminated from the conditions for getting married, and "not truthfully providing information regarding one's serious disease" is relegated to be a ground for revoking the marriage (article 1053); the commencing date of the preemption period for the right to revoke is modified (article 1052(3)); a ground for claiming compensation for damage in divorce is added (article 1054(2)).

In the Chapter on Family relations, "the power of agency from cohabitation to enter into transactions to provide the necessities of life" is added (article 1060); the rule for distinguishing between community property and individual property is improved (article 1062(1)); in adopting the provisions already enshrined in the 'Interpretation of the Supreme People's Court on Issues concerning the Application of Law in the Trial of Cases Involving Marital Debt Disputes', a rule for determining the community debts is added (article 1064); the rule for partition of the community property, that previously existed in a judicial interpretation only, is adopted (article 1066); in addition, the rule for affirmation or denial of maternity or paternity is also added (article 1073).

In the Chapter on divorce, the most significant modification concerns the insertion of a "divorce cooling-off period", which consists of two consecutive periods of thirty days (article 1077). The new divorce cooling-off period helped deal with the rising divorce rate, reduce the number of impulsive, rash and hasty divorces, and encourage the parties to deal with the conflicts between husband and wife calmly and rationally.[50] In contrast, the Civil Code has to some extent relaxed the criteria for granting a divorce in litigation, solving the problem of a long mandatory preliminary mediation period: "where, after a judgment has been made against divorce and the spouses have been separated for one more year, such divorce shall be granted where one of the spouses files again for divorce with the people's court" (article 1079(5)). In adding a provision for favoring the no-default party (article 1087) and a catch-all situation

50 See Huang Wei, *Interpretation of the Civil Code of the People's Republic of China* (Law Press China 2020) 2037 (黄薇主编, 中华人民共和国民法典释义, 法律出版社).

upon which the no-default party may claim compensation for damage upon divorce (article 1091), civil sanctions on the party at fault are strengthened. This suggests that, although the Chinese Civil Code does not require the condition of 'default' in granting a divorce in litigation, it does require such a condition when it comes to civil liability, so as to protect the interests of the non-defaulting party. In addition, the situations for granting compensation upon divorce are extended beyond the situation of separate property to other situations, and household chores are considered as a more important factor in partitioning property upon divorce (article 1088).

In the Chapter on Adoption, the major modification lies in the extension of the scope of adoptees, through the deletion of the prohibition of adopting children over fourteen years old. Plus, in order to strengthen the protection of minors, the condition that "the adopter does not have criminal record that is detrimental to the healthy growth of the adoptee" is added (article 1098). Likewise, the requirement "where a person without a spouse intends to adopt a child of a different gender, the prospective adopter shall be at least forty years older than the adoptee", is made clear (article 1102) and a process of adoption evaluation is added (article 1105(5)). These modifications signify a general tendency for protecting minors.

Although the compilation of the Civil Code is problem-driven and experience-driven, the official elaborating book reveals that a large amount of foreign legislation has been consulted, especially that of civil law countries like Germany, Japan, France, Italy, South Korea, and Russia; in comparison, the law of common law countries were consulted less. The consultation of the foreign laws often provided arguments useful to support the legislative revision.

5 Conclusion

From the perspective of knowledge genealogy, the Book on Marriage and Family of the Chinese Civil Code is less a product of legal transplantation than that of local resources. From the compilation of the 1950 Marriage Law, to the compilation of the 1980 Marriage Law, to the revision of Marriage law in 2001 and eventually to the enactment of the 2020 Civil Code, Chinese legislators accumulated much experience in legislating on marriage and family. However, for a long time, little concern was given to the science behind this legislation. Even the drafting of the 1950 Marriage Law, which at first glance emulated Soviet family law, was based on a formal consultation of Soviet sources instead of a substantive one. After the 'reform and opening up', both at the level of positive law and academic thinking, Chinese family law has always been on the path of returning to its tradition of modeling on civil law countries. Legislation and theories of other civil law countries have provided Chinese legislators with beneficial support to summarize and refine Chinese local experience through the terminology and rules derived from Roman law. However, it important to note that after getting rid of the yoke of Soviet doctrine and legislation, legislation of Chinese family law has never taken inspiration from a specific country. Thus, the lynchpin lies in the extent to which a specific foreign legislation is useful in solving a Chinese issue and the extent to which the foreign legislation is consistent with Chinese experience. Therefore, even family law provisions that are inspired by foreign sources, they never present the typical features of passive legal transplantation.

CHAPTER 13

Marriage and Family in the Civil Code of the PRC: Outer Perspectives

Nicoletta Patti and Antonello Miranda

1 Family Law and the Hybridisation of Models*

Chinese family law, both in terms of formal rules and social practices, has received limited attention in comparative legal studies. However, recent developments, encourage researchers to engage in the investigation. The function and structure of the family in the People's Republic of China have changed radically over the years, hand in hand with the evolving concept of the family in society. The drafting of the new code and the inclusion of the discipline of family law within it constitute one of the milestones of such an evolution. During the codification process, marriage and family have been the subject of lively debate concerning the adhered-to family model, underlying conceptions, systematic structure of the book, and relationships between marriage and divorce.[1] The resulting Book V from this debate clearly illustrates the multifaceted articulation of legal sources in this country, re-introducing many of the contaminations previously experimented within Chinese private law.[2] First, a link emerges between the Chinese legal system and the Roman legal tradition, of which the very term 'code' is a well-known by-product. However, the peculiarities of China's historical and cultural events have influenced the content of the code not only through Roman law, but also through numerous other elements, such as traditional Chinese law, that was long governed by custom, the law of the so-called socialist countries, and the 20th century Western

* Nicoletta Patti is the authors of Sections 1, 2, 3, 3.1, 3.2, 3.3, 4 and 5; Antonello Miranda is the author of Section 6.

1 Meiling Huang, 'Alcuni problemi del Libro sul diritto matrimoniale e di famiglia nel Codice civile cinese' (2020) 10 Bullettino dell'Istituto di Diritto Romano "Vittorio Scialoja" 143.

2 For a broader analysis of the hybridisation of legal models within the Chinese civil code, see Marina Timoteo, 'Il nuovo codice civile cinese: prime riflessioni', in Antonio Saccoccio and Stefano Porcelli (eds), *Codice Civile cinese e sistema giuridico romanistico* (Stem Mucchi 2021) 89–100; Camilla Crea and Oliviero Diliberto, 'The Chinese Civil Code and 'Fascination' with Roman Law. A Conversation with Oliviero Diliberto' (2021) 7 Ital L J 1–10.

 DOI:10.1163/9789004704428_014

legal tradition.[3] The presence of such heterogeneous contributions shows that China wants to address its issues by drawing on solutions from other legal systems whilst stimulating interest in studies on the subject.

Before delving into the analysis of Book V of the Chinese Civil Code, a preliminary remark is necessary. This essay aims to offer some points of comparative reflection on family and marriage, as regulated within the newly-formed code, starting from the English version of the text that has been circulating in the Western world since its approval.[4] The existence of this linguistic limitation must be borne in mind in the analysis we are about to undertake.

2 General Rules on Marriage and Family

The newly-formed Code first and foremost, in relation to the positioning of the discipline, demonstrates its departure from the Soviet model – which considers the rules relating to the family to be extraneous to civil law as a whole, as a social formation substantially detached from economic issues – to adhere to the Pandectist, and therefore Romanist, model of family law.[5] The subject matter in question, as already mentioned, is regulated in Book V of the Code, entitled "Marriage and Family",[6] and is divided into five chapters dealing respectively with: general provisions; marriage; family relations; divorce; adoption.

The presence of general provisions at the opening of the book under review immediately emerges as a divergence compared to the Italian Civil Code.[7] This is an abstracting legislative technique that makes abundant use of general definitions and mainly draws inspiration from European civil law in the Pandectist tradition. Such provisions are not even found in the German Civil Code (BGB),

3 P. Lo Iacono, 'La sorprendente "sinfonia" tra Chiesa cattolica e Repubblica Popolare Cinese', in Saccoccio and Porcelli (eds) (n 2) 296–297.

4 The English version of the Civil code of the people's Republic of China is available at <http://www.npc.gov.cn/englishnpc/c23934/202012/f627aa3a4651475db936899d69419d1e/files/47c16489e186437eab3244495cb47d66.pdf> (accessed January 15, 2023).

5 Lo Iacono (n 3) 298.

6 This locution brings out a difference with that used in most codes (including the Italian one) where everything is included in 'family law', of which the institution of marriage is a part. See Huang (n 1) 144–145.

7 Meiling Huang conducted a statistical survey and found that among sixty-seven continental law countries analysed, thirty-two of them have a general family law section. These include, for example, Japan, South Korea, Vietnam, Mongolia, Russia, the Netherlands, Belarus, Moldova, Hungary. On the other hand, thirty-five countries have no such general part, such as Spain, Italy, Germany, Greece, and Colombia. See Huang (n 1) 146–147.

the mature product of German pandectics[8] which, while providing for a general part in Book I (*Allgemeiner Teil*) common to the entire codified structure, does not provide for anyone within the individual books. In other words, we can observe how on this point the Chinese Civil Code is more in line with the Pandectistic approach than the BGB itself.[9] As others have argued, these general provisions appear to our eyes similar to a manual.[10] Through these provisions, it is also possible to identify the objectives pursued by the Code: to promote the exercise of virtues related to the family sphere, to encourage a correct family lifestyle based on good values, to increase the level of protection of the elderly and minors and maintaining harmonious and civilised relations between family members (article 1043). From the point of view of content, those listed seem to be meta-legal values deeply embedded in local traditions that make the boundary between ethics and law somewhat uncertain. In other words, those notions appear to the 'Western civilian' as belonging to a distant and unknown world, foreign to the categories ordering the system of civil relations in which moral rules belong to the subjective, intimate and private sphere of the persons involved and not to normative regulation.[11]

Chapter One, containing the general provisions, identifies the fundamental characteristics of marriage and kinship relations within the family.

On the first aspect, the combined provisions of articles 1041 and 1042 of the Code come to the fore. This set of rules reveals how marriage is characterised, similarly to the Italian Code, by freedom of consent, monogamy, and equality between the spouses. Here the Chinese legislator reaffirms the "definitive repudiation of the traditional vision of marriage, strongly influenced by Confucianism, centred on specularly opposite principles: the admissibility of matrimonial coercion; the legitimacy of polygamy; the superiority of man over woman".[12] On the second aspect, article 1045 of the code defines the kinship system by stating that: "Relatives include spouses, relatives by blood, and relatives by marriage. Spouses, parents, children, siblings, paternal and maternal grandparents, and paternal and maternal grandchildren are close relatives.

8 For a comprehensive discussion on the German Civil Code and the pandectist school, see Vincenzo Varano and Virginia Barsotti, *La tradizione giuridica occidentale* (Giappichelli 2018) 140–149.

9 Domenico Dursi, 'Il Codice Civile Cinese: tra tradizione romanistica e socialismo con caratteristiche cinesi' (2021) 13 Igor: rivista di scienze della comunicazione e di argomentazione giuridica 180–181.

10 Ibid., 181.

11 Lo Iacono (n 3) 308; Giulia Terlizzi, 'Una nuova era del diritto civile? Prime riflessioni sul codice civile della Repubblica Popolare Cinese' (2020) 6 Politica.eu 1, 10.

12 Lo Iacono (n 3) 298.

Spouses, parents, children, and other close relatives living together are family members." Although the attempt at definition is commendable, the letteral provision of article 1045 nevertheless presents some issues. First of all, the expression 'close relatives' does not belong to the traditional civil law system, it is neither scientific nor accurate, and it is not helpful in international dialogue. Secondly, the system of degree and kinship lines has not been included. A purpose-specific taxonomy should provide detailed lists of relatives and the relationships between them, which would also help to improve the successions provisions.[13]

3 Marriage

The Code goes on to regulate marriage analytically, from the point of view of the regime of the act (Chapter II, articles 1046–1054), the set of effects that ensue from it (Chapter III, articles 1055–1075) and the dissolution of the bond (Chapter IV, articles 1076–1092), but, like the Italian Civil Code, it does not offer a definition of marriage and its legal qualification does not seem clearly stated either. In fact, the Chinese lawmaker, on the one hand, refrains from qualifying marriage as a contract (as it would have had to if following the common-law model) and, on the other, does not even bring it back to the sphere of the juristic act (as sustained by Italian legal scholarship).[14]

Given this gap, which will be the task of the interpreters to bridge, the following sections will analyse the formal aspects relating to the constitution of the conjugal bond, the personal and patrimonial effects arising from it, and the pathological or physiological (in case of mutual dissent) phase of the relationship between the spouses that is regulated by the legal instrument of divorce.

---

13 Xia Li and Ruina Feng, 'Reform of the Marriage and Family part of the Civil Code in China', in Margaret Brinig (ed), *International Survey of Family Law 2020* (Intersentia 2020) 59, 60 and 61.

14 The concept of juristic act – developed by the German legal scholarship and erected as an ordering category of the civil law system – is structured in such a way as to cover the entire area within which the constitution or modification or extinction of legal relationships is, to varying degrees, left to the free determination of private individuals. It is an extensive concept that reduces to conceptual unity every possible manifestation of private autonomy, thus identifying a common thread between marriage, will and contract. In contrast, in the common law system we find the lowest degree of abstraction. For a deeper insight see Antonello Miranda, *A Short Introduction to the Italian Legal System* (Giappichelli 2014) 95–133; Giovanni Criscuoli, *Il contratto* (Cedam 1992).

3.1 *Constitution of Marriage*

With regard to the elements of the conjugal bond, the first requirement is the consent of both spouses, who must marry freely without being subjected to pressure or conditioning by third parties (article 1046). Furthermore, in establishing the conditions to which entitlement to the *ius connubii* is subordinate, it is specified that the betrotheds are to be of a minimum age, which differs according to whether they are male or female: twenty-two for the former and twenty for the latter (article 1047). This provision sets a marriage age that is not in line with the General Rules of Civil Law on capacity to act, requiring a greater capacity for marriage than that required for other types of conduct, which is contrary to the tradition of civil law.[15] Moreover, the differentiation in age requirements for men and women is a source of inequality and contrary to the proclamation of equality between husband and wife contained within the general provisions at the opening of Book V.

The codified provisions reveal that the Chinese marriage and family system does not explicitly recognise engagement. Instead, this period is taken into consideration by Italian law for the purposes of regulating the 'promise' to get married and the fate of the gifts that the betrotheds have exchanged with a view to marriage. The dissolution of the promise often leads to property disputes that must be resolved. In our legal system, the spouses are free to revoke their choice to get married until the celebration of the marriage. However, this choice is not without legal effects: the promisor may, within a year of the refusal to get married, request the restitution of the gifts made on account of the promise to marry. If the promise was made by a formal deed or results from the request for publications, the promisor who, without just cause, refuses to execute the promise is obliged to compensate the other party for the damage caused by the expenses he/she incurred because of the promise.[16] Certainly, the absence of legal regulation of this phase in the Chinese Civil Code is in line with the free revocability of consent to marry (which the legislature may have wanted to safeguard as a priority). However, by introducing a similar provision, the law could ensure proper conduct during the engagement and set rules for the restitution of gifts in the event of its dissolution.

Regarding the formalities through which the union can be validly established, the Chinese Civil Code provides only one formality: the man and the woman wishing to marry must have their marriage registered at a special office, which is obliged to check that all the requirements of the law are met.

---

15 Xia Li and Ruina Feng (n 13) 63.

16 See articles 80 and 81 of the Italian civil code.

In the case of a positive outcome, the parties are entitled to registration and the issue of the relative certificate: the status of spouse is acquired with the completion of the registration procedure.[17]

As far as the cases of invalidity of marriage are concerned, it is interesting to focus attention on the terminology used in the Chinese Code, which is more analytical than the one adopted by the Italian legislature. The latter, in fact, in Section VI of Chapter III of Book I, under the common heading of 'the nullity of marriage', has included textual references to both the nullity and the annulability of the marriage. The reasons for the lack of a rigorous distinction are of a historical order and depend on a twofold suggestion that influenced the Italian legislature: that of Canon Law, which only recognises the category of nullity (marriage being a sacrament, the act by which it is consecrated can only be valid or invalid in absolute terms, a situation of mere annullability not being conceivable), and that of French law, which, as in contractual matters, adopts the unitary category of nullity. It was legal scholarship that subsequently carried out a systematic reorganisation of the framework of marriage invalidity.[18] Conversely, the Chinese Civil Code, echoes German pandectistics on this point, clearly distinguishing the cases of nullity (provided by article 1051) from the figures of annulability (listed in articles 1052 and 1053). The first category includes the tie of previous marriage, kinship ties and the violation of age limits provided by law. On the other hand, hypotheses of annulment of marriage include marriage contracted under coercion or deprivation of personal liberty, and the fact that one spouse suffers from a serious illness pre-existing the marriage and unknown to the other spouse. These invalidity figures appear to fall within the category of vices of the consent (duress and error) provided for in article 122 of the Italian Civil Code. In both legal systems, these vices must be asserted within one year from when the violence ceased or from the date on which the party knew or should have known the cause of the annulment.

3.2 *Effects of Marriage*

Turning to the analysis of Chapter III (effects of marriage), it should be pointed out as of now that articles 1055–1066 (Section I, Chapter III, Book V) of the Code lay down the fundamental principles concerning the relations between spouses, while articles 1067–1075 (Section II) outline the relations with children and other 'close' relatives.[19]

---

17 Articles 1049–1050 Chinese Civil Code.

18 For a reconnaissance of matrimonial invalidity in Italy, see Gilda Ferrando and Agnese Querci, *L'invalidità del matrimonio e il problema dei suoi effetti* (IPSOA 2007).

19 See *infra*, Section 4.

Once again, it seems useful to elaborate on the first article of this part of the code, article 1055, which contains a statement of principle that reinforces what is already provided in the general provisions: "husband and wife are equal in marriage and in the family" (and article 1056 of the Chinese Civil Code states that husband and wife have the right to use their own surname and name). As mentioned earlier, article 1055 establishes the definitive departure from the traditional view of family relations, deeply rooted in the patriarchal values of Confucianism that placed women in a position of subordination to men. There seems to be a parallelism with the historical events that have affected our legal system. Similarly, the Italian Civil Code now states as the first and fundamental regulating principle of marital and family relations that "by marriage, husband and wife acquire the same rights and assume the same duties" (article 143(1) of the Civil Code), in line with the provisions of article 29 of the Italian Constitution, according to which marriage "is ordered on the moral and legal equality of the spouses". This provision, introduced with the family law reform of 1975, supersedes the vision of the original text of the Civil Code, which, previously upheld the supremacy of the husband, identified as the head of the family, holder of the 'marital power' over his wife. It is clear that both systems recognized the need for a regulatory intervention that would eliminate the discrimination between the position of the husband and the wife, both in their mutual relations and in relation to their offspring.

A comparative reading reveals the shared obligation of assistance and economic solidarity deriving from marriage in both legal systems. The matrimonial property regime also appears to be similarly regulated in both systems. Article 1062 of the Chinese Civil Code regulates 'joint property', much like the Italian framework, wherein not all assets belonging to each spouse automatically enter into community of property. This pertains mainly to the assets acquired by the spouses during the marriage (although not all of them), including salaries and wages as well as bonuses and other remuneration received from services rendered (which in the Italian code would fall under the '*comunione de residuo*'); proceeds obtained from production, business operation, and investment; proceeds arising from intellectual property rights; except as otherwise provided in Subparagraph (3) of article 1063 of the Code, property acquired from inheritance or given as a gift; and other property jointly owned by the spouses. Husband and wife have equal rights when disposing of the community property. On the other hand, the following remain exclusive ownership of each spouse: premarital properties of one spouse, compensation or indemnification received by one spouse for injury inflicted upon him, properties that belongs to only one spouse as provided in a will or gift contract, goods exclusively used by one spouse for daily life, and other properties that shall be owned by one spouse. Article 1065 then, evoking the discipline of marriage agreements adopted by the Italian legislature,[20] allows husband and wife, through a written agreement, to partially deviate from the established property regime, providing that their premarital property and the property to be acquired by them during their marriage may be owned by them separately or jointly, or partially owned separately and partially owned jointly. Common assets are automatically divided after the death of one of the spouses or the termination of the marriage bond. Similarly echoing the Italian code, article 1066 offers the option of judicial asset division in cases of mismanagement by one spouse or when one spouse refuses to contribute to medical expenses in the event of the other's illness.[21]

3.3 *Dissolution of Marriage*

The most controversial area of the new law regulating marriage and the family perhaps is to be found in the provisions on divorce,[22] contained in Chapter IV. In particular, the Code offers two methods of divorce: official registration of divorce at the joint request of the spouses or divorce proceedings in court. In the case of divorce by mutual consent (*fuqi shuangfang ziyuan lihun*), which is governed by articles 1076, 1077 and 1078, the legislator provides that the divorce may be approved and registered with the competent administrative body if both parties voluntarily accept it, draw up and sign their divorce agreement in writing, submitting the relevant application. However, article 1077, inspired by the experiments of 'cooling-off' periods conducted in some court pilot projects, introduces further requirement for divorce by mutual consent: a thirty-day delay period from the date of filing the application. During this period, either spouse may withdraw the divorce application. Moreover, if the couple does not appear at the local office to request a divorce certificate within thirty days of the expiry of the cooling-off period, the application is considered withdrawn. This provision seems more in line with the Chinese tradition than with westernisation and it is a legislative response to concerns about the rising rate of divorces.[23] According to this official view, the end of a marriage is not an

---

20 See article 162 of the Italian Civil Code.

21 See article 1066 of the Chinese Civil Code.

22 He Xin, Maria Federica Moscati, Michael Palmer, 'China's family law in action: an introduction' (2020) 15(2) J Comp L 17.

23 It is estimated that the number of divorces has risen from about 2.5 million in 2010 to about 4.7 million in 2019, of which about 80 per cent are consensual divorces and appear to be growing steadily. See He Xin, Moscati, Palmer (n 22) 17.

entirely private matter, as there is a public interest in avoiding the harmful impact of divorce on society and other family members.

In judicial divorce proceedings, pursuing the same objective, the court will initially act as a mediator in the hope of obtaining an agreement between the spouses that avoids divorce. If the mediation intervention is ineffective and the marriage is deemed to be irreparable, the court will grant the divorce,[24] provided that the conditions listed in article 1079 are met (one spouse commits bigamy or cohabits with another person; commits domestic violence or abuses or abandons a family member; abuses drugs or gambles; the spouses have been separated for at least two years or there are other circumstances where mutual affection between the spouses no longer exists). There is also a limitation, in that a husband cannot apply for divorce if his wife is pregnant and six months have not elapsed since the end of the pregnancy, unless the People's Court deems it appropriate to hear the divorce petition.

Article 1091 regulates cases where the divorce is to be attributed to the fault of one of the spouses for conduct contrary to the duties arising from the marriage.[25] Similarly to our legal system, such fault determines effects on the property level, giving the 'innocent' spouse the right to claim damages. As far as child relationships are concerned, divorce doesn't dissolve the parent-child bond; both parents retain rights and obligations of raising, educating, protecting, and supporting their children. The code states that if the divorcing spouses have a child under the age of two, custody generally rests with the mother; if, on the other hand, the child is between two and eight years old and the parents cannot reach an agreement, the decision on custody rests with the court. If the child is older than eight, their wishes must be duly taken into account. The non-custodial parent will have visitation rights and will have to pay maintenance. This does not appear to be in line with the one adopted in Italy, where sole custody is characterised as a case of exception. The Italian Law no. 54/2006 introduced shared custody as the preferred solution, in order to guarantee the minor child a balanced and continuous relationship with each of the parents, to receive care, education and upbringing from both of them and to maintain significant relationships with relatives of each parental branch.

Lastly, the comparative analysis of this section reveals how the innovative thrust guiding the drafting of the code is not fully accomplished in the

24 ibid.

25 Specifically, article 1091 provides that "A no-fault spouse has the right to claim compensation where divorce is caused by one of the following acts done by the other spouse: (1) has committed bigamy; (2) has cohabitated with another person; (3) has committed domestic violence; (4) has maltreated or deserted a family member; or (5) has acted with other serious faults".

regulation of family and marriage. In the book on the family, there is no provision on *de facto* cohabitations and unions between persons of the same sex, unlike Italy – which introduced their legal regulation with the Law no. 76/2016 – and most European countries. On this point, the Commission that dealt with the drafting of the code ruled out greater openness and tolerance, declaring that the current rule is "in line with national conditions and China's historical and cultural traditions":[26] offering legal protection to these new family models would create a serious impact on the institution of marriage, as traditionally conceived. However, it is considered that the solution adopted does not respect social and cultural pluralism and it distances China from the legal rules of the rest of the world, unreasonably restricting the freedom of individuals to choose their own family lifestyle.[27]

4 Parent-Child Relationship

The legal relationship between parents and children is regulated by Section Two, Chapter III, Book V of the Code, based on the principles of equality of duties and prerogatives of parents. The provisions, similarly to the Italian legislation, outline a unitary discipline of the relationship between parent and child, regardless of whether they are children born in or out of wedlock.

The *status* of child brings with it a set of legal effects. On the one hand, parents have the duty to educate and protect their children and to support them until they are economically self-sufficient; on the other hand, children have the duty to respect their parents and not to interfere with their parents' divorce or subsequent married life, moreover, adult children are obliged to support parents who are unable to work or who are in a financial difficulty. These rights and obligations also extend to mutual relations between grandchildren and grandparents and between siblings in the event of parents' death. The rules briefly sketched out are different from those set out in the Italian code: in the Italian legal system while children are entitled to full maintenance, from birth and until they reach full economic independence, parents are only entitled to

26 Wang Chunxia, '全国人大法工委回应民法典草案六大问题，多个涉及婚姻家庭' ['The National People's Congress Law and Industry Commission responded to six major questions about the draft civil code'] (2020) China Women's Daily, May 14, 2020, at <https://www.women.org.cn/art/2020/5/15/art_22_164373.html> (accessed January 15, 2023).

27 On the same lines, see Terlizzi (n 11) 9; Xin, Moscati, Palmer (n 22) 19; Li and Feng (n 13) 64–65; Huang (n 1) 148–149.

assistance from their children if they are in a real and persistent state of need and are without a spouse who can provide for their needs.[28]

In this section, reference must also be made to adoption, which can be defined as the legal relation of filiation established between persons not related by blood, the in-depth analysis of which would require much more space. We shall, therefore, limit ourselves to focusing on the key aspects of the discipline and, in particular, on the changes that were made from the previous PRC Adoption Act. Firstly, the code revised a basic principle: article 1044(1), placed under the general provisions, incorporates the principle of the best interests of the child provided in the United Nations Convention on the Rights of the Child, and states that adoption should follow the principle of "benefiting the adoptee to the greatest extent". Similarly to what is provided for in the Italian legal system – where the discipline of child adoption is found in a special set of rules outside the code (Law no. 184/2003) – the adoption aims to achieve the child's right to have a family, i.e. as an environment where he or she can receive all appropriate care and education, in line with the principles enunciated by international sources. Consequently, according to article 1098 of the Chinese Code, the family should be concretely able to raise, to educate and protect the adopted child. Adoption, in accordance with the Italian regulations, is allowed for minors who are in a state of abandonment or whose natural parents are unable to raise him/her due to difficulties that cannot otherwise be overcome (article 1093).

The examination of the provisions on filiation in China clearly reveals some gaps. Unlike the solution adopted by our legislature, the presumption of paternity or maternity is not defined, the action of disavowal, the action of claiming or contesting the status of child is not regulated, nor is there a rule concerning the proof of the status of child. The system of confirmation and denial of child status is found in article 1073 of the Chinese Code. It is a laconic provision, more akin to a procedural rule, which empowers the People's Court to confirm or deny the parent-child relationship, but without specifying the necessary elements and requirements for its implementation. Consequently, too much freedom seems to be allowed for judicial interpretation in an area where the rules should instead be of legislative origin, to avoid reconstruction difficulties. This is part of a broader context in which there is a rejection of artificial procreation techniques: no provision, in fact, refers to children born through

28 See Salvatore Casabona, *Il dovere di assistenza verso i genitori in stato di bisogno* (Edizioni Scientifiche 2008).

assisted procreation.[29] Progress in medical science has offered new and effective remedies against sterility and infertility. These methods, however, so far as they affect a delicate sphere such as procreation, raise serious moral and legal questions. Assisted procreation practices through medical intervention have been widespread for many years now and it is necessary that the legal vacuum be filled. This process remains complicated and can take a long time. For instance, in the Italian legal system this happened at the end of a twenty-year parliamentary debate with the Law no. 40/2004, which regulates the entire subject of medically assisted procreation.[30]

5 An Appraisal

In the light of the aforementioned, what is certain is that the Western reader of the Chinese civil code transitions from a sense of familiarity concerning certain concepts to one of bewilderment and surprise when confronted with rules and provisions belonging to unfamiliar categories.[31] The text of the code, in fact, is a blend: as it was observed, the code is peppered with expressions, terms, and concepts rooted in Chinese cultural traditions[32] (such as references to good family values and harmony among family members), while also revealing the influence of the Western legal tradition. It seems to be fair to say, therefore, that we are faced with a Romanist family civil code with Chinese characteristics.[33]

Undoubtedly, the new code is an important milestone in the development of Chinese private law and an important component of the governance system providing certainty and clarity.[34] However, our comparative analysis of family law has shown on the one hand how the terminology is often too vague and

29 It is possible that the failure to introduce rules on access to medically assisted procreation techniques is part of China's population containment policy. Although there is no trace of birth planning regulations in the newly formed code, it is, in fact, important to remember that since at least the early 1970s the People's Republic of China has pursued population control policies.

30 For a critical approach to the Italian Act on Surrogacy, see, among others, Antonello Miranda, 'Surrogate Motherhood in Italy', in Françoise Monéger (ed), *Gestation pour autrui: Surrogate Motherhood* (Société de Législation Comparée 2011) 187–197.

31 Terlizzi (n 11) 10.

32 ibid.

33 Dursi (n 9) 184.

34 Jacques Henri Herbots, 'The Chinese new Civil Code and the law of contract' (2021) 49 China-EU Law Journal 39, 48–49.

undefined, using non-specialised concepts, and on the other hand, how some aspects of family law still require innovative intervention more in line with the social needs of the time (especially with reference to the legal recognition of new family models).

Incidentally, it should not be overlooked that after promulgation, the time of interpretation and enforcement begins. As has been stated, "attempts at such reform in a society of China's size and complexity, entrenched patriarchal familial consciousness (in which relationships within the family were governed by ethical as well as legal norms), and strong historical awareness have been, and still are, difficult to put into effect".[35] While the shaping of family relationships from a top-down perspective is undeniably significant, the local filtration, evasion, or rejection of this law by judicial decisions and social practices influenced by customary norms and traditional ideals must also be taken into consideration. This is particularly true in the family context, which constitutes an aspect of social life strongly influenced by the culture in which it is embedded.[36] Consequently, after analysing the legal framework of the family, we think it is appropriate to wait for the moment when the rules are concretely applied in action. The weak point of the code may be that these provisions have been imported from various foreign legal systems without perhaps taking due account of the historical, social and cultural peculiarities of the Chinese reality into which they have been transplanted and, therefore, without evaluating whether and how they can actually operate.[37]

6 The Risks of Importing Models and the Role of Comparison: A Critical Reflection

The aforementioned observation warrants further, albeit brief, deliberation. Family law, and matrimonial law in particular, is a field in which the application of comparative methodology finds its ideal terrain also in the perspective of preventive control and critical verification of the circulation and transposition of models and institutions. Too often legislators (and their advisors) either do not make use of the indications that can come from comparative law or, worse, use them randomly. The Chinese legislator, at least with regard to the family law provisions in the new code, also seems to have fallen into the same error of perspective.

---

35 Xin, Moscati, Palmer (n 22) 2.

36 ibid 1–3.

37 See Section 6 below.

Studying a legal solution adopted in one country and contemplating its transplantation into another legal system without taking into account the systemic differences and the evolution of that specific legal order or considering the cultural, social, economic and political background of each country, is the best way to obtain no results at all or, worse still, to obtain unexpected results. This approach also risks missteps in the reconstruction and evaluation of the legal datum. To be clear, this is also a common pitfall in the Western traditional comparative approach to family law (and to law in general). The lack of awareness of the substantial diversity in the way law is perceived across diverse global systems often leads to analysis and classifications unaware of the fact that those achievements stem from a 'Western' vision of law (and of jurists) that is not present in other systems. Just as 'exporting democracy'[38] presents challenges, it must be admitted that one cannot study legal systems with the spectacles of the Western jurist and vice versa study legal systems with the spectacles of the Oriental. Doing so would result in observing everything in shades of a specific colour, akin to the Wizard of Oz's emerald green perspective.

Indeed, Western legal systems have in common an idea of law that no one else in the world has. For us, the law is something that is self-generating and self-justifying, something that is free, indeed completely free from dependency on religious, moral or ethical precepts. Something in which nothing is created, nothing is destroyed, but everything is transformed by society and without the interference of the legislator, except to a limited extent and in particular situations (it goes without saying that for us law does not coincide or end with statutory laws). In other words,[39] in the Western legal tradition, law is secular and, above all, self-sufficient. It is secular because the legal rules were established spontaneously and evolved with society without depending on or descending from the 'will' of a God or a philosophy or a political creed, or ethical or moral issues. Western law is secular and self-sufficient, capable of addressing gaps via its principles and mechanisms, imbued not solely by the legislator's will, but also the product of pre-existing factors resistant to legislative influence. Furthermore, it is somewhat contentious to focus only on State law when all societies show that, despite the provision of the sanction or the use of the 'force of the State', societies follow and put into practice an array of differently regulated behaviour. The comparatist knows that the legal norm does not end

38 Mauro Bussani, 'Deglobalizing Rule of Law and Democracy: Hunting Down Rhetoric Through Comparative Law' (2019) 67 American Journal of Comparative Law 701.

39 Those of Tito Ravà, *Introduzione al diritto della civiltà europea* (Cedam 1982), and of Mauro Bussani, *Il diritto dell'Occidente. Geopolitica delle regole globali* (Einaudi 2010).

with the requirement of the legislator or the precedent of a court or the intuition of a jurist, but one must also observe what practices are followed by the people, what rules are 'established' in society, regardless of their 'recognition' by the state. All societies move and act by obeying or disobeying the rules not so much when certain behaviours are explicitly foreseen and permitted and others forbidden; they move and act by obeying or disobeying the rules when there is a 'convenience' to do so. A convenience that is not merely economic (it is useless to think of a simple cost-benefit analysis) but of 'pleasure', enjoyment, satisfaction, reward, 'improvement of the quality of life', even if neither material or immediate.[40]

Therefore, if a given society decides to follow a model or to be 'contaminated' by a foreign model, it may do so regardless of the actual 'transplantation' by the legislature. This is the case of the 'stinging' of rules, i.e. the discolouration of the national regulatory structure due to the 'stain' or discolouration produced by foreign rules that are, however, really operating in the same society. As a result, the presence of 'foreign' behaviour and rules spreads over the national regulatory structure, effectively altering it and giving rise to something new and different, even in the presence of the 'old' legislative rules, but also in the presence of the new regulatory and behavioural elements that have not yet been 'verbalised' or transposed into an act.[41] Conversely, when the legislative and political powers decide to emulate a model, they should first check the efficiency and effectiveness of their choices and the risks involved with that transplant or imitation.[42]

On closer inspection, what is striking in reading the provisions of the Civil Code on family matters is, on the one hand, the presence of rules mainly relating to the 'patrimonial' and economic aspects of the relationship between husband and wife, and, on the other, the absence not only of the definition of marriage, but also of any provision on the content of the relationship. Although

---

40 Mauro Bussani, 'Strangers in the Law: Lawyers' Law and the Other Legal Dimensions' (2019) 40 Cardozo Law Review 3127.

41 Cf Antonello Miranda, 'The Bleeding of Legal Rules Between Rights and Limits, in the Age of Migration Flows and the Crisis of the Nations' (2018) 4 Ital L J 23.

42 In view of the complexity of the Chinese context and the diversified presence of various ethnic groups, religions and social needs, Prof. Lei Chen observed that "China has a long history with many ethnic minority groups living in the territory. Over time these groups have developed their local customs, some of which are still functioning today. These local customs have been disregarded and overlooked, as they were external to China's unitary national statutory system. With time pressure to complete codification on time, the much-needed surveys on local customs have not been conducted". Lei Chen, 'Continuity and change: some reflections on the Chinese Civil Code' (2021) 29 Asia Pacific L Rev 287, 301.

at the beginning of Book Five of the Chinese Civil Code, article 1040 states that "[t]his Book regulates the civil-law relations arising from marriage or family", while article 1043 provides that "[f]amilies shall establish good family values, promote family virtues and enhance family civility" and that "[h]usband and wife shall be loyal to each other, respect each other, and care for each other"; but what the marriage relationship actually is and covers has, perhaps prudently, been left open.[43]

Additionally, with regard to family harmony, in some ways evoked by article 1043, its protection is limited to the issue of domestic violence, which in turn is very difficult to implement precisely because of the strong social and even political resistance, preferring even on the part of the legislature and local administrations to safeguard the abstract 'integrity' of the family rather than protect victims.[44] What happens if a spouse does not respect the "family virtues" or depreciates family civility (assuming it is clear what civility is) or, worse, still does not "maintain a marital relationship of equality, harmony and civility" remains entirely vague.

Undoubtedly, the most 'innovative' part provided for in this book of the Chinese Civil Code is certainly that relating to the divorce provisions. In this respect, although there is no trace of possible pre-, post- and para-marital contracts, the rules seem to have been more systematically conceived. Yet, the desire to 'positively' provide for all possible aspects resulted in the creation of a complex set of rigid rules that invite many interpretative uncertainties. This is precisely what happens when the legislator imports models by adapting them without taking into consideration the source and target context. Among other things, it seems that Chinese lawmakers have not taken into account what has already happened in the Westen legal systems that appear to have inspired them. For instance, in Italy the introduction of 'no-fault' divorce has led to the creation of complex relationships such as extended families, while social evolution has caused an enormous reduction in both religious and civil marriages and the growth of de facto relationships, making the matter of divorce residual and at the same time increasing the demand for protection of de facto relationships.

It remains to be seen whether abstraction will prevail or, if once again, reality will outshine the legislator's imagination.

43 It may be that the Chinese codifier followed the old Italian proverb, according to which between husband and wife you would better not to put your finger: Antonello Miranda, 'Tra moglie e marito non mettere il dito', in Renzo Cavalieri and Giorgio F. Colombo (eds) *Il Massimario. Proverbi annotati di diritto comparato* (Giuffrè 2013) 165–171.

44 Xin, Moscati, Palmer (n 20) 12.

CHAPTER 14

The Innovations of Succession Part in the Civil Code of the People's Republic of China

汪洋 *Wang Yang and* 尹思雨 *Yin Siyu*

1 Introduction

The Civil Code of the People's Republic of China (hereinafter referred to as the 'Civil Code') is the first civil code in the past seventy years since the foundation of the People's Republic of China (hereinafter referred to as 'PRC'). The sixth Book of the Civil Code is devoted to 'Succession'. In terms of its structure, the Book follows the old Succession Law issued in 1985 (hereinafter referred to as the '1985 Succession Law') and includes four chapters, entitled respectively 'General Rules', 'Intestate Succession', 'Testate Succession and Testamentary Gift' and 'Disposition of Estates'; the number of articles has increased from the thirty-seven articles of the 1985 Succession Law to the forty-five articles of the current Book Six. The Succession Part of the Civil Code provides for a series of new institutions and systematically integrates the wisdom and achievements of the legislation and judicial practice in the area of succession since the foundation of the PRC. This chapter introduces the innovations and improvements of the Chinese succession system, brought by the Civil Code following the order of chapters in the Succession Book.

2 Amendments and Improvements for the 'General Rules'

2.1 *Complementing the Scope of the Estate*

Confined to a situation where people had a small number and few kinds of personal property, the 1985 Succession Law generally provided in its article 3, that the estate was lawful personal property left behind by a person upon their death. It then listed in detail what the notion of lawful personal property included: namely, a person's income; houses, savings, and household goods; trees, livestock, and poultry; cultural relics and books; means of production lawfully owned by the person; property rights pertaining to the person's copyright and patent rights; and other lawful property. Besides, the 'Opinions on Issues Concerning the Implementation of the Succession Law of the People's

 | DOI:10.1163/9789004704428_015

Republic of China' issued by the Supreme Court (hereinafter referred to as 'Opinions on the Succession Law') specified additional types of property falling into the scope of the estate, such as negotiable securities and contract revenues. Such legislative approach had two big drawbacks: firstly, since the law cannot enumerate all possible things, it had to end with a miscellaneous provision; secondly, the attempt to list all the items that might have fallen into the estate was, in terms of costs of legislative drafting, counterproductive, since it might have produced misunderstandings about the types of the estate which were not listed in the law.[1]

Along with the social and economic development and the increase in the number and types of people's property in China, especially due to the emergence of new types of property such as game accounts and data, these drawbacks have become increasingly obvious. By the time the Civil Code was drafted, it was clear that the existing legislative enumerations were not able to cover all the scope of estates, and could not meet the new needs of the public to inherit private property. Therefore, article 1122 of the Civil Code provides it as follows: "The estate refers to the property lawfully owned by a natural person upon death. The estate not inheritable according to the provisions of law or based on the nature of the property may not be inherited". The Civil Code changes the way in which the law defines the scope of estates, moving from an approach of 'general rule + enumeration list' to an approach of 'general rule + exclusion clause'. This means that, people's inheritable property can be included into the scope of the estate to the maximum extent. Not only does this choice save legislative resources, but also avoids the possibility of omissions caused by gaps in the enumeration. The new provision also corresponds with the provision of article 124 of the Civil Code according to which "[p]rivate property lawfully owned by a natural person can be inherited in accordance with law".

2.2 *Refining the System of Accepting and Disclaiming Succession and Testamentary Gifts*

The 1985 Succession Law did not specify the way of disclaiming succession. Articles 47 and 48 of the Opinions on the Succession Law provided that, a person disclaiming succession shall do so in writing; a person could disclaim succession orally only if the disclaimer was acknowledged by the person himself or was proven by other evidence. However, the 1985 Succession Law did

1 Yang Lixin, 'Improvements of the Succession System of China and Its Application' (2020) 4 China Leg Sci 88, 89 (杨立新，我国继承制度的完善与规则适用，《中国法学》).

not help in cases where the successor went back on his word after disclaiming succession orally. In order to reduce disputes and guide people to disclaim succession by legal means, article 1124(1) of the Civil Code specifies that disclaimers of succession shall be made in writing. Besides, article 1124(2) amends the period of time for making an expression of intent to accept or disclaim a testamentary gift, replacing the "two months" period provided in article 25 of the 1985 Succession Law to "sixty days", so as to avoid that the period varies depending on the year or month of the decedent's death and to ensure the uniformity of the length of the period.

2.3 *Supplementing the Statutory Circumstances of Disinheritance and Conditions for Pardon*

The 1985 Succession Law provided that a will made by the decedent under fraud or duress was invalid, but did not classify the coercive or fraudulent behavior as a circumstance for disinheritance. Although this behavior did not result in a material change of the will performed by the perpetrator personally, making the testator express an untrue expression of intent for the disposition of the estate through fraud, duress and other means, was also a serious violation of the law which illegally modified the will of the testator. The fact that the successor who concealed the testator's will or infringed the testator's testamentary freedom by fraud or duress, was nevertheless a successor created legislative loophole.[2]

Article 1125(1), subparagraph 4 and 5, of the Civil Code adds to the list of circumstances of disinheritance the following: "concealing the will and circumstances are serious" and "through fraud or duress compelling or interfering with the testator to write, alter, or revoke a will, and the circumstances are serious". This is done to protect the decedent's testamentary freedom and to sanction illegal acts, as well as to avoid the contradictory situation where the will is invalid but the successor who has committed fraud or duress can still inherit the estate according to the law. Overall, the statutory circumstances of disinheritance now include: (1) intentionally killing the decedent; (2) killing any other successor in fighting over the estate; (3) abandoning the decedent, or maltreating him and the circumstances are serious; (4) forging, tampering with, concealing, or destroying the will, and the circumstances are serious; (5) through fraud or duress, compelling or interfering with the testator to write, alter, or revoke a will, and the circumstances are serious.

2 Wang Geya, 'Civil Code – Succession Part: Improvements of Institutions and Refinements of Norms' (2020) 1 Seeking Truth 88 (王歌雅,〈民法典·继承编〉：制度补益与规范精进,《求是学刊》).

There are two types of disinheritance: absolute disinheritance and relative disinheritance. The former means that the successor is disinherited when a statutory circumstance of disinheritance occurs, while the latter means the successor may not be disinherited despite the occurrence of a statutory circumstance of disinheritance when certain conditions are met, such as being pardoned by the decedent. Article 1125(2) of the Civil Code clearly identifies the conditions for absolute and relative disinheritance. The successor will be disinherited absolutely if he intentionally kills the decedent or kills any other successor in fighting over the estate. The successor will be disinherited relatively if he abandons the decedent or maltreats him and the circumstances are serious; or forges, tampers with, conceals, or destroys the will, and the circumstances are serious; or compels or interferes with the testator to write, alter, or revoke a will through fraud or duress, and the circumstances are serious. Under the circumstances of relative disinheritance, if the decedent expressly shows his pardon or, in the knowledge of such circumstances, still lists the successor as an heir in a later will, the successor will not lose his right to succeed. When the decedent and the successor are related by blood or have a special kinship, allowing the decedent to pardon the successor who has made a mistake is not only in line with folk custom, but also reflects that the Civil Code respects the free will of the decedent to dispose of his estates[3] and advocates the good morality of 'nothing is better than correcting the mistake that a person himself has made'.

3 Amendments and Improvements for 'Intestate Succession'

3.1 *Expanding the Scope of Heirs in Subrogation to the Children of Siblings*

The Book on Succession of the Civil Code maintains the provision of the 1985 Succession Law which only provided for two orders of intestate successors. Under the 1985 Succession Law, the only intestate successors were spouses, children, parents, siblings, paternal and maternal grandparents. The disadvantage was that, with the scope of intestate successor being too narrow, there was a substantial possibility that the estate was left without successors. As a supplement to intestate succession, article 11 of the 1985 Succession Law provided the lineal descendants of the decedent's predeceased child as the heir in subrogation, which was still relatively narrow in scope. This system couldn't

3 Yang (n 1) 90.

meet the realistic needs of families who lost their only child and of people who were unmarried or had no children to devolve the estate to their descendants.

The Civil Code essentially expands the scope of intestate successors by enlarging the scope of heirs in subrogation. Article 1128 adds the inheritance right in subrogation of collateral relatives by blood: "[w]here a decedent is predeceased by a sibling of his, the children of the predeceased sibling shall inherit in subrogation". It also further clarifies the share of inheritance in subrogation: "[s]uccessors who inherit in subrogation generally may only take the share of the estate per stirpes". This amendment effectively adapts the law to the status quo, insofar as having siblings in the family has gradually become the norm of family life after the abolition of the 'one-child' policy. The modification can also help the subrogation system perform its function to keep the decedent's estate within the family whose members have blood relations and flowing downward so that the estate will not be left unattended. The disadvantage is that since the children of siblings are included in the scope of heirs in subrogation, the lineal descendants of siblings should all be recognized as heirs in subrogation without discrimination, otherwise it would be contradictory to the goal of inheritance in subrogation system.[4]

3.2 *Expanding the Scope of People Who Shall Be Given Estates at Discretion*

In article 14 of the 1985 Succession Law there were two types of people that should be given estates at discretion: one was the person other than successors who had been a dependent of the decedent, provided that the person was unable to work and had no source of livelihood; and the other was the person other than successors who had made considerable contributions in supporting the decedent. This meant that a person who had been a dependent of the decedent was entitled to be given the estate at discretion only if he met the conditions of being 'unable to work' and 'having no source of livelihood' at the same time. However, with the change of family values, the phenomenon of long-term non-marriage cohabitation had increased in real life. In the past, even when cohabitants formed an interdependent relationship of support, they could not participate in the distribution of the estate of each other

4 Chen Wei and He Haiyan, 'On the Legislative Ideas and New Provisions in the Succession Part of the Civil Code' (2020) 11 Hebei L Sci 32 (陈苇, 贺海燕, 论民法典继承编的立法理念与制度新规,《河北法学》).

because they were neither the other party's intestate successors, nor people who were unable to work and had no source of livelihood.[5]

Article 1131 of the Civil Code eases the restrictions for people who shall be given estates at discretion and provides that "[a]n appropriate share of the estate may be given to a person, other than a successor, who has been a dependent of the decedent, or to a person, other than a successor, who has made considerable contributions in supporting the decedent". It deletes the qualification of being 'unable to work and having no source of livelihood', and keeps the requirement of the stability of support relationship formed during the lifetime of the decedent, encouraging mutual support among those who have established support relationship. The new provision is also conducive to achieving a balance of interests between the supporter and the decedent, and motivating people other than successors to join in the sequence of supporters and caregivers.

4 Amendments and Improvements for 'Testate Succession and Testamentary Gift'

4.1 *Adding the Testamentary Trust*

As the number of people's private property increases, their needs to plan for the inheritance of their property after death, to professionally manage their estate, keep and increase its value, to use the estate to support specific person, and to avoid the successors or legatees from squandering the estate, become increasingly urgent. Compared with article 16 of the 1985 Succession Law, article 1133(4) of the Civil Code adds the provision of testamentary trust, which is meant to fill a legislative gap and to respond to the realistic needs of people inasmuch as inheritance of property is concerned.

Testamentary trust, also known as a post-mortem trust, is a trust in which the trustor makes a will in advance to arrange the affairs of the management, distribution, application, and payment of the estate after the trust is delivered; when the will takes effect, the trust property is transferred to a trustee, who will manage and dispose of the trust estate according to the contents of the trust. In the testamentary trust, the trustor is the decedent; the trustee (who may be a lawyer, an accountant, a trust investment institution or other professionals or professional institutions) is the executor of the will; the beneficiary

5 Wang Geya, 'Civil Code – Succession Part: Disputes about the Draft and the Selection of Institutions' (2020) 1 Leg Forum 115 (王歌雅,〈民法典·继承编〉:编纂争议与制度抉择,《法学论坛》).

is the successor, who may be one or more of the intestate successors, or an organization or individual other than the intestate successors designated by the testator.[6]

As a combination of testament and trust, the testamentary trust can not only solve problems of property inheritance, but also make up for the deficiency of successors' ability to manage money through the executor's expertise and professionalism. It can also reduce disputes arising from the succession because the intervention of a neutral executor can make the liquidation and partition of the estate fairer, and can better protect the interests of estate creditors. It is foreseen that in the future testamentary trust will gradually become one of the main methods of estate disposition.

4.2 *Supplementing the Forms of the Will*

The 1985 Succession Law did not provide for the will to be made in printed form; the reason underlying this was that computers were not popular at the time in which the law was drafted and writings in printed form were still relatively rare in China. In judicial practice, there was much controversy about the validity of a will made in printed form, with some considering it as a holographic will and others considering it as a will written on behalf of the testator. In view of the increasing popularity of wills in printed form, article 1136 of the Civil Code provides that "[a] will in printed form shall be attested by two or more witnesses. The testator and the witnesses shall sign and specify the year, month, and day on each page". The will in printed form is different from the holographic will, since it entails the process of transformation from electromagnetic media to paper, and therefore is exposed to a heightened risk of forgery and alteration. This is why, in order to ensure the authenticity of the will, stricter conditions of validity are prescribed by the law for wills in printed form than those required for wills written on behalf of the testator.

The will made in the form of an audio or video recording is a new type of will, which refers to the will narrated by the testator and recorded in the form of an audio or a video. Article 17 of the 1985 Succession Law did not provide for the will made in the form of a video recording, but foreseen a will made in the form of an audio recording, thus establishing relatively simple conditions for its validity: a will made in the form of an audio recording was valid as long as two witnesses were present. In the silence of the 1985 Succession Law, wills made in the form of an audio recording were used as an auxiliary tool or evidence to verify the authenticity of a holographic will, or of a will written on

6 Chen and Haiyan (n 4) 32.

behalf of the testator, which was not treated as an independent form of will. In judicial practice, courts could only apply the rules of the will made in the form of an audio recording or the nuncupative will by analogy to judge the requirements for validity of a will made in the form of a video recording. However, this easily led to the will being considered as invalid because of lacking formal elements. This conclusion was clearly sub-optimal insofar as it was not conducive to protecting the testator's true expression of intent.

Article 1137 of the Civil Code now adds the will in the form of a video recording as a new type of will; at the same time, the provision specifies that "the testator and the witnesses shall record their names or likeness in the recording and specify the year, month, and day of its making", in addition to the existing requirement that the will "shall be attested by two or more witnesses". The article thus provides a legal basis for judicial practice to determine the characteristics and validity of the will in the form of a video recording.

4.3 *Expanding the Scope of Unqualified Witness to a Will*

A witness to a will is a third person who is present at the time of making the will and testifies to the authenticity of the will. The civil capacity and credibility of the witness and the authenticity of the evidence are directly related to the validity of the will. Article 1140 of the Civil Code provides: "[n]one of the following persons is eligible to act as a witness to a will: (1) a person with no or limited capacity for performing civil juristic acts, or a person otherwise incompetent to attest a will; (2) a successor or a donee-by-will; or (3) a person having an interest with a successor or a donee-by-will". The article has now an open-ended provision according to which the list of persons not eligible to witness a will includes any "person otherwise incompetent to attest a will". The category of any "person otherwise" refers to people who have full capacity for performing civil juristic acts, and nevertheless do not have the capacity to witness. This may for instance be the case of people who cannot read or write, people who do not have sufficient knowledge of the language used in the will (such as in cases in which such language is a minority or foreign language, Braille, sign language, or the like) and people who cannot understand or comprehend what is happening because of physical handicaps (such as people who are deaf, blind, mute or anyway do not have the ability to see or hear).

4.4 *Confirming the Principle of Post-Established Will Prevailing in Validity*

Article 20(2) of the 1985 Succession Law provided that "if there are several wills, the last will shall prevail if their contents are in conflict"; at the same time, article 20(3) provided that "the holographic will, the will written on behalf of the testator, the will made in the form of an audio recording, and the nuncupative will shall not revoke or change the notarized will", thus establishing the principle of priority of notarized wills. Now article 1142(3) of the Civil Code cancels this principle and establishes the rule that the last will prevails.

The provision that no other form of will shall change or revoke a notarized will may absolutize the validity of a notarized will, even when the latter does not necessarily represent the testator's final and true expression of intent. Since its establishment, change or revocation of a notarized will has to be done under the complicated procedures prescribed in the law, such as the Notary Law and the Rules for Notarizing the Will. Thus, the party has to pay certain notarial fees, as it is not easy for a testator to revoke or change a previously established notarized will before their death. Therefore, the principle that the notarized will always prevails, does not only limit the testator's freedom to change or revoke their will, but also increases the financial cost and difficulty of making a will. The rule now enshrined in article 1142(3) of the Civil Code rightly affirms the prevalence of the last will, whatever its form.

4.5 *Improving the System of Withdrawal of Will*

Article 1142 of the Civil Code replaces the expression "revocation of will" used in article 20 of the 1985 Succession Law with the expression "withdrawal of a will". Revocation is the denial of an expression of intent that has already taken effect, while withdrawal is the denial of an expression of intent that has not taken effect. After the making of a will and before the death of the testator, the will is not yet into effect; consequently, if the testator cancels his will before death, this cannot but be a 'withdrawal' of the will. The amendment of the Civil Code makes the legislative expression more precise and scientific.

After a will is made, according to the principle of freedom of will, the testator has the right to withdraw his decision of disposition. The testator may withdraw the testamentary disposition either expressly or by making a new will that contradicts with the previous one. At the same time, because the will does not restrict the testator's disposition of his property before his death, the testator may still perform an act contrary to the will. A contrary act, also known as an act in conflict with the contents of the will, is an act of the testator that results in the presumed withdrawal of the will other than making a new will.[7]

Article 1142(2) of the Civil Code adds a contrary act as a statutory circumstance for withdrawing a will: "Where a testator who, after making a will, acts

7 See Lin Xiuxiong, *Handouts of the Succession Law* (Taiwan Angle Publishing Ltd 2017) 259 (林秀雄, 继承法讲义, 元照出版社); Shi Shangkuan, *On Succession Law* (China University of Political Science and Law Press 2000) 477 (史尚宽, 继承法论, 中国政法大学出版社).

inconsistently with the content of his will, the pertinent part of the will is deemed to be withdrawn". After making a will, the decedent's property is not fixed but in a floating state. Whether a change of property has an effect on the validity of the will mostly depends on the type of testamentary disposition. For wills with specific property as the object of disposition, the loss of the property may have an effect on the validity of the will exclusively.

5 Amendments and Improvements for 'Disposition of Estates'

5.1 *The Establishment of New Rules on the Estate Administrator*

Articles 1145–1149 of the Civil Code create the new system of the estate administrator. The system realizes a relative separation between the estate and successors' property and is of great significance for improving the status of the estate creditors in the disposition of the estate. The estate administrator is a person who acts in the interests of both successors and creditors, and bears the responsibility for properly handling the claims and debts of the estate, as well as safeguarding the interests of the successors and creditors. In order to ensure the neutrality of the estate administrator, the administrator is in principle elected by the successors, but is subject to the statutory duty of performing its role in accordance with the law.

Articles 1145 and 1146 of the Civil Code deals with the selection of estate administrator. First of all, after the opening of the procedure for estate disposition, the executor of the estate is also the administrator of the estate. In coordinating the functions of the executor with those of the administrator, these provisions aim to respect both the parties' intent and the law. No matter the form the decedent used in a will to designate the executor, the functions of the latter automatically expand according to the law to include those of the administrator; yet, the scope of the management of the estate should be subject to the unanimous consent of successors. Secondly, successors may also decide to appoint another person as the estate administrator or to jointly serve as the estate administrator; in the latter case, they will set up a group with the nature of an 'interpersonal cooperation'. Although the decisions made by successors to appoint an estate administrator or to jointly manage the estate have the nature of a resolution, they should be adopted through the procedure of unanimous consent. The successors or administrators may reach agreements on the rules of procedure, but major issues such as the disposition of the estate and the determination of the order of payment of estate debts should be agreed on by at least half of the members. Thirdly, according to the last sentence of article 1145, where there is no successor or where all of the successors disclaim inheritance, the civil affairs department of the government or the villagers' committee in the place where the decedent was domiciled at the time of his death, should serve as the estate administrator. Finally, it is also possible to let a court appoint the estate administrator. Courts shall apply special procedures and should not mechanically comply with the last paragraph of article 1145 to designate other organizations as the estate administrator, but should rather consider the living conditions of the deceased before his death, and take the situation of the estate into account.[8]

Article 1147 of the Civil Code provides for the duties of the estate administrator by way of enumeration. In particular, an estate administrator shall "(1) verify and make an inventory of the estate; (2) report to the successors about the inventory of the estate; (3) take the necessary measures to prevent the estate from being destructed, damaged, or lost; (4) clear the decedent's claims and debts; (5) partition the estate in accordance with the will, or in accordance with law; and (6) perform any other act necessary for managing the estate". The list omits two important duties, namely those of examining the will and of notifying creditors about the opening of the estate administration and the need to declare their rights. Likewise, the provision of "making an inventory of the estate" is too simple. It would have been better to draw on the experience of comparative law and of the relevant provisions of the bankruptcy administrator, and the custodian for property in China to conceive an estate inventory system so as to promote the open and orderly administration of the estate. The disposition of claims and debts of the estate should be based on the notification of creditors' declarations of rights, which affects both the extent of realization of creditors' requests and the scope of the estate acquired by successors. Regardless, the estate administrator shall perform his duties with faithfulness and diligence, make all the necessary dispositions, and report the status of the estate and the progress of disposition to the successors or creditors in a timely manner.[9]

If the successors and the administrator agree on the latter's remuneration, duties and liability, the administrator shall be liable to the successors for breach of contract according to the relevant provisions of the 'entrustment contract'. Under this circumstance, since the misbehavior of the estate administrator

8 Wang Baoshi and Wu Yunying, 'Study on the System of Estate Administrator in the Civil Code' (2020) 6 L & Econ 51 (王葆莳、吴云煐,〈民法典〉遗产管理人制度适用问题研究,《财经法学》).

9 Chen Wei and Liu Yujiao, 'The Systematic Establishment of Inventory of the Estate in the Succession Part of the Civil Code' (2019) 5 Mod L Sci 58 (陈苇，刘宇娇, 中国民法典继承编之遗产清单制度系统化构建研究,《现代法学》).

may also give rise to his tort liability, the successors may claim liability against the administrator either in contract or in tort.

5.2 *Improving the Rules of Responsibility for Paying off Debts of Estate*

The determination and change of the order in which the debts of the estate are to be paid, involve many dimensions – the conceptual one, the normative one, and the technological one. Limiting the individual enforcement of estate and replacing it with a collective payment procedure in itself is a socialized arrangement. Defining the order in which the debts of the estate should be paid essentially entails how a mechanism to allocate risk is determined. Any modification into such an order must be done considering the impact of the change on the expectations and actions of each party.

The 1985 Succession Law did not offer any instruction about how to pay off the debts of the estate; article 62 of the 'Opinions on the Succession Law' only provided an ex post facto remedial rule about the allocation of liability for cases in which the estate has been partitioned without paying off the debts. Article 1163 of the Civil Code, adds a new rule on the allocation of responsibility between the successors and legatees while paying off the debts of estate, extending their liability from the situation where "the estate has been partitioned without paying off the debts" to the entire process of estate partition. The new rule can prevent successors from evading the payment of debts and infringing on the interests of the creditors after the partition of the estate.

5.3 *Adding the System of Subsuccession*

Subsuccession refers to the cases in which the successor dies after the death of the decedent and before the partition of the estate; in such cases, the share of the estate to which the successor was entitled is transferred to his legal successors. The 1985 Succession Law did not expressly provide for the subsuccession. Article 52 of the 'Opinions on the Succession Law' provided for such a system, responding to a high demand for the application of the subsuccession in succession activities and judicial practice. Article 1152 of the Civil Code adds a new provision of subsuccession: "Where, after a succession opens, a successor who has not disclaimed inheritance dies before the estate is partitioned, the share that he should have inherited shall be inherited by his successors, unless otherwise provided in the will". The provision clarifies that the subsuccession applies to both intestate succession and testate succession. However, if the will contains other arrangements, the testate succession applies preferentially. This amendment does not only respect the decedent's free will to dispose of the estate, but also helps reduce disputes.

5.4 *Expanding the Scope of the Obligor of the Agreement on Testamentary Gift for Inter Vivos Support*

Article 31 of the 1985 Succession Law provided that agreements on testamentary gifts for inter vivos support could only be signed with collective organizations acting as supporters; other subjects could not be the supporters in a legacy-support agreement. The provision particularly did not include organizations with elderly care function as potentially legitimate supporters. This was a problem insofar as there was a real demand for social and commercial pensions of old people who have lost their only child, and of the 'empty-nest elderly' arising from economic development and related migration of workers.

Article 1158 of the Civil Code now expands the scope of supporters to all natural persons, legal persons, and unincorporated organizations other than successors. The rule strengthens the possible use of the complementary functions of agreements on testamentary gift for inter vivos support for family and social security pensions.

5.5 *Clarifying the Use of the Estate Escheated to the State with Neither a Successor nor a Donee-by-Will*

Given the narrow scope of intestate successors, there is a great chance that in China, there will be estates with neither a successor nor a donee-by-will. Article 32 of the 1985 Succession Law did not provide for the use of the estate escheated to the State or collectivity with neither a successor nor a donee-by-will. The first sentence of Article 1160 of the Civil Code now provides that "an estate with neither a successor nor a donee-by-will shall be escheated to the State for public interest purposes". Therefore, even if the private estate is escheated to the State, it can only be used for the legitimate purpose of public welfare. The rule promotes the development of social welfare and reflects the people-oriented concept of the State. It also implements the policy of 'taking from the people and using it for the people' and favors the maximization of the social utility of estates with neither a successor nor a donee-by-will.

5.6 *Relationship between the Testate Succession and Testamentary Gifts*

The Civil Code distinguishes between testate succession and testamentary gifts depending on whether the receiver of the estate is "within the scope of the intestate successors"; on this basis, the Civil Code provides for different ways to exercise the right of testate succession and testamentary gifts. The Code does not distinguish testate succession and testamentary gifts from the perspective of paying off the debts of the estate, which is different from what happens according to other models in comparative law. Compared with article 27 of the 1985 Succession Law, article 1154 of the Civil Code adds the rule that the part of the estate lost by a legatee shall be dealt with in accordance with the rule of intestate succession. The rule corresponds to article 1125(3) which provides that "a donee-by-will who has committed the act listed in the first paragraph of this article loses his right to receive the testamentary gift".

Article 29 of the Property Law provided that "[w]here a real right is acquired through succession or testamentary gift, the real right as inherited becomes effective at the time when the succession opens". Article 230 of the Civil Code has now removed the mention to testamentary gifts. In general, the Civil Code seems to treat the change of property rights arising from testate succession and the one arising from testamentary gifts differently. This choice causes unnecessary problems in the overall understanding of the change of property rights of the estate. For the sake of consistency and coordination between the Book on Real Rights and the Book on Succession, it would be better to return to the position of the Property Law and interpret the word "successor" in article 230 of the Civil Code in an expanded manner so as to include into the scope of the "successor" the donee-by-will.[10]

6 Conclusion

Compared with the background of the 1985 Succession Law, the level of social development and the total value of social wealth and per capita value in the era of the Civil Code have changed dramatically. The change is clearly bringing out demands for more specific and detailed norms on the disposition of the estate. However, it should be noted that, after more than thirty years of application of the 1985 Succession Law, the majority of the public has already accepted and become accustomed to the existing system of succession. Thus, the social cost of changing the existing rules would be great. This explains why the Book on Succession of the Civil Code makes some complements and improvements to the chapters of the 1985 Succession Law on "General Rules", "Intestate Succession" and "Testate Succession and Testamentary Gift", while leaving the succession system basically unchanged. The most important modifications are those concerning the chapter on "Disposition of Estates". It is

10 Wang Yang, 'Change of Property Rights Arising from the Testamentary Gift in Chinese Law' (2020) 9 L Sci Magazine 62, 74 (汪洋, 中国法上基于遗赠发生的物权变动,《法学杂志》).

especially worth highlighting the revision of the rules of the administration of estate and in the establishment of a brand new estate administrator system. The new rules try to maintain the stability of the basic succession system in China while adapting it to the changes of the whole society at the same time.

CHAPTER 15

Comparative Perspectives on the Law of Succession in China

Grzegorz J. Blicharz

1 Introduction

The law of succession is most embedded in the traditions of a given society. It reflects the culture and history of a nation sometimes even more than property or family law do. As Andrzej Stelmachowski, the eminent Polish civil law scholar who witnessed the transformation from communism to democracy, famously declared: the most difficult to reform is the law of succession, because the effects can be judged at the earliest in the third generation.[1] Roman law of succession was a source of innovative solutions, providing a testing ground for new dogmatic constructions, also because it frequently involved large transfers of property. The complexity, flexibility, and subtlety of the law of succession in the Western legal tradition has been a function both of citizen's wealth and of a mentality focused on the long-term development of individuals, families and communities. Hence, it is much to the point that the regulation in Book Six of the Chinese Civil Code,[2] which represents traditional Chinese values, seeks to promote and protect them by modelling law on Western principles of both civil and common law, and Roman law. Sometimes it happens that the pedigree of Roman law appears by surprise, or Roman law terminology even helps properly translate Chinese legal notions.[3] A comparative perspective teaches

1 Andrzej Stelmachowski, *Zarys teorii prawa cywilnego* (PWN 1998) 23.

2 The analysis is carried both on the original Chinese version of the Code as well as an official English translation (at <http://www.npc.gov.cn/englishnpc/c23934/202012/f627aa3a46514 75db93689d69419d1e/files/47c16489e186437eab3244495cb47d66.pdf> (accessed December 9, 2022)) which was confronted with non-officials translations into Italian (the first that was published) by Oliviero Diliberto, Domenico Dursi, Antonio Masi (eds), *Codice civile della Repubblica Popolare Cinese* (Meiling Huang transl, Pacini 2021), and into English by Jiangqiu Ge, Jian He, Qiao Liu, Zhicheng Wu, and Bingwan Xiong (eds), *The Civil Code of the People's Republic of China* (Brill 2022).

3 Jing An and Jiahui Sun, 'Translation strategy of legal terms with Chinese characteristics in Civil Code of the People's Republic of China based on Skopos theory' (2022) 17(9) PLoS ONE e0273944.

 | DOI:10.1163/9789004704428_016

one to look at the regulation of the law of succession using a conceptual framework that is based precisely on the principles and values.[4] Adopting this optic, proposed and elaborated by Franciszek Longchamps de Bérier, a synchronous analysis will be carried out to capture the main comparative features between Book Six of the Code and the Western law of succession extended by a diachronic comparison with Roman law.

2 Structure of the Book Six

2.1 *Modest Regulation*

The law of succession is regulated almost at the end of the Code, which might be thought to resemble a Pandectist's systematics, an idea which is also reinforced by the presence of a general part (Book One) and the placement of marriage and family law before the law of succession itself. The Code, however, eludes clear-cut classification, as it draws on many different models: only after the law of succession, in the last book, that 'torts' are regulated, implying the adoption of the division into contracts and torts instead of the uniform regulation of the law of obligations. The Book Six we are concerned with is not extensive compared with the other books of the Code. It consists of 45 articles (from article 1119 to article 1163) out of a total of 1260, and is indeed one of the shortest books of all, ranking just behind Book Five on marriage and family, which has 55 articles. One should note that, not just in terms of its proportion to the other books, but more generally in comparison to other contemporary civil codes, this Book must be considered very modest in terms of its size and, therefore, in the detail of its regulation. The book on the law of succession in the Italian Civil Code consist of 354 articles out of nearly 3000 in the whole code; in the Austrian Allgemeines bürgerliches Gesetzbuch (ABGB), it covers more than 320 sections out of 1503; in the Polish Kodeks cywilny (KC) 167 articles out of 1088; and similar proportions are found in the French Civil Code, the German Bürgerliches Gesetzbuch (BGB), the Dutch Burgerlijk Wetboek (BW), and the Swiss Zivilgesetzbuch (ZBG). The proportion of the Chinese Civil Code is similar to that of the Russian Civil Code (76 articles out of 1600), although in the Russian Code the regulations are much more elaborate.

4 Franciszek Longchamps de Bérier, *Law of Succession. Roman Legal Framework and Comparative Law Perspective* (Wolters Kluwer 2011) 52–53.

2.2 *Interconnectedness and Terminology*

In the Chinese Civil Code, however, the regulation of the legal effects of death and inheritance is not limited to Book Six. More than 30 articles in the other books of the Code deal with these effects: in the general part (articles 10, 16, 39, 50, 51, 52, 53, 101, 115, 173, 175), property law (articles 230, 369, 370, 371), contract law (articles 664, 732, 934, 935, 936, 977), personal property law (articles 992, 994), matrimonial and family law (articles 1061, 1071, 1074, 1075, 1108) and torts (article 1181). Such a legislative technique, taking advantage of the interconnectedness of the books of the Code is consistent with the art of codification. A minor issue that concerns the official English translation is the inconsistent use of the concept of heir: the term 'heir' appears in the translation only in articles 664, 935, 936, while in Book Six it is only the term 'successor' that is used. However, this difference does not appear in the original version of the Code, which always uses the same phrase – 继承人; that this is a genuine inconsistency in the official translation is confirmed by a recent English translation of the Chinese Civil Code. Thus, one should not conclude from the original translation that Chinese law clearly distinguishes an heir from a successor, but neither does this necessarily signify that it expresses the same concept of heir as in the Western legal tradition.[5]

2.3 *Internal Structure: Italian Influence*

The internal structure of the Book does not differ from the typical layout of other modern codes, although it does favor regulating first intestate succession, and thus differs from, for example, the ABGB or the Russian Civil Code. From the point of view of structure, the Chinese Civil Code seems most similar to the Italian and Polish Civil Codes. The Chinese legislator, arranging the structure of the book in four chapters, uses a division exactly the same as that of the Italian Civil Code: it begins with general provisions (7 articles), then moves on to intestate succession (also 7 articles), testate succession (12 articles) and disposition of estate (19 articles). It confirms the crucial and longstanding influence of Italian legal academics and also Roman law experts on the Chinese legal scholarship. The Chinese regulation ends with provisions on disposition of the estate – similar, as it happens, to those in the ZGB, while the Italian one contains provisions on donations and the Polish one on special rules for inheriting farms. The Polish Code is made up of as many as 10 titles but takes up successive issues in the same order as the Chinese one. Due to

5 Li Fan, 'The orientation and characteristics of the inheritance agreement in China and Russia: comparative legal research' (2021) 4 Legal Science in China and Russia 26, 28.

the small size of Book Six of the Chinese Civil Code, many issues that in other codes (e.g. Polish) are the subject of separate chapters or titles are dealt with in the Code in one or more articles that are small enough not to require a separate unit of text – for example, those concerning liability for inheritance debts (article 1163). The formal structure itself proposed by the Chinese legislature, as well as the thoroughness of the regulation of the various inheritance matters, is not accidental. The fact that the last two chapters cover more than two-thirds of the provisions of Book Six (31 articles) confirms something apparent in the very content itself of the regulation, i.e. the increased importance of testate succession and the issues regarding distribution of estate between heirs.

3 Principles and Values: A Framework

Principles work both as a legal order's foundations and as rules which are, nevertheless, open to limitations (exceptions). At the same time, principles comprise a reference to certain values which they try to foster and protect. The observed diversity of the regulation of the law of succession within the Western legal tradition testifies to the fact that it is difficult to find a consensus on the basic underlying values and principles of the law of succession.[6] This is very often due to the historical background, and resulting 'conservatism' of inheritance law, which causes the relatively slow changes in this legal area.[7] Although different legal orders emphasize differently the principles and values of inheritance regulation, one can nevertheless grasp an underlying conceptual constancy within legal thought.[8] In the historical evolution of the law, the same ideas and discussions recur time and again, there is no simple linear progression but rather contemplation of principles and values that are fixed and that, thanks to the genius of Roman jurists, have already been proclaimed explicitly in our legal history. Thus, the law of succession is characterized by both volatility and stability, which often means – fortunately – a constant chance for the return of well-attested historical solutions.[9] A highly instructive

6 Longchamps de Bérier (n 4) 9.

7 Kenneth G.C. Reid, Marius J. de Waal, Reinhard Zimmermann, 'Testamentary Formalities in Historical and Comparative Perspective', in Kenneth G.C. Reid, Marius J. de Waal, Reinhard Zimmermann (eds), *Comparative Succession Law: Volume I: Testamentary Formalities* (OUP 2011) 432, 471.

8 Thomas Rüfner, 'Intestate Succession in Roman Law' in Kenneth Reid, Marius de Waal, Reinhard Zimmermann (eds), *Comparative Succession Law: Volume II: Intestate Succession* (OUP 2015) 2.

9 Longchamps de Bérier (n 4) 23–24.

example from the perspective of Chinese law is given by the history of Polish law. Even the communist era that followed World War II did not eradicate the persisting Western foundations of the Polish law of succession. Its resilience is also, however, accompanied by variability, though often, ironically, as a result of the recurrence of 'eternal solutions':[10] even today, after 'three generations' since the political transformation, the Polish law of succession marked the return from the past of the *legatum per vindicationem*, *donatio mortis causa*, and the expansion of the circle of statutory heirs. The clarity, practicality and apolitical nature of the construction of Roman law vis-à-vis the patchwork of solutions of modern legal orders motivates one to evaluate Chinese regulation using the Roman principles and values, supplemented by criteria developed in comparative law.

4 *Nemo pro parte testatus pro parte intestatus decedere potest* – An Eternal Principle

In the Western legal tradition, the reference point for all inheritance law is the old Roman principle that 'nobody may leave his property partly by will, and partly by intestate succession' (Justinian Institutions – ad I. 2.14.5). Unlike in Roman law, in modern legal orders this serves only as an organizing principle, i.e. it designates the two main modes of inheritance: testate and intestate. Answer to the question of what happens to the inheritance after a person's death should be sought either in the will of the deceased himself or in the will of the legislature. These two pillars are, indeed, accepted almost everywhere, but they are not mutually exclusive.[11] In fact in Rome itself, from the time of Antoninus Pius (2nd century A.D.) to the Justinian period (6th century A.D.), the law did not set these two modes of inheritance in opposition to one another and allowed many exceptions to this rule.[12]

The Chinese Civil Code builds succession law on the basis of the same two universal pillars of inheritance, as expressed in article 1123, where it mandates that inheritance be carried out either according to intestate succession or

10 Franciszek Longchamps de Bérier, 'The Historical Lawyer and the Goals of Legal Education' (2022) 72 (3) Zbornik PFZ 777, 783–784.

11 Kenneth G.C. Reid, Marius J. de Waal, Reinhard Zimmermann, 'Intestate Succession in Historical and Comparative Perspective', in Kenneth G C Reid, Marius J. de Waal, Reinhard Zimmermann (eds) (n 8) 442, 445 fn 17.

12 Longchamps de Bérier (n 4) 57–58.

according to testate succession. However, as in the Western legal tradition, it allows the two modes of succession to be combined with regard to a particular single inheritance, as evidenced by article 1163, which resolves the manner of liability for the deceased's debts and taxes owed in situations where intestate succession, testate succession, and testamentary gift concurrently exist.

4.1 *Inheritance Agreement for* Inter Vivos *Support: A Creative Chinese Solution*

Additionally to these two universal bases, the Code seems to provide for a third pillar of inheritance law: in article 1123, it is permitted to carry out inheritance in accordance with the agreement on testamentary gift for *inter vivos* support. The so called legacy–support agreement does not in fact correspond to the role that the 'inheritance agreement' plays in countries of Germanic tradition (ABGB, BGB, ZGB), i.e. as a third way of disposing the estate. It more closely resembles the deathbed gift, *donatio mortis causa*, well known to the countries of the Roman tradition. The Chinese testamentary gift corresponds to what Justinian described as 'a kind of gift from the deceased' (I. 2.20.1), which, according to Chinese regulation, is either provided for in the will, constituting a legacy, or is provided for by an agreement for *inter vivos* support. The Chinese solution seems unique with regard to its onerous nature: the obligation to support the future decedent during that person's lifetime and attend to his interment after death, has *inter vivos* effect, and, with regard to the transfer of property, *mortis causa* effect. Moreover, the beneficiary is not considered an heir because, as article 1158 stipulates, such an agreement can only be made with an organization or individual other than a successor. Consequently article 1163 asserts that such a beneficiary is not liable for the deceased's debts. The solution, oriented towards caring for elderly, can be considered the inverse of the retained life estate in property known in civil law and common law, which consists in the providing lifetime maintenance to the future decedent in exchange for the transfer of real property which, however, takes place *inter vivos*.[13]

The Chinese solution is unusual in that the beneficiary must wait for the testamentary gift until the death of the person concerned but is assured that the agreed gift will be received, since he can initiate succession proceedings. We learn from European history that the retained life estate in property is readily used formerly in rural relations only, nowadays it is found in urban relations as

13 Adam G. Province, 'Killing Me Softly: A Comparative Review of Chinese Inheritance Law to Address the Problem of Elder Abuse and Neglect in the United States', (2012) 22 Ind Int'l & Comp L Rev 71, 84–85.

well. Although testamentary gifts for *inter vivos* support serve as an important supplement to the social welfare system, and may be competitive to making a will, however, the deferred effect of the caregiver's acquisition of property raises greater concerns about the 'longevity' of the future testator's life and in practice causes conflicts over financial management.[14]

4.2 *No Accruals: Like the Old Common Law*

One of the consequences of the principle of *nemo pro parte testatus pro parte intestatus decedere potest* is the law of accrual: in Roman law, the undistributed portion of the inheritance, or the share of the appointed heir which such appointee does not want or cannot inherit, accrued to the remaining heirs either in testate or intestate succession. The law of accrual is also an expression of the construction of universal succession, i.e., that the inheritance must be disposed of in its entirety as one thing. In contrast to the Western legal tradition, the Chinese Civil Code does not provide for the right of accrual at all – a significant departure from the mechanism used in the West. It is understandable when a portion of estate was not disposed of by the will, since in modern European orders, the law of accrual is still used, but only in the case of testate succession with regards to heirs and legatees (e.g. in Polish law article 965 ex. 973 KC), and even so with certain limitations. Only recently in common law some advocate for different solution in the case of incomplete wills, that the court should use will as a blueprint for the whole estate,[15] a solution well known in Roman law. However, in common law, accepting the law of accrual took longest to pave its way in the event of lapse of bequest for devisee or failure of testamentary provision for legatees.[16] From a comparative perspective, therefore, the Chinese regulation is closest to the old common law version, which always provided lapsed portion to statutory heirs, most often due to primogeniture interests, instead of granting it to another devisee appointed in will. But this rule has long since been reversed in the U.S. by specific statutes or common law courts. In the Chinese regulation (article 1154) a portion of the estate affected for different reasons than incompleteness of will, i.e. when it was disclaimed, heir or legatee was disinherited or predeceased, or will was partially invalided, an intestate succession occurs with respect to it. This solution limits the impact of the testator's will itself. In common law

---

14 Cfr. an example in Siyi Lin, *The Law of Unjust Enrichment in China: Necessary Or Not?* (Springer 2022) 103–104.

15 Adam J. Hirsch, 'Incomplete Wills' (2013) 111 Mich L Rev 1423, 1473–1474.

16 Jesse Dukeminier and Stanley M. Johanson, *Wills, Trusts, and Estates* (4th ed., Little Brown 1990) 341.

the testator himself is encouraged to establish substitutes or exclude statutory heirs in the event of lapse. Civil law orders also provide for an accrual in such cases, unless a testator decides to exclude the law of accrual (article 965(3) KC; § 2094 BGB, article 674 CCI). The situation seems more unclear under article 1154 when there is a testate succession and legatee disclaims legacy. If intestate succession occurs to that portion, it is a reminiscent of the old inadequate common law solution which questions the status of intestate heirs as universal successors.

4.3 *The Anti-lapse Solution for the Protection of Private Property*

The Chinese rejection of the law of accrual is puzzling because in the general rules of the Book Six, the Chinese legislature has provided for the typical anti-lapse solution widely used in the United States. According to article 1121, when persons with the right to inherit each other's estate die in the same incident and it is difficult to determine the time of each person's death, then it is assumed that the first to die is the one who had no other heirs.

The solution serves, first, to protect the right of inheritance, and, second, to keep property in private hands, a typical anti-escheat solution. If there is a difference of generations between the deceased in common peril and they both have heirs, then the classical rules already known to Roman law decide, i.e. the representatives of the older generation are assumed to have died first, and, when both belong to the same generation, then there arises the case of *commorientes*, resolved just like in Roman law by applying the fiction of a joint death and the simultaneous opening of both inheritances independently. This regulation thus suggests that the Chinese legislature is aware of anti-lapse solutions but does not apply them indiscriminately.

5 Freedom of Testation

5.1 *Appreciated Yet Underdeveloped Principle*

The Chinese Civil Code highlights the freedom of testation: a hallmark of the Roman law tradition which passed over the old Germanic customs and common law favoring intestate succession. First, it gives priority to inheritance based on a will (article 1123). Second, it requires only full capacity for performing *civil juristic acts* to make a last will (article 1143). Third, it allows a broad disposition of property by instituting heirs even outside the circle of statutory heirs, by giving legacies with possibility of imposing an obligation of performance on them, and by creating testamentary trust (article 1133). Testamentary trust being an import from common law operates in China for two decades and confirms the possibility of employing it in civil law orders (cfr. Czechia or Hungary), but raises questions about the implications for property issues,[17] since common law solutions are always embedded by using Roman framework.[18] There are however no rules on testamentary substitutions which diminishes anti-lapse effect. Fourth, the Code increases the accessibility and ease of drafting an act of last will by allowing many ordinary forms of wills (articles 1134–1139), including the holographic will (article 1134), listed first and intuitively regarded as the basic form, like in many countries in the civil law and common law orders and in mixed-jurisdictions.[19] Besides three other ordinary forms of wills: allographic, printed, and audio-video, the oral will is, just like in other legal systems, an extraordinary or special form which falls when the immediate danger threatening the testator passes (article 1138). Novel, but not-so-precise audio-video form, requires the recording of witnesses and the date, and though is easy to make (e.g., by using Jitterbug cell phones adapted to elders), it is questionable whether this form fosters virtues of cautionary, protective, and evidentiary will. Fifth, the lack of specific requirements as to the content of a will makes it likely that it may be drafted in three words, just as in ancient Roman oral will (D. 28.5, pr.-1). More likely, since there are no rules or requirements to disinherit in a will statutory heirs. Practice suggests that in China, like in many other countries, testators dispose of individual assets either by establishing an heir *ex re certa* or creating legatees.[20] Sixth, the Chinese code follows the Roman principle that a will is changeable until the very end of life (D. 34.4.4), permitting the testator to change the content of the will also by later acting inconsistently with the content of his will (article 1142), and settles the priority of wills dependent on chronology rather than type of will.

5.2 *Upside Down: Public Entities as Testamentary Heirs*

After explaining in article 1133 that one can appoint in the will some of statutory heirs, which should be obvious, but represents also the testamentary practice in the Western countries, legislator provides in an unexpected order, other

17 Lusina Ho, Rebecca Lee, Jin Jinping, 'Trust Law in China: a critical evaluation of its conceptual foundation' in Lusina Ho and Reveca Lee (eds), *Trust Law in Asian Civil Law Jurisdictions: A Comparative Analysis* (CUP 2013) 98.

18 Domenico Dursi, 'Il Codice Civile Cinese: tra tradizione romanistica e socialismo con caratteristiche cinesi' (2021) 13 (2) Tigor 177, 184.

19 Longchamps de Bérier (n 4) 169.

20 '遗嘱怎么写法律才有效（立遗嘱最新法律规定)来源：法大大 发布时间', November 9, 2022, at <https://www.fadada.com/notice/detail-14131.html>.

possible heirs: the State or a collective, or an organization or individual other than intestate heir. In the West inheritance is always linked to private property, hence it is unintuitive to appoint the state, to which taxes are paid during one's lifetime, and to which the estates escheat only as a last resort. The Code places emphasis on the fact that public entities from different levels of state organization also have the capacity to testacy which, in fact, is also true for the Western tradition where making bequests to public entities: associations (*collegia*) and municipalities (*municipia* or *civitates*) was steadily accepted in Roman law.

5.3 *Confused Wording: The Universal Succession Mechanism*

Some confusion is caused by a prima facie conceptual inconsistency that occurs in the wording and translations of the article 1133: statutory heirs can be *designated to inherit estate* (将个人财产指定; *designare quali successori del patrimonio personale*), and testator can *donate estate* (将个人财产赠; *assegnare il proprio patrimonio*) to other entities. Does the Code differentiate statutory heirs (法定继承人) from testamentary devisees like in common law? Does universal succession mechanism operates in both cases? Although the Code does not contain any reference to universal succession, like in Western law, it indicates it since debts are the responsibility of heirs and legatees, and are not the burden of the estate, although there is the administrator of estate, and the liability within the estate's inventory is a rule. Also naming convention for appointed in the will is not discriminating since article 1154 refers to them as testamentary heirs (遗嘱继承人). Although different verbs are used, the same phrase 个人 财产 (patrimony of a person – article 1133) describes the object of testate succession, and the same serves to define inheritance (遗产 – article 1122), so this does not constitute a common law distinction between real and personal property, and treats inheritance as one asset. The scope of inheritance is limited either by nature of rights – a well-known limitation of inheritance to patrimonial rights (cf. article 992 on personality rights, article 934 on the entrustment contract with exceptions, article 173 on the agency agreement, article 39 on guardianship) or results from the statutory exclusion of certain rights or property (article 369 on the right of habitation or article 1153 on common family property).

6 Principle of Family Solidarity

6.1 *No Compulsory Portion Yet Extremely Limited Necessary Portion*

The principle of family solidarity is extended in the Code to solidarity outside kinship and even in society *en large*. It interferes with the freedom of testation by a reservation of necessary portion, and the lack of accrual. The Code provides the right to necessary portion very narrowly only for an heir who has neither the ability to work nor the source of income (article 1141). Preserving the Inheritance Law of 1985 solution fits perfectly into the heated debate whether mandatory family protection still has a *raison d'être*.[21] The Code, in this regard, presents a mixture of various traditions: either of socialist flexible approach to care for those in need (especially elderly), but expect able ones to work for themselves, or of a holistic approach of Chinese culture.[22] Even in Western legal orders, however, it is undisputed that such family members should be supported by higher compulsory portion. In the Code peculiarly there is no indication what necessary portion means, and although in practice it may be estimated as a portion of intestate share,[23] it represents the early version of Roman *pars legitima* which was judged case by case.[24] Contrary to Western law, the Code allows *any successor* to receive necessary portion, and not specific family members.[25] The omission to reserve a necessary portion does not invalidate a will, since it may be provided later at the time of distribution of estate (article 1130). Surprisingly, the Chinese legislator excludes from inheritance and from necessary portion by using disinheritance – and not as usually in forced heirship regimes by unworthiness – only in circumstances enlisted in article 1125 (ex lege *loses his or her right to inherit* – see article 1144). The testator, however, was granted the chance to forgive such a person with two exceptions (article 1125, subparagraph 1–2). It may be done implicitly, by later appointing this person as an heir, only if the then disinherited truly repented and amended his ways. This unprecedented in the Western law requirement indicates Chinese peculiarity.

6.2 *More Solidarity than Family*

The principle of family protection operates primarily in intestate succession. The Code indirectly extended the modestly broad circle of statutory heirs by allowing representation in the case of descendants of predeceased children and siblings, allowing *per stirpes* distribution (article 1128). Unusually, it divides

---

21 Longchamps de Bérier (n 4) 74–77; Alexandra Braun, *Forced Heirship in Italy*, in Kenneth G.C. Reid, Marius J de Waal, Reinhard Zimmermann (eds), *Comparative Succession Law: Volume III: Mandatory Family Protection* (OUP 2020) 109–110.

22 Knut Benjamin Pißler and Timo Kleinwegener, 'Necessary Portion in China' in Kenneth G.C. Reid, Marius J de Waal, Reinhard Zimmermann (eds) (n 22) 623.

23 Pißler and Kleinwegener (n 22) 610.

24 Longchamps de Bérier (n 4) 72.

25 Pißler and Kleinwegener (n 22) 608.

the statutory heirs into two circles. With no surprise siblings and parental or maternal grandparents inherit when there are no heirs from the first circle (article 1227). Amusingly, however, when the inheritance falls to the first circle it is distributed equally to spouse, children and parents (article 1130). It confirms the broad conception of multigenerational family which is taken to extreme by a broad definition of children, parents and siblings (article 1127) which extends them to stepchildren, but only those who were raised by the deceased, stepparents who raised the deceased, stepsiblings who supported or were supported by the deceased. They all inherit on an equal footing which shows how solidarity goes beyond blood ties. The right of stepchildren in the Western legal tradition is shaped differently, since they usually inherit only ahead of the state. The Chinese legislator, however, unlike Polish law (article 934(1) KC), limits the stepfamily rights by requiring a special relationship with the deceased. The Code went further to reconceptualize the 'family' as bound closely together by a feeling of sacrifice and assistance towards each other. This allowed to grant right to inherit based on affinity relationships between parents-in-law and children-in-law (article 1129). This is less surprising given some U.S. states laws, for example, in California which however is based on anti-escheat mentality.[26] In China, the reason is to provide substantial support for the parents-in-law (article 1229), only then children-in-law may inherit, amusingly, in the first circle, provided they are also widowed.

6.3 *Flexible Distribution of Estate: Judge's Discretion vs. Testator's Wishes*

The rules on intestate succession begin with the widely used Justinian principle that men and women have the same right to inherit (article 1126). The inclusion of so many persons in the first circle and the principle of solidarity *en large* lead to a very flexible mechanism unknown to Western legal tradition for modifying the equal distribution of shares. Statutory heirs are entitled to agree after the death of *de cuius* on the unequal distribution of shares (article 1130), a solution which perhaps was even exceptionally applied in Roman law (Justinian in Edict 3: *De Armeniorum successione*, 535 AD). This provision seems to allow through a contractual distribution of the estate to modify the intestate succession. Certainly, such competence is vested into the judges' hands who not only can provide necessary portion for an heir in need if there was no will, or it did not cover it, but also may modify shares of other heirs.

26 Grzegorz Blicharz, *Udział państwa w spadku. Rzymska myśl prawna w perspektywie prawnoporównawczej* (Od. Nowa 2016) 406–407.

When heir rebels against decedent and circumstances are serious operates disinheritance by law, but when there is less serious lack of solidarity, failure to fulfill the duty to support, to show solidarity, the code allows to adapt accordingly the disposition of shares. It is doubtful that at this stage an heir can be deprived of the title, thus it resembles the Roman *incapactias*, which only prevents from acquiring share or part of share. Similarly, those who supported or lived with the deceased either not only may acquire their share, but also obtain more, just like in the Roman *caducum* regime. Following the principle of solidarity *en large* allows a judge to grant a share to a person who is not an heir, but was maintained by the deceased or substantially supported the deceased (article 1131). Behavioral based distribution of estate is not totally surprising since in the United Kingdom and Australia it may happen, but only as a last resort, when the estate escheated or became *bona vacantia*, so the state can provide property to certain individuals or organizations.[27] In China unprecedented judges' discretion in adjudicating inheritance cases may flexibly adjust intestate succession, but may also significantly interfere with respecting the testator's will.

7 Respect for a Dead Person's Wishes

The principle of respect for the will of the testator is essentially an interpretive principle, as made clear by Longchamps de Bérier. The Code is parsimonious when it comes to regulating how to interpret a will, however it expresses the respect rooted in Roman law, that a will must manifest the genuine intention of the testator (article 1143), that a very last will counts, any intermingling with the freedom of testation may lead either to the invalidity of will, or to disinheritance by law, respecting the will can mean declaring the invalidity only of the part that was tampered with. Chinese law finds a specific solution for situations where the obligation imposed on heir or legatee has not been performed, on the one hand, allowing as in Roman law, *iusta causa* of non-performance to be invoked, on the other hand enabling deprivation of his right to inherit by an intervention of a third party or an organization interested in fulfilling the obligation (article 1144).

27 Blicharz (n 26) 509–510.

8 *Semel Heres Semper Heres*

The principle of 'he who once an heir, always an heir' makes it impossible in Western legal tradition to add dissolving conditions to provisions in a will. In Chinese law, as a rule, an heir's position is permanent but both the principle of respect for the will of the testator and the principle of family solidarity can lead to a violation of the position of the heir. The Chinese legislature explicitly affirms permanency in the case of a spouse, who may freely distribute the inherited share even if he or she chooses to remarry (article 1157).

9 *Nasciturus pro iam nato habetur, quotiens de commodis eius agitur*

The universal principle of protecting the interests of unborn children, developed in Roman law, has been upheld in the Code. It is elevated to the general principle of the entire civil law (article 16 in the General Part), following some of Western regulations, and is repeated in the law of succession (like ZGB, CCI). In the distribution of estate, a portion shall be retained for the fetus (article 1155), just like in Roman law (D. 37.9.1.1). The broad protection of the *nasciturus*, however, does not effectively affect the question of regulating abortion.[28]

10 The Principle of State's Share in Inheritance

Roman law developed two facets of the principle of state's involvement in inheritance either through escheat or through inheritance tax – as an exceptional or broad share in inheritance. The Code explicitly gives the state the right to escheat only in an exceptional situation where there are no heirs (article 1160), preserves legacies (article 1160), and directs the property 'for the needs of the common good;' which resemble a general Spanish regulation ('to pay off the public debt') rather than specific solutions of some American states. Priority to unclaimed estate granted to the collective organization to which the deceased belonged, is reminiscent of Roman privileges in favor of associations or *civitates*, or modern priority of county or district. This is coherent with an obligation of the villagers' committee in the place where the decedent was domiciled to administer such estate. Like a Roman *gens*, the villagers' committee is a primary-level self-governing organization (articles 101 and 264).

28 Longchamps de Bérier (n 4) 85.

The second facet of state's share in succession is inheritance tax which, despite some drafts, was not introduced in China which confirms soft version of applying this principle.

11 Conclusion – Rule of Law and Rule of Virtues

The panoramic analysis of legal principles allows to see what values they refer to. In the Code, we encounter well-known Western values and specific Chinese ones. It confirms that the Code belongs to Roman legal tradition mixed with Chinese characteristics expressing both traditional and socialist background.[29] Among the first group we can enlist: the designation of an heir, so that 'no one dies without an heir'. Chinese counterpart would be designating a solidary heir. In both traditions the mutual services among community members encourage *mortis causa* compensation for such services. Another set of values are: Western based desire to influence the world of the living after one's own death, which is mitigated by Chinese value of caring for elderly incapable decedent. The right to inherit depends on the conformity to socialist morality. Invariably, heirs or legatees are also free to accept the inheritance or other dispositions of the testator, although unlike in European orders the legatee has to be active to acquire the bequest (article 1124). Family is also a value to be protected although more appreciated is solidarity and protecting the more needy, especially the elderly and the sick. Protection of the community at many levels is certainly aimed at taking care of the stability and security of the social, political and economic structure. A manifestation of the protection of the deceased's creditors is certainly the institution of administrator of estate, regulated in some detail along with the liability of the administrator for any damage caused to creditors as well. Based on the so-called seven virtues of testamentary formalities which legal order foster,[30] one can distinguish four virtues (cautionary, protective, discoverability, evidentiary), which argue for a relatively high level of formality and three (facilitative, cheapness, secrecy) encouraging low level of formality. The Code changed from promoting highly conservative virtues into virtues allowing flexibility which implies risks and uncertainty but perhaps may give boost to testamentary succession, and long-term development of society, maintaining the impact on the world of the living,[31] and to regard with favor the intention of the testator.

29 Dursi (n 18) 184.
30 Reid, de Waal, Zimmermann (n 7) 468–469.
31 Rüfner (n 8) 2.

CHAPTER 16

The Structure and Contents of the Book on Tort Liability of the Chinese Civil Code

方新军 *Fang Xinjun*

1 The Historical Evolution of the Book on Tort Liability

The Chinese Civil Code is divided into seven books, the last of which is the Book on Tort Liability. The Book on Tort Liability consists of 95 articles (Articles 1164 to 1158), which are mainly derived from the Tort Liability Law (ninety-two articles in total) that came into effect in 2010. Compared to the Books on Property Rights and Contracts, the Book on Tort Liability has made relatively fewer changes to its preceding legislation, though the changes are nevertheless notable.

The Book on Tort Liability of the Chinese Civil Code keeps the same name as the Tort Liability Law, which implies the reason for not establishing a separate Book on Obligations in the Chinese Civil Code. During the drafting process of the Tort Liability Law, there was a debate over the name of 'Tort Liability Law' and 'Law of Tortious Acts', in which the core issue was whether tort should be seen as one of the causative events of an obligation.[1] Furthermore, as a consequence of this argument, if tort is considered to give rise to an obligation, then tort should be seen as one of the causative events of an obligation, therefore in the system of the Chinese Civil Code, tort should be provided in a separate Book on Obligations. If tort is considered to give rise to liability, then tort is not one of the causative events of an obligation, and in the system of the Chinese Civil Code, tort should be separated from the Book on Obligations and become an independent book.[2]

Scholars who advocated the name of 'Law of Tortious Acts' believed that, according to the civil law tradition, tort is a factual act and one of the causative events of an obligation. Tort law should therefore constitute the obligation law

1 Zhang Xinbao, 'General Provisions of Tortious Act Law' (2001) 4 Chinese J L 42 (张新宝, 侵权行为法的一般条款，《法学研究》).

2 Wang Liming, 'Rediscussion on the Competition and Cooperation of Liability for Breach of Contract and Liability for Tort' (continuation) (2001) 4 China's Foreign Trade 27 (王利明, 再论违约责任与侵权责任的竞合, (续)《中国对外贸易》).

 | DOI:10.1163/9789004704428_017

system of the Chinese Civil Code together with contracts, negotiorum gestio and unjust enrichment (among others). Scholars who advocated the name of 'Tort Liability Law' believed that tort does not give rise to a legal relationship of obligation, but rather to liability.[3] Consequently, the so-called 'Law of Tortious Acts' should have been more appropriately named 'Tort Liability Law'. The Tort Liability Law, effective in 2010, adopted this view, and the Book on Tort Liability of the Chinese Civil Code continues this practice. This also explains why the Chinese Civil Code does not adopt a book devoted to obligations as it happens in other civil codes of the civil law tradition, but instead contains the Books on Contracts and Tort Liability as separate books and includes unjust enrichment and negotiorum gestio as quasi-contracts in the Book on Contracts. Although there is still controversy in the academic community, the fact that the Chinese Civil Code does not establish a separate book on obligation has been settled, which will make it more challenging to interpret specific provisions of the Chinese Civil Code in the future. The challenge stems from the Chinese Civil Code not formally establishing an autonomous book on obligation, whilst it clearly provides contents on the obligation law in substance. The extent in which the contents of the General Rules in the Book on Contracts can serve as the general rules of obligations and produce effects on torts, needs to be interpreted on a case-by-case basis. Meanwhile, many articles in Chapter 8 on "Civil Liability" in the Book on General Provisions and Book IV on "Personality Rights" of the Chinese Civil Code are related to tort liability.

2 The Structure of the Book on Tort Liability

The Book on Tort Liability of the Chinese Civil Code is divided into ten chapters; two less than the Tort Liability Law. Chapter 12 of the Tort Liability Law contained the Supplementary Provision on the effective entry into force of the Tort Liability Law, and the deletion of this chapter did not involve legal issues. The other deleted chapter in the Chinese Civil Code is Chapter 3 of the Tort Liability Law on 'Circumstances of Immunity of Liability and Deduction of Liability'. Although the chapter has been formally deleted, its specific contents have not been deleted, with the relevant provisions being simply moved elsewhere.

3 Xie Hongfei, 'Reconstitution of the Concurrent Theory of Liability for Breach of Contract and Liability for Tort' (2014) 6 Global L Rev 5 (谢鸿飞，违约责任与侵权责任竞合理论的再构成，《环球法律评论》).

The Book on Tort Liability of the Chinese Civil Code can be divided into two parts. The first part comprises of the general rules on general tort liability, including Chapter 1 on Basic Rules, Chapter 2 on Damages, and Chapter 3 on Special Rules of Tortfeasors. The second part comprises of the rules on special tort liability, including Chapter 4 on Product Liability, Chapter 5 on Liability for Motor Vehicle Traffic Accidents, Chapter 6 on Liability for Medical Malpractice, Chapter 7 on Liability for Environmental Pollution and Ecological Destruction, Chapter 8 on Liability for Ultra-Hazardous Activity, Chapter 9 on Liability for Damage Caused by Domestic Animal, and Chapter 10 on Liability for Damage Caused by Building or Object.[4]

Although the title of Chapter 1 on 'Basic Rules' of the Book on Tort Liability of the Chinese Civil Code remains the same as that of the Tort Liability Law, there's a stark contrast between the specific contents of Chapter 1 of the former with its predecessor. All of the five articles in Chapter 1 of the Tort Liability Law have been deleted and replaced by the fifteen articles of Chapter 1 of the Book on Tort Liability of the Chinese Civil Code, mainly concerning the doctrine of liability fixation for tort liability (ie, the issue of fault-based or non-fault based liability, and the issue of proving fault by evidence or presumption), tort liability involving multiple parties, and tort law defenses. This chapter is composed of some provisions from Chapter 1 and Chapter 3 of the Tort Liability Law.

Compared with Chapter 2 on 'Constituent elements of a tort liability and methods of bearing liability' of the Tort Liability Law, Chapter 2 on 'Damages' of the Book on Tort Liability of the Chinese Civil Code shows not only a change in the title, but also a very significant change in its content. Chapter 2 of the Tort Liability Law had twenty articles in total, while Chapter 2 of the Book on Tort Liability of the Chinese Civil Code has only nine articles. Since the doctrine of liability fixation for tort liability and liability involving multiple parties has been moved to Chapter 1, the rest of the Chapter focuses on damages.

Chapter 3 on 'Special Rules on Tortfeasors' of the Book on Tort Liability of the Chinese Civil Code contains fourteen articles, with five articles being added compared with the Tort Liability Law. The most significant changes are the refinement of the content of network torts and the addition of new provisions on tort liability, such as those referring to the liability of entrusted guardians and of ordering parties in contracting activities.

There are fifty-seven articles on special tort liability in Chapter 4 to Chapter 10 of the Book on Tort Liability of the Chinese Civil Code; six articles have been

---

4 For a scholar-friendly translation of the Chinese Civil Code, see Chen Lei et alii, *The Civil Code of the People's Republic of China* (Brill Nijhoff 2022).

added compared with the Tort Liability Law. While the overall framework has not changed much, some very distinctive provisions have been added. This is for instance the case with article 1217 on liability for a lift with good intentions (good Samaritan), article 1232 on punitive damages for environmental tort, article 1234 on alternative restoration for environmental torts and article 1235 on the determination of specific losses in cases of environmental torts.

3 The Characteristic Contents of the Book on Tort Liability

Compared with the Tort Liability Law, the changes in the Book on Tort Liability of the Chinese Civil Code are generally not radical. Yet there have been some changes that are noteworthy and deserve to be highlighted.

3.1 *Changes to the General Clause on Tort Liability*

Article 1165(1) of the Chinese Civil Code provides that "[a] person who is at fault for infringing a civil right or interest of another person, causing damage, shall be liable in tort". Compared with article 6(1) of the Tort Liability Law, the expression of "causing damage" has been added. The above change is remarkable because article 1165(1) of the Chinese Civil Code serves as a general clause on tort liability.

In the process of drafting the Tort Liability Law, there has been a dispute about whether the general clause on tort liability should follow the German or the French model of general clauses. The German model is characterized by having three separate general clauses: one for the infringement of absolute rights and interests (breach of protected interests), one for the violation of a statute protecting others (breach of legislative protective norm), and one for the intentional violation of good morals (intentional harm). In contrast, the French model has only one holistic general clause. Lawyers favoring the German model think that it provides a good distinction between the protection of rights and interests, and overall makes the law more operable in judicial practice. Lawyers favoring the French model think that the German model is too rigid to cope with various new types of rights and interests emerging from socioeconomic life. Thus, in theory, article 106(2) of General Principles of the Civil Law (now the same provision as in the Book on General Provisions of the Chinese Civil Code) adopted the French model of general clauses, with article 6(1) of the Tort Liability Law following suit.

After the Tort Liability Law came into effect, its doctrine has been highly debated in regards to which model of protection of rights and interests should be chosen between the model of equal protection and the mode of differentiated protection.[5] The core issue is how to protect those interests which are not explicitly recognized by law as "rights". There is no doubt that, with the development of social and economic life, new types of interests continue to emerge; it is equally beyond doubt that it is impossible for the law to protect all the interests that could be claimed by the parties. The core task of tort liability law is to strike a balance between social security and freedom of behavior. Since Roman law, the function of tort liability has shifted from punishment to compensation, and its overall rationale has moved from liability for consequences to liability for fault. All this indicates that the overall trend of tort liability law is to pay more attention to the freedom of conduct of civil subjects. However, with the emergence of liability for presumptive fault and liability without fault, tort liability law also shows a trend of constantly expanding the scope of protection.[6] Likewise, the problem is that article 2(2) of the Tort Liability Law listed eighteen kinds of named rights, but did not specify the scope and the way to protect interests, thus raising many questions in judicial practice.

The protection of interests other than rights has always been a difficult problem in judicial practice. Since the promulgation of the General Principles of the Civil Law, the Supreme People's Court has touched upon this issue in its 'Judicial Interpretation on Compensation for Personal Injury' and 'Judicial Interpretation on Compensation for Emotional Damages and Official Replies'. The Judicial Interpretations are applicable in many cases, but lack systematic and in-depth research. The Chinese Civil Code now expands the enumeration of rights and legal interests provided in Chapter 5 on 'Civil Rights' of Book First on General Provisions and Book Four on Personality Rights. Such a choice may, to a certain extent, alleviate the difficulty of protecting interests other than rights. However, due to the assumption of the legislature's bounded rationality, the legislator can never anticipate the developments of social and economic life, and therefore can never provide a complete list of rights and interests that should be protected by law. When one claims that his civil interest other than rights is infringed, demanding the tortfeasor to assume the tort liability, the

5 Cao Xianfeng, 'The Tort Composition Model of China's Tort Liability Law—Centering on the Positioning and Functional Analysis of "Civil Rights and Interests"' (2013) 6 Chinese J L 88. (曹险峰，我国侵权责任法的侵权构成模式——以"民事权益"的定位与功能分析为中心，《法学研究》).

6 Wang Liming, 'On the characteristics of the scope of protection in China's Tort Liability Law' (2010) 4 J Renmin U China 2 (王利明，论我国〈侵权责任法〉保护范围的特色，《中国人民大学学报》).

court will be faced with the difficult problem of justifying why it should decide in favor of them or against them.

Compared with article 6(1) of the Tort Liability Law, article 1165(1) of the Chinese Civil Code adds to the list of protected rights and legal interests in the expression "causing damage", which does not substantially change the constitutive elements of general tort liability. Based on a textualist interpretation of article 1165(1) of the Chinese Civil Code, the constitutive elements of general tort liability include: (1) an act of infringement; (2) the infringement of rights and interests; (3) a causal connection between the act of infringement and the infringement of the civil right or interest and (4) fault. If damages are to be claimed, the following shall be added: (5) a damage and (6) causation between the infringement of the civil right or interest and the damage. The infringement of a right or interest may not necessarily cause damage; in such a case, the victim of the infringement may not be able to claim damages. Therefore, if a civil subject suffers a harm because of the infringement of his lawful rights and interests, he can claim compensation.

The term 'unlawfulness' does not appear in article 1165(1) of the Chinese Civil Code. Yet, this does not mean that Chinese law does not adopt the element of unlawfulness, rather the element of the infringement of rights or interests can be seen as another way to express the element of unlawfulness. As such it can be said that, rights and law are two sides of the same coin. Objective law is the legal norm, while subjective law is the right. Therefore, the element of unlawfulness is presumed whenever there is an infringement of a right. As to interests, not all interests can be protected by law; only if lawful interests are within the scope of protection of law. Therefore, when a civil subject claims that a certain interest should be protected by law, he must prove that this interest is lawful. Thus, it implies that rights and interests should be protected in a differentiated manner. If a law clearly provides for the protection of some interests, such as personal freedom and personal dignity under articles 109 and 990(2) of the Civil Code, or personal information under articles 111 and 1034, it is clear that, although these interests are not manifested as rights, they are not different from rights in terms of protection under the Tort Liability Law. As a result, such a conclusion is based on explicit stipulations of the law, therefore there is no dispute that these interests are lawful interests, and the rest can be left to interpretation. By contrast, whenever a civil subject asserts an interest that is not clearly provided by law, the civil subject has to seek a specific basis for his claim and the judge has to seek persuasive grounds for adjudicating in favor or against the protection of that interest. The overall situation is problematic under many perspectives.

First, when a civil subject puts forth a claim that a certain interest has been infringed, judges should consider whether this interest has been expressed as a right in the law, or whether the law has clearly provided for protection of such an interest. Judges cannot create rights that the law does not provide for; yet, they can protect interests other than rights. By highlighting the formalistic standard of the protection of rights, it only solidifies the judge's duty of justification in the protection of interests.

Second, if the law does not directly provide for the protection of an interest, judges need to consider whether such an interest can be included in the types of rights or interests that are defined by the Book on Tort Liability of the Chinese Civil Code. This interpretation must respect the limits of textualist interpretation, otherwise it is tantamount to the judge directly creating rights that are not clearly provided by the law.

Third, if the above interpretation is not possible, judges should consider whether private law norms outside the Book on Tort Liability of the Chinese Civil Code protect this interest.

Fourth, if there are no such private law norms, judges need to consider whether there are public law norms protecting such interests. Public law norms, constitutional and criminal norms, in principle, are considered unable to protect personal interests, so that they cannot be conceived of as laws protecting others in the sense of private law. Judges are not allowed to directly cite constitutional and criminal law norms when judging infringement cases, but they are not excluded from referring to the value of these norms through the basic principles or general clauses of civil law in the reasoning part of their judgments. Administrative regulations are the primary law protecting others in the sense of private law. In determining whether an administrative regulation is a law protecting others, the judge shall consider the hierarchy status of the administrative regulation in question; conversely, the judge shall consider whether that administrative regulation is aimed at protecting personal interests, whether the person claiming the interest is the person whom such administrative regulation is intended to protect, and whether the interest claimed by civil subjects belongs to the scope of the interests that such administrative regulation is intended to protect.

Fifth, if there is no public law that protects a certain interest, judges should consider whether a certain interest should be protected by law based on the judgment of the internal system of the civil law. The Chinese Civil Code is a synthesis of an internal system and an external system. The external system is the system of norms, and the internal system is the system of principles. The distinctive feature of the Chinese Civil Code is that articles 3 to 9 of the Book on General Provisions enumerate eight basic principles in detail. Judges can deliberate and decide whether an interest claimed by civil subjects should be protected by law through the value notion mentioned by the above basic principles. If, according to this value judgment, a certain interest should not be protected by law, then this interest is in the lawless space.[7]

3.2 *Changes to Defenses against Tort Liability*

Chapter 3 of the Tort Liability Law on "Circumstances of Immunity of Liability and Deduction of Liability" disappears in the Chinese Civil Code. The Book on Tort Liability no longer includes "Circumstances of Immunity of Liability and Deduction of Liability" as a separate chapter. Some of the circumstances that were mentioned in Chapter 3 of the Tort Liability Law – namely, "force majeure", "self-defense" and "necessity" – are now provided in Chapter 8 on "Civil Liability" of the Book on General Provisions, while others – i.e., "negligence offset", "the victim's intentional default" and "a third party's causation" – are provided in Chapter 1 on "General Rules" of the Book on Tort Liability which also adds provisions for the "victim's voluntary assumption of risk" and "self-help behavior".

Yet, notwithstanding the evolution of these provisions from the Tort Liability Law to the Civil Code, there are still many problems affecting the coherence of the system arrangement of defenses against tort liability. In China's current legal system, the legislative mode of defenses belongs to the model of 'specific provisions plus general provisions'.

The original 'general provisions plus special provisions' refers to the general provisions regarding the grounds for exemption in Chapter 3 of the Tort Liability Law, and the special provisions regarding the grounds for exemption in special causes of action for tort liability. When applying the provisions of grounds for exemption in the Tort Liability Law, the special provisions should have been applicable first; if there were no special provisions, then the general provisions should have been applied. If the special provisions had excluded the application of the general provisions, naturally, the grounds for exemption set forth in the general provisions could not be applied. After the promulgation of the Chinese Civil Code, the relevant provisions in Chapter 8 on "Civil Liability" of the Book on General Provisions, are in a more general position than the provisions of the Tort Liability Law.[8] Therefore, there have been some

---

7 Fang Xinjun, *Interpretation of the Interests' Protection of Tort Liability* (Law Press China 2021) 280 (方新军, 侵权责任利益保护的解释论, 法律出版社).

8 Yang Lixin, 'The Autonomous Legislative System of China's Tort Liability Law Constructed by the Civil Code' (2023) 1 J Shanghai U Pol Sci & L (The Rule of Law Forum) 55 (杨立新, 〈民法典〉构建的我国侵权责任法自主立法体系, 《上海政法学院学报(法治论丛)》).

changes in the relevant system arrangement and contents of provisions of the Chinese Civil Code.[9]

The title of Chapter 3 of the Tort Liability Law no longer exists and defenses were moved into Chapter 1 on "Basic Rules" in its entirety, which can be taken to mean that legislators adopted the view that defenses are the negative constituent elements of tort liability. Since force majeure is provided in article 180, self-defense in article 181, and necessity in article 182 of the Book on General Provisions of the Chinese Civil Code, the above-mentioned defenses are deleted from the Book on Tort Liability. Meanwhile, the provisions of article 1176 on the "victim's voluntary assumption of risk" and article 1177 on "self-help behavior" have been added in the latter Book. However, there are many problems in dealing with the relationship between general provisions and special provisions in the Tort Liability Law, with no fundamental change having been made in the Book on Tort Liability of the Chinese Civil Code.

In terms of legislative technique, the general provision is an abstraction of common factors, which should be applicable to the law as a whole if there is no particular reason.[10] The defenses are exceptions to the general constituent elements of tort liability, and the defenses in special tort liability are exceptions to the general defenses. Such exceptions come in two forms, the first of which is constituted by a more specific provision; the second by a more special provision, such as excluding the application of general defenses to a certain special tort liability. Therefore, in the case of special tort liability, if there is no special provision, the general defenses should be applicable in their entirety, and if there are special considerations, exception provisions should be added specifically.

As an example of exceptions due to a more specific provision, the Chinese Civil Code does not provide a defense of the 'consent of the victim'. However, the notion can be derived from the general theory on civil juridical acts, and moreover the provision of explicit consent of the patient in article 1219 of the Chinese Civil Code can be considered as a more specific requirement of a broader principle.

An example of exceptions because of a special provision is the relationship between article 1175 of the Chinese Civil Code and articles 1204, 1233, and

9 Yang Lixin, 'The Construction and Application of the System of Reasons for Exemption of Tort Liability in the Civil Code' (2022) 5 Seeking Truth 107 (杨立新, 民法典侵权责任免责事由体系的构造与适用,《求是学刊》).

10 Jiang Qiang, 'Legislative Purpose and Legislative Technique of Tort Liability Law' (2010) 3 The People's Judicature 11 (姜强, 侵权责任法的立法目的与立法技术,《人民司法·应用》).

1250 of the Tort Liability Law. While the former provides that "a third party's causation" is a general defense, the latter specifically provided that the act of a third party did not act as a defense in cases of product liability, liability for environmental pollution and liability for damage caused by domestic animals, respectively. Article 1220 of the Chinese Civil Code, which provides that the consent cannot be obtained in cases of an emergency, is by contrast an example of exceptions because of a more specific provision with respect to the general (unwritten) defense of the consent of the victim.

The above provisions follow the logical relationship between the general provisions and the special provisions relatively well. In the above instances of specific cases for tort liability, if no special provisions are made for other defenses, we may assume that all other defenses are applicable. However, the incoherence of the system arrangement is obvious in Chapter 8 on 'Liability for Ultra-Hazardous Activity' of the Book on Tort Liability of the Chinese Civil Code.

Taking the general defense of 'force majeure' as an example, article 1237 of the Chinese Civil Code provides that "the business operator of the civil nuclear facility shall not bear tort liability if it can prove that the damage is caused by a situation such as war, armed conflict, riot and so forth or by the victim intentionally". This could be considered a narrowing of the scope of force majeure by the legislator, and it is reasonable to narrow the scope of grounds for exemption since the danger of nuclear facilities is very high. The provision of article 1238 on liability for damage caused by civil aircraft makes no reference to force majeure, therefore we can assume that there is no special provision, and force majeure is certainly applicable as a ground of exclusion. Moreover, this provision is reasonable in terms of value judgments, since the danger of a civil aircraft is obviously lower than that of a civil nuclear facility, and therefore the scope of the ground of exemption shall be broader. However, in the subsequent articles 1239 (on "liability for damage caused by ultra-hazardous materials") and 1240 ("liability for damage caused by an aerial work, high tension work, underground excavation or high-speed rail transport vehicle"), force majeure is enumerated as a ground of exclusion. This puts it into question whether force majeure is applicable as a ground of exemption in the preceding article 1238. It will be more reasonable to delete force majeure from articles 1239 and 1240. In addition force majeure is already provided as a general defense in article 180 of the Chinese Civil Code (specifying that the rule applies "except as otherwise provided by law"). With the deletion of force majeure from articles 1239 and 1240, it would clarify that force majeure can be a ground of defense in the whole of Chapter 8. With the exception of article 1237 which is a special provision, force majeure could be applied as a defense to any other liability for ultra-hazardous activity.

Articles 1237, 1238, 1239 and 1240 of Chapter 8 of the Book on Tort Liability of the Chinese Civil Code also provide an exemption from liability for cases of the victim's intentional act. This exemption could be deleted as well, since article 1174 of the Chinese Civil Code already provides the victim's intentional act as a general ground of exemption. Otherwise, the question may arise as to whether the fact that the victim's intentional act is not provided by subsequent articles 1241, 1242 and 1243 means that these articles shall not apply to the victim's intentional act as a ground of exemption.

The provisions of Chapter 8 of the Chinese Civil Code concerning defenses are not absolutely without merit. The second sentence of article 1239 provides that "[i]f the victim is grossly negligent as regards the occurrence of the damages, the liability of the possessor or user may be reduced". This sentence is very much in line with the criterion of coherence: all other things being equal, the more analytical relationships there are between statements belonging to a theory, the more coherent the theory becomes. The sentence clearly distinguishes between intention and gross negligence, avoiding the dogma of 'gross negligence is equivalent to intention', and thus falls within the exception to article 1174. At the same time, this sentence also clearly distinguishes gross negligence from general negligence, and therefore belongs to the exception of article 1173. That is to say, in the case of "liability for damage caused by ultra-hazardous materials", if the victim only has general negligence as regards the occurrence of the damage, the liability of the possessor or user shall not be reduced.

In article 73 of the original 'Tort Liability Law', the ground of reduced liability for damage caused by an aerial work, high tension work, underground excavation or high-speed rail transport vehicle was the victim's negligence as regards the occurrence of the damage. If only negligence was required, then this sentence could be deleted, because article 26 of the Tort Liability Law provided negligence offset, and as such, this sentence did not constitute an exception. However, a question immediately arises. These activities all belonged to the category of ultra-hazardous activities. Yet, it remained unclear why, in the case of liability for damage caused by ultra-hazardous materials, if the victim was grossly negligent as regards the occurrence of the damage, the liability of the tortfeasor might have been reduced, but, in the case of liability for damage caused by an aerial work, high tension work, underground excavation or high-speed rail transport vehicle, the liability of the operator might have been reduced if the victim was simply negligent as regards the occurrence of the damage. Therefore, article 1240 of the Chinese Civil Code changes the ground of reduced liability in article 73 of the Tort Liability Law to "the victim's gross negligence as regards the occurrence of the damage". Thus, a reasonable change.

Likewise, articles 1241, 1242 and 1243 of the Chinese Civil Code (on liability for damages caused by ultra-hazardous things that are lost, abandoned, illegally possessed or unlawfully obtained) do not specify the effect of the victim's fault on liability for damages. It may be argued that the provisions of articles 1173 and 1174 could be applied to the above special forms of tort liability. Yet, it is also true that there is no difference in nature between the dangerousness of these special forms of tort liability and liability for ultra-hazardous activities provided in articles 1239 and 1240. Therefore, it should be added in articles 1241, 1242 and 1243 that the tortfeasor who is grossly negligent as regards the occurrence of the damage may assume reduced liability.

The incoherence of this system of defenses has been laid down in Chapter 3 of the Tort Liability Law. Article 26 of the Tort Liability Law provided that "[w]here the victim of a tort is also at fault as to the occurrence of the damage, the liability of the tortfeasor may be reduced". Fault as a superior concept included intention, gross negligence, general negligence and slight negligence. However, article 27 provided that "[t]he actor shall not be liable for any damage that is intentionally caused by the victim". This leads to a logical contradiction. When there was a victim with intent, it was uncertain whether the liability of the tortfeasor should have been reduced or exempted. Therefore, it was more reasonable to change the term "fault" in article 26 to "negligence". Unfortunately, the above systemic incoherence remains unchanged in the Chinese Civil Code.

3.3 *Substantial Changes to Provisions on Apportionment of Loss*

Article 1186 of the Chinese Civil Code provides that "[w]here neither the victim nor the actor is at fault when damage occurs, both of them shall share the loss in accordance with provisions of law". Compared to article 24 of the Tort Liability Law, the expression "based on the actual situations" has been replaced by "in accordance with provisions of law". This change greatly limits the discretion of judges, since previous judicial practice tended to interpret broadly both article 24 of the Tort Liability Law and article 132 of the General Principles of the Civil Law, thus softening the doctrine of the liability for fault. The amendment of article 1186 of the Chinese Civil Code is meant to change this situation.

Article 132 of the 1987 General Principles of the Civil Law provided that "[w]here neither the victim nor the actor is at fault when damage occurs, both of them shall share civil liability according to the actual circumstances". Article 24 of the 2010 Tort Liability Law amended "share civil liability" to "share the loss", which actually indicated that apportionment of loss was not an independent doctrine of liability fixation, but rather a supplement to the existing doctrine of liability fixation. However, this change merely solved a theoretical controversy about whether apportionment referred to liability or to the loss, but did not prevent judges from applying the above-mentioned provisions broadly according to the actual circumstances.[11]

From the perspective of comparative law, China is almost unique in providing such general clauses of apportionment of loss in the General Principles of the Civil Law and in the Tort Liability Law. During the drafting process of BGB, some scholars also proposed that a general clause on fair liability should be provided, and the Second Draft of BGB even accepted this suggestion, however it was removed from the final text that went into force. The principle of fair liability was also initially provided in the civil codes of the former Soviet Union, but was removed in the 1960s. There are many reasons against the generalization of fair liability in legislation. First, it is unclear what positive basis makes a person bear liability in the absence of fault. Likewise, the legal ambiguity of the articles on fair liability is intolerable, since the benchmark of 'fairness' is unclear, and it clearly undermines the clarity and stability of the law. In addition, when applying fair liability (or apportionment of loss), courts mainly consider the property status of the parties; therefore, the amount of property becomes a doctrine of liability fixation for civil liability, with the result that "the obligation arises out of affluence".[12] In practice, the presence of a rule on apportionment of loss may lead to a situation in which courts do not carefully determine whether a person is at fault, or whether the operation engaged is ultra-hazardous, but instead directly apply the article on the apportionment of loss leniently based on convenience, human sympathy or other factors; thus it implies a failure of both liability for fault and liability without fault to play their due normative functions, and overall softens the system composition of the doctrine of liability fixation in the tort law.

The expression "[i]n accordance with provisions of law", now inserted in article 1186 of the Chinese Civil Code, mainly refers to the following articles of the Chinese Civil Code:

---

11 Yang Lixin, 'The successful transformation of civil Code to the protection method of civil rights in China' (2022) 4 J National Prosecutors College 133 (杨立新, 民法典对我国民事权利保护方法的成功改造,《国家检察官学院学报》).

12 Wei Zhenying, 'Civil Liability as stipulated in the General Principles of Civil Law—From the Property Law to the Civil Code' (2006) 5 Mod L Sci 45 (魏振瀛,〈民法通则〉规定的民事责任—从物权法到民法典的规定,《现代法学》).

- article 182(1) and (2), according to which, whoever triggers an emergency shall bear civil liability for the damage so caused in necessity. The person who caused damage in necessity shall not bear civil liability if the emergency is triggered by natural reasons, but the People's Court may, at its discretion, order him or her to pay a reduced sum of money to the aggrieved party;
- article 183, according to which, where one suffers damage due to his or her act of protecting another's civil rights or interests, the tortfeasor shall bear civil liability, and the People's Court may, at its discretion, order the beneficiary to pay a reduced sum of money to the victim. In the case of no tortfeasor, absconding tortfeasor, or tortfeasor unable to bear civil liabilities, the beneficiary shall pay a reduced sum of money to the victim at the People's Court's discretion if the victim does claim for such remedy;
- article 1188, according to which, where a person without the civil capacity to carry out juridical acts or with limited civil capacity to carry out juridical acts causes damage to another person, the guardian shall be liable in tort. If the guardian has fulfilled the guardian's duties, tort liability may be reduced. Where a person without civil capacity to carry out juridical acts or with limited civil capacity to carry out juridical acts, who has assets causes damage to another person, the compensation shall be paid out of his or her own assets. The guardian shall make up any shortfall in the compensation;
- article 1190(1), according to which, where a person with full civil capacity to carry out civil juridical acts causes damage to another person as the result of temporary loss of consciousness or loss of control, if the actor is at fault, the actor shall bear tort liability; if the actor is not at fault, the actor shall compensate the victim appropriately depending on the actor's economic condition;
- article 1192(2), according to which, where, during the provision of labor services, any damage caused to the party providing labor services due to an act of a third party, the party providing labor services shall be entitled to ask the third party to bear tort liability, or be compensated by the party receiving labor services. The party receiving labor services that has paid compensation may be reimbursed by the third party;
- article 1254(1), according to which, it is forbidden to throw anything out of a building. Where anything thrown out of a building or falling off a building causes damage to another person, the tortfeasor shall bear tort liability. Where, upon investigation, it is hard to determine

the specific tortfeasor, all the users of the building who could possibly have committed the tort except those who can prove that they are not the tortfeasor shall compensate the victim. After paying compensation, the users of the building who could possibly have committed the tort shall be reimbursed by the tortfeasor.

CHAPTER 17

A Swiss Perspective on the Book on Tort Liability of the Chinese Civil Code

Franz Werro

1 Introduction

The present contribution comments on Dean Xinjun Fang's chapter "The structure and contents of the Book on Tort Liability of the Chinese Civil Code".[1] While it offers an insight into the doctrinal discussion surrounding this part of the Chinese Civil Code, this chapter does not address any analysis of the cases these rules have triggered so far. This is no doubt a deliberate and legitimate choice. While a legal realist would claim that codified rules do not reveal how the law actually works, I appreciate that their presentation finds an interesting academic justification. Indeed, I think that, as it is, the chapter reveals some of the legislator's fundamental choices.

Xinjun Fang, who I will refer to as the author, begins his analysis with a few remarks on the structure of the Chinese Civil Code and its seventh Book on Tort Liability. What immediately strikes the European civilian eye is the separation of that Book from the rest of the law dealing with obligations. While I cannot appreciate the reason for that legislative choice, I gather that it is the obvious output of a historical development. To me, it would certainly have been interesting to know what in the history of Chinese law and its law of obligations and tort led to that choice. However, this was not the focus of the author's presentation. As a consequence and leaving aside the structure of the book that the author explains in detail, I will limit my remarks to the content of the codified rules in the book of tort liability as the author presents them.

The author's paper concentrates on the novelties of these rules. I will not depart from that choice. In the light of the order the author chose to make his own presentation, and gathering some thoughts on selected aspects only, I will first focus on the general clause on tort liability (Section 2). I will then address defenses against tort liability (Section 3) and apportionment of loss (Section 4). I will end with a few concluding remarks (Section 5).

1 See Xinjun Fang's chapter, above in this book.

 | DOI:10.1163/9789004704428_018

2 The General Clause on Tort Liability

The general clause on tort liability finds expression in article 1165 (1) of the Chinese Civil Code (hereinafter: CCC).[2] Article 1165 (1) CCC states: "[a]n actor who through his fault infringes upon another person's civil-law rights and interests shall bear tort liability". One important feature of this provision lies in its adhesion to the model of § 823 of the German Civil Code (hereinafter: BGB).[3] Indeed, very much like that BGB provision, article 1165 CCC contains an explicit reference to the protected rights whose infringement must have occurred for a tort claim to exist.[4] The author writes that "[s]ince article 106(2) of General Principles of the Civil Law [...] belongs to the French model of general clauses in theoretical framework, [...] the Tort Liability Law [...] adopted the French model, on the basis of simply following the existing path". While I agree that the Chinese provision is a general clause of liability,[5] I do not find it to correspond to the French one.[6]

Contrary to article 1240 of the French Civil Code (hereinafter: CCfr),[7] a careless act or fault (*'faute'*) under the CCC alone does not prompt liability. Very much like the drafters of the European Draft Common Frame of

---

2 All translations in English of the Chinese Civil Code are provided by the official translation of the People's Republic of China, available at <https://english.www.gov.cn/archive/lawsregulations/202012/31/content_WS5fedad98c6d0f72576943005.html> accessed 9 October 2023. The editors of this book kindly provided this link.

3 For more details, see Gert Brüggemeier, 'European Civil Liability Law outside Europe. The Example of the Big Three: China, Brazil, Russia' (2011) J Eur Tort L 1–22.

4 § 823 BGB states: "(1) A person who, intentionally or negligently, unlawfully injures the life, limb, health, freedom, property or some other right of another person is liable to provide compensation to the other party for the damage arising there from. (2) The same duty is incumbent on a person who commits a breach of a statute that is intended to protect another person. If, according to the contents of the statute, it is possible to violate it also without fault, then liability to compensation only exists in the case of fault" (the translation is available at <https://www.gesetze-im-internet.de/englisch_bgb/englisch_bgb.html#p4209>, accessed 9 October 2023).

5 Xinjun Fang (n 1).

6 Article 1165 (2) CCC also provides that "[w]here an actor is presumed to be at fault according to the provisions of law and is unable to prove that he is not at fault, the actor shall bear tort liability". To me, this does not appear to add much if anything to what the provisions of law referred to, and article 1165(1) CCC already say. In the absence of further knowledge, I will assume that article 1165(2) CCC only has some pedagogical value.

7 Article 1240 CCfr states: "Any human action whatsoever which causes harm to another creates an obligation in the person by whose fault it occurred to make reparation for it" (the translation is made by David Gruning, Alain R. Levasseur, John Randy Trahan, Estelle Roy, 'Traduction du Code Civil français en anglais version bilingue' (2015), available at <https://shs.hal.science/halshs-01385107/document>, accessed 9 October 2023).

Reference (hereinafter: DCFR; see article VI.-1:101 DCFR, that refers to "legally relevant damage"), the Chinese legislator appears to have found inspiration in the German model.[8] That model imposes a duty of care principally with respect to losses resulting from the infringement of certain goods or that of a written (or unwritten) 'protective norm' ('*Schutznorm*') of behavior. While French law aims to repair all reasonably foreseeable losses that result from careless behavior, German law, and thus Chinese law as well, exclude compensation for pure economic losses as a matter of principle.[9]

In the words of the author, the choice of the legislator results from a balance between social security and freedom of behavior.[10] Indeed, the Chinese legislator chose to "pay more attention to the freedom of conduct of civil subjects".[11] However, as the author also notes, the difficulty did not end here, as the trend has also consisted in a slow but steady expansion of the scope of protection under Chinese tort law.[12] One learns that article 2(2) of the Tort Liability Law listed eighteen kinds of named rights.[13] This list contains many more indeed than the ones listed in the BGB[14] or recognized in Swiss practice, for example.[15] As the author notes, article 2 of the Tort Liability Law leaves it to judicial practice to define the meaning and the scope of these rights.[16]

One knows of the rigidity of the German law of tort, as articulated in the BGB, and of all the complications it led to, including the creation of judicial

---

8 Article VI.-1:101 DCFR: "(1) A person who suffers legally relevant damage has a right to reparation from a person who caused the damage intentionally or negligently or is otherwise accountable for the causation of the damage. (2) Where a person has not caused legally relevant damage intentionally or negligently that person is accountable for the causation of legally relevant damage only if Chapter III so provides".

9 For a comprehensive comparative approach on the issue, see Mauro Bussani and Vernon Palmer (eds), *Pure Economic Loss in Europe* (Cambridge University Press 2003; Chinese version by Law Press China 2005).

10 Xinjun Fang (n 1).

11 ibid.

12 ibid.

13 ibid.

14 Unlike § 823 BGB, article 41 of the Swiss Code of Obligations does not contain a list of rights. Caselaw essentially limits them to the right to property and personality rights. That notion remains in the hands of judicial practice but refers not only to life, as well as physical and mental integrity, but also to a person's honor, privacy and other personality entitlements.

15 Under Swiss law, the protected rights are the so-called 'absolute' rights, that is those rights protected by the entirety of the legal order, independently of any contractual arrangement. See, for example, Franz Werro, *La responsabilité civile* (3rd edn, Stämpfli 2017) 105 ff.

16 Xinjun Fang (n 1).

doctrines of various kinds.[17] It would have been interesting to learn why the Chinese legislator preferred the German model to the French one. In the absence of a reference to protected rights in article 1240 CCfr , the French system, as well as the tort law of the EU, as it emanates from the European Court of Justice (hereinafter: ECJ), arguably offer a substantial advantage in flexibility.[18]

While open flexibility in the legislative framework might trigger the fear of a 'flooding' tort system, it may also increase legal certainty. Indeed, systemic rigidity bears the risk of unexpected exceptions and thus of a certain legal uncertainty. Indeed, courts may want to bypass the limits the system wishes to impose and ignore the absence of an infringement to a protected right in order to avoid that a pure economic loss caused carelessly remains uncompensated for. As we know, judges in Germany and Switzerland have often 'invented' protective norms, so as to make sure that unfair losses resulting from a careless behavior do not remain uncompensated for.[19] Arguably, this expansion of the tort boundaries often remains uncertain if not arbitrary.[20] Swiss practice shows this uncertainty with the somewhat random finding of protective norms as well as of doctrines such as liability based on disappointed expectations ('*Vertrauenshaftung*', '*la responsabilité pour la confiance déçue*') or other schemes expanding the scope of contractual protection.[21]

Be that as it may, choosing a model over another does not happen by chance. As law is culture, just as culture is law,[22] legal choices are path dependent,

17 Gerhard Wagner, 'BGB §823 Schadenersatzpflicht', in Franz Jürgen Säcker, Roland Rixecker, Hartmut Oetker, Bettina Limperg (eds), *Münchner Kommentar zum BGB* (5th edn, Beck 2009) 142–145; Melanie Mathis, 'BGB §823 Schadensersatzpflicht', in Sabine von Göler (ed), *BGB-online Kommentar* (von Göler Verlagsgesellschaft 2023) 36.

18 For the European approach, see European Court of Justice, case C-46/93 and C-48/93, *Brasserie du Pêcheur* [1996] ECR I-01029.

19 ATF (Arrêts du Tribunal fédéral suisse) 101 Ib 252; ATF 102 II 85.

20 Swiss practice shows that judges have found norms to be protective of financial interests but have rejected others to be the same. There is no way to rationally explain their choices, other than through opportunistic or political preferences. For a seminal study, see Peter Gauch and Justin Sweet, 'Deliktshaftung für reinen Vermögensschaden', in *Feschrift Max Keller zum 65. Geburtstag* (Schulthess 1989), 117–140; for further studies, see, among many others, Franz Werro, 'Tort Liability for Pure Economic Loss: A Critique of Current Trends in Swiss Law', in Efstathios K. Banakas (ed), *Civil Liability for Pure Economic Loss* (Kluwer 1996), 183–196. I would want to add at this point in time that these preferences are unavoidable and even acceptable, at least as long as they follow a certain coherence and a transparent justification.

21 ATF 120 II 331, Journal des Tribunaux 1995 I 359; ATF 121 III 350. On that subject, see the many contributions in Christine Chappuis and Bénédict Winiger (eds), *La responsabilité fondée sur la confiance. Journée de la responsabilité civile 2000* (Schulthess 2001).

22 See Werner Menski, 'Plural Worlds of Law and the Search for Living Law', in Werner Gephart (ed), *Rechtsanalyse als Kulturforschung* (Vittorio Klostermann 2012) 71–88.

culturally and politically, and no rationalization will help legislative choices in that regard.[23] I have long advocated the proposition that the French model was preferable for Swiss law, and this effort found expression in article 46 of the draft of model Code 2020 (hereinafter: CO2020).[24] However, that effort remained without success, because the majority of jurists in Switzerland have found inspiration in German legal thinking for more than a century. I finally realized that I could only lose my cause when the guardians of the legal temple warned me against the dangers of an innovation they saw as a dangerous deviation.[25] For similar reasons, '*Brasserie du Pêcheur*', a major ECJ case that triggered the hope of some to contribute to the unification of tort law in Europe,[26] has only found very limited acceptance, if any, in Germany and elsewhere. One of the reasons is that '*Brasserie du Pêcheur*' espoused a French approach to tort law, and not at all a German one.[27]

3 Defenses against Tort Liability

From the Chapter III of the Tort liability Law, defenses moved to Chapter I of Book Seven of the CCC, under the 'Basic Rules'. As the author notes, the legislator added two provisions in the Book on Tort Liability: article 1176 CCC deals with the victim's voluntary assumption of risks and article 1177 CCC deals with

23 For an in-depth study, see Mauro Bussani and Marta Infantino, 'The many Cultures of Tort Law', in Mauro Bussani and Anthony J. Sebok (eds), *Comparative Tort Law. Global Perspectives* (2nd edn, Edward Elgar 2021) 11–38; Mauro Bussani and Marta Infantino, 'Tort Law and Legal Cultures' (2015) 63 Am J Comp Law 77–108.

24 Article 46 CO2020 states: "A person who infringes upon a duty of care without justification is liable for damages." For a commentary, see Walter Fellmann, Christoph Müller, Franz Werro, 'Des obligations résultant d'actes illicites', in Claire Huguenin and Reto M. Hilty (ed), *Code des Obligations Suisse 2020. Projet relatif à une nouvelle partie générale* (Schulthess 2013) 152, 156 ff.

25 See Bruno Schmidlin, 'Das Schweizer Obligationenrecht 2020' (2015) 111(2) Schweizerische Juristen-Zeitung 25–34, severally criticizing the proposition made in the draft revision to the CO in this respect.

26 See Walter van Gerven, 'The ECJ Case-Law as a Means of Unification of Private Law', in Arthur S. Hartkamp et al. (eds), *Towards a European Civil Code* (3rd edn, Ars Aequi-Kluwer 2004), 101–123, at 107 ff.

27 On the limits of the impact on the transformation of the national law of the Member States in the European Union of that decision, see Franz Werro, 'European Private Law: Quo Vadis?', in Thibaut Massart and Abdoulaye Mbotaingar (eds), *Liber Amicorum en l'honneur du professeur Joël Monéger* (LexisNexis 2017) 809–819, at 814.

self-help.[28] While these changes seem structural, they also raise substantive issues with respect to the relationship between the general provisions and these special provisions.

One cannot however assess these difficulties without more knowledge about Chinese civil law, and I confess having trouble understanding the incoherences the author denounces in his paper.[29] The job is all the more difficult that the defenses are scattered in various chapters of the code.[30] There are certainly good reasons for this legislative technique, but it takes an insider to grasp them and relate to their place in the code. An outsider like me remains at a loss.

In any event, the author explains that the provisions dealing with defenses in the CCC have some merit.[31] To give an example, he refers to article 1239 CCC that deals with the "gross negligence" of the victim.[32] He points out that the term was carefully chosen and that it must be distinguished from intention and other forms of fault.[33] With respect to liability for damage caused by "ultra-hazardous materials", this means that general carelessness of the victim will not reduce the amount of damages the victim can claim.[34]

---

28 Article 1176 CCC states: "[w]here a person voluntarily participates in a recreational or sports activity with certain inherent risks and thus suffers damage due to another participant's act, he may not request the other participant to bear tort liability unless the damage is caused by the latter's intentional act or by his gross negligence. The liability of an organizer of the activity shall be governed by the provisions of articles 1198 through 1201 of this Code". Article 1177 CCC states: "[w]here a person's lawful rights and interests are infringed upon and he may suffer irreparable harm if actions are not immediately taken because the situation is urgent and no protection from the State organ is immediately available, he may take reasonable measures such as seizing the property of the tortfeasor to the extent necessary for protecting his lawful rights and interests, provided that he shall immediately thereafter request the relevant State organ to handle it. A victim who has taken an improper measure so that damage is caused to another person shall bear tort liability".

29 Xinjun Fang (n 1).

30 ibid.

31 ibid.

32 Article 1239 CCC states: "[w]here the possession or use of flammable, explosive, highly toxic, highly radioactive, strongly corrosive, highly pathogenic, or other ultrahazardous things causes damage to another person, the possessor or user thereof shall bear tort liability, provided that such a possessor or user shall not assume any liability if it can be proven that the damage was intentionally caused by the victim or caused by force majeure. Where the infringed person is grossly negligent for the occurrence of the damage, the liability of the possessor or user may be mitigated".

33 Xinjun Fang (n 1).

34 ibid.

This approach reminds me of the choice the French legislator made in the '*Loi Badinter*' with respect to road accidents.[35] Indeed, this French statute forbids the defendant to raise carelessness of the victim as a defense. When the victim has acted in a faulty manner, not only will damages not be reduced (as it would be the case under Swiss law);[36] but exclusion of liability will only be possible in cases of exclusive and intentional fault.[37] French courts have applied this exception to liability quite restrictively, stressing the importance of the protection granted to victims of an ultrahazardous activity such as the operation of an automobile.[38]

4 Apportionment of Loss or of Damages

Under this title, the author analyzes the important changes that the Chinese legislator has made with respect to the apportionment of loss.[39] As he explains, article 1186 CCC provides the general rule on apportionment in cases provided for by law.[40] According to this provision, "[w]here neither the victim nor the actor is at fault when damage occurs, both of them shall share the loss in accordance with provisions of law".

The author further explains what "provisions of law" are referred to by article 1186 CCC[41] – an issue that I will leave aside here. He makes the point that this provision limits judicial discretion more than in the past, because the former rule on apportionment (article 132 of the 1986 General Principles of the

35 Article 2 ff, *Loi n° 85–677 du 5 juillet 1985 tendant à l'amélioration de la situation des victimes d'accidents de la circulation et à l'accélération des procédures d'indemnisation* (hereinafter: *Loi n° 85–677*).

36 Article 59(1) of the Swiss Road Traffic Act ('*Loi fédérale sur la circulation routière*') provides that the guardian is not liable if the accident finds its cause in force majeure, the gross fault of the victim or of as third provided he has been faultless and that his vehicle was not defective. Article 59(2) of the Swiss Road Traffic Act adds that, if the keeper cannot escape liability under the circumstances set forth in the first paragraph, but proves that the victim was at fault, the judge will assess damages in the light of the circumstances.

37 Article 3, *Loi n° 85–677*.

38 Cour de Cassation, Chambre civile 2, 28 April 1986, 85–11.175, 261; Cour de Cassation, Chambre civile 2, 19 February 1986, 84–17.795, 552.

39 Xinjun Fang (n 1).

40 ibid.

41 ibid.

Civil Law) made it possible to apportion liability on the basis of the "actual circumstances" of the case.[42]

The author remarks that China is almost unique in providing this system of apportionment of loss in tort law.[43] He explains that scholars had proposed a general clause during the drafting process of the code, but that the legislator did not accept it.[44] The author mentions that the same provision existed in the former Soviet Union Civil Code, but that the lawmaker abandoned it in the 1960s; the author then goes on to explain why.[45]

From my perspective, these observations are quite interesting, because somewhat like Chinese law, Swiss law rejects the idea of an 'all or nothing' system of liability. It does so by refusing to cover the full amount of the victim's loss in certain situations and accordingly allows for a reduction in damages. Indeed, articles 43 and 44 of the Swiss Code of Obligations (hereinafter: CO) provide that the judge has to apportion damages taking into account the gravity of the defendant's fault and circumstances (article 43 CO) as well as other mitigating factors (article 44 CO).[46]

Under the heading 'Determining compensation', article 43 CO states the following:

> 1. The court determines the form and extent of the compensation provided for damage incurred, with due regard to the circumstances and the degree of culpability.
>
> 1bis. Where an animal kept as a pet rather than for investment or commercial purposes has been injured or killed, the court may take appropriate account of its sentimental value to its owner or his dependents. [...]
>
> 2. Where damages are awarded in the form of periodic payments, the debtor must at the same time post security.

Under the heading 'Grounds for reducing compensation', article 44 CO provides:

> 1. Where the person suffering damage consented to the harmful act or circumstances attributable to him helped give rise to or compound

42 ibid. Under article 132 of the 1986 General Principles of Civil Law, "[w]here neither the victim nor the actor is at fault when damage occurs, both of them shall share civil liability according to the actual circumstances".

43 Xinjun Fang (n 1).

44 ibid.

45 ibid.

46 The following translation of articles 43 and 44 CO is provided by the Federal Department of Justice and is available at <https://www.fedlex.admin.ch/eli/cc/27/317_321_377/en>, accessed 9 October 2023.

the damage or otherwise exacerbated the position of the party liable for it, the court may reduce the compensation due or even dispense with it entirely.

2. The court may also reduce the compensation award in cases in which the damage was caused neither willfully nor by gross negligence and where payment of such compensation would leave the liable party in financial hardship.

This is not the place to analyze in detail what Swiss practice has made of these provisions. A few remarks may however be useful to bring some additional insight.

Firstly, the factors listed in these two provisions overall lead judges to take into account equitable and social considerations in the assessment of damages.[47] While some still play a role, others have lost their importance, especially where insurance schemes help the defendant (with liability insurance) or the victim (with first-party mandatory insurance). That explains for instance why taking into account financial hardship has become obsolete in practice, as most defendants have liability insurance.[48]

Secondly, the idea of determining damages according to the importance of fault – or 'culpability', as the English translation by the Federal Department of Justice unfortunately suggests – only plays a limited role.[49] Courts do take that circumstance into account when it comes to measuring children's liability. The importance of fault also plays a role in a case of several tortfeasors. The extent of the regress that one of them will have against the others will be measured in accordance with the importance of their respective fault.[50] For the rest, the idea of measuring damages in relation to fault remains largely dead letter.

Thirdly, under the notion of "circumstances" within the meaning of article 43 CO, case law has included gratuity or the desire to help reduce damages owed by the wrongdoer. Courts have at times also considered the privileged financial situation of the victim or even their imminent death. Further, when applying article 44 CO, courts have taken into account the preexisting condition of the victim[51] or their own assumption of risk.[52] While new insurance

47 Werro (n 15) 376 ff, 404; see also ATF 104 II 184.

48 See for instance ATF 103 II 330 (part 4).

49 ATF 112 II 138.

50 ATF 104 II 184; ATF 100 II 337 (part 3a).

51 ATF 113 II 86; TF 4C.416/1999 of 20 February 2000; ATF 131 III 12.

52 See Werro (n 15) 375; Stephan Weber, 'Umstände für die der Geschädigte nicht einstehen muss' (2007) 1 HAVE/REAS 108–111.

schemes have made some of the circumstances traditionally listed less relevant than they were in times without insurance, courts still like to assess damages in the light of equitable considerations.

Fourthly, contributory fault also plays an important role in this context. In cases in which the victim contributes to the occurrence of the damage by acting in a careless way, a court may take this into account when determining the damages (article 44(1) CO).

Furthermore, the tortfeasor may be entirely exempt from their liability if the victim's fault constitutes gross negligence or the victim's fault is so important that it interrupts proximate causation between the tortfeasor's action and the harm.[53] However, as mentioned above, article 59(1) of the Swiss Road Traffic Act, for example, makes that exclusion of liability more difficult as it requires for the defendant or persons, he is liable for, not to be at fault. According to the same provision, defectiveness of the vehicle will also rule out an exclusion of liability.[54]

Finally, the victim may also have a duty to contain the harm by taking appropriate and reasonable measures after it has occurred. Courts base this duty on the principle of good faith.[55] Whether and to what extent judges will impose this duty will depend on the circumstances of the case.[56] For example, an injured person who does not seek medical help may lose the right to receive full compensation.[57]

5 By Way of Concluding

This short text does not do justice to the wealth of information in Xinjun Fang' chapter. Nevertheless, it provides, I hope, an example of an outsider's partial

53 ATF 142 IV 237 (c. 1.5.2); ATF 133 V 14, c. 10.2.

54 Article 59(2) of the Swiss Road Traffic Act states: "[if,] however, the keeper cannot be released under para. 1, but proves that the injured party was at fault, the court will set the compensation, taking all the circumstances into account" (author's own translation).

55 In its unofficial translation (available at <https://www.fedlex.admin.ch/eli/cc/24/233_245_233/en>, accessed 9 October 2023), article 2 of the Swiss Civil Code states: "1. Every person must act in good faith in the exercise of his or her rights and in the performance of his or her obligations. 2. The manifest abuse of a right is not protected by law".

56 Annick Achtari, *Le devoir du lésé de minimiser son dommage: étude en droit des obligations* (Schultess 2008) 71 ff; see also Pascal Pichonnaz, 'Le devoir du lésé de diminuer son dommage', in Franz Werro (ed), *La fixation de l'indemnité. Colloque du droit de la responsabilité civile Fribourg 2003* (Stämpfli 2004) 109–134.

57 See Werro (n 15) 377.

reaction. By definition, a comparatist approaches foreign law as an outsider. Instead of ignoring or fighting it, the comparatist should embrace this position and accept that their investigation will be fragmentary. Furthermore, their investigation will rest on cultural biases and other preferences, but indeed offer a picture of that foreign law an insider's representation would not. This is what I did here no doubt, without even seeing what will probably appear strange to Xinjun Fang.

In the future, it would be interesting to expand the scope of the study of tort law under the Chinese Civil Code and to analyze how practice and caselaw have dealt with it in general. It would also be interesting to see how the new codified rules have triggered outcomes the old rules had not. Admittedly, the task of the comparatist will then become more difficult. Indeed, interesting comparative work requires, in my opinion, the knowledge of the language of the law under study so as to minimize the distortions translation brings about. Also, I think that without the help of another discipline, which provides a broader understanding of the law and grasps what makes foreign law different, legal comparison is likely to remain bookish. Comparatists may want to render practical services, but they will only do so if they engage in theory, with critical lenses.

Acknowledgements

I wish to thank Andrea Chawla, BLaw, research assistant at the Faculty of Law of the University of Fribourg (Switzerland) for her precious help in finalizing this paper.

PART 3

The Outer Significance of the Chinese Civil Code

CHAPTER 18

The Significance of the Chinese Civil Code in the Special Administrative Regions of Macao and Hong Kong

唐曉晴 *Io Cheng Tong*

1 Introduction: The Chinese Civil Code and the Civil Laws of Macao and Hong Kong

The Civil Code of the People's Republic of China (hereinafter the 'Chinese Civil Code') was enacted on May 28, 2020 and entered into force on January 1, 2022, fulfilling the aspirations of legal modernization which were pursued by several generations of Chinese legal scholars over the past a hundred years. During the last decades of the 19th century, with the Qing Dynasty facing internal and external challenges, the Qing Imperial Court decided to carry out political and economic reforms, which included the reform and modernization of the legal system.[1] Such reform and modernization drew inspiration from the influential legal traditions found in different jurisdictions around the world. The model provided by some jurisdictions of civil law traditions was judged more suitable for China's conditions, and was chosen as a benchmark for the reform endeavor.[2] Particularly, the adoption of a series of systematic and complete codes, especially the civil code, usually found in jurisdictions of civil law tradition, such as those of continental Europe, was considered an important objective of the reform. Therefore, the codification of civil law entered the agenda of Chinese legislators, setting off a process that lasted for the past century.

The successive versions of the Chinese Civil Code, regardless of the era in which they were drawn up and regardless of the nature of the government that drew them up, clearly reflected the influence of some civil law systems of continental Europe, namely Germany, France and Switzerland, and of Japan. The newly adopted Chinese Civil Code is no exception. The design of its seven books not only follows the modern Continental Civil Code structure

---

1 Ma Zhe, 'Uma Breve Introdução da História da Codificação do Direito Civil Chinês' (2021) 49 Boletim da Faculdade de Direito da Universidade de Macau 177–187.

2 Percy R. Luney, 'Traditions and Foreign Influences: Systems of Law in China and Japan' (1989) 52 L & Cont Probs 129–150.

 | DOI:10.1163/9789004704428_019

comprising a general part and several special parts,[3] but also adopts some basic concepts and institutions of civil law, such as the concepts of 'legal person', 'legal transaction', unjust enrichment and real rights. Alongside this civil law heritage of various origin,[4] it is believed that some values labelling the Chinese characteristics have also found expressions in the new Chinese Civil Code. For example, Article 1186 of the new Chinese Civil Code retains the unique doctrine of 'liability in equity': once an injury occurs, the party who caused the injury is partially liable, even though he was not at fault. This reflects the concept of distributive justice derived from Chinese moral philosophy.[5] However, compared with the old rules, the new Civil Code has also amended the concept of 'liability in equity' from "based on the actual situations" to "in accordance with the law", thus changing the way the rule of equitable contribution to loss is applied.[6] Another instance concerns ownership of land, and the traditional Chinese principle that land cannot be privately owned.[7] In 1986, General Principles of the Civil Law established a land usufructuary rights with socialist characteristics, land contracted management rights, which contracted state-owned land to individuals. In order to increase the circulation of land in the market, the new Chinese Civil Code provides for a new land management right in Articles 339–342, which is based on the socialist market economy with Chinese characteristics. Finally, another example worth of mention is the setting apart of personality rights as an independent part of the new Chinese Civil Code, comprising 51 articles, which is remarkably unlike any other civil code. This innovation came about after decades of debate around

3 Although the Chinese Civil Code also has its own characteristics: in addition to the general part, it consists of six (instead of four) special parts, which regulate respectively rights *in rem*, contracts, rights of personality, marriage and family, succession and civil liability.

4 Among which the Portuguese/Macau Civil Code and Portuguese legal scholarship also played a role. See Io Cheng Tong, 'O Código Civil Português e o seu impacto na recodificação do direito Civil de Macau e na codificação em curso na República Popular da China', in António Pinto Monteiro (ed), *50 Anos do Código Civil* (Almedina 2019) 425–439.

5 See Hao Jiang, 'The Making of a Civil Code in China: Promises and Perils of a New Civil Law' (2021) 95 Tulane L Rev 782 –783.

6 See Xiaojian Zheng, 'Liability in Equity, Sharing of Damages and the Science of the Civil Code – The "Origin" and "History" of Article 1186 of the Civil Code' (2022) 1 L Rev 90.

7 In Macao and Hong Kong, the land and natural resources shall be State property, with the exception of the private land recognized as such according to the laws in force before the establishment of the Macao Special Administrative Region. See Basic Law of the Macao Special Administrative Region of the People's Republic of China, Article 7; Basic Law of the Hong Kong Special Administrative Region of the People's Republic of China, Article 7.

previously existing Chinese rules of tort law, and their limits in apprehending new instances of tort liability.[8]

Against this backdrop, this chapter examines the relevance of the Chinese Civil Code for the peculiar legal systems of the Hong Kong Special Administrative Region (hereinafter, Hong Kong) and the Macao Special Administrative Region (hereinafter, Macao) (together, the SARs). The SARs retain their specific legal heritage, which are the result of their history, and are currently granted legislative and judicial autonomy by the PRC's central government under the principle of 'One country, two systems' enshrined in their respective Basic Laws.

The legal system of Hong Kong testifies of its past under British occupation, and has existed as a different and separated system from the one of the Qing Dynasty since 1841. Along with its Basic Law and Statutes,[9] the legal systems of Hong Kong retains the characteristics of a common law jurisdiction, including a system of common law, rules of equity, the doctrine of precedent and the connection with other jurisdictions pertaining to the same legal tradition whose decisions are of persuasive authority within the adjudicatory process of the courts of Hong Kong. The Hong Kong legal system is unique in that the common law system operates under the civil law system of China.[10] As such and as a jurisdiction pertaining to the common law tradition, Hong Kong provides a gateway to investigate how the common law legal tradition may respond to the modernization of civil law in PRC.

Similarly, Macau has a specific legal heritage, influenced by its historical past. Macau's legal systems is largely of Portuguese origin, and therefore bears similarities with both the Germanic system and the Roman law tradition. The current Civil Code of Macao very closely replicates the structure and most of the provisions of the 1966 Portuguese Civil Code. The 1966 Civil Code differed significantly from its predecessor, the 1867 Civil Code, in terms of form and structure. Although the idea persists that the reform process of the 1966

---

8 See Liming Wang, 'On the Reason for taking the Personality Right Law as an independent part in the Civil Code' (2017) 6 L Rev 1. See also Lixin Yang, 'Innovative Development of Personality Rights Legislation in Chinese Civil Code' (2020) 4 Studies in Law and Business 18; Jun Xue, 'Two Basic Theoretical Models of Personality Rights and Chinese Legislation on Personality Rights' (2004) 4 Studies in Law and Business 63.

9 With respect to civil matters, Relevant legal provisions are sparsely found in different sections of Hong Kong Ordinance: Conveyancing and Property Ordinance (Cap. 219); Contracts (Rights of Third Parties) Ordinance (Cap. 623); Personal Data (Privacy) Ordinance (Cap. 486); Marriage Ordinance (Cap. 181); Probate and Administration Ordinance (Cap. 10).

10 See Stefan H C Lo, Kevin Kwok-yin Cheng, Wing Hong Chui, *The Hong Kong Legal System* (2nd ends, Cambridge University Press 2020) especially in the preface to the Second Edition.

Portuguese Civil Code was only formally inspired by the German legal tradition, while the spirit of roman law lingered on, the adoption of a five-book system of general and special provisions, along with the use of concepts and institutions such as 'capacity', 'legal personality' and 'legal transactions', clearly testify the influence of the German Civil Code on the Portuguese reform, and by extension, the Civil Code of Macau. Under this perspective, the new Chinese Civil Code and the Civil Code of Macau share an important source, the systematic approach and concepts of continental Europe, which creates the crucial and foundational conditions for a dialogue between the two jurisdictions. However, there are certain differences between the two systems:

- From the formal or structural perspective, the Chinese Civil Code has six Special Provisions under the General Provisions: Real Rights, Contracts, Personality Rights, Marriage and Family, Succession, and Tort Liabilities. By contrast, the Macao Civil Code, like the BGB, has just four Special Provisions: the law of obligations and property law, and the family law and succession law. Under the General Provisions, the four Special Provisions form two levels, two by two.
- From the substantial perspective, the divergence between the Chinese Civil Code and the Macau Civil Code are obvious at least in the provisions about preliminary contract, unjust enrichment, transfer of ownership and possession (and *usucapio,* which is provided in the Macau Civil Code but not in the Chinese Civil Code).

Finally, a few aspects that are specific to the geographical region of the Greater Bay Area, comprising the Chinese Province of Guangdong, Hong Kong and Macao (the GBA), have bearing on the significance of the Chinese Civil Code for the two SARs. Within the GBA, increased economic integration will lead to and ever-closer interaction and mutual influence of the three legal systems of civil law and common law tradition, against the backdrop of the overarching jurisdiction of China and the influence of the Chinese Civil Code. In addition, the GBA harbors interesting potentialities for legal integration, such as the Guangdong-Macao Hengqin Deep Co-Operation Zone, currently under construction. Such experiment of integration at the administrative and economic level could bring about the convergence of civil and commercial rules towards the Macau model, offering a livable and business-friendly legal environment, on par with international standards. Another instance of convergence and integration within the GBA could be represented by Hong Kong SAR acting as a platform for investment into China and out of China. The traditional financial prosperity, openness and safety guaranteed in Hong Kong SAR are bound to attract growing investment from both Mainland China and foreign jurisdictions, fostering the likelihood of a greater relevance of Chinese Law, and the Chinese Civil Code in particular, in the legal operations taking place in Hong Kong.

Taking into account this background, this chapter proceeds to briefly discuss the political, cultural and judicial significance of the Chinese Civil Code for the legal systems of Hong Kong and Macao.

2 Political Significance: The Chinese Civil Code and the Principle 'One Country, Two Systems'

As it has been pointed out, legal systems are simultaneously the seed and the fruit of a mixture of economic, religious, and social factors.[11] The three legal systems of the Mainland China, Hong Kong and Macao are no exception. As an additional layer, the diversity and integration of these three legal systems find a political overtone in the principle of 'One country, two systems', which governs the relations between, on the one hand, Mainland China and, on the other hand, each of the two special administrative regions of Hong Kong and Macao.

In a nutshell, under such principle, the unity of the PRC is ensured, while the two SARS maintain a high degree of autonomy, including regarding their own civil and criminal laws. Under the principle of 'One country, two systems', Macau and Hong Kong apply civil and commercial rules that are different from those in the Chinese Civil Code.

The principle of 'One country, two systems' was the result of a political decision made by the PRC in the negotiations regarding the return of the territories of Hong Kong and Macao. In the mutual understanding that the PRC reached with Portugal, respecting the *status quo* of Macau was paramount as a way of maintaining the historical and cultural heritage of the city.[12] In accordance with Article 31 of the Constitution of the PRC,[13] and Chapter I (General Principles, Articles 2–11) of the Basic Law of the Macau Special Administrative

11 Mauro Bussani, 'Democracy and the Western Legal Tradition', in Mauro Bussani and Ugo Mattei (eds), *The Cambridge Companion to Comparative Law* (Cambridge University Press 2012) 384, 390.

12 Io Cheng Tong and Yanni Wu, 'Legal Transplants and the On-Going Formation of Macau Legal Culture' (2010) 1 Isaidat Law Review 614.

13 Constitution of the People's Republic of China 2018, Article 31: "The state may establish special administrative regions when necessary. The systems to be instituted in special administrative regions shall be prescribed by law enacted by the National People's Congress in the light of the specific conditions".

Region of the People's Republic of China,[14] China's socialist economic system will not be practiced in Macao, while Macao enjoys a high degree of autonomy in all matters, except foreign and defense affairs, until at least 2049, i.e. fifty years after the handover to the PRC. Thus, the previous economic, legal and social systems of Macau was preserved thanks to the principle 'One country, two systems'.[15]

According to Article 18 of the Basic Law of Macau, two types of Chinese national laws are applicable in Macau SAR: the Chinese national laws listed in Annex III,[16] and the Chinese national laws that the Central People's Government orders to apply in Macao in situations of war or state of emergency.[17] An equivalent arrangement is in place with Hong Kong.[18]

These arrangements and the 'One country, two systems' principle allowed the continuous application of different rules of civil law in the two SARs. As mentioned, Macao has its own civil code, the 1999 Macau Civil Code,[19] which is an updated and 'localized' version of the 1966 Portuguese Civil Code, reflecting the German law turn that took place in Portuguese legal scholarship at the beginning of the 20th century. Similarly, the Chinese Civil Code is not applicable in Hong Kong, where the principles of the common law, along with relevant Statutes, continue to apply in civil matters.

As it appears from this brief review, the principle 'One country, two systems' is a new and successful governance initiative, deeply entrenched in the PRC's

14 Basic Law of the Macau Special Administrative Region of the People's Republic of China, Article 11: "In accordance with Article 31 of the Constitution of the People's Republic of China, the systems and policies practiced in the Macau Special Administrative Region, including the social and economic systems, the system for safeguarding the fundamental rights and freedoms of its residents, the executive, legislative and judicial systems, and the relevant policies, shall be based on the provisions of this Law. No law, decree, administrative regulations and normative acts of the Macau Special Administrative Region shall contravene this Law".

15 Yash Ghai, 'The Basic Law of the Special Administrative Region of Macau: Some Reflections' (2000) 49 Int'l &Comp L Q 183.

16 Annex III of Basic Law of Macau includes the Resolution on the National Capital, Calendar, National Anthem, and National Flag of the People's Republic of China, Nationality Law of the People's Republic of China, Regulations of the People's Republic of China Concerning Diplomatic Privileges and Immunities, etc.: see Annex III of Basic Law of Macau. Since the Chinese Civil Code is not listed in Annex III, it is not applicable both in Macao. A similar reasoning can be made for Hong Kong.

17 Basic Law of the Macau Special Administrative Region of the People's Republic of China, Article 18.

18 Basic Law of the Hong Kong Special Administrative Region of the People's Republic of China, Article 18.

19 Civil Code of the Macau Special Administrative Region (Decree - Law No. 39/99/M) 1999.

system of socialism with Chinese characteristics. It simultaneously allows for the rational combination of the highly autonomous exercise of legislative, administrative and judicial power of Hong Kong and Macau, while making it possible for these two special regions to actively and continuously contribute to and be integrated with the central State. And, building on 'One country, two systems', these three legal systems of different nature can coexist and support each other, which provides the conditions for China's pluralistic rule of law.[20]

As a consequence, the Chinese Civil Code is not applicable in Hong Kong and Macau. Nevertheless, the enactment of the Chinese Civil Code carries important messages to the two SARS: PRC formally enters into an era of rights; private life finds its protection in an intensive and systematical manner. At this respect, mainland China and its two SARS now stand on the same level.

3 Cultural Significance: The Chinese Civil Code within the Composite Culture of the Greater Bay Area

The Chinese Civil Code has the potential to contribute to the cross-cultural dialogue among the three legal systems of Mainland China, Hong Kong and Macao. Such dialogue and the resulting legal evolution will be visible in the shifting language and legal categories used by legal professionals, and within the circles of legal learning. The cultural impact will be particularly visible in the GBA, the geographical area comprising the two SARS and the Chinese Province of Guangdong.

3.1 *Cultural Integration of Rights Thinking*

Rights discourse and rights thinking were introduced in China in the 19th century through different channels,[21] and the Chinese term chosen to translate these concepts has undergone thorough debate.[22] Both Macau and Hong Kong have been influenced by non-Chinese legal systems before their reunification with China. Macau with its Portuguese heritage, and Hong Kong, with its

---

20 Dayuan Han, 'On the Civilized View of "One Country, Two Systems" and Its Contemporary Significance', Calaw, July 3, 2021, at <http://www.calaw.cn/article/default.asp?id=14184> (accessed November 27, 2022).

21 Xiaoqing Tang and Wen Wen, 'The Topic of Rights Under the Chinese Context and the Evolution of Roman Law IUS Tradition – Focusing on the Rational Use of Several Technical Terms' (2020) 2 SJTU L Rev 7.

22 Xiaoqing Tang and Mingze Tang, 'How is a Quanli without a sense of Good and Just possible?' (2021) 3 Xiamen U L Rev 9–24.

British heritage, share as a common feature the centrality of individual rights. And this cultural feature is also accepted and protected by the Basic Laws of the two SARs, and implemented within their respective legal rules. Article 103 of the Macau Basic Law and Article 105 of the Hong Kong Basic Law provide that each SAR shall, in accordance with its law, protect the right of individuals and legal persons to the acquisition, use, disposal and inheritance of property.[23] In addition, the Macao Civil Code also places great emphasis on the protection of individual rights. For example, Book II of the Macao Civil Code provides in detail for the protection of personality rights of natural persons, and separately sets up a part on the exercise and protection of rights, with special provisions on the abuse of right, and the conflict of rights. Hong Kong, on the other hand, protects rights to property and the corresponding legal remedies under the rules of the common law. In addition, relevant statutes have been introduced for the protection of certain personality rights. For example, as early as 1995, Hong Kong adopted the Personal Data (Privacy) Ordinance, which attached great importance to the protection of personal information.

With the enactment and implementation of the Chinese Civil Code, the relevance of the rights' discourse has been enhanced within the legal system of Mainland China. The Chinese Civil Code is based on the foundational idea of the protection of private rights, further promoting in the Mainland the development of a legal culture that values individual rights. Indeed, two of the most important innovations introduced by the Chinese Civil Code specifically relate to individual rights. First, and unlike civil codes found in other jurisdictions, the Chinese Civil Code provides for 'Civil law rights' in a separate chapter. This chapter enumerates the personal rights and property rights enjoyed by individuals. The collocation of the chapter on 'Civil law rights' in the General Part of the Chinese Civil Code not only demonstrates the rights-based thinking of the Civil Code, but also embodies the structure of a rights-based systems by listing the object of such rights. This plays a crucial role in setting the rights in specific provisions, promoting a better cultural understanding of the types of individual rights that are protected.

Second, the Chinese Civil Code has an independent book on personality rights, which fully reflects the great importance attached to the protection of such rights within the legal systems of Mainland China. The promulgation and implementation of the Chinese Civil Code will certainly foster the public's understanding of personality rights, and in particular will promote awareness regarding the importance of their protection in modern societies. Such

---

23 The Basic Law of Macao SAR, Article 103; The Basic Law of Hong Kong SAR, Article 105.

protection certainly resonates with the legal systems and culture of Macau and Hong Kong, which emphasize the protection of personality rights. As mentioned, Hong Kong has an established regime of privacy protection, under the 1995 Personal Data (Privacy) Ordinance. Similarly, Macau's rules on privacy are long-standing and influenced by the Portuguese Personal Data Protection Law of 1998, including the current Macao Personal Data Protection Law of 2005.

Law is a reflection of the customs and convictions of a society, sometimes referred to as the 'spirit of a people', which constantly interacts with the community.[24] The manifestation of rights thinking in the Chinese Civil Code reflects the fact that the legislator has recognized the changing habits, awareness and needs of the people, and further deepened the people's acceptance of the rights discourse and thinking. As for their side, Macau and Hong Kong have been influenced by non-Chinese legal systems and maintained a capitalistic organization. In this context, traditionally both SARs have attached great importance to the protection of individual rights, which are also nowadays recognized and protected under the respective Basic Laws of the SARs. The introduction of a renewed era of rights in Mainland China, trough the adoption of the Chinese Civil Code, has triggered a series of cultural repercussions in both the academic and social spheres. Against this backdrop, many subscribe to the view that the rights discourse and thinking of the Mainland, Hong Kong and Macau will become increasingly consistent over time. In turn, growing consistency will support the achievement of a full integration of the underlying legal cultures, prompting the harmonious development of the GBA region and the country as a whole.

3.2 *Language and the Legal Profession*

As mentioned, under the principle of 'One country, two systems', most of the laws of mainland China are not applicable in Hong Kong and Macao, and the three jurisdictions are able to maintain different legal traditions as far as civil and commercial matters. In addition to and as a consequence of the existing differences within the three legal systems, there are also some differences in the languages used by the legal professional communities in these three regions. Chinese is the only official language in mainland China, and usually, the legal professional community in Mainland uses Chinese and mandarin as written and spoken language respectively. Conversely, in Hong Kong and Macao, due to their post-colonial heritage, bilingualism remains the official policy.[25] Specifically, in Hong Kong, legislation is enacted in both Chinese and

24 See Tong and Wu (n 12) 619–675.

25 The Basic Law of Hong Kong SAR, article 9; The Basic Law of Macao SAR, article 9.

English, and the legal professional community uses Chinese and English as written languages, while Cantonese and English are used as spoken languages. In Macao, where legislation is enacted in both Chinese and Portuguese, the legal professional community normally uses Chinese and Portuguese as written languages, but Cantonese and Portuguese as spoken languages.[26]

The differences in historical background, law applicable and language leads to many differences in the legal culture between Hong Kong, Macao and Mainland China. However, with the construction of the GBA, qualified lawyers from Hong Kong and Macao who are able to write legal documents in Chinese and conduct business activities in Mandarin are allowed to handle some civil and commercial affairs subject to the laws of Mainland China, in nine cities within the GBA. Along with the economic growth and integration of the GBA, this possibility of cross-border legal practice will gradually foster exchange and cooperation among civil legal practitioners in these three regions. Under this perspective, the Chinese Civil Code, which systematizes previously scattered civil legal rules, has the functions of rationalizing the legal system and facilitate the search and application of laws.[27] Undoubtedly, the Chinese Civil Code shall be a more familiar tool for legal practitioners from Hong Kong and Macao, for their better and faster integration into the civil and commercial legal services of the GBA, thereby promoting the convergence of civil legal rules and mechanisms between Guangdong, Hong Kong and Macao.

In addition, although the Chinese Civil Code is drafted and enacted in the Chinese language, it is provided almost immediately with an official English translation, which will support non-Chinese speaking practitioners in the GBA and beyond, promoting a better understanding of the civil legal system of Mainland China. Legal practitioners based in Hong Kong and Macao, who are unable to practice in Mainland China due to identity, language or any other reason, will be able to access the rules of civil law of Mainland China systematically and comprehensively, through the Chinese Civil Code English translation. From this point of view, the enactment and enter into force of the Civil Code shall promote the convergence of legal cultures between Mainland China, Hong Kong and Macao.

26 Io Cheng Tong, 'Linguistic Pluralism and the Legal System of Macau' (2020) 7 J Int'l& Comp L 183.

27 Liming Wang, 'The Systematic Function of the Civil Code and its Realization' (2021) 38 Studies in Law and Business 3.

3.3 *Law Teaching and Learning*

Legal culture is greatly intertwined with the teaching and learning of law in a given jurisdiction. On one hand, the Chinese Civil Code is the reflection of a theoretic consensus among researchers and scholars with expertise in civil law. On the other hand, codification and interpretation of civil law shape law students' education within law schools. In the GBA, and particularly in Hong Kong and Macao, the spillover effects of the adoption of the Chinese Civil Code in legal education are gradually emerging.

The methodology of legal education adopted in law schools teaching the law of a jurisdiction of civil law tradition is substantially different from the one adopted in jurisdictions of common law tradition, in particular given that the civil and common law systems rely on different sources of law as the basis for those operating rules.[28]

With its British heritage, Hong Kong is part of the common law tradition. Accordingly, the curriculum of law schools and professional certifications for the admission to the practice of law (PCLL) are designed to expose students to practice before they gain admission to the Bar.[29] For example, the LLB syllabus at Hong Kong University (HKU), includes several courses in the area of civil and commercial matters, such as the Law of contract I/II, Law of Tort I/II and Land Law I/II, with an emphasis on cases and judicial precedents as essential course materials.[30] As for Macao, one can see that the Portuguese civil law system continues to shape legal education in law schools. Following the approach to teaching of systems pertaining to the civil law tradition, such as Portugal, Macao law students learn civil law principles through an overview of the entire system; more specifically, the teaching methodology originated from general doctrine of legal relation.[31] In Macao, just like in Portugal and other continental law jurisdictions, law students are generally not exposed to

28 Rodrigo Sadi, 'Legal Education and the Civil Law System' (2017–2018) 62(1) NY L Sch L Rev 165–182.

29 See Luke Marsh and Michael Ramsden, 'Developments in Hong Kong Legal Education' (2016) 3(2) Asian J Leg Ed 144–159. See also Andrew Godwin and Richard Wai-Sang Wu, 'Legal Education, Practice Skills, and Pathways to Admission: A Comparative Analysis of Singapore, Hong Kong, and Australia' (2017) 66(2) J Leg Ed 212–236.

30 See the website of the Faculty of Law of the University of Hong Kong, at <https://dm.law.hku.hk/content/uploads/LLB_regulations_syllabus_2022-23.pdf> (accessed November 27, 2022).

31 See Kee Kee Ng, 'Teaching and Research on the General Theory of Civil Law in Macao: Plan, Content and Methodology' (2020) 51 Faculty of Law Newsletter (Supplement) University of Macau 30.

practical problems and thinking before they have thoroughly studied the theoretical framework of civil law rules.[32]

One of the purposes of legal education is to build a body of common knowledge shared by legal professionals. In the landscape of the GBA, the enactment of the Chinese Civil Code will serve to catalyze consensus among legal professionals and education institutions in Mainland China and the two SARs, and bring about subtitle changes in the teaching and learning methodology of the law schools established across the GBA. For example, the civil law of Mainland China has become an important part of learning for law students in Hong Kong. The LLB syllabus of HKU includes at least 6 elective courses on PRC civil law, including Chinese family law, property law and tort law. The courses introduce the fundamental legal concepts relating to civil relations and the principles underlying such area of law.[33] Likewise, the civil law teaching system in Macau also responded to the increasing importance of the civil rules of Mainland China for law students and future legal professionals. The University of Macau has set up a new Bachelor of Laws program which will admit students in 2023, named 'Bachelor of Laws (Chinese and Global Law)'. The curriculum of Civil Law is similar to that of Mainland law schools, with General Civil Law in first year, Contract Law and Tort Law in second year, and Property Law and Succession Law in third year.[34] In this Bachelor Program, students shall also be exposed to the common law and more global topics such as international business law.

As mentioned, under the principle of 'One country, two system', Macao and Hong Kong both maintained the legal systems inherited from Western traditions. However, in the context of the GBA, law schools and educators are called to imagine and design new teaching methods that will support students in gaining an understanding of the legal systems of all jurisdictions of the GBA, ie Mainland China, Hong Kong and Macau. Predictably, in the coming years, the law programs of Hong Kong and Macao will increasingly evolve with a view to equipping law students with new professional skills, which will include knowledge and cross-cultural communication skills across the three legal systems of the GBA.

---

32 Sadi (n 28) 165–182.

33 See the website of the Faculty of Law of the University of Hong Kong at <https://dm.law.hku.hk/content/uploads/LLB_regulations_syllabus_2022-23.pdf> (accessed November 27, 2022).

34 See the website of the Faculty of Law of the University of Macau, at <https://fll.um.edu.mo/wp-content/uploads/2022/09/BLC23-Study-Plan.pdf> (accessed November 27, 2022).

4 Juridical Significance: The Greater Bay Area and the Choice of Law Problem

The GBA combines three different legal systems within the same country. Yet, the intense and continuous commercial and social interchange between the people of the three regions has created conditions for many instances of conflict-of-laws. Such conflicts are prompted by the diversity of the rules of civil law coexisting in the region, and many of them may affect the interest of residents living in the three regions in different ways. For example, the *bona fide* acquisition rule provided for by the Chinese Civil Law Code is a general rule, while the *bona fide* acquisition rule provided for by the Macao Civil Code is only exceptionally applicable, namely for the protection of transferees under specific circumstances.[35] Again, for the transfer of property rights, the Chinese Civil Law Code adopts a system depending on registration and delivery, while the Macao Civil Code adopts a the so called *consensualisme* system. These differences have provoked the need for pertinent rules to fix issues of applicable law and jurisdiction, and for smoothing cross-border cooperation and circulation, which obviously would involve action in terms of drafting and enacting laws, law enforcement frameworks and mutual assistance in justice matters.[36]

Currently, Guangdong, Hong Kong and Macao have various frameworks in place that allow governance of the cross-border relations, including the Mainland and Hong Kong Closer Economic Partnership Arrangement (CEPA), the Framework Agreement on Guangdong-Hong Kong-Guangdong Cooperation, and the State Council on Issuing the Framework Plan for China (Guangdong) Pilot Free Trade Zone. On September 5, 2021, the Central Committee of the Communist Party of China and the State Council issued the General plan for building a Guangdong-Macao in-depth cooperation zone in Hengqin, which proposed to gradually build a harmonize body of civil and commercial rules, which is compatible to Macao law and to international standards.

With regard to the approaches to the solution of the conflicts-of-laws, scholars have put forward solutions along two main axes. On the one hand, it would be possible to look for a common ground in matters relating to civil and commercial transaction, and adopt *ad hoc* legislation independently, as

35 Io Cheng Tong, 'The effect of possession and the protection of possession – focusing on the possession regime of Macau Civil Code' (2012) Revista da Promoção de Direito de Macau 22 –24.

36 Yi Dong, 'Specificity and Coordination of the Development of the Guangdong-Hong Kong-Macau Greater Bay Area' (2022) 4 Legal Issues in the Governance of Cooperation 1–15.

authorized by the National People's Congress. Another proposal would be to solve the conflict-of-laws along the lines of origin, thus treating agents from the Mainland, Macao and Hong Kong differently, according to the law applicable in their place of origin.

We are of the view that conflict-of-laws in the fields of civil and commercial matters between the three regions of the GBA need to be approached through various methodologies, such as coordination of substantive laws, coordination of conflict-of-laws rules, and the strengthening of mechanisms of mutual judicial assistance. Perhaps at a later stage of integration in the GBA, it is conceivable that the time will be ripe for a more radical type of harmonization, based on a model of central unified legislation. Following this line, the PRC's legislator could decide to enact a 'Uniform Interregional Conflicts of Laws' instrument that would serve as the basic norm regulating China's interregional conflicts. In the long run, legislation aimed at putting into place more integrated mechanisms of cooperation and collaboration seems to provide the most direct way to achieve convergence of civil and commercial law rules, and is also the inevitable result of the path of integration of the GBA.[37]

5 Conclusion

The evolutionary trajectory of the relationship between Mainland China and Hong Kong and Macao, coupled with the future outlook of the region, seems to suggest ample potentialities for the Chinese Civil Code in terms of impact on Hong Kong and Macao, due to ever closer political, economic, social and cultural ties. We can expect that civil and commercial activity as well as the way of life in the GBA shall proceed to the direction of deeper integration.

The Chinese Civil Code may subsequently have a substantial influence on the legal profession and the relevant legal studies, along with fostering a culture of rights discourse across the legal system, judgments by courts, mediation and dispute resolution.

37 Ke Li, Io Cheng Tong, 'Hengqin Guangdong-Macau In-depth Cooperation Zone: Conceptual Innovation and Institutional Construction' (2022) 1 Hong Kong and Macao Studies 13–24.

Acknowledgements

The author would like to thank cordially the help of Prof. Sara Migliorini, Prof. Wang Xing, Prof. Chen Yi, Dr. Li Ke, Dr. Ma Zhe, Dr. Ho Lok Sum, Tang Mingze, Du Yaqing, Yuen Zheng, for their great contributions in the preparation and revision of the present work.

CHAPTER 19

Legal Musings about Environmental Jurisprudence in the Civil Code of China and India: Peeking through a Tortious Liability Lens

Manjeri Subin Sunder Raj and Ujal Kumar Mookherjee

1 Introduction

India and China, two giants situated in Asia, have for long had a bitter-sweet relationship. While the legal systems that exist in both these countries can be said to be poles apart – at least based on the principles that they fall back on –, similarities do exist. The nature of legal systems present in a country is shaped by numerous factors, and often do borrow facets from different legal systems across the globe. Albeit the fact that the nature of legal systems is a tad different, in the two countries, the very basis of the same, surely, does have scope for an enquiry.

This chapter aims to bring about a comparative analysis of the Chinese Civil Code and the India counterpart. Since the scope of the Chinese Civil Code is vast and because of the fact that the Indian legal system does not squarely have a comparable civil code – rather, it has such aspects which are mentioned in different laws, under different heads, the chapter aims to specifically look into two aspects and compare its scope under both the legal systems. The present chapter therefore will first look into tortious liability under the Chinese Civil Code and in India. After locating the general structural differences between the two systems, the focus will specifically be on the issue of tortious liability for environmental damage.

2 The Chinese Civil Code and Tortious Liability

The Civil Code of the People's Republic of China is divided into seven books. While Book 1 of the same deals with general provisions of civil law, the remainder of the civil code may be classified under various heads like provisions relating to property law, contractual law, personality rights, family law, succession and liability for tort. The new Civil Code brings all sectoral codification efforts together under the same head albeit providing for certain new provisions

 | DOI:10.1163/9789004704428_020

warranted by the changing nature of the Chinese society and economic system. The first substantive books of the Code deal with property rights and contractual obligations, while the interrelated personality rights, rights relating to family and succession come in next. The part on tortious liability comes in at the last which deals primarily with remedies for both the personal and proprietary injuries.

2.1 *Origin and Development of Tort Law in China*

Yan Zhu has classified the genesis of tort law in China into three distinct phases.[1] The origin of tort law in China can be traced back to the days of the Qing dynasty; however, it was the Chinese Civil Code of 1933 that recognised fault-based liabilities. The development of tort law in China hit a roadblock from 1949 to 1980s owing to the adoption of Soviet styled economic model in China.[2] It was only after the Cultural Revolution that the General Principles of Civil Code (GPCL) were promulgated and the development with regards to civil law in China resumed. Besides retaining fault-based liability as the basis, the GPCL also contained some principles relating to strict liability in a handful of cases like road traffic accidents, highly dangerous activities and in relation to environmental damage. Since the GPCL was concerned with laying down the general principles applicable to civil cases in general, scant attention was paid to specific remedies that are available under tort law. Yang Zhu identifies the last stage of development of tortious liability in China in the enactment of the Tort Liability Law (TLL) in 2009.[3]

Besides the Tort Liability Law, some aspects of tortious liability can be found in laws like the Unfair Competition Law of 1993 and the Anti-Trust Law of 2007. The Supreme People's Court of China (SPC), from time to time, issues certain judicial interpretations, which serve to fill up the gaps in the regime.

2.2 *Tortious Liability under the Chinese Civil Code*

Book Seven of the Civil Code of 2020 contains provision relating to tortious liability. The Civil Code repeals all previous laws with regards to the subject matter dealt with under it, including the GPCL and the TLL. By and large, the civil code incorporates the provisions of the 2009 Act. However, some new provisions relating to tortious liability also finds place in the civil code.

---

1 Yan Zhu, 'The Bases of Liability in Chinese Tort Liability Law: Historical and Comparative Perspectives', in Lei Chen and C.H. van Rhee (eds), *Towards a Chinese Civil Code: Comparative and Historical Perspectives* (Martinus-Nijhoff 2012) 336–341.

2 *Ibid* at 339.

3 *Ibid* at 341.

Book Seven is divided into ten Chapters. Chapter 1 of the Book contains general provisions relating to tortious liability.

Article 1165 of the Code lays down that a person, who, because of fault on his part infringes upon the civil rights and interests shall bear tortious liability. The exact connotation of civil rights and interests has not been defined under the Code. The TLL, under Article 2 defined "civil rights and interests" to include rights like right to life, to health, to name, reputation, honor, self-image, privacy, marital autonomy, guardianship, ownership, usufruct, security interest, copyright, patent right, exclusive right to use a trademark, right to discovery, equities, succession, and other personal and property rights and interests.

The Code has brought certain important interventions in the field of tortious liability in China. It introduces the self-risk rule. Article 1176 of the Code holds that, if a person has participated in any sporting or recreational event voluntarily, he cannot claim compensation from the other participants. However, if the damage is caused by intentional act or gross negligence on the part of the other party, tortious liability will still arise. The Code also introduces a self-help rule. As per Article 1177, in case a person's rights and interests are infringed and he may suffer an irreparable damage owing to that, then he may take such measures as maybe reasonable in order to avoid such damage. Such measures include seizure of property of the tortfeasor. The precondition, however, to take such a measure is immediate unavailability of the State organ to tackle such a situation. As regards to compensation, the Code provides for nutritional and food allowances for hospitals to be made a part of compensation payable. Punitive damages for environmental pollution are another important import of the Code. Punitive damages can be claimed by the victim if the tortfeasor has acted intentionally in polluting the environment and that has resulted in serious consequences, though no formula for compensating for the same has been provided under the Code.

One of the issues that the Code suffers from is that several clauses of the Code remain vague in terms of its language. Ascertainment of the exact rights that are sought to be protected under Book 7 remains vague. Scholars attribute the same to the difficulty in bringing pre-existing laws together in a Code.[4] In this context, it is the judicial interpretations given by the Supreme People's Court of China that have to be relied upon to ascertain the exact scope of some of the provisions used in the Code are.

4 Hao Jiang, 'The Three Myths of Tort Law in the Chinese Civil Code' (2021) 7(2) Italian L J 713–716.

3 Indian Tort Law: An Overview

More than one hundred and fifty years of British rule in India implies that tort law in India bears distinct common law imprint. In fact, in India, instead of a separate branch of law, there exists the common law of tort, Indianised by the courts of the country through the application of principles of justice, equity and good conscience.[5] Some aspects of torts are dealt with under criminal law in the country. A number of sectoral statutes govern some aspects of tortious liability.[6] The enforcement of civil rights in general, is done through filing civil suits before the civil courts.[7] As early as in 1772, through Warren Hastings's Judicial Plan, India imported common law features by distributing powers amongst the courts, outlining role of judges and their power of precedent setting.[8] One distinct advantage however that courts in India had over their English counterparts was the non-separation of the law and equity jurisdiction. So, courts in India, through the application of common law and principles of equity at the same time could Indianise the same and build up a strong bulk of precedents which effectively constitutes the Indian tort law. These have continued to be in force even after enactment of the Indian Constitution.[9]

Tort litigation in India has however remained scant over the years, owing to the lack of awareness of the laws, high litigation costs coupled with the socio-economic conditions and less than effective enforcement measures.[10] As such the institutional structure of the Indian judicial system fails to inspire enough confidence in the mind to people to pursue civil action, particularly if alternative modes of remedy remain available. The role of the judiciary in India becomes significant in this regard. On one hand, the Courts of the country have enlarged the ambit of constitutional rights through creative interpretations, one the other hand, tortious rights have been combined with constitutional rights, thereby affording compensation to the victims of tortious actions.[11]

---

5 Marc Galanter, 'Review of The Common Law in India by M.C. Setalvad' (1961) 10(3) Am J Comp L 292 (1961).

6 Several legislations like Air (Prevention and Control of Pollution Act), 1981, Water (Prevention and Control of Pollution Act), 1974, the labour laws of the country, The Railways Act, 1989 etc.

7 C. M. Abraham and Sushila Abraham, 'The Bhopal Case and the Development of Environmental Law in India' (1991) 40 Int'l & Comp L Q 334, 354.

8 *Ibid.*

9 See, Article 372, Constitution of India, 1949.

10 S.K. Bhatia, 'Specific Problem of Tort Law in India' (1969) 11(4) J Indian Law Institute 510–519. See also Abraham and Abraham (n 7) 352–355.

11 Abraham and Abraham (n 7) at 360–365.

It is pertinent in this context to examine the role played by the Indian judiciary is enlarging the ambit of constitutionally guaranteed fundamental rights on one hand and also the broadening of the definition of 'State' on the other, to afford protection to victims of torts.

3.1 *Supreme Court of India and Broadening of the Ambit of Fundamental Rights*

The Supreme Court of India being the Apex court of the country, its decisions are binding on all courts of India.[12] Power of judicial review by the Supreme Court and High Courts in the country is inherent in the Constitution. While Article 13 of the Indian Constitution invalidates any State made law abridging fundamental rights, Article 32 and 226 of the Constitution gives right to a person whose fundamental[13] or any other right[14] stands violated, to move the Supreme Court or the High Court for enforcement of the same. The courts, through the broadening of the ambit of right to life and personal liberty by including other rights within its ambit has amplified the extent of fundamental rights.[15] It can be said that it was the Supreme Court's interpretation of the term 'life' in Article 21 as right to live with human dignity and all the incidents of the same, laid down the foundation for further developments.[16] Personal liberty was also given a wider interpretation. Using these enumenrated rights, rights such as right to healthcare,[17] right to education,[18] right to food,[19] right to clean and safe

---

12 See Article 141, Constitution of India, 1949.

13 Supreme Court of India can be moved under Article 32 only for violation of fundamental rights. See Article 32, Constitution of India, 1949.

14 The High Courts can be moved under Article 226 for violation of fundamental or any other rights. See Article 226, Constitution of India, 1949.

15 Often this development has taken place through the tool of Public Interest Litigations. A Public Interest Litigation implies a lot of things at the same time. It implies (a) flexibility with regards to rules of standing to move a court, (b) flexibility with regards to rules of procedure to be adhered to in cases, (c) a creative and activist interpretation of rights, and (d) flexibility as to the remedies that can be awarded. So essentially, wherever there is a "vacuum in governance", the Courts can fill it, owing to the broad powers that Public Interest Litigations give them. For more on Public Interest Litigations, see Anuj Bhuwania, 'Public Interest Litigations as a Slum-Demolition Machine' (2016) 12 Projections: MIT J Planning 68–69.

16 See, *Francis Coralie Mullin* v. *Union Territory of Delhi* AIR 1981 SC 746; *Maneka Gandhi* v. *Union of India* AIR 1978 SC 597.

17 See *Parmanand Katara* v. *Union of India* AIR 1989 S.C. 2039; *Consumer Education and Research Centre* v. *Union of India* AIR 1995 SC 922.

18 See Article 21 A of the Constitution of India, 1949.

19 *In re Problems and Miseries of Migrant Labourers*, Writ Petition (Civil) no 6 of 2020.

drinking water,[20] right to privacy,[21] right to clean and healthy environment,[22] right to livelihood[23] and most recently, personality rights[24] have been held to be included within the ambit of the terms 'life' and 'personal liberty' and hence entitled to constitutional protection.

Another unique constitutional innovation of the Indian Supreme Court is the 'golden triangle jurisprudence'.[25] In *Maneka*,[26] the Supreme Court in India laid down that if any rights infringing measure had to take away from the Constitutional right to life and personal liberty, the measure has to satisfy not only the stipulated requirements for restriction of rights[27] provided under Article 21, but also requirements under Article 14[28] and 19.[29] This decision has had a tremendous effect on strengthening the fundamental rights protection through court mechanisms and the later decisions of the Supreme Court and High Courts have built further on this brick.

The Indian courts have also evolved a strong compensatory jurisprudence. In *Rudul Shah*, the Supreme Court held: "One of telling ways in which the violation of that right can reasonably be prevented [...] is to mulct its violators in payment of monetary compensation".[30]

The courts have awarded compensation for violation of fundamental rights by the State or its instrumentalities in a number of judicial decisions.[31] In many of these cases, the infringement of rights has been caused by agents of the

20 *Subhas Kumar* v. *State of Bihar* AIR 1991 SC 420.
21 *K.S. Puttaswamy* v. *Union of India* (2017) 10 SCC 1.
22 *Subhas Kumar* v. *State of Bihar* AIR 1991 SC 420.
23 See *Olga Tellis* v. *Bombay Municipal Corporation* AIR 1986 SC 180.
24 Lucy Rana and Shilpi Sharan, 'Protection of Personality and Image Rights in India – Trademark – Worldwide', at <https://www.mondaq.com/india/trademark/1211056/protection-of-personality-and-image-rights-in-india> (accessed November 30, 2022).
25 Chintan Chandrachud, 'The Four Phases of Constitutional Interpretation', *The Hindu*, January 25, 2020, sec. Lead., at <https://www.thehindu.com/opinion/lead/the-four-phases-of-constitutional-interpretation/article30653706.ece> (accessed November 30, 2022).
26 AIR 1978 SC 597.
27 *Maneka Gandhi* v. *Union of India* AIR 1978 SC 597.
28 Article 14 deals with right to equality. It allows classification amongst people. But the same must have a reasonable nexus with the object sought to be achieved and must be based on intelligible differentia. See *State of West Bengal* v. *Anwar Ali Sarker* (1952) S.C.R. 284. It must not also be arbitrary. See *E.P. Royappa* v. *State of Tamil Nadu* AIR 1974 SC 555.
29 *Maneka Gandhi* v. *Union of India* AIR 1978 SC 597.
30 (1983) 4 SCC 141.
31 *Nilabati Behara* v. *State of Orissa* (1993) 2 SCC 746.

State, but, utilising the common law principle of vicarious liability, the State has been asked to provide compensation.[32]

3.2 *Horizontality of Rights in India*

The classical idea of fundamental rights is that they are enforceable only vertically, i.e. against the State. However, this idea of a strict demarcation of the public from the private has been subject to a number of criticisms. Even in India, over the course of time it has been realised that a perfectly horizontal model of fundamental rights is ineffective to meet the present demands.[33]

Under Article 12 COI, 'State' means the Central and State Governments and Legislatures as well as local or other authorities in India or under the control of Government of India. However, through a catena of judicial decisions, the ambit of the term 'State' has been broadened, to assimilate otherwise private bodies within the definition of State as well.

It is the interpretation of the term 'other authorities' that has managed to widen the definition of State. A broad test for the same was adopted in the *International Airport Authority of India*[34] case. The court held that if a body is an agency or instrumentality of government, it may be called an 'other authority'. Some tests were laid down to determine instrumentality or agency, like extent of funding by State, extent of State control over affairs, functional character and whether the authority holds a monopoly status which government grants or protects.[35]

Using these tests a number of authorities have been included in the term 'State', like cooperative societies,[36] public sector undertakings,[37] life insurance corporations,[38] educational institutes,[39] government companies,[40] registered societies,[41] private universities under the University Grants Commission Act,[42] have all been held to be a 'State'.

---

32 See *Rooplal* v. *Union of India* AIR 1972 J&K 22; *N. Nagendra Rao & Co.* v. *State of Andhra Pradesh* (1994) 6 SCC 205.

33 Gautam Bhatia 'Horizontality under the Indian Constitution: A Schema', Indian Constitutional Law and Philosophy (blog), May 24, 2015, at <https://indconlawphil.wordpress.com/2015/05/24/horizontality-under-the-indian-constitution-a-schema/> (accessed November 30, 2022).

34 AIR 1979 SC 1628.

35 *Ibid.*

36 *Dukhoram* v. *Cooperative Agricultural Society* AIR 1961 MP 219.

37 *Sukhdev* v. *Bhagatram* AIR 1975 SC 1331.

38 *Ibid.*

39 B.S. *Minhas* v. *Indian Statistical Institute* (1983) 4 SCC 582.

40 *Som Prakash Rekhi* v. *Union of India* AIR 1981 SC 212.

41 *Ajay Hasia* v. *Khalid Mujib* AIR 1981 SC 487.

42 *Janet Jeyapaul* v. SRM *University* AIR 2016 SC 73.

4 Comparing Tort Law in China and India

The new Chinese Civil Code has dropped the definition of 'civil rights and interests', which was earlier available under Tort Liability Law of 2009. Article 1165 of the Code simply says that whoever infringes the 'civil rights and interests' of individuals shall bear tortious liability. This creates a confusion as to what are the exact ambit of rights that are protected under Book 7. The question remains whether only the rights and interests mentioned in the Code are, or are other constitutional rights also safeguarded thereunder.[43] The introduction of a separate section on 'personality rights' further adds to this confusion. As a general opinion, the scholars commenting on Chinese tort law have opined that rights protected by public law do not fall within the scope of the rights protected under the Tort Liability Law.[44] On this question the Supreme Peoples's Court had issued a judicial interpretation holding that the same could be imposed. However, this interpretation was discontinued by the Supreme Court.[45] On the contrary, as discussed above, the Supreme Court of India, in a country where tort related litigation remains low affords protection to victims of tort, by bringing civil rights and interests within the ambit of constitutional rights.

The Chinese Civil Code introduces an entire section on personality rights. Part 4 of the Civil Code now talks about four kinds of personality rights, namely; right to life, health and physical integrity, right to name, right to one's image, right to one's reputation and honour and right to privacy and data protection. Many of these rights are also constitutional rights found under the Constitution of the PRC. Transplanting the same into the Civil Code implies that the same are protected through civil law also. In India, however, these rights are not dealt with under the civil law. There exists no tort of privacy, or a tort of image. Even constitutional right to privacy in the country has only been recently established as full constitutional right.[46] Defamation is primarily a crime in India dealt with under the provisions of the Indian Penal Code. Increasingly however, more and more civil suits are being filed for claiming compensation for defamation.[47] This is generally in line with the English

43 Jiang (n 4) 716.
44 *Ibid.*
45 *Ibid.*
46 *K.S. Puttaswamy* v. *Union of India* (2017) 10 SCC 1.
47 *Ram Jethmalani* v. *Subramaniam Swamy* AIR 2006 Delhi 300.

common law practice. A tort of privacy, till date remains unrecognised within the English common law.[48]

Recognition of new tort through the judicial mechanism is a long and cumbersome process. The recognition of such torts within the Chinese civil code is a progressive step and one in which the Indian legal system is lagging behind the Chinese system.

5 Liability for Polluting the Environment and Damaging Ecology: An Overview of the Chinese Civil Code

In the Chinese Civil Code, Chapter VII of Book 7 specifically deals with the concept of Tort Liability for damaging the environment. The code specifically mentions that a person who has polluted the environment or harmed the ecological system will be cast upon with a tortious liability.[49] The burden of proof is also placed on the wrong-doer in such instances and he should prove either his innocence or the fact that his liability can be mitigated or that there absolutely is no connection whatsoever between his act and the damage caused.[50] Extension of liability if there are more than one culprit too has been mentioned and various factors which help in determining the same are the type, concentration, and quantity of discharge of the pollutants, the way, scope, and degree of damage to the ecological system, and the impact of the act on the consequences of damage.[51]

Intentional pollution of the environment or the harming of an ecological system is treated with a high level of importance and the person responsible for it can be asked to pay punitive damages by a person whose rights has been infringed.[52] However, if the damage is caused by a third party's fault, the compensation can be claimed from either the tortfeasor or the third party – and in the case of the former, the tortfeasor can exercise his right to indemnification.[53]

48 Gert Brüggemeier, 'Protection of personality rights in the law of delict/torts in Europe: mapping out paradigms', in Gert Brüggemeier, Aurelia Colombi Ciacchi, Patrick O'Callaghan (eds), *Personality Rights in European Tort Law* (Cambridge University Press 2010) 5, 25–28.

49 Article 1229 of the Chinese Civil Code.

50 Article 1230 of the Chinese Civil Code.

51 Article 1231 of the Chinese Civil Code.

52 Article 1232 of the Chinese Civil Code.

53 Article 1233 of the Chinese Civil Code.

If damages are caused, the state authorized agencies or other organizations which have been legally authorized so, can request the tortfeasor to bear the responsibility of restoration – and the same has to be carried out within a specific time period. If the tortfeasor fails to restore it, the said agencies or organizations can go forward with such actions either on its own or entrust it to some other, and in the case of the latter the expenses have to be taken care of by the tortfeasor.[54]

The law also mandates that when ecological damage is caused, the state authorized agencies or organizations do possess the right to request the tortfeasor to make good the loss. Article 1235 lays down five different heads under which this right can be exercised.[55]

6 The Indian Environmental Legal Regime – An Overview

As noted earlier, British colonial legacy runs deep in the Indian legal system – and obviously so –, after being subjected to colonial rule for over two centuries. The common law concept of nuisance is the basis from which environmental law in India grew. Both public as well as private nuisance played a significant role in Indian jurisprudence, and they did develop over time. While the former dealt with interventions in re the use of land, the latter dealt with interventions with the general public's common right. Both private as well as public nuisance form part of the Indian legal system and the Code of Civil Procedure has provisions wherein two or more persons could sue with the consent of the court. While the Advocate General's consent was earlier required, it was done away with by the 1976 amendment.

Public nuisance was held to be a combination of both civil and criminal characteristics – warranting civil and criminal prosecution, in *Perumal Naicker* v. *Rathina Naicker*.[56] S. 91 of the Code of Civil Procedure, which dealt with *class*

---

54 Article 1234 of the Chinese Civil Code.

55 Article 1235 of the Chinese Civil Code: "Where ecological damage is caused in violation of the State regulations, the State authorized agencies or the organizations authorized by law have the right to request the tortfeasor to compensate the following losses and expenses: (1) losses caused by loss of service function from the time the ecological environment is damaged to the time the restoration is completed; (2) losses caused by permanent damage to the function of the ecological environment; (3) expenses for investigation, appraisal, and assessment of the damage to the ecological environment; (4) expenses for cleaning-up the pollution and restoring the ecological environment; and (5) other reasonable expenses incurred to prevent the occurrence or aggravation of the damage".

56 AIR 2004 Mad. 492.

action, was discussed and the court delved into it being used as a possible remedy for environmental harms.

Another noticeable aspect of Indian jurisprudence is the presence of the Indian Penal Code (IPC) of 1861, which lays down punishments for harm caused to the environment. Negligent acts which are dangerous to life,[57] adulteration of food, drinks and drugs,[58] contaminating water of public springs or reservoirs,[59] polluting the atmosphere,[60] are all treated as punishable offences. This Code lays down the punishments which are to be meted out as well, should these offences be committed.

The Code of Criminal Procedure, under S. 133, deals with public nuisance. It lays down that an Executive magistrate can interfere and remove a public nuisance in the first instance with a conditional order and then a permanent order. It is pertinent to note that this was the provision of law that was put to use by courts to secure environmental protection before the coming into existence of specific laws which aimed at protecting the environment.

Govind Singh v. *Shanti Swaroop*[61] was the earliest case in India to take a peek into the Code of Criminal Procedure and search for possible remedies. A bakery owner was at the receiving end of a litigation that had been instituted against his establishment due to the smoke that emanated from it, which caused public nuisance. The *Ratlam Municipal Council* v. *Vardichand* case[62] started off judicial activism in India. Residents were in a state of trouble due to the unclean drains and slums – and the municipality did not take any steps to correct it despite orders of the local magistrate. The Supreme Court of India laid down that the local municipality administration was responsible to ensure a clean environment. A social justice component was very much prevalent under S, 133, and the court laid down that urgent actions should be taken to ensure environmental protection.

Civil remedies are present for environmental hazards as well, wherein the law mandates that affected persons can seek remedies for infringement of their civil rights – which obviously would include damages as well. A law on public nuisance was developed in *State of AP* v. *M V Nayadu*,[63] and it was held to be possessing persuasive value.

57 Ss. 269, 270 IPC.
58 Ss. 272–276 IPC.
59 S. 277 IPC.
60 S. 278 IPC.
61 AIR 1979 SC 143.
62 AIR 1980 SC 1622.
63 AIR 1999 SC 812.

6.1 *The Constitutional Perspective of Environmental Damage*

While the original Constitution did not have any specific provision regarding environment protection, public health was a matter of concern.[64] Later in 1972, Mrs. Indira Gandhi, the Indian Prime Minister, spoke at the Stockholm Conference and raised concerns about eco-imbalance and pollution. India was a party to the Stockholm Declaration and passed the 42nd Constitutional Amendment in 1976, which inserted Article 48A and Article 51A(g). The former placed responsibility on the state – Directive principles of State Policy and the latter was a fundamental duty placed on citizens.

Later decisions like *Sachidananda Pandey* v. *State of West Bengal*,[65] *RLEK, Dehradun v. UP*[66] and *Indian Council for Enviro-Legal Action* v. *UOI*[67] were some of the decisions which highlighted this aspect; and the courts wanted to put into effect these aspects. In *RLEK* v. *State of UP*, Justice R.N. Mishra threw light on *Article 51-A(g)*. In *Shri. Sachidanand Pandey* v. *State of West Bengal*, the Supreme Court opined that the court should recall Arts 48-A and 51-A (g) in all matters related to ecology.

The Seventh Schedule has three Lists based on the power to legislate – List I – matters where only the Parliament can enact laws, List II where only the State Legislature can enact laws, and List III – wherein both can enact laws, but the Parliament made laws would supersede. It is also to be noted that the Parliament can legislate in national interest on matters laid down in List II under Article 249. Article 51(c) puts across that international law and treaty obligations should be followed. In light of such commitments that India entered into internationally, the same was to be read as part of Indian national law. Art 253 also does ensure that such international laws are made part of domestic laws. Entry No. 13 and Entry No. 14 of List I specifically give these powers. The Supreme Court in in *PUCL* v. *UOI*[68] held that the International Covenants to which India is a part of can be read into Indian Law. They are in addition to the rights that are present and can be made enforceable. In *Vellore Citizens Welfare*

64 Article 47, Indian Constitution (Duty of the State to raise the level of nutrition and the standard of living and to improve public health): "The State shall regard the raising of the level of nutrition and the standard of living of its people and the improvement of public health as among its primary duties and, in particular, the State shall endeavour to bring about prohibition of the consumption except for medicinal purposes of intoxicating drinks and of drugs which are injurious to health".

65 AIR 1987 SC 110.

66 AIR 1988 SC 2187.

67 AIR 1996 SC 1446.

68 (1997) 3 SCC 433.

Forum v. UOI[69] the Supreme Court held customary International Laws which are in line with domestic law can be relied on by Indian courts. They will be treated as having being read into and as part of domestic law.

All these led to the expansion of the right mentioned under Article 21. As mentioned above, the Courts in this country broadened the ambit of fundamental rights like the "right to life" under the Constitution and incorporated civil rights within its ambit. This managed to afford protection to the victims of environmental damage to be duly compensated for their loss.

6.2 *Doctrine of Absolute Liability: A Unique Innovation by the Indian Judiciary*

One of the major innovations of the Indian Courts in the context of fixating liability in cases of ecological damage is the introduction of the principle of absolute liability, an Indianised strict liability rule. The Bhopal Gas Leak Disaster in Madhya Pradesh in India is considered as one of the worst industrial disasters in human history. The leakage of MIC from a plant of the Union Carbide Corporation of India Ltd. (UCIL), a subsidiary of the multinational corporation Union Carbide Corporation (UCC), killing atleast 3800 people immediately, besides causing severe morbidity and premature death of many more.[70] In December of 1985, another similar incident of leakage took place in Delhi. The leakage caused the death of an advocate practicing in a court nearby along with several others. A writ petition was filed and eventually the matter came before a three judge bench of the Supreme Court.[71] The case was essentially related to what should be the tortious liability of a corporation who is engaged in an ultra-hazardous activity. In its judgement, the Supreme Court emphasised the need to move beyond the English jurisprudence of strict liability that was developed in the 19th Century and was unfamiliar with the realities of the 20th Century. The court talked about the need to develop an Indianised jurisprudence tailored to the needs of the country.[72] The court held:

> any enterprise which engages in any hazardous or inherently dangerous activity which may be a potential threat to the safety and health of the workers and the people in the vicinity owe a "absolute and non-delegable

69 (1996) 5 SCC 647.

70 Edward Broughton, 'The Bhopal disaster and its aftermath: A Review' (2005) 4(6) Environmental Health: A Global Access Science Source, at <https://ehjournal.biomedcentral.com/articles/10.1186/1476-069X-4-6> (accessed November 30, 2022).

71 *M.C. Mehta* v. *Union of India* (1987) 1 SCC 395.

72 *Ibid.*

> duty" to the community to ensure no harm results therefrom. Such activities have to be performed with highest standards of safety and that the enterprise shall be made absolutely liable to compensate for any harm that results therefrom. It will be no defense for the enterprise against liability to plead that all reasonable care had been taken on its part and that the harm had occurred without any negligence on their part.[73]

It is pertinent to mention in this regard that the common law rule of strict liability or what is popularly regarded as the Rylands vs. Fletcher rule[74] provides certain grounds on which liability may be excused of a person who brings on his own land, for his own purpose, anything that may cause mischief if it escapes. They are force majeure, act of a stranger, plaintiffs' own default and statutory authority.[75] The principle evolved by the Indian Supreme Court in *Mehta*, excludes all such excuses. Further, the court further said that in computing the compensation to be paid by such an enterprise, the magnitude and capacity of the enterprise have to be considered, so as act as a deterrent. This decision has ever since been affirmed and followed in a number of decisions of the Indian courts.[76]

The doctrine of absolute liability remains a unique innovation of the Indian courts in the area of allocating tortious liability. The decision was crafted out by the Indian Supreme Court keeping the socio-economic peculiarities of a developing country like India in mind, which was gradually opening up its doors to economic liberalisation.[77]

The tortious liability under Chinese Civil Code recognised three kinds of liabilities: fault based liability, no-fault liabilities in some cases and liability in equity in some cases.[78] Where damage is caused by a third person, it shall be the third person who shall bear tortious liability.[79] Where an employee infringes civil rights and interests of another in course of employment, the

---

73 *Ibid.*

74 (1866) LR 1 Exch 265, (1868) LR 3 HL 330.

75 Bryan McMahon and William Binchy, *Law of Torts* (Bloomsbury Professional 2013) 1041–1044.

76 See *Indian Council for Enviro Legal Action* v. *Union of India* (1996) 3 SCC 212 and *Klaus Mitterbachert* v. *East India Hotels* AIR 1997 Delhi 201.

77 The Economic Times, 'On This Day in 1991: A Landmark Budget That Changed India's Fortunes', July 24, 2022, at <https://economictimes.indiatimes.com/news/economy/policy/on-this-day-in-1991-a-landmark-budget-that-changed-indias-fortunes/articleshow/93090439.cms> (accessed November 30, 2022).

78 Jiang (n 4) 713 –716.

79 Article 1166 of the Chinese Civil Code.

employer bear primary tortious liability, though any compensation paid can be recovered from the employee later.[80] No fault liability has also been recognised under Chapter V of the code dealing with motor vehicle accidents. Article 1230 introduces the concept of *res ipsa loquitur* or reverse burden of proof. When a person pollutes the environment or causes ecological damage, it shall be upon that person to prove that he should not be held liable, or that his liability should be mitigated.[81] If a person intentionally pollutes environment or causes ecological harm, then punitive damages may be recovered from that person.[82] In case the pollution/harm is owing to the act of third party, compensation may be claimed against either the third person or the tortfeasor. The tortfeasor can recover the same from the third person.

As may be apparent, in case of ecological damage, the Chinese Civil Code follows a mixed fault-based liability and strict liability regime. In case of ultra-hazardous activities where the rule of strict liability is more strongly followed,[83] circumstances are outlined where such liability maybe excused, like armed conflict, riot or other like circumstances or where the victim causes the damage intentionally.[84] Force majeure has also been recognised as an excuse.[85] Act of stranger has also been included as a parameter for mitigating liability.[86]

The doctrine of absolute liability remains a distinct feature of Indian jurisprudence relating to environmental damage and hazardous activity and has been instrumental in development of tort law and environmental laws in the country.

7 Afterthoughts about the Chinese and the Indian Perspectives

Lack of codification of tort law in India has been identified as one of the major reasons behind scanty tortious litigation in the country. On the other hand, efforts at codifying the civil law in China started long back. Now the law of tortious liability has been incorporated within the Civil Code of the country, integrating it with other branches of civil obligations. It makes the exact scope and nature of Chines tort law more easily accessible and ascertainable. Further, the

80 Article 1191 of the Chinese Civil Code.
81 Article 1230 of the Chinese Civil Code.
82 Article 1232 of the Chinese Civil Code.
83 Article 1237 of the Chinese Civil Code.
84 Article 1237 of the Chinese Civil Code.
85 Article 1239 of the Chinese Civil Code.
86 Article 1243 of the Chinese Civil Code.

incorporation of a separate chapter on 'personality rights' means that several new tortious liabilities, like liability in case of privacy infringement, infringement of right to health, education etc. can now be easily enforced in the country. In India, the recognition of any new kind of tort is a time taking process given the judiciary-centric enforcement that is prevalent in the country.

The judiciary in India plays a really robust role. Through incorporating civil rights within the ambit of Constitutional rights and through enlarging the definition of the State, the judiciary has managed to extend a wide ambit of protection to the victims of torts as well. The doctrine of absolute liability developed by the Indian courts, keeping the socio-economic conditions of the country in mind remains a piece of judicial innovation that is absent in any other legal system, including China's. One of the reasons why their counterparts in China have not managed to pursue such a course of action is the lack of a system of uniform judicial interpretation in China. Firstly, as per the Constitution of the PRC, it is the Standing Committee of the National People's Congress that has the powers to interpret the Constitution of China.[87] Although such power was later delegated partially to the Supreme People's Court,[88] the Supreme Court's judicial interpretations do not have any precedential value. These interpretations are regularly published and publicised. The lower courts tend to take these into consideration while interpreting laws, but they are not binding in nature.[89] Uniformity in judicial interpretations has always been an Achilles heel for the Chinese structure, and it is probably because of this reason that the promulgation of a single Civil Code is of such vital importance for China.

As regards to liability for damaging the environment, the principles on which the Indian environmental legal landscape is based on is spread across not just the Constitution of India, but also in various legislations, policies and rules. The Chinese Civil Code in that aspects seems to be a one stop shop for matters relating the environment. This is an aspect that is worth emulating in India. The Chinese Civil Code has been able to bring under its ambit, in a single place, environment related protection that has to be afforded. This would definitely ensure that a certain legal mechanism exists – coupled with the fact

87 Article 67 of the Constitution of the People's Republic of China.

88 Resolution of the NPCSC on Statutory Interpretations, 1955 and Resolution of the NPCSC on Strengthening the Work of Statutory Interpretations, 1981.

89 For more discussion on Supreme People's Court role in uniform judicial interpretation, see Zhenbao Jin, 'From a Supplementary Legislator to a Legitimate Judicial Lawmaker: On the Role of the Supreme People's Court in Developing the Law in Mainland China', in Lei Chen and C.H. van Rhee (eds), *Towards a Chinese Civil Code: Comparative and Historical Perspectives* (Martinus-Nijhoff 2012) 32–44.

that a justice delivery system too exists independently and is able to render justice. In India, one of the major problems is that there are a number of adjudicating institutions, but the presence of a number of laws, and a number of adjudicating bodies that exist under these laws, does, to a certain extent, create confusion as well as a 'not my jurisdiction' syndrome.

All said and done, a mutual exchange of ideas present, it is felt, would be of immense help in reinvigorating the legal regimes that exist in both India as well as in China.

CHAPTER 20

The 2020 Chinese Civil Code: Some Comparative Legal Challenges from a Russian Law Perspective

William E. Butler

1 Introduction

Russian, Soviet, and post-Soviet approaches to civil law offer instructive perspectives on the 2020 Civil Code of the People's Republic of China (hereinafter: 2020 Chinese Civil Code). That Code also raises general comparative legal issues of considerable interest.

One of those issues has occupied mainstream western comparative legal studies for a considerable period: legal transplants. At one level, the reception of European legal institutions and codifications in China via the former Soviet Union remains understudied and underappreciated. To the extent that Western legal sinologists have considered the question, their discussion has remained outside western comparative legal analyses of transplants.

What the 2020 Chinese Civil Code may represent is the third stage of a massive reception of European (and in the third stage, also Anglo-American) legal values and techniques by one of humankind's most venerable distinctive approaches to law and philosophy. This is a hypothesis which the present chapter will pursue in main outline.

Painting with very broad strokes, Karl Marx and Friedrich Engels offered a critique of the society contemporary to them and held out a vision of a future society in which law and State would become redundant. No detail was offered as to how precisely law and the legal system would exist and operate once Revolution was achieved and through what stages, if any, societal development would pass. The Bolshevik movement in Russia once in power, in the absence of a legal blueprint except of the most general variety, was forced to improvise and experiment. Russian Soviet experience, deeply influenced, *inter alia*, by Marxian perceptions of the Paris Commune and short-lived episodes in Hungary, Weimar Germany, and an incipient albeit specialized success in Mongolia, was known to the Chinese revolutionary movement and duly made available by a combination of offer and invitation. Thus was born the Chinese Soviet Republic as an exercise in legal reception and transplantation.

 | DOI:10.1163/9789004704428_021

2 The Chinese Soviet Republic

That Russia (including the former Soviet Union) would be a significant resource and source of inspiration for the Chinese architects of the Civil Code is hardly surprising. Whatever indigenous and foreign influences may have existed prior to 1949 in mainland China (traditional Ch'ing, Kuomintang, American, German, Japanese, or others), the communist movement drew upon the example of the RSFSR directly and through the Communist International (Comintern) and benefited from the experience of Soviet legal advisors during the late 1920s-early 1930s.[1] A comparison of Soviet Russian and Chinese enactments during the Chinese Soviet Republic (CSR) era gives evidence of convergence and divergence. Some enactments were so detailed and so close to Russian legislation that one assumes the texts of the codes must have been consulted by Chinese drafters or their advisers. Not to be excluded is the possibility that CSR institutions could have emerged spontaneously as part of the dynamics of a Marxian revolutionary movement.

Even when evidence of Soviet Russian influence on CSR legislation is overwhelming, it does not necessarily follow that the Russian Soviet rules and institutions received were necessarily those in force in the Soviet Union in 1931. Land law was a domain in which the pattern of Chinese enactments between 1928 and 1931 moved away from the USSR pattern of the late 1920s to something more akin to Russian legislation just after 1917 or even legislation of the Provisional Russian Government. Different periods or eras of Soviet Russian experience were drawn upon without evident regard for mechanistic comparative periodizations of the developmental stages of the Russian and Chinese revolutions.

The evidence of a 'reception' of law in the CSR was most thoroughly documented in the field of land law. That reception, however, was neither a mechanical transplantation nor a case of drawing upon Soviet Russian legislation of the

1 William E. Butler (ed), *The Legal System of the Chinese Soviet Republic 1931–1934* (Transnational Publishers 1983). The contributors to the volume were Stuart Schram (1924–2012), John N. Hazard (1909–1995), William B. Simons, Hiroshi Oda, Ivo Lapenna (1909–1987), Marinus J. Meijer, Sybille van der Sprenkel, G.P. van den Berg, and Paul Ch'en. The volume contains translations of twenty CSR enactments from the Russian language. No mention is made of the Chinese Soviet Republic experience in P. V. Krasheninnikov and L. Iu. Mikheeva (eds.), *Основные положения ГК КНР. Сравнительно-правовой анализ. Сборник статей* [Basic Provisions of the Civil Code of the Chinese People's Republic: Comparative Legal Analysis. Collection of Articles] (Statut 2022). For a critique of earlier experience, see Jedidiah J. Kroncke, *The Futility of Law and Development: China and the Dangers of Exporting American Law* (OUP 2016).

early 1930s. Unlike the reception of CSR legislation determining State structure, and under Comintern guidance, the 1931 CSR Land Law more closely approximated the land policies of the earliest stages of revolution in Russia, including the pre-Bolshevik period. As for family law reforms in the CSR, emphasis was placed on liberating the woman in the family and modifying the status of parents and husband, thereby laying the groundwork for further reforms. It is noteworthy that the 2020 Chinese Civil Code incorporates family legislation.

Labor law in the CSR gave evidence of strong Soviet Russian influence as reflected in Comintern directives and textual comparisons of RSFSR and CSR labor legislation. CSR labor legislation operated in primarily a rural environment, and there was adaptation to local conditions. In the domain of criminal law and procedure, however, Soviet Russian influence was present but selective and Chinese reshaping was substantial. Not surprisingly, Soviet Russian influence was paramount in CSR legislation governing the structures of the State apparatus.

After the establishment of the present Chinese People's Republic, the primary foreign legal model was the former Soviet Union, especially from 1950 to the early 1960s. Substantial numbers of Chinese jurists studied in the Soviet Union and had an excellent command of the Russian language; early Chinese legislation was indebted to Soviet legal models.

3 Socialist Legal System with Chinese Characteristics

In China it has been accepted for some time that China has a socialist legal system with 'Chinese characteristics' – whatever precisely those may be. In October 2017 the XIX Congress of the Communist Party of the People's Republic of China formally embodied that characterization in the Constitution, or Charter, of the Communist Party.

The question of 'Chinese characteristics' is therefore multi-dimensional. At one level it was and remains a prescriptive policy issue: what in the legal fabric comprises those elements that distinguish a socialist legal system from a non-socialist legal system and when and how should those elements be introduced? For those intent upon achieving a 'socialist revolution', what precise measures need to be introduced, and in what sequence, to achieve 'socialism' – however defined – or 'communism'.

At another level this is an analytical category: in the domain of comparative law, for example, on the basis of what criteria do we distinguish a 'socialist legal system' individually or as part of a 'family' from all others? It is in this latter sense that we approach the issue in the present article or, more precisely, in what sense or in what respects does the Chinese Civil Code give expression to or reinforce the proposition of a socialist legal system with Chinese characteristics.

Although comparatists share different views with regard to what the distinguishing indicia of a socialist legal system were/are, the following would figure in the discussion:[2]

(1) private ownership of the means of production leads to the exploitation of man by man and should be replaced by socialist, State, and social forms of ownership, usually achieved by the nationalization of private property and State predominance in the economy;
(2) capitalist anarchy in production and distribution relations is replaced by State economic planning and centralized distribution; five-year and one-year economic plans are issued in the form of a law;
(3) antagonistic class elements are eliminated or isolated through various means of legal discrimination (deprivation of some civil rights, class justice);
(4) the laboring masses comprise the people and those who use hired labor for their personal enrichment do not fall within the concept of the "people";
(5) class struggle is the driving force of historical change, and class enemies may take the form of exploiters or enemies of the people;
(6) members of the working proletariat are accorded certain advantages in comparison with the peasantry and intelligentsia, at least in principle;
(7) the Communist Party or leading party under another name plays the role of vanguard in the State and enjoys a monopoly of political power;
(8) social (that is, non-State) organizations must be under Party direction; religious organizations may be tolerated, but are not encouraged, and experience various levels of persecution;
(9) Marxism-Leninism operates as the official State and Party ideology, in some countries complemented by the doctrinal writings of indigenous leaders;

2 These are abstracted and conflated from a number of works by, principally but not exclusively, Soviet and post-Soviet comparatists, but set out in my own formulations. All are legitimately the subject of discussion and would generate disagreements or reformulations in the hands of any general comparatist.

(10) drawing upon the experience of the Paris Commune in the early 1870s, the foundation of the State system is the "soviets", or councils, which acted as agencies of State power (as distinct from agencies of State administration);
(11) the separation of powers is recognized, but not the principle of checks-and-balances;
(12) the principle of democratic centralism within the State system means that medium-level and local soviets are subordinate to superior soviets, and the principle of dual subordination means that executive committees of soviets are subordinate to their own soviet and to their superior executive committee;
(13) courts at the lowest levels are elected directly by citizens and at the higher levels by the respective soviets. The principle that judges may not be removed is not recognized in socialist legal culture;
(14) the exercise of rights and freedoms is subject to the cause of achieving socialism or communism and to the leading role of the Party;
(15) the distinction between public and private law is not recognized;
(16) unequal forms of ownership, discouragement of personal enrichment, cooperative marketing of goods; civil marriage; duty to rescue socialist property; greater emphasis given to crimes against the State and ideological crimes; discouragement or prohibition of strikes in labor relations; and many others are features of the socialist legal tradition.

4 Typologies of the Chinese Legal System

When the comparative method is used to classify similarities and differences among legal systems, there is an inclination – perhaps drawing on the natural sciences – to achieve hard and fast conclusions as to typologies, to treat classifications as legal fact rather than angles of vision or perspectives. The question is whether the adoption of the Chinese Civil Code does or should alter our perception of the place of the Chinese legal system on the world map of legal systems. To draw upon some of the perspectives the present author has found insightful with respect to the contemporary Russian legal system, consider the following.

Chinese Legal System in the Romano-Germanic Family. When evaluating Soviet claims to have created an entirely new and qualitatively-superior family of legal systems, of which Soviet civil law was a leading component, the late Albert Ehrenzweig (1906–1974) observed that if the Soviet legal system could validly be segregated as unique in the traditional realm of private law, he would be obliged "to abandon the philosophical pattern of two and one-half millennia and the comparative concern of a thousand years". Although there might well be innovations in public law, he considered that the "essentially civilian structure" in the law of the family, property, succession, contract, and tort remained unchanged, and he perceived only minor changes in established European patterns of criminal law and procedure.[3] Others suggested that the Soviet legal system was merely a variant of the European Romano-Germanic civil law system embellished with ideological encrustations[4].

For China, the question becomes whether the enactment of the Civil Code moves its legal system into the Romano-Germanic legal tradition sufficiently to reclassify the China as becoming part of the Romano-Germanic legal tradition. In early 2020 the present writer happened to be in Moscow acting as the Honorary President of the Mozolin Readings at the Kutafin Moscow State Law University. A senior Chinese civilist present for the occasion informed me that the imminent and long-awaited adoption of a fully-fledged Civil Code in China would contain a significant measure of Russian influence. I replied that presumably this influence would reflect the transitional elements of the Civil Code of the Russian Federation.[5] Not so much, he replied; more familiar to me would be the administrative-command elements of the 1964 Civil Code of the RSFSR, which he said would be very much present in the new Chinese Code.

To those comparatists for whom none of the Russian Soviet models of civil legislation represented a substantive move away from the classical Romanist model, Chinese recourse to the administrative-command model of a civil code represented nothing new and placed China in the mainstream of that portion of the achievements of world legal civilization. Those who view the administrative-command model as a serious departure from the

3 See Ehrenzweig's review of Hazard in Albert A. Ehrenzweig, 'Book Review. Communists and Their Law: A Search for the Common Core of the Legal Systems of the Marxian Socialist States by John N. Hazard' (1970) 58 Cal L Rev 1005, at 1007.

4 Frederick Henry Lawson (1897–1983), cited in the preface to John. N. Hazard, William E. Butler, Peter B. Maggs, *The Soviet Legal System* (3rd edn, Oceana Publications 1977) vi. This section of the present article draws upon my earlier reflections on the subject. See, in particular, William E. Butler, *Russian Law and Legal Institutions* (3rd edn, Talbot Publishing 2021) 1–21; William E. Butler, 'Україна на правовій карті світу' ['Ukraine on the Legal Map of the World'], in Vasil Ia. Tatsyi et alii (eds), *Правова доктрина України* [*Ukrainian Legal Doctrine*] (O.V. Petryshyn 2008) (for the English version of the article see William E. Butler, 'Ukraine on the Legal Map of the World', in William E. Butler (transl & ed), *Ukrainian Legal Doctrine* (Wildy, Simmonds & Hill Publishing 2015) I, 179–190).

5 See William E. Butler (transl & ed), *Civil Code of the Russian Federation* (2021), 2 vols.

Romano-Germanic civil code will see the equation differently. Beyond dispute, however, is that the Chinese legislator has based the Chinese Civil Code upon advanced civil law models from throughout the world and sought to introduce the most advanced elements consistent with Chinese economic, political, and moral values. One might at a minimum see the Chinese legal system as 'gravitating' towards the Romano-Germanic legal tradition in a distinctively Chinese fashion and in its own way as forwarding the processes of globalization.

It is my impression that Chinese civilists have been catholic in their study of foreign approaches to the codification of civil law to their considerable benefit. Several years ago I was approached by a Chinese civilist about permission to translate my English version of the Civil Code of Turkmenistan into the Chinese language. My translation of the Civil Code of that post-Soviet Central Asian jurisdiction had been undertaken as part of a larger project on my part to translate the principal post-Soviet civil codes. Turkmenistan was among the Central Asian jurisdictions which had accepted law reform consultations from German legal scholars that included a full civil code based on German legal experience and the latest thinking in the field, but adapted to Turkmenistan conditions. This model differed from that accepted by the other four Central Asian countries (Kazakhstan, Kyrgyzia, Tadzhikistan, Uzbekistan), which mostly follow a mixture of a Model Civil Code adopted within the Commonwealth of Independent States for guidance and/or the Russian Federation Civil Code.

The Turkmenistan version will have represented a challenge to the Chinese translators, whether in the Turkmen or Russian languages. I assume that my English translation, which followed the original text very closely as is my practice, will have been easier to work with. Whatever the thinking, in due course a Chinese translation of the Turkmenistan Civil Code based on my English translation from the Russian duly appeared. My presumption is that the Chinese translation was part of, or became part of, the drafting exercise of the Chinese Civil Code. If so, this would confirm that the Chinese drafters of their Civil Code reached widely throughout the international community to find and consider the experience of other jurisdictions in adopting a civil code.

Chinese Legal System as Transitional. Transition in the sense of change is inherent in the Marxist-Leninist perception of the nature, role, and purpose of law. Society is postulated to have passed through and to be continuing to pass through stages of development that are shaped by and shape legal development. Modern Chinese legal doctrine recognizes these processes, so to say that Chinese law is 'transitional' in this sense is accepted as normal, although some of the transitions have been distinctively Chinese. The Chinese Civil Code is part of transitional processes. Unlike Russia, however, which is transitioning away from Soviet socialism, China is professedly moving in the opposite direction and striking its own balance between, for example, elements of a socialist planned economy and a market economy. The Chinese Civil Code is an integral part of that balance. In this sense, among others, the Chinese legal system may be classified as transitional.

Chinese Legal System as Totalitarian or Authoritarian. In the post-Soviet period some jurists have classified the Soviet legal system as a 'totalitarian' system that was never truly "socialist" and which, in their view, belonged to a separate family of legal systems. This classification has not been widely accepted in comparative legal studies because it turns upon a perception of the political characteristics of leaders rather than legal principles or institutions. Some have perceived this as an 'ideological' classification and others have collapsed the two classifications into one and refer to a 'legal system of totalitarian socialism'.[6]

Although examples of 'totalitarian' legal systems routinely cited in the literature happen to be associated with a particular ideology, the presence or absence of an ideology does not appear to be decisive. The 'seeds of totalitarianism' have been traced back to China in the years 258 to 210 BC[7]. Such legal systems, in Lafitsky's view, are built on the denial of spiritual (ethical) values.[8]

Chinese Legal System as Technocratic. The observation has and is being made in comparative legal circles that most legal systems in the twenty-first century are becoming increasingly 'technocratic'. This is understood to mean greater reliance on normative legal acts drafted in the style of 'technical documentation' than in the style of 'legislation'. Details become so excessive that they lose all touch with reality, reflecting, as Lafitsky aptly expressed the position, "the illusions of their compilers".[9]

This becomes an exercise in 'over legislation': a technocratic legal system moves away from setting out general principles of law in legislative texts and adopts too many legislative acts. In part this trend emerges from the absence of clear doctrine and principle limiting the power of the State to interfere in

---

6 See, for example, Veniamin E. Chirkin, *Основы сравнительного правоведения* [*Foundations of Comparative Law*] (Voronezh 2014) 315–330; Vladimir I. Lafitsky, *Сравнительное правоведение в образах права* [*Comparative Jurisprudence in the Images of Law*] (Statut 2010–2011) II, 394.

7 Lafitsky (n 6) II. Also see Weitseng Chen and Hualing Fu (eds), *Authoritarian Legality in Asia* (Cambridge University Press 2020), where an authoritarian political perspective is applied to China, Singapore, Taiwan, Hong Kong, Japan, Vietnam, and South Korea: authoritarian legality "falls between liberal rule of law […] and lawless autocracy". *Ibid.*, 17.

8 Lafitsky (n 6) I, 99.

9 Lafitsky (n 6) II, 394.

domains of social life where such interference is inappropriate, or harmful, or senseless. Legal theorists undertake to hypothesize the 'perfect legal system' to which ideal legislation should correspond. In practice, legislation becomes increasingly fragmentary and less cohesive. In a technocratic legal system the language of legislation becomes less comprehensible, and judicial practice follows. The courts move away from applying sound principles of law and instead apply technicalities of construction that defy sound reason.

Chinese Legal System as 'Formalist'. Modern legal systems not only engender staggering numbers of normative legal acts, but also may be characterized by the way in which those acts are interpreted and applied. One feature of the administrative-command approach in a Planned Economy is an inherent reliance upon 'extreme formalism' in the pattern of thinking about what law is and how it should be understood.

Elements of formalism are contained in Article 142 of the 2020 Chinese Civil Code, which in the English translation provides that when an expression of intent is made by one person to another, "the meaning of the expression shall be interpreted according to the words and sentences used, with reference to the relevant terms, the nature and purpose of the civil juristic act, the custom, and the principle of good faith". That formulation gives priority to the literal meaning of the words and expressions and secondarily to the factors which follow.

For the Planned Economy component of the Chinese national economy, the rationality of the 'command system' of normative legal acts is essential. The discretion of actors within that system must be necessarily limited, with narrow scope for human volition lest the symmetry of planning relations be disturbed. Formalism requires strong adherence to 'law in the books', however imperfect it may be, and requires that the legal emphasis be placed upon administrative and criminal law to enforce compliance. The Chinese formulation of Article 142 comes as no surprise.

Formalism is also expressed in the balance in any civil code between imperative and dispositive provisions – the extent to which parties to transactions are given discretion or options to make choices between alternatives in their own interests. The transition of the Russian Federation from a socialist to a market economy has been expressed, in the view of many Russian civilists, in the balance between imperative and dispositive provisions in the Civil Code of the Russian Federation.[10] A market economy gives greater freedom to the parties to transactions to negotiate their own provisions. There is no absolute

10 See Butler (n 5).

formula as to what the precise balance should be, and the Chinese will need to determine by way of own experience whether the proper balance has been achieved.

China: Socialist System with Chinese Characteristics or Chinese Legal System with Socialist Characteristics. As noted above, the official ideological position of the Chinese Communist Party is that China is a socialist legal system with Chinese characteristics. In a comparative legal analytical context, that leads to the question of what precisely are the 'socialist' characteristics, the 'Chinese' characteristics, and how does the content and correlation of these change over time as Chinese society matures.

Insofar as a 'family of socialist legal systems' is postulated to exist, China is the undoubted paragon of that system, together arguably with North Korea, Vietnam, Cuba, Laos, and arguably others. The precise threshold for determining who is within this family has never been agreed by comparatists, and there is a strong view that the criteria turn more on public than on private law criteria. Of the jurisdictions mentioned, each would have a case in support of the perception that each has national features that distinguishes them within the socialist family. The level of monolithicity is open to discussion.

China as a 'Mixed' Legal System. There is no such thing, and perhaps in the history of humankind never has been, a 'pure' legal system. All legal systems are 'mixed' systems; that we employ analytical classification categories in comparative legal studies, including notions of 'families of legal systems', to distinguish between 'civil law' and 'common law' groupings or features, or other combinations of factors that influence the configuration of legal systems (religion, philosophy, ideology, ethnic composition, tribal, socialist, geographical, and the like), is a matter of intellectual organization rather than empirical fact.

China is multi-jurisdictional, and for that reason alone is 'mixed'. Hong Kong laws, for example, continues to contain British elements. But it is always the nature, sources, and correlation of the components that comprise of mixture which are of interest. And in that respect, it may be argued that all legal systems are unique despite an overlapping of commonality.

5 Perspectives

One would like to suppose that the entry into force of the 2020 Civil Code of China marks a new step forward in the globalization of civil law and signifies a growing rapprochement with the domain of private-law relations in China and a satisfactory balance between the Chinese variant of a socialist Planned Economy and other forms of entrepreneurship. For China the reception of

European legal models occurred on a comprehensive scale with the introduction of Soviet legal models in the Chinese Soviet Republic in the late 1920s. This was an invited reception, not an imposed one. It was far-reaching insofar as the fields of legislation addressed were fundamental to any developing and modernizing society, but the legislation was piecemeal and did not reach the level of code-formation.

The next significant level of legal reception occurred during the 1950s, when Chinese students and legal scholars were sent to the Soviet Union for advanced training and Soviet legal scholars visited China as advisers and lectured in Chinese law faculties. This was a time when the Russians themselves were in the process of de-Stalinizing and replacing codifications of the 1920s with post-Stalin variants. China confined itself to introducing individual legislative acts partly influenced by Soviet models. But this too was invited reception, and not imposed.

In the aftermath of the Cultural Revolution, China introduced civil-law reforms on a gradual basis by the adoption of individual enactments on family law, general principles of civil law, succession, security, contract, tort, and ownership – all of which have been superseded from 1 January 2021 by the 2020 Civil Code. The fascinating issue now becomes whether the elevation of civil legislation to the status of a cohesive, symmetrical, interconnected conception of civil law relations within a socialist planned economy in the form of a Code will take on a life of its own and advance economic and social relations in a positive way within China and improve foreign economic and investment relations.

This may depend in significant part on the next step – the emergence of Chinese commentaries on the Civil Code analyzing judicial and arbitral developments together with doctrinal writings that constructively advance the values inherent in systematization and codification as major achievements of human civilization.

CHAPTER 21

The Significance of the Chinese Civil Code in Europe

Marie Goré

1 The Long March towards the Chinese Civil Code

The Civil Code of the People's Republic of China was eagerly awaited.

It was so, in the first place, because the current codification was preceded by numerous attempts, a few of which are worth mentioning to highlight the importance of this Code for China and for Europe. China had a tradition of written law. From the time of the Warring Kingdoms onwards, each dynasty wanted its own code, but the codifications that were adopted contained little more than administrative or criminal provisions. In the run-up to the 1911 revolution, the government of the Qing dynasty intended to put an end to the unequal treaty regime: the counterpart demanded by the great Western countries was the improvement of China's judicial and legal system. This triggered what came to be known as the period of modern codification, under the impetus of Shen Jiaben. In this period, Chinese experts already drew on comparative law.[1] In fact, inspiration was drawn from the laws of continental Europe – German, Swiss, French and Austrian – and from Japanese law. The effort was slowed down by the advent of the Republic of China, which took up the initiative. Here again, many projects were started under the influence of many European traditions, but these projects were brought to a halt by the promulgation of the People's Republic of China in 1949.

History teaches us that the methods and techniques used to draw up legal texts, akin to codification, had more to do with rules relating to the administration of the country than with private law, which clearly gained in autonomy with the Civil Code. This shows that Chinese law belongs to continental law. In fact, for historical reasons, the laws of the Romano-Germanic family were primarily designed to regulate relations between citizens: civil law is the seat

1 Roscue Pound, 'Comparative Law and History as basis for Chinese Law' (1948) 61(5) *Harvard Law Review* 749–762; Taisu Zhang, 'The development of Comparative Law in China', in Mathias Reimann and Reinhard Zimmermann (eds.), *Oxford Handbook of Comparative Law* (2nd edn, OUP 2019) 228–251.

 | DOI:10.1163/9789004704428_022

par excellence of the science of law. On the other hand, the rules governing the administration of justice, procedure and evidence are at the origin of common law, whose primary concern was to resolve disputes and restore disturbed order, not to establish the foundations of society. Indeed, the origins of common law are linked to royal power. The common law is first and foremost a public law derived from procedure, since disputes between private individuals could only be submitted to the common law courts insofar as the interests of the Crown were at stake. In the formation and development of English law, a public law based on procedure, the Romanists' science, based on civil law, played only an infinitely subsidiary role.

The fact that, in the civil law tradition, law is primarily conceived as a model of social organization, prescribing the rules to which individuals must obey in their social behaviour, is due to the fact that it was born in universities. This trait also marks another difference with English law. It is worth pointing out that the Chinese Civil Code was the fruit of important work by a number of Chinese universities, in particular Renmin University of China, and the Chinese Civil Law Association, chaired by Professor Wang Liming. In China, too, codification is the natural outcome of a conception of law nurtured in the universities. In the current European context, it is worth remembering that law must not be imposed from above but must be the fruit of reflection on the core of the legal system.[2]

Secondly, the Chinese Civil Code was eagerly awaited because China's participation in economic globalization and the internationalization of law called for the construction of Chinese law that was no longer passive, in the sense of an almost docile, atonic adaptation to foreign or international standards, but dynamic, i.e. taking into account China's legitimate needs and its role in the construction of a law common to all civilizations.[3] In fact, the launch of the New Silk Roads (BRI), by land and sea, is intended to place China at the heart of the planisphere and strengthen its connection to the rest of the world. Chinese law has made real progress since the policy of opening up and reform initiated by Deng Xiao Ping. The reforms accelerated with China's accession to the WTO on December 11, 2001, forcing Chinese law to adapt to the constraints laid down in the accession protocol, particularly with regard to uniformity of application of the law, its transparency, legal certainty, and improvement of the jurisdictional system.[4] However, these achievements have not been without

2 Bruno Oppetit, 'Droit commun et droit européen', in *L'internationalisation du droit. Mélanges en l'honneur de Yvon Loussouarn* (Dalloz 1994) 311–320.

3 Bin Li, *Légitimité, légalité, et effectivité. La protection de la propriété en Chine* (L'Harmattan 2011, 2 vols).

4 Jianfu Chen, *Chinese Law: Context and Transformation* (revised edn, Brill 2008) 5–40.

drawbacks, firstly in terms of the legibility and accessibility of the law, and secondly in terms of the inner coherence of the legal infrastructure. As others have already been pointed out, "the house of Chinese law is a bit like a building whose floors are piled up while the foundations are forgotten".[5]

The Civil Code builds on these foundations. China's commitment to the very principle of a Civil Code is therefore essential. To borrow a sporting idiom, with the Civil Code, China is changing gear.

2 The Purposes of the Code

In 2020, the time was ripe for a Chinese Civil Code. As Portalis said of the French Civil Code, there comes a time when 'we can afford to regulate things and men with the wisdom that presides over lasting establishments'. Codification is needed when social upheavals have receded, and the country has once again become stable. With the entry into force of the Chinese Civil Code, European jurists will find the constants of all great codification. In fact, the Chinese Civil Code serves a dual purpose, both technical and political.

The technical purpose is obvious. The primary aim of the Code is to rationalize the law in response to the need for legal certainty, and to remedy the chronic legislative inflation, disorder, and confusion in the sources of the law. The multiplicity of Chinese legal sources has already been mentioned. Contract law is a good example. Before the enactment of the current Civil Code, to understand the positive law of contractual relations, lawyers had to consult no less than 5 texts.[6] In addition to this multiplication of texts, lawyers also had to take into account the interpretative explanations of the Supreme Court on the 1999 Contract Law, that were as numerous as they were voluminous.[7] The Code's normative clarification is therefore to be welcomed, as article 1260 provides for the repeal of all previous texts, the list of which is specified. Achieving the goal of rationalizing the law obviously takes time, as this is a delicate undertaking. If the genesis of the Chinese Civil Code was difficult, it is because it was

5 Yves Dolais, 'Conclusion: La sécurité juridique existe-t-elle en RPC?', in *L'actualité du droit des affaires en Chine. Colloque du 14 novembre 2003* (Société de Législation Comparée 2004) 130, 132.

6 These laws were: the Economic Contracts Law of 1981, the Foreign Economic Contracts Law of 1985, the Provisions in the General Principles of Civil Law of 1986, the Technology Contracts Law of 1987, the Contract Law of 1999. On these legal sources, see Jacques H. Herbots, *Contracts in the People's Republic of China* (Die Keure 2018).

7 Jiayou Shi, 'La rédaction du code civil chinois: entre la compilation et l'innovation' (2019) 71(4) Rev Int Dr Comp 945, 950.

linked to the evolution of economic reforms, necessarily long and non-linear, and the gradual affirmation of a market economy. This temporal dimension is inherent to all codifications. The Dutch Civil Code required thirty years' work before coming into force in 1992. The French Civil Code – supposedly written in 6 months – is an exception because it was preceded by a wealth of doctrinal work.

However, the singularity of the Chinese Civil Code, with regard to the clarification operation, must be pointed out from the outset, as the normative role of the Supreme People's Court must continue to be reckoned with. One might have thought that, with the entry into force of the Civil Code, the explanations of the Supreme People's Court would no longer be necessary. Not so. In fact, no less than five interpretations of the Court were published on December 29, 2020 and came into force on January 1, 2021, exactly at the same time as the Civil Code. They deal respectively with the following points: marriage and family (Book IV), successions (Book VI), property (Book II), securities (L.II, Title IV), and the application over time of the Civil Code. In addition, a new interpretation on the application of Book I, devoted to general provisions was published on February 24, 2022. In other words, the Chinese Civil Code can only be read in the light of these interpretations, which, it should be remembered, blur the boundary between legislative and judicial power, and undermine legal certainty through inconsistencies and contradictions between the law and its interpretation. Added to this are the groups of model cases relating to the implementation of the Civil Code already published by the Supreme Court, that are selected decisions, formalized as Guiding cases, with imperative effect, a kind of Chinese-style precedent which is "just another form of explanation or brief and rapid judicial interpretation".[8] In the context of the new Silk Roads (BRI), China's trading partners need to be aware of the limits of legal clarification, in terms of legal certainty, legibility and accessibility. This should lead them to reflect upstream on the choice of law applicable to international contracts with China, as well as to dispute settlement methods.

The political purpose of codification is also decisive. The success of a codification depends on the determination of an enlightened sovereign, eager to enshrine a legal order, and even to leave his name on it. We immediately think of one man, Napoleon. By contrast, the Prussian code, the *Allgemeines Landrecht* of 1794, a gigantic work of 19,208 articles initiated by Frederick the Great, lacks any real ambition. The *Bürgerliches Gesetzbuch* (BGB) did not

8 Shigang Li and Mengchao Cui, 'Cas directeurs dans les affaires civiles', (2019) 71(4) Rev Int Dr Comp 925, 928.

appear until the early 20th century, precisely because Germany was beginning to achieve political unity. The German Empire was created in 1871, and it was then that the Criminal Code appeared, followed by the codes on civil and criminal procedure in 1877, by the Commercial Code in 1897, and finally by the BGB, which was promulgated in 1896, but came into force on January 1, 1900, a date chosen for its particular symbolism. The link between the Italian unity and the codification of 1865 is also worth noting. From this point of view, the Chinese Civil Code marks the unity of a great country, a great economic power.

This political purpose is clearly expressed in China. The very wording of Article 1, in the General Provisions, is perfectly clear in this respect. "The present Code is formulated in accordance with the Constitution, with the aim of protecting the legitimate rights and interests of legal subjects, regulating civil relations, maintaining social and economic order, meeting the requirements of the development of socialism with Chinese characteristics, and promoting the fundamental values of socialism". This echoes Article 1 of the Constitution of the People's Republic of China, which states: "[t]he People's Republic of China is a socialist state of people's democratic dictatorship led by the working class and founded on the alliance between workers and peasants. The socialist system is the fundamental system of the People's Republic of China. It is forbidden for any organization or individual to undermine the socialist system". This reference is highly symbolic and ideological.[9] And we also understand that codification can only be specific to a country, because it reflects its identity. This is an essential point. "A codification is, in fact, always directly dependent on the political construction it is intended to achieve".[10] This must be borne in mind by those who wish to persevere in the construction of a Europe-wide code.

3 The Code and the Civil Law Tradition

Today, the Chinese Civil Code is the most recent in the long list of codes from countries with a continental tradition.[11] On reading it, the European observer will have little hesitation in asserting that Chinese law is irreversibly anchored in the continental law family, whose diversity it nourishes. In our opinion,

9 Remy Cabrillac, 'Le symbolisme des Codes', in *Mélanges en hommage à François Terré* (Dalloz-PUF 1999) 211.

10 Yves Lequette, *Défense et illustration de l'ordre civil français* (Dalloz 2023) 320.

11 Frédéric Zenati-Castaing, 'La portée de la codification chinoise' (2021) 73 Rev Int Dr Comp 253–287.

it is precisely one of the advantages of the Chinese Civil Code that it offers European jurists an opportunity to become aware of the pluralism of continental law. No one would dispute that common law also comes in the plural. American law has emancipated itself from the "mother order"[12] of English law. India has not experienced the distinction between common law and equity, and has had to come to terms with Indian realities, but there is no denying that India belongs to the common law tradition through its techniques, its judicial function and its concepts. In fact, the common law family expresses itself only in English, which is its common denominator and tempers its possible diversity. At the same time, the diversity of continental law is expressed in several languages, including Mandarin, the world's second most widely spoken language.

This diversity, it should be stressed, is also due to the resources of comparative law. All the major modern codes have been drawn up, more often than not, on the basis of comparative law.[13] This reliance on comparative law is a constant in the law of the Romano-Germanic family. It prohibits any focus on one's own national law and leads to the advancement of legal science. The Chinese Civil Code is no exception to this rule. In the Code, there are numerous borrowings from French law: quasi-contracts, economic loss, identification of joint debts between spouses, hardship, right of unilateral termination in open-ended contracts. Common law mechanisms are rarer, but they do exist, as shown by the discipline of the anticipatory breach of contract. Added to this, and this is a common feature of modern codifications, are references to international sources. These include the Vienna Convention on the International Sale of Goods and the UNIDROIT Principles of International Commercial Contracts.[14]

4 The Originality of the Code

The diversity to which the Chinese Civil Code contributes can be illustrated by three observations relating to the Code's structure, its recipients, and its scope.

With regard to the structure of the Code, it is not new to note that its general plan is German-inspired. It is so at least in two respects. Book I, the general

12 Konrad Zweigert, 'Des solutions identiques par des voies différentes (Quelques observations en matière de droit comparé)' (1966) 18(1) Rev Int Dr Comp 5, 15–18.

13 Louis Vogel, 'Le monde des codes civils in 1804–2004', in *Le Code civil. Un passé, un présent, un avenir* (Dalloz 2004) 789, 797.

14 ibid.

part, is devoted to the legal institutions that transcend all branches of private law and apply to the matters covered by the other parts of the Code. Then there is the fact that each book follows the same method, beginning with a chapter devoted to general rules or general provisions. But that is also where the analogy ends. Unlike its German counterpart, the Chinese Code begins with the law of property and does not devote a book to the law of obligations, preferring to treat in two separate books the law of contract and the law of torts. Another original feature is the presence of a book devoted to personality rights, which German law had refused to include in the BGB, with the exception of the right to a name.

European lawyers will be familiar with the particularity of the general part. It is not an introductory section proposing principles of interpretation or proclamations of a moral or social nature: it is a true body of rules, constituting positive law, the mastery of which is indispensable for anyone wishing to know Chinese private law. However, one cannot help seeing it as a heterogeneous book. Some rules, such as article 115 on the definition of movables and immovables, could have been included in the book on property. The same criticisms as those levelled at the German Civil Code by Konrad Zweigert and Hein Kötz would be welcome. A different example comes from the difficulty relating to the transfer of ownership of a sold good. In order to understand when and how property passes, Chinese lawyers must refer to the following provisions: (1) articles 137 and following in Chapter 6 of the General Part, (2) articles 463 and following in the general part of Book III on contracts, (3) articles 595 and following in the special part of Book III on contracts of sale, (4) articles 209 and following of the general part of Book II on transfer of ownership. In other words, lawyers need a great deal of expertise and experience to handle the Chinese Civil Code.

This obliges the European jurist to ask himself who the Code is intended for. For whom was this Chinese Civil Code written? In Portalis' eyes, a Civil Code represented 'the greatest good that all men can give and receive'. He saw it as a mark and reflection of civilization. This is undoubtedly also true of the Chinese Civil Code. Portalis' view also highlights the profound significance in Europe of the rule of law, which must express the culture, spirit, and values of those for whom it is intended, and not reason in purely quantitative and material terms.[15] In our view, this makes the possibility of a European Civil Code unrealistic, and even less desirable.[16]

---

15 Oppetit (n 2).

16 See Yves Lequette, 'Défense et illustration de l'ordre civil français' (Dalloz 2023) 327 and following; Rodolfo Sacco, 'Non, oui, peut-être', in *Mélanges Christian Mouly* (Litec 1998, I) 163.

This calls for a comment on the legislative style of the Chinese Civil Code. The Chinese Civil Code contains just 1,260 articles, whereas the French Civil Code has more than twice that number. For instance, there is a quantitative discrepancy in the treatment of the law of succession, to which the French Civil Code devotes 200 articles, excluding the will regime, and the Chinese Civil Code only 45 articles, including the will regime.[17] However, in some cases the Chinese Civil Code adopts more and longer articles than its French counterpart. For instance the Code contains long norms with numerous details relating to offer and acceptance, and the exception of non-performance, on which the original French Civil Code was notoriously silent.[18] Style is undoubtedly linked to language, grammatical structure and vocabulary, and it is always tricky, even misleading, to judge legislative art on the basis of translations. We may well wonder whether the drafting of the Civil Code gave rise to a deliberate choice of writing style for the norm, or whether it follows the pattern of any Chinese legal provision. But we must not draw hasty conclusions from the Chinese language. In fact, it would suffice to open the Taiwanese Civil Code, based on the German model, to observe that the Chinese language does not prevent highly detailed and meticulous drafting. A reading of the Chinese Civil Code suggests that there is no extreme casuistry as in German law. Rather, French jurists will find a rule of conduct that is familiar to them, admittedly less abstract and concise than that of the 1804 Code, but that similarly appeals to the reasonableness of the '*bonus pater familias*'.

This leads to a more direct comment on the true addressees of the Civil Code. The terms used to designate its intended addressees – subject of civil law, subject of law – contrast with the subject of administrative law, and of public law in general. Behind these expressions, who is the beneficiary of the norm? Is it the legal professional, concerned with technique and detail as in the German Civil Code and in Anglo-American law, or is it the Chinese citizen who has just conquered new rights, such as the right of use, the right of personality, and the right to environmental protection? This would suggest that the Code is intended to develop legal awareness in Chinese individuals, as evidenced by the campaigns to promote, disseminate, and explain the contents of the Civil Code to the general public. Moreover, the emblematic creation of the

---

17 Michel Grimaldi, speech delivered at the 'Conférence du 16 octobre 2023 Pékin-Shanghai. Le code civil Chinois. Regards croisés Chine-France', on file with the author.

18 Charles Gijsbers, 'Evolutions en matière de négociation précontractuelle et similarités avec le droit français des contrats' (2021) 74 Courrier du centre sino-français de formation et d'échanges notariaux et juridiques à Shanghai (available at <http://www.cnfr-notaire.org/Article.List5.f.asp?id=1070>, accessed 30 October 2023).

book on personality rights certainly reflects the desire to place people at the centre of society, to show the interest of the Chinese legislator in the effective protection of individual rights, and also to take into account the risks raised by new technologies.

What about the scope of the code? Any codification raises the question of its scope, and the Chinese Civil Code is no exception. On reading the Chinese Civil Code, a continental lawyer would be circumspect. On the one hand, the Chinese Civil Code includes administrative contracts, while administrative bodies retain the status of ordinary civil law subjects for the activities specified in the Code. Also administrative liability is governed by the Chinese Civil Code. This inclusion of administrative contracts in the Civil Code is probably a sign that the autonomy of civil law in China has not yet been fully achieved. Also noteworthy is the surprising inclusion in the Civil Code of Contracts for the Supply and Consumption of Electricity, Water, Gas, or Heat. The role of the State is recurrent throughout these provisions. While it is understandable that the general interest or the interest of the State, for example, limits the contractual sphere, the overarching presence of the state in the structure of the Civil Code is probably linked to the fundamental characteristics of the Chinese political system and to the risk of discretionary exercise of power by the administration.

On the other hand, the Civil Code includes provisions which, in countries where the distinction is made, are more akin to commercial law, and therefore could belong to a separate codification – the Commercial Code. Legal persons and their classification, including for-profit entities, are described in the general part. According to article 125, the 'persons of the civil law' enjoy shareholder rights and other investor rights in accordance with law. Issues related to commercial law are therefore considered as special civil rights. Certain types of commercial contracts, such as contracts for financing lease, factoring contracts, partnership contracts, entrustment contract, transport contracts and many others, are included in the book devoted to contracts. As in Italy and now in Argentina, there is therefore no distinction between the Civil Code and the Commercial Code. Of course, in comparative law, some countries have never made the distinction, while others have abandoned it (such as, for instance, Switzerland, where the merger of civil and commercial law was justified by the country's federal structure). Last but not least, environmental protection is a recurring theme of the Chinese Civil Code, as demonstrated by the several provisions (e.g., articles 9, 509(3), 294, 346, and 1232) that mention it.

Can we consider this Chinese civil code to be the common law of China? Following the example of the 1804 Civil Code, could we claim that it constitutes "the prestige of being common law, holding the lexicon of stem words and the stock of principles that are the sediment of legal memory"[19]? Is it based on a certain conception of the human being, in terms of the Chinese people and their aspirations, and as such a symbol of the unity of the Chinese nation? This is doubtful.

5 The Future of the Code

It would be wrong to believe that codification freezes the law, and this would be even truer in the Chinese context. In the Code, there is a constant search for a more precise match between the abstract rule and living reality, which provides a very useful lesson for Western jurists. One of China's greatest characteristics is actually its incessant change, with society evolving in several strata, at several speeds. This rules out any systematization of law making in the broadest sense of the term. The abstract, unconditional rule is not favoured – quite the opposite. Hence a 'propensity for flexibility', as the rigid application of a standard to diverse realities can only lead to 'disorder'. The approach to law is therefore anything but dogmatic: on the contrary, it is as close as possible to concrete reality and to the needs of actual circumstances; no truth is established in advance. Inheritance law is a perfect illustration of this. An heir's inheritance rights may be increased or reduced according to the assistance they have or have not provided to the deceased. According to article 1130 of the Chinese Civil Code, "[w]hen distributing an estate, due consideration shall be given to a successor who has special financial difficulties and is unable to work. When distributing an estate, a successor who has made predominant contributions in supporting the now decedent, or who has been living with the now decedent may be given a larger share. When distributing an estate, a successor who had the ability and was in a position to support the now decedent but failed to fulfil the duty of support shall be given no or a smaller share". Flexibility is a constant feature of Chinese law. Even before the advent of the Civil Code, the construction of Chinese law was characterized by multifaceted normative experimentation through interim, trial regulations, adopted according to the different branches of law and geographical areas of application.

19 Jean Carbonnier, 'Le code civil', in Pierre Nora (ed), *Les lieux de mémoire* (Gallimard 1997, I) 1342.

6 Conclusions

How can we conclude? It is still too early to assess the impact of the Chinese Civil Code on China and the rest of the world. Could the Chinese Civil Code be a useful model for Europe? We do not think so. Firstly, because of its imperfections, but also and above all because traditions differ, and in particular the place of the individual, exalted here, dependent on the group there. Nevertheless, the very existence of the Chinese Civil Code should provide food for thought for Western, and particularly European, jurists.

First of all, the Chinese Civil Code demonstrates the importance of codification, which can only reflect a specific legal culture, a fundamentally unique civilization. This condemns any idea of a European code, be it a civil code or a business code. Secondly, European jurists must be aware of the profound legal transformations taking place in Asia. They need to be aware of the extent to which the creation of standards can nowadays come from outside Europe, and of the need to decompartmentalize the classical, i.e. Euro-centric, vision of legal systems. We need to recognize the legitimate refusal of Asian countries to subscribe to whole swathes of Western law. It is also time to properly appreciate the impact of legal cooperation in Asia. From a political, economic and legal standpoint, the Belt and Road Initiative (BRI), launched in 2013 by President Xi Jin Ping, goes beyond the construction of a gigantic infrastructure network to pragmatically and progressively make China – and its legal model – the leader of the global legal order currently in the making. It is often stressed that codification is established in a major country, exerting an influence on other countries that cannot shirk.[20] The circulation of civil law has developed mainly in the field of private law, while the circulation of American law has mostly occurred in the field of constitutional law. But does this mean that this new Chinese 'private' law is sufficiently legible and accessible worldwide to inspire other laws? Nothing is less certain, given China's political system and its emphasis on administration and authority. Thanks to the Chinese Civil Code, the rule of civil law has undoubtedly gained exclusivity for the whole of China. It is not a given that it has gained in legitimacy.

20 René David, Camille Jauffret-Spinosi, Marie Goré, *Les grands systèmes de droit contemporains* (12 edn, Dalloz 2016) n° 48.

CHAPTER 22

The Significance of the Chinese Civil Code in Africa

Salvatore Mancuso

1 A Short Preamble

On May 28, 2020, the National People's Congress passed the long awaited Chinese Civil Code.[1] It represents a milestone in the development process of the Chinese legal system, being the Code is "[t]he first Chinese law to carry the title 'code' since the founding of the People's Republic of China in 1949".[2] The code is also considered part of a broader political project that links the code to the theory of the socialist rule of law with Chinese characteristics, since "the Civil Code is expected to comprehensively strengthen the protection of people's various rights and improve the Chinese socialist system of laws".[3] The Civil Code entered into force on Jan 1, 2021.

The Chinese Civil Code puts systematically together all the existing legal norms concerning civil law matters, being it "a re-grouping of existing mini-codes, a compilation without touching the essence of the existing articles. It was no remodeling of the private law, no rethinking of the existing texts – what implies innovation, endorsing a unifying idea",[4] but includes also several interesting novelties. It continues the development of the Chinese legal system in the ambit of the civil law tradition (Mainland China is a civil law jurisdiction since the beginning of the Republic), as it can be noted through the structure of the Code (having a strong German influence), which is divided in seven Books: General Provisions, Property, Contracts, Personality Rights, Family Law, Succession, and Torts.[5]

---

1 For a brief history of the Chinese Civil Code see Eric Lin *et al.*, 'The adoption of the Chinese Civil Code and its implications on contracts relating to China', at < https://www.reedsmith.com/en/perspectives/2020/06/the-adoption-of-the-chinese-civil-code-and-its-implications-on-contracts> (accessed October 19, 2022).

2 The State Council of the People's Republic of China, *Civil Code of the People's Republic of China*, at <https://english.www.gov.cn/archive/lawsregulations/202012/31/content_WS5fedad98c6d0f72576943005.html> (accessed October 19, 2022).

3 *Ibid.*

4 Jacques H. Herbots, 'The Chinese new Civil Code and the law of contract' (2021) 7 China-EU L J 39.

5 See more in Marina Timoteo, 'China Codifies. The first book of the civil code between Western models to Chinese characteristics' (2019) Opinio Juris in Comparatione, at

 | DOI:10.1163/9789004704428_023

Moving from the consideration that "any general statement on the C[hinese] C[ivil] C[ode] solely concentrating on the paper rules would fail to capture a complex reality without paying regard to the underlying social, economic, and political contingencies",[6] it is necessary to go beyond the law in the book in order to imagine how the Chinese Civil Code could possibly be significant in Africa.

Indeed, if an African jurist is asked what are the influences that the Chinese Civil Code can exercise in his country, he will answer that there cannot be any, because his country already has its own legal system, and the Chinese Civil Code is intended to operate only in China. A similar answer will be provided by a Chinese jurist.

This observation would seem to foreclose the matter. But if the barriers of the mere juridical element are overcome, and the phenomenon of the enactment of the new Chinese Civil Code is framed in the more general context of the relations between China and Africa, then different scenarios can be delineated. In particular, the enactment of the new Chinese Civil Code shall be considered in the ambit of the more general discourse concerning the Chinese legal diplomacy and how it is used in the ambit of the China-Africa relations.

Since his election as leader of China, Xi Jinping abandoned Deng Xiaoping's foreign policy approach of 'keeping a low profile'. He inaugurated a new phase of the Chinese diplomacy, in which all actions are subordinated to China's foreign policy goal of regaining its superpower status. This means that China is engaged in bringing changes in the global system, which has been traditionally dominated by the West. In that sense, Chinese diplomacy is characterised by continuity as far as the goal of regaining the superpower status is concerned, but the ways to achieve this goal have been changed. China announced new diplomatic slogans, promoted cooperation forums and institutions, and continued to expand its geographical engagement beyond Asia.[7]

<http://www.opiniojurisincomparatione.org/opinio/article/view/129> (accessed October 22, 2022). On the development of the civil law tradition in China see Lei Chen, 'The Historical Development of the Civil Law Tradition in China: A Private Law Perspective' (2010) 78 Leg Hist Rev 159.

6 Lei Chen, 'Continuity and change: some reflections on the Chinese Civil Code' (2021) 29 Asia Pacific L Rev 287.

7 Justyna Szczudlik, 'Towards a "New Era" in China's Great Power Diplomacy', The Polish Institute of International Affairs, Policy Paper no. 1(161), March 2018, at <https://pism.pl/publications/Towards_a_New_Era_in_Chinas_Great_Power_Diplomacy> (accessed October 22, 2022); Tim Rühlig, 'China's international relations in the new era of Xi Jinping – implications for Europe', EU-Asia at a Glance, European Institute for Asian Studies, March 2018, at <https://www.eias.org/wp-content/uploads/2016/03/EU_Asia_at_a_Glance_Ruhlig_2018.pdf> (accessed October 22, 2022).

This new approach is visible both in theoretical and practical terms, as Chinese diplomacy is becoming more and more innovative. China has recently engaged in the extensive promotion of its new diplomatic pillars, among which 'new model of international relations', and 'Chinese solution' are at the forefront. While the first is one of the cornerstones of the new Chinese approach to diplomatic relations, the second is a concept indicating that Chinese values and standards based on Asian philosophy are effective in solving global problems: more broadly, those concepts are considered as the Chinese contribution to the theory of international relations.[8]

Such 'new model of international relations' is based on pillars like avoidance of conflicts and confrontations, mutual respect, win-win cooperation, fairness and justice. Such concept arises directly from the Chinese vision of international relations, which must be beneficial to China and its goal of being a superpower. The key point for China is the 'mutual respect', a concept that refers to a list of issues that China views as non-negotiable.[9] 'Chinese solution', on the other hand, has been used extensively by Chinese leaders in their speeches and official documents to show the superiority of Chinese values, norms and standards, purporting the idea that the 'socialist market economy with Chinese characteristics' works well as it is proved by the continuous Chinese GDP growth.[10]

The idea is therefore to consider to which extent the Chinese Civil Code can be used as a tool for Chinese 'legal diplomacy' in Africa, an element of the new way of conducting foreign policy by China that has been named "great power diplomacy with Chinese characteristics".[11] After a short overview of the concept of 'legal diplomacy' and how it has been used by China, the chapter will discuss the implications of legal diplomacy on China-Africa relations. Then, a consideration on the role that the Civil Code can play in this respect will come after, followed by a short conclusion.

8 See more in Szczudlik (n 7) 3; Olivier Sempiga, 'Does China offer a new narrative and an alternative voice in International Relations?' (2017) 3 J Int'l Rels, Peace Stud & Dev, Article 4.

9 The list of core interests is open-ended, but undoubtedly includes Taiwan, Hong Kong, Tibet, and the disputed islets of the South and East China Seas. See again Szczudlik (n 7) 4 ff.

10 Matt Ferchen, 'China, Economic Development, and Global Security. Bridging the Gaps' (2016) Carnegie–Tsinghua Center for Global Policy, at <https://carnegieendowment.org/files/CP_289_Brief_Ferchen_China.pdf> (accessed October 22, 2022).

11 Justyna Szczudlik, 'Towards Great Power Diplomacy under Xi Jinping', The Polish Institute of International Affairs, Policy Paper no. 9(111), April 2015, on file with the author.

2 The Meaning of Legal Diplomacy

In a nutshell, diplomacy is the instrument that facilitates peaceful relations between States.[12] There are different perspectives of diplomacy (economic, cultural, political), but among them legal diplomacy is definitely a new concept. Traditionally, there has not been too much connection between law and diplomacy, being State relations based on different grounds, like negotiations, and – more in general – on politically oriented instruments. More recently, when the outcomes of diplomatic negotiations have been formalized into instruments that can be considered as law, the latter started to be part of diplomacy.[13] With the new approaches to global governance and the increasing move toward legal globalization the connection between diplomacy and law became stronger and the expression 'legal diplomacy' started to appear.[14]

Legal diplomacy is a kind of diplomatic activity that is based on the content, use and approach to law. It aims at instilling legal concepts – and in particular that of rule of law – in diplomatic activities, so that diplomatic issues, foreign affairs and diplomatic disputes are dealt with and solved using legal avenues. It covers not only traditional diplomatic activities – like, for example, negotiation and ratification of treaties, judicial assistance, international relations – but also public diplomacy and people-to-people diplomacy where law plays a fundamental role in diplomatic activities.[15] In this respect, States need to introduce the concept of the rule of law in diplomatic activities, to have a legal agenda in diplomacy, to convert relevant political, economic, cultural, and military issues into legal issues, and to resolve disputes using the appropriate legal procedures.[16]

Legal diplomacy can take different forms. In diplomatic or foreign affairs, actors can use law – even if not explicitly – as their framework of reference (law-based diplomacy); diplomatic activities can be vested in legal form, as

12 Ivor Roberts, *Satow's Diplomatic Practice* (6th edn, OUP 2009) 3.

13 On the European human rights law (and the European Convention for the Protection of Human Rights and Fundamental Freedoms – ECHR) as a form of 'legal diplomacy', see Mikael R. Madsen, ''Legal Diplomacy' – Law, Politics and the Genesis of Postwar European Human Rights', in Stefan-Ludwig Hoffmann (ed), *Human Rights in the Twentieth Century* (Cambridge University Press 2010) 62.

14 Zhipeng He, 'Legal Diplomacy and the Possible Approach of China', in Naren Chitty *et al.* (eds), *The Routledge Handbook of Soft Power* (Routledge 2017) 166.

15 He (n 14) 166.

16 Wenxian Zhang and Zhaomin Gu, 'China's Law Diplomacy: Theory and Practice' (2013) Glob Rev 48, also published as a booklet with the same title: (China Law Society Press 2013) 22.

in the case of international treaties or dispute resolution by using peaceful instruments like arbitration or judicial organs (law-formed diplomacy);[17] law can also be the content of the diplomatic activities to achieve specific objectives of the negotiating countries, like regional integration, development of the legal systems, judicial and legal assistance (law as the content of diplomacy).[18]

Generally, the concept of legal diplomacy is used mainly in international relations. It is the process which focuses on the legal obstacles hampering peace and recommends the adoption of all possible legal measures that may be undertaken in order to restore and maintain peace across the world, since an engagement based on legal diplomacy will enable policymakers to better identify legal responses to peace issues in line with international law standards, building on common understandings of international law.[19] However, through the development of the Chinese presence in international relations, the concept assumed also a different connotation: it indicates the promotion of the Chinese legal model as a tool to promote the Chinese culture and solutions to legal issues as an alternative to the Western ones. It is with reference to this meaning that the concept will be used in the present discourse.

3 China and Legal Diplomacy

The Chinese legal diplomacy program is the result of the new role taken by China in the international arena and is based on the Chinese increased use of soft power instruments in international relations.

3.1 *China in the International Arena*

In the ambit of international relations in present times there is a great number of global, regional, and bilateral issues where China should take its position by voting in the related decision-making designated places, others where China exercises its own (geo)political influence, other directly affecting the country.[20] Chinese leaders have consequently recognized the necessity and importance of participating in global governance.

---

17 An example in Fernanda G. Nicola, 'Legal Diplomacy in an Age of Authoritarianism' (2021) 27 Colum J Eur L 152.

18 He (n 14) 168 ff.

19 Brian Egan, 'International Law, Legal Diplomacy, and the Counter-ISIL Campaign: Some Observations' (2016) 92 Int'l L Stud 235.

20 He (n 14) 171.

Since law is playing an increasing important role in a broader scope and at a deeper level, China promotes the adhesion to the path of peaceful development, carving out a role for itself as a force driving the world towards multipolarity. This because China's rise as an economic power has deep and far-reaching worldwide implications, in view of a transformation of the world toward a greater and more general balance of power, thus creating a favourable international context for law diplomacy. On the other hand, China wants to promote its image of a responsible major power steered to maintaining a peaceful and stable world and to promoting the world order and the international system to evolve in the direction of becoming more just and equitable.[21]

This explains why the Chinese position from the perspective of international law is based on the assumption that "the Chinese government attaches greater importance to the international rule of law and consciously practices it".[22] The goal is clear: "[T]he role of China should change from a student to a teacher in the field of international rules. However, you have to be a student of international rules first if you want to be a teacher in it".[23]

The key element in this discourse is China's use and promotion of soft power at national and international level. Chinese leaders and scholars, being attached to historical and cultural values, did not consider democracy, individual freedom and openness in culture as components of soft power. They were more attracted to the idea that "soft power provided a way of influencing other states through non-coercive means".[24] This gave to China the possibility of creating its own definition of soft power based on three components of attraction: benignity, brilliance, and beauty.[25] According to Chinese leaders, China's soft power is based on benign values, traditions, and approaches as evidenced in the writings and teachings of Confucius; brilliance derives from China's economic model and growth through which it survived the global financial crisis, played a major role in the global economic recovery during the post-crisis phase, and pulled many of its citizens out from poverty conditions; while the beauty of Chinese soft power is embodied in the manifestation of its

21 Zhang and Gu (n 16) 23.

22 Zhang and Gu (n 16) 31.

23 Zhongtao T. Zhang, 'China's Road to Participate in the International Rule-Making' (2016) 12(4) Canadian Social Science 51, at <http://www.cscanada.net/index.php/css/article/view/8329> (accessed October 24, 2022).

24 Joseph S. Nye Jr, 'Soft Power and American Foreign Policy' (2004) 119 Pol Sci Q 255.

25 Alexander L. Vuving, 'How Soft Power Works' (2009), paper presented at the panel 'Soft Power and Smart Power', Toronto, September 3, 2009, at <https://apcss.org/Publications/Vuving%20How%20soft%20power%20works%20APSA%202009.pdf> (accessed October 25, 2022).

unique model of development that is attractive despite differences in culture, political, and economic systems.[26]

Then, soft power in China is based on the Chinese culture itself,[27] a sort of "soft power with Chinese characteristics".[28] It can be summarized in two levels. The first refers to Chinese values, thinking ways, ideas and norms. The second is institutional and is revealed in its output of policies, strategies, rules, and institutions: a series of concepts based on "harmony", like the peaceful rise, peaceful development, and the harmonious world can be regarded as diplomatic strategies to realize the Chinese goal to be a world power, and can be looked upon as cases to examine the cultural soft power and its applications at national and international level.[29] In particular, the concepts of harmonious society and harmonious world are the desired domestic order and international order that China intends to build.[30] The approach aiming at "establishing a 'harmonious society' domestically and establishing a 'harmonious world' internationally" is considered as providing a "comprehensive framework for the ongoing development of China's soft power".[31] Furthermore, such soft approach showing obedience to legal principles couples perfectly with China's "go global" economic strategy since protects China's image internationally and facilitates to realize the role of law in helping Chinese companies and people "go global" and to attract more investments to China.[32]

26 Muhammad Nadeem Mirza, Hussain Abbas, Muhammad Qasim Nizamani, 'Evaluating China's Soft Power Discourse: Assumptions, Strategies, and Objectives' (2020) 5 Glob Strategic & Sec Stud Rev 40.

27 Huning N. Wang, '作为国家实力的文化:软权力' ('Culture as National Soft Power: Soft Power') (1993) 3 复旦学报 (J Fudan U) 91; You Wu, 'The Rise of China with Cultural Soft Power in the Age of Globalization' (2018) 8 J Lit & Art Stud 763. Actually, even if the importance of culture has apparently got the support of the Chinese leadership, not all scholars agree that it is the core of soft power. The minority view does not deny the importance of culture, but purport that the state's political power and not its culture or attractiveness, is the essence of soft power. See Bonnie S. Glaser and Melissa E. Murphy, 'Soft power with Chinese characteristics the ongoing debate', in Carola McGiffert (ed), *Chinese soft power and its implications for the United States* (Center for Strategic and International Studies 2009) 10.

28 Glaser and Murphy (n 27) 12.

29 Ying Zhou, 'Assessing China's Soft Power Diplomacy and its Implications on Asia Cooperation', at <http://www.waseda-giari.jp/sysimg/imgs/200908_si_st_09zhou_paper_f.pdf> (accessed October 24, 2022).

30 Ying (n 29) 14.

31 Changping Fang, '中美软实力比较及其对中国的启示' ('Comparison of Chinese and U.S. Soft Power and Its Implications for China') (July 1, 2007) 世界经济与政治 (World Economy and Politics) 287, quoted by Glaser and Murphy (n 27) 20.

32 Zhang and Gu (n 16) 27 ff.

China's preference for using soft power in international relations is greatly manifested in its diplomatic strategy. This is achieved through the Beijing consensus, partnership initiatives, and spread of cultural values using the Confucius institutes;[33] being the common feature of such policy the focus upon the mechanisms of attraction. On the diplomatic side, this has been developed through a 'charm offensive' towards partners and by creating a confidence in Chinese policy, discourses, culture and models. Furthermore, China has developed different activities to promote cultural, economic and trade initiatives to establish its soft power.[34] However, China's soft-power policy main objective continues to be that of disproving the China-threat theory and to promote a different image of the country.

3.2 *Chinese Legal Diplomacy*

Chinese legal diplomacy can be framed within the more general context of the cultural diplomacy.

China is actively focused on the promotion of the Chinese social, and cultural development to the world, mainly through the action of the Confucius Institutes which create an attraction towards Chinese culture through various activities and encourage students to participate in cultural and educational exchange programs.[35]

With reference to law, the decision of the CPC Central Committee on "Major Issues Pertaining to Comprehensively Promoting the Rule of Law" stated: "vigorously participate in the formulation of international norms, promote the handling of foreign-related economic and social affairs according to the law, strengthen our country's discourse power and influence in international legal affairs, use legal methods to safeguard our country's sovereignty, security and development interests".[36]

Having considered all circumstances indicated above, Chinese jurists put forward the concept of "law diplomacy" to offer a new perspective to deal with

33 About the importance attached to the Confucius Institutes in the Chinese soft power approach, see Ying Zhou and Sabrina Luk, 'Establishing Confucius Institutes: a tool for promoting China's soft power?' (2016) 25 J Contemp China 628; Rui Yang, 'Soft power and higher education: an examination of China's Confucius Institutes' (2010) 8 Glob, Soc & Ed 235; James F. Paradise, 'China and International Harmony: The Role of Confucius Institutes in Bolstering Beijing's Soft Power' (2009) 49 Asian Surv 647.

34 Nadeem Mirza, Abbas, Qasim Nizamani (n 26).

35 Osamu Sayama, 'China's Approach to Soft Power. Seeking a Balance between Nationalism, Legitimacy and International Influence' (2016) Royal United Services Institute Occasional Paper, on file with the author.

36 The decision is cited in Zhang (n 23) 51.

diplomatic issues and a new and different dimension for managing foreign relations.

Legal diplomacy can be counted among the instruments to exercise soft power, which refers to the ability to obtain preferred outcomes through appeal attraction rather than coercion and rests primarily on three resources: the culture (that it is attractive to others), the political values (that are followed at home and abroad), and the foreign policies (that are seen as legitimate and having moral authority) of a country.[37]

Chinese legal diplomacy is based on the call on the jurist academia and law professionals in all countries to increase exchange and communication and to better understand each other's laws and regulations, so as to provide a strong and firm guarantee for the sustainable development and common prosperity in the global economy. At the same time, Chinese jurists involved in these issues are of the opinion that "different legal systems, legal units, and legal institutions are showing signs of convergence to a certain degree. It facilitates the mobility of jurists and law professionals among countries, explores and diversifies the channels and means of legal services, draws closer the legal ideas, notions, and basic legal values of different countries, provides infinite opportunity for law diplomacy, and enrich the form and substance of law diplomacy".[38]

According to the Chinese scholars, the importance of legal diplomacy can be seen at least from six perspectives.[39]

First, in the ambit of an international governance system respecting the rule of law, legal diplomacy favours the management of international issues from the legal point of view, transforming political, economic, cultural, military, and environmental issues into legal ones.

Second, legal diplomacy is consistent with the Party and government's policies and is the direction of the Party's vision on the world trends and future architecture.

Third, legal diplomacy contributes to China's efforts in building a socialist country under the rule of law and to its proactive involvement in constructing international rule of law. In particular, through legal diplomacy China develops studies on its domestic experience, puts forward its legal culture, and, at the same time, learns extensively from other countries' legal expertise and experience in the rule of law, and conducts legal exchanges with other countries.

37 Joseph S. Nye, *Soft power: the Means to Success in World Politics* (Public Affairs 2004).

38 Zhang and Gu (n 16) 24.

39 Zhang and Gu (n 16) 29 ff.

Fourth, legal diplomacy is considered the necessary choice of elevating China's international standing by promoting the exchange between China and the rest of the world on the rule of law, and the diplomatic work of China to a higher level.[40]

Fifth, legal diplomacy is considered a valid support to drive away misunderstandings and suspicions about China and to challenge the so-called "China threat" theory. This theory is based on the economic growth of China that is so fast to possible undermine other economies, on the Chinese military strength sometimes felt as a threat, and on the large population and high energy consumption of China which is considered a threat to the rest of the world and detrimental to China's development. The Chinese view is that the observance of and respect for law will strengthen the confidence and belief in China as a responsible major power, loving peace, honouring its engagements and never seeking hegemony.

Sixth, legal diplomacy protects Chinese interests and facilitates the smooth advancement of all its ventures, since legal diplomacy not only improves international legal standards, but also helps safeguard Chinese national interests.

In a nutshell, from the Chinese point of view, "the promotion of law diplomacy plays an important strategic role in establishing a fair and just international order and system and building a harmonious world of enduring peace and common prosperity".[41]

3.3 *The Chinese Way to Conduct Legal Diplomacy*

Since the power of a country determines its influence on international law,[42] for a large developing country such as China the participation in the international rule-making process, is considered an inevitable requirement of economic globalization and regional economic integration, an indispensable way to be involved in international affairs, a necessary policy to protect the national interests.[43]

China conducts legal diplomacy at different levels and in various forms. They range from the work of Chinese delegations in multilateral organizations

40 Here it is very interesting the comparison with the Roman empire (and the consequent point of view) made by Zhang and Gu (n 16) 32 ff, where they observe that "[t]he Roman Empire conquered the world for three times, the first by war, the second religion, and the third law".

41 Zhang and Gu (n 16) 29.

42 Chongli L. Xu, 论文题目：软硬实力与中国对国际法的影响 (*Hard and soft power and China's impact on the international law*) (dissertation Law School of Xiamen University 2012) 151.

43 Zhang (n 23) 51.

and in the dispute resolution arena, to the establishment and promotion of new Chinese international commercial courts, the brand-new framework provided by the Belt and Road Initiative for bilateral relations in the legal field and others. Having considered the scope of the present work, attention will be paid only to those aspects of Chinese legal diplomacy relevant to the export of the Chinese pattern abroad, with particular reference to Africa.

Law diplomacy involves official and people-to-people diplomacy. With reference to official diplomacy, the Ministries of Foreign Affairs, Justice and Education, the Supreme People's Court and other government agencies launched relevant programs and sponsored related events. As far as people-to-people diplomacy is concerned, people-to people-exchanges and interpersonal relations have gained a prominent part in the establishment of the country's soft image using several platforms to promote its culture, language and traditions to the world through cultural exchange programs, as well as countless governmental and non-governmental seminars, conferences and dialogue centres for the interaction, cooperation and discussion of the Chinese people with the outside world.[44] Chinese legal organizations such as the China Law Society and the China Society for Human Rights Studies are also actively engaged in legal diplomacy activities. Through this system China wants to have a more proactive role in participating in legislative and treaty-making processes of international organizations, promote the formulation of international and global laws and regulations and the expansion of international legislation. Participating in the formulation of legislation at international level is considered by China as an opportunity to express its positions, opinions, national interests and core values, and to contribute to the achievement of a worldwide harmony.[45]

Practically, the Chinese way to conduct legal diplomacy is based on continuous exchanges on domestic laws and on international law. Such exchanges are made by academic conferences and seminars, by sending Chinese students and scholars abroad to better understand foreign laws and international law and by inviting foreigners to learn more about Chinese laws and regulations, by supporting mutual visits and inspections of judges, procurators, lawyers, policemen, legal workers to exchange views on different legal issues and enhance coordination, by providing legal assistance in various forms with the aim of spreading the Chinese legal culture: the idea is that China can exercise more extensive and deeper influence on other nations by exporting its legal

44 Nadeem Mirza, Abbas, Qasim Nizamani (n 26) 45.
45 Zhang and Gu (n 16) 36.

thoughts and experience in practicing the rule of law, maintaining full respect for the sovereignty and cultures other nations.[46]

So far, the China Law Society has been the main actor in putting forward Chinese legal diplomacy. In particular, the China Law Society has focused its activities into people-to-people diplomacy and academic diplomacy and the compilation of textbooks on legal diplomacy has been started.[47]

4 Legal Diplomacy to Export the Chinese Pattern in Africa

From the description made above, two points deserve particular attention: the fact that through legal diplomacy China wants to put forward its legal culture, and the promotion of legal exchanges between China and the rest of the world.

Since participating in the international rule-making activities can be understood as international legislative cooperation, China considers itself entitled to make its own proposals and ideas for the construction or the reform of specific legal systems, as well as on settlement of international disputes.[48] Actively participating in international legislation, jurisdiction, and law enforcement is considered a priority by China.[49]

China wants to give the message that it is a State with proper legal culture, based on its own history and tradition, to disprove one of the strongest stereotypes that Westerners have on China, in line with its image-building policy to create a new world image using soft power diplomacy.[50]

Since its inception, the effective practice of Chinese legal diplomacy, exemplified by the establishment and sustained development of the different Fora initiated under the initiative of the China Law Society (like the China-ASEAN Legal Forum, the BRICS Legal Forum, and the Legal Forum under the Forum on China-Africa Cooperation), has given a significant contribution to the enrichment of the theory and practice of the Chinese legal diplomacy.

The Forum on China-Africa Cooperation (FOCAC) is the main vehicle for China to support cooperation with African countries. Along with FOCAC,

46 Zhang and Gu (n 16). Interestingly, this part does not appear in the booklet published by the China Law Society, but it is in the other version of the same work published in (2013) Glob Rev 48–50.

47 For an exhaustive list of the activities done by the China Law Society in the ambit of legal diplomacy project see again Zhang and Gu (n 16) Section IV. Gu is the former Secretary General of the China Law Society.

48 He (n 14) 171.

49 Zhang and Gu (n 16) 36.

50 Ying (n 29) 2.

China has a major diplomatic presence in Africa: Beijing, which has diplomatic relations with 49 African countries, maintains an embassy with an accredited ambassador in all of them. In this ambit, China-Africa legal cooperation is one of the areas where the Chinese orientation to legal diplomacy showed to be very strong.

The establishment of the 'Forum on China-Africa Cooperation-Legal Forum' as a clear sign of the development of China-Africa relations represents a solid foundation for China-Africa legal diplomacy in Africa. The promotion of legal diplomacy, the development of dialogues, exchanges, and cooperation between the legal academia and legal professionals of China and Africa, and the application of legal diplomacy to disputes involving Chinese and African parties, is considered of great importance to strengthening China-Africa friendship, guaranteeing Sino-African trade and investment, and the common prosperity of China and Africa.

The promotion of legal diplomacy has been inserted into the Constitution of the Guiding Committee of the Legal Forum under the Forum on China-Africa Cooperation, the first time to expressly indicate the legal diplomacy as a common mission of the legal academia and legal professionals of the concerned.

In the ambit of this extended project, China engaged in different legal capacity building programs. China has brought a lot of scholars and students from Africa (and beyond) to learn Chinese legal system and culture, sending Chinese legal professional, government officers, scholars and students to Africa to study the legal systems of African countries, organizing conferences and seminars on Sino-African legal relations. After the Center for African Laws and Society at Xiangtan University, the Chinese government authorized the opening of several other centers in other Chinese university to study African law and legal culture. In general, short-term training programs organized by China are most likely the largest in the world; in addition to bringing officials and other professionals to China, the Chinese government trains people in their home countries, and Confucius institutes play a major role in this respect.[51]

On the other side, China opened Confucius Institutes in every African country with whom it has diplomatic relations. After the first Confucius Institute established in Africa in Nairobi in 2005, as of November 2021 China maintains 61 Confucius Institutes and 48 Confucius Classrooms in Africa.[52] As mentioned

51 Samuli Seppanen, 'Chinese Legal Development Assistance: Which Rule of Law? Whose Pragmatism?' (2021) 51 Vand L Rev 101.

52 Xinhuanet, '61 Confucius Institutes, 48 Confucius Classrooms established in Africa: white paper' (2021), at <http://www.news.cn/english/2021-11/26/c_1310334064.htm> (accessed October 27, 2022).

above, the main mission of the Confucius Institutes is to spread the Chinese culture and language worldwide. In the ambit of this mission, legal scholars have been sent to Africa (and beyond) to teach Chinese law and many local law students learned the Chinese language in view of possible future graduate studies in China. China also sponsored the creation of an arbitration Centre in Johannesburg aiming at dealing and solving with Sino-African commercial disputes.

The effort in promoting legal diplomacy, mainly conducted by the China Law Society is considered still not adequate. So, there is an internal demand for China to further improve the construction of legal diplomacy. The theoretical research outcomes are considered still preliminary, there is an urgent need to determine how to translate research outcomes into concrete policies, and a further effort for the international promotion of the research outcomes of Chinese law diplomacy is considered necessary.[53]

The further implications of this further strategy are clear from the words of the high-ranking executives of the China Law Society when they say that "[i]n order to promote the building of a harmonious world of lasting peace and common prosperity, law diplomacy must be treated as a national strategy and an organic part of China's soft and smart power. Law diplomacy has an irreplaceable promotional role in China's economic growth and elevating its discourse power. Therefore, starting from the overall national strategy of development, we should work out a detailed and balanced plan to promote law diplomacy both at the governmental and non-governmental levels to advance China's peaceful rise under the rule of law and realize the Chinese dream and the dream of the rule of law, providing legal support and guarantee for the Chinese discourse system in international rule of law and for the building of a just and reasonable international order and system as well as a harmonious world of common prosperity".[54]

The language issue is strictly connected to this approach. Since at present English is the vehicular language of the international society, the international rule-making process is also conducted using this language. China wants to gradually introduce the use of Chinese in this process to support the use of the Chinese models, to give to its people more opportunities to be present in the key position of international organizations, to ultimately have an always increasing voice in the international arena. The activity of the Confucius

53 Zhang and Gu (n 16) 46.

54 *Ibid.*

Institutes to bring the Chinese language worldwide can also be framed in the ambit of this general vision.

The ultimate goal of the legal diplomacy is then very clear: China shall become the key country to consider when discussing about rule of law and legal reforms. The Chinese pattern shall be presented and promoted as a viable and sustainable alternative to the Western model and subject to be adopted by those countries (especially the developing) aiming at imitating China's economic rise. As a direct consequence, the Chinese approach to the rule of law discourse (the so-called "rule of law with Chinese characteristics"[55]) shall become an alternative approach to the Western one, on the basis of the same value and dignity between the two.

5 The Chinese Civil Code as a Tool for Legal Diplomacy in Africa

From the scenario outlined above, it can be understood how the discussion about the significance of the Chinese Civil Code in Africa cannot be seen from the law in the book perspective (which is reductive and not that relevant), but it must be considered in the more general discussion concerning legal diplomacy and the promotion of the Chinese pattern in Africa.

Africa is undergoing a profound phase of legal reform aiming at modernizing legal systems that are often outdated and dating back to the end of the colonial period, when the leaders of the new independent African countries decided to maintain the legal system inherited from the colonial administration.[56] Such process of legal reform undergoes social and political influences and is affected by the presence of movements promoting the 'decolonization' of African law, its detachment from the European pattern and, more in general, of the African countries from the influence of the former colonial powers. The latter resulted, for example, in Zimbabwe cutting of relations with Great Britain during the Mugabe's administration or – more recently – in Central African Republic, Mali and Burkina Faso coups, whose common line can be detected in the intention to break the ties with France.

---

55 On the Chinese approach to the rule of law, see Randall Peerenboom, *China's Long March toward Rule of Law* (Cambridge University Press 2002); Ignazio Castellucci, 'Rule of Law with Chinese Characteristics' (2007) 13 Ann S Int'l & Comp L 35.

56 On the reasons that determined the retention of the legal systems after the colonial administration see Charles M. Fombad, 'Fostering a Constructive Intra-African Dialogue in Post-Colonial Africa' (2022) 66 J African L 1.

The African legal history tells us that these kinds of sudden political changes are accompanied by reforms of the country's legal system. This happened – for example – very often in the 1960s and 1970s of the past century during the cold war times when African rulers were frequently changing from the Western capitalist to the socialist pattern, and vice-versa, to position their country under the control of one or the other of the two blocs.[57]

The situation we are living in the present days is not that different from the one of the historical periods referred above. China proposes itself as leader of the developing countries bloc, as opposed to that of the developed Western countries. China argues that it is still a developing country who reached a higher level of development thanks to the strict compliance with its pattern. With African countries China upholds that their adoption of the Western patterns has not produced too many results in terms of development for them: therefore, China[58] proposes to African countries the adoption of its model under its guidance to support their development. This includes the adoption of the Chinese pattern.

Law-related foreign development assistance embraces at least three different dimensions. The wording 'legal technical assistance' has been used to describe aid comprising: (i) technical assistance for the drafting of laws and regulations and technical advice for substantive law reforms, (ii) support for the court system and the legal profession, and (iii) assistance for the development of legal information systems.[59] The focus here will be on the first of these three dimensions.

The main issue is to ascertain even some elementary facts about the size and type of China's legal development assistance. In general, this would be a simple task in many other jurisdictions. In China, collecting even basic information about foreign development assistance constitutes a formidable

57 Among the several cases of political change followed by a reform of the legal system (mainly remained at the level of the law in the books), it is worth mentioning those of Ethiopia and Somalia, since the changes between the two blocs was one of the main factors determining the Somali defeat in the 1977 Ogaden war with Ethiopia. See more in Francesco M. Mengo, 'Il Derg, Siad Barre e l'Ogaden. Due diverse concezioni di dittatura militare e il loro scontro in una guerra per procura' (2015) 24 Diacronie, at <https://journals.openedition.org/diacronie/3832?lang=es> (accessed October 31, 2022).

58 With reference to the Chinese foreign development assistance to Africa (without a legal focus), see Deborah Brautigam, *The Dragon's Gift: The Real Story of China in Africa* (OUP 2011); David Haroz, 'China in Africa: Symbiosis or Exploitation?' (2011) 35 Fletcher Forum World Aff 65; Uche E. Ofodile, 'Trade, Empires, and Subjects-China-Africa Trade: A New Fair Trade Arrangement, or the Third Scramble for Africa?' (2008) 41 Vand J Transnat'l L 505.

59 Seppanen (n 51).

challenge, especially if it not possible to count on some 'insider' support. This because information about Chinese foreign development assistance is considered a state secret.[60]

Even if law has been considered having a marginal role in Chinese foreign development assistance,[61] China has been very active as an actor for legal reforms in Africa. Considering the kind of China-Africa relations, it can be understood how this happened mainly in the area of commercial law.[62] China has signed treaties and agreements with a number of African countries covering commercial and judicial technical assistance,[63] and is actively engaged in supporting African judicial systems and arbitration and mediation as disputes resolution mechanisms for Sino-African commercial controversies.[64] The China Law Society – through the Center for African Laws at Xiangtan University – offered its contribution to help OHADA[65] for the reform and update of some uniform acts; but China has get to the point of imposing legislative requirements on developing countries in specific projects.[66] Furthermore, in

60 Seppanen (n 51); Brautigam (n 58).

61 Seppanen (n 51).

62 Salvatore Mancuso, 'China in Africa and the Law' (2012) 18 Ann Surv Int'l & Comp L 243. See also Frédérique Youmbi Fasseu, 'La joint-venture dans le contexte sino-africain: éléments pour une lex mercatoria sino-africaine' (2012) 1 Revue de l'ERSUMA, at <https://revue.ersuma.org/no-1-juin-2012/etudes-13/LA-JOINT-VENTURE-DANS-LE-CONTEXTE> (accessed October 31, 2022).

63 Won L. Kidane, 'Agreements and Dispute Settlement in China–Africa Economic Ties', in Arkebe Oqubay and Justin Y. Lin (eds), *China-Africa and an Economic Transformation* (Oxford University Press 2019) 216.

64 Moses N. Kiggundu, 'China-Africa Legal and Judiciary Systems: Advancing Mutually Beneficial Economic Relations' (2013) 4 Beijing L Rev 155; Weidong Zhu, 'Arbitration as the Best Option for the Settlement of China-African Trade and Investment Disputes' (2013) 57 J African L 149.

65 OHADA is the acronym for *Organisation pour l'Harmonisation en Afrique du Droit des Affaires*, a system of harmonized business law presently in force in 17 African countries, on which see the resources at <www.ohada.org> and <www.ohada.com> (accessed November 1, 2022).

66 This was the case with a mining and infrastructure agreement between the Democratic Republic of the Congo (DRC) and a group of Chinese state-owned companies, where the agreement between the DRC and the Chinese companies included a requirement for the DRC to adopt legislation that gave the Chinese companies the benefits of all existing DRC regulations and the freedom to transfer funds abroad free of charges and transfer controls. See the *Convention de collaboration entre la République Démocratique du Congo et le Groupement d'Entreprises Chinoises: China Railway Group Ltd Sinohydro Corporation relative au développement d'un projet minier et d'un projet d'infrastructures en Republique Démocratique du Congo*, Article 15.1, at <http://static.tijd.be/pdf/congochina.pdf> (accessed November 1, 2022).

2014 Chinese agricultural experts took an active part in providing expertise the drafting of Benin's Agricultural Law and Agricultural Administration Law, in connection with Chinese investments into agricultural land in that country.[67]

Another example of the legal influence exercised by China on African countries regards the Special Economic Zones. After the end of the Maoist times, Special Economic Zones played an important role in the development of the Chinese economy, since through them the Chinese government was able to check the results of economic reforms and to attract foreign investments to targeted areas, thus favoring their development.[68] When Chinese companies started their activities in Africa, the Chinese government supported African countries in the establishment of Special Economic Zones to host Chinese companies there. Chinese-supported SEZs have been established in several African countries, and some of these countries reportedly modeled their SEZ laws on the Chinese example.[69]

If all the above-described aspects are considered, it can be understood how the new Chinese Civil Code could represent a further step in the more general discourse of the Chinese legal diplomacy in Africa and the China-Africa legal cooperation.

The Code is clearly too new to measure any kind of direct influence in Africa at present. However, if we consider that – according to the China-Africa Cooperation Action Plan 2022–2024 – "[t]he two sides will strengthen exchanges and cooperation between the leadership, special committees, and bilateral friendship groups of the National People's Congress of China and parliaments of African countries to enhance mutual understanding and friendship and promote exchanges and mutual learning in such areas as legislation", and

67 The People's Republic of China, China's Foreign Aid White Paper (2014), at <https://perma.cc/9F4A-Z3BC> (accessed November 2, 2022).

68 Brautigam (n 58).

69 This is the case at least for Angola, Djibouti, Egypt, Ethiopia, Nigeria and Tanzania. See Bryan Robinson, *African Special Economic Zones. Lessons and Investments from China* (Springer 2022); Jan Knoerich, Liliane Chantal Mouan, Charlotte Goodburn, 'Is China's Model of SEZ-Led Development Viable? A Call for Smart Replication' (2021) 50 Journal of Current Chinese Affairs 248; UNCTAD, *Handbook on Special Economic Zones in Africa. Towards Economic Diversification across the Continent* (UNCTAD 2021), at <https://unctad.org/system/files/official-document/diaeia2021d3_en.pdf> (accessed November 6, 2022); Deborah Brautigam and Xiaoyang Tang, 'China's investment in special economic zones in Africa', in Thomas Farole and Gokhan Akinci (eds), *Special Economic Zones: Progress, Emerging Challenges, and Future Directions* (The International Bank for Reconstruction and Development/The World Bank 2011) 69; Deborah Brautigam and Xiaoyang Tang, 'African Shenzhen: China's special economic zones in Africa' (2011) 49 J Mod Afr Stud 27.

that "[t]he two sides will encourage the National People's Congress of China and parliaments of African countries to jointly hold bilateral and multilateral seminars, strengthen human resources cooperation, and promote capacity building of legislative bodies",[70] it is not difficult to predict that the Code will be part of the discussions in any future legislative support programs by China on matters contemplated therein.

A further signal in this direction can be seen in the insertion of legal training on the Chinese Civil Code in the 7th and 8th Course of China-Africa Legal Professionals Exchange Program, hosted by China Law Society in 2020 and 2021 respectively.[71] Courses on Chinese law including the main features of the Chinese Civil Code have been already organized in African universities.[72] This will imply that African legal professionals trained in the ambit of these activities will bring their 'Chinese experience' in the legal discourses concerning civil law matters.

6 Conclusions

The Chinese legal diplomacy program (with particular reference to Africa) can be seen in the ambit of the wider objective of the Chinese soft power policy to promote Chinese socialist market values and the Chinese development model as an alternative to Western values and support to development.[73]

Should this endeavor have success, the West will lose its monopoly over the export of patterns and legal solutions, having a strong (and in many cases more appealing) competitor in a world where the economic implications of legal rules play a decisive role in their adoption and formulation.[74]

70 Forum on China-Africa Cooperation Dakar Action Plan (2022–2024), paragraphs 2.2.2 and 2.2.3, at <http://www.focac.org/eng/zywx_1/zywj/202201/t20220124_10632444.htm> (accessed November 6, 2022).

71 The program of the 7th Course of China-Africa Legal Professionals Exchange Program is available at <https://www.oam.org.mz/wp-content/uploads/2020/08/China-Africa-Legal-Professionals-Exchange-Program.pdf> (accessed November 6, 2022), while I directly received the program of the 8th from the China Law Society. The program of the 2022 Course was not available at the time of writing.

72 See, for example, the courses organized at the University of Cape Town in South Africa at <http://www.lawatwork.uct.ac.za/lw/courses> (accessed on November 6, 2022).

73 Such idea is also proposed in Glaser and Murphy (n 27) 11.

74 The theme of the importance of the economy over the law today, and how law must serve economic objectives is developed in Salvatore Mancuso, *Liquidità e comparazione* (Pacini 2018).

The present work tried to demonstrate how the issue of the significance of the Chinese Civil Code in Africa is an example of the fact that it is not possible to discuss about the circulation of the legal models merely looking at the law in the books and that it is necessary to pay attention at the different legal formants[75] acting in a given 'lawscape'.[76] Following this path the discourse about the (possible) significance of the Chinese Civil Code in Africa assumes a different connotation based on the broader Chinese design of strengthening its footprint in Africa also using legal cooperation mechanisms.

Therefore, the real significance of the Chinese Civil Code in Africa shall be measured in a medium, or even long, term perspective looking at how – and to which extent – the African legislator will be receptive to – and be further influenced by – the Chinese pattern.

"The international law and the internal law are both the important legal sources of the socialist legal system with Chinese characteristics. Just like a pair of wings, they will make a great contribution to the realization of the Chinese Dream".[77]

---

75 On the concept of legal formants, see Rodolfo Sacco, 'Legal Formants: A Dynamic Approach to Comparative Law' (1991) 39 Am J Comp L 1 (Part 1) and 343 (Part 2).

76 On the concept of 'lawscape', see Salvatore Mancuso, 'Law and Glocalization', in Victor N. Roudometof and Ugo Dessì (eds), *Handbook of Culture and Glocalization* (Edward Elgar, 2022) 76.

77 Zhang (n 23) 52.

CHAPTER 23

'Obvious Unfairness' and 'Unconscionability': An (Indirect) American Connection to Chinese Contract Law

James Gordley and 蒋昊 Hao Jiang

1 Introduction

As one of us observed elsewhere, Chinese Civil Code is a product of Western legal transplants and Chinese ingenuity.[1] Yet, the Western influence came mainly from the German tradition and sporadically from French, Soviet and Roman law. American law is a significant source of inspiration for Chinese corporate and securities law. There is an indirect connection to the doctrine governing fairness in contract law. As recognized by leading Chinese scholars such as He Jian, Han Shiyuan and Wang Yi, the Chinese doctrine of 'obvious unfairness' is like the American doctrine of 'unconscionability'. He Jian identified the two doctrines.[2] He considers both of them to be a compromise between the general principles of fairness and autonomy: the fairness principle requires substantive fairness and autonomy requires bargaining equality and freedom from exploitation.[3] Han Shiyuan recognized unconscionability in American law as the common law counterpart of obvious fairness doctrine.[4] He believes that exploitation or bargaining inequality indispensable and denies that substantive fairness is an independent ground for relief.[5] In his words, *laesio*

1 Hao Jiang, 'The Making of a Civil Code in China: Promises and Perils of a New Civil Law' (2021) 95 Tul L Rev 777.

2 贺剑, '《合同法》第54条第一款第2条 （显失公平制度）评注' (2017) 法学家 [He Jian, 'Commentary on Obvious Unfairness under Article 54 of Contract Law' (2017) Jurists] 155 (in the English abstract of the commentary, He wrote that "[i]t is widely accepted in the case law that unconscionability, despite the disputes among scholars, has both a substantive and procedural elements"; here, the term 'unconscionability' was the translation of the Chinese term 'obvious unfairness').

3 He (n 2) 155–156.

4 韩世远, 合同法总论 (法律出版社 2018) [Han Shiyuan, *The Law of Contract* (Law Press 2018)] 290.

5 Han Shiyuan, 'Regulating Unfair Contract Terms under Chinese Law', in Mindy Chen-Wishart and Stefan Vogenauer (eds), *Contents of Contracts and Unfair Terms. Studies in the Contract Law of Asia* (OUP 2020) 44.

 | DOI:10.1163/9789004704428_024

enormis – relief was given simply because a price is unfair – does not have a place in Chinese law.[6] Moreover, fairness is "a matter of subjective evaluation" of the parties.[7] It would be paternalistic for courts to exercise their judgment over the fairness of terms.[8] Wang Yi treated obvious unfairness as one of the two "constitutive elements" of exploitation (the other being one party taking advantage of the other's distress).[9] The mainstream view of American jurists is the same. 'Substantive unfairness' alone does not warrant relief. The disadvantaged party must also prove 'procedural unfairness': bargaining inequality manifested by oppression or surprise. In this chapter, we will see that the parallel is real but that it goes beyond American law.

2 The Origin of the Problem

In borrowing this solution from the West, China imported the problem it raises. Why should substantive unfairness not be a sufficient ground for relief? Before the 19th century, Western legal systems did recognize it as a sufficient ground. During the 19th century, they said that a contract could not be substantively unfair, or, if it could be, its unfairness should not matter. Chinese and American law have arrived at an uneasy and perhaps inconsistent middle position: substantive unfairness matters but does not by itself warrant relief.

In the 19th century, the idea of fair exchange went out of fashion when Western jurists started to embrace will theories of contract. These theories defined contract solely in terms of the will of the parties. Relief for unfairness violated the principle that the parties were bound by whatever terms they had willed. Also, it made no sense because, according to the 19th century jurists, it was meaningless to speak about fair terms. Value was relative. The value of a performance differed from one party to the next.

Before the 19th century, relief for unfairness had been given in both civil and common law without raising these concerns. Roman law gave relief to a person who sold land for less than half its fair price. Medieval French law adopted this rule. The medieval *ius commune*, the version of Roman law accepted in throughout much of continental Europe, extended this remedy to give relief leases as well as sales, to buyers as well as sellers, and to all goods and services.

6 *Ibid.*
7 Han (n 5) 45.
8 Han (n 4) 292.
9 Wang Yi, 'Duress and Exploitation in Chinese Contract Law', in Mindy Chen-Wishart and Stefan Vogenauer (eds), *Invalidity. Studies in the Contract Law of Asia* (OUP 2020) 57.

In England before the 19th century, courts of equity had given relief when a contract was 'unconscionable', which, according to the courts, meant that it was extremely unfair. It was "unreasonable",[10] "unjust",[11] "unequitable and unconscientious",[12] "hard and unequal",[13] or entered into for "inadequate" or "grossly inadequate" consideration[14] or through "imposition".[15]

In the 19th century, jurists wondered why the law should ever give relief for unfairness. The French Civil Code had preserved the traditional rule giving relief to sellers of land. Some jurists claimed that the relief was given, not on account of unfairness, but because the disadvantaged party had been the victim of mistake or fraud or duress. In much of Germany, Roman law remained in force until the enactment of the German Civil Code in 1900. Jurists agreed that relief for *laesio enormis* could not be reconciled with the principles of contract law. Some said it was given out of 'humanity'. Anglo-American courts of equity continued to give relief when a contract was 'unconscionable'. As Simpson notes, a disparity in price came to be considered as "evidence of fraud, not as an independent substantive ground, and not as constituting hardship".[16] While the fraud theory never swept the field,[17] it found its way into many treatises beginning with the early one by Powell in 1790.[18] Courts of equity nevertheless continued to give relief, perhaps as generously as they would have if the theory had not changed.[19]

---

10 *Earl of Arglasse v Muschamp*, 1 Vern 237, 238–39; 23 Eng Rep 438, 439 (1684); *Earl of Chesterfield v Jannsen*, 2 Ves Sen 125, 130, 28 Eng Rep 82, 85 (1750–51) (argument for plaintiff).

11 *Earl of Chesterfield v Jannsen*, 2 Ves Sen 125, 130, 28 Eng Rep 82, 85 (1750–51) (argument for plaintiff).

12 *Chesterfield v Jannsen*, 2 Ves Sen 125, 155, 28 Eng Rep 82, 100 (1750–51).

13 *Kien v Stukeley*, 1 Bro. 191, 192, 1 Eng Rep 506, 507 (H.L. 1722) (argument for defendant).

14 *Gwynne v Heaton*, 1 Bro. C.C. 1, 6, 28 Eng Rep 949, 951 (1778).

15 *Earl of Chesterfield v Jannsen*, 2 Ves Sen 125, 145, 152, 156, 28 Eng Rep 82, 94, 98, 100 (1750–51); *Nichols v Gould*, 2 Ves Sen 422, 423, 28 Eng Rep 270, 270 (1752).

16 Alfred W.B. Simpson, 'The Horwitz Thesis and the History of Contracts' (1979) 46 U Chi L Rev 533 at 569.

17 See also, e.g., Theophilus Parsons, *The Law of Contracts* (4th edn, Little, Brown 1860) I, 362–363; John Norton Pomeroy, *A Treatise on the Specific Performance of Contracts as it is Enforced by Courts of Equitable Jurisdiction in the United States of America* (2nd edn, Banks & co 1897) 274–275.

18 See, e.g., John J. Powell, *Essay Upon the Law of Contracts and Agreements* (Chamberlaine and Rice 1790) II, 157–158; for additional references, see James Gordley, Hao Jiang, Arthur Taylor von Mehren, *An Introduction to the Comparative Study of Private Law. Readings, Cases, Materials* (2nd edn, OUP 2021) 200.

19 James Gordley, 'Equality in Exchange' (1981) 69 Cal L Rev 1587 at 1650–1655.

3 Two Paths Not Taken

3.1 *French Law: Relief Denied in Principle but Given in Practice*

In the 20th century, many French jurists continue to claim that, in principle, relief for unfairness interferes with freedom of the will, with "the act of will of a capable, enlightened, and free individual",[20] with "the healthy principle according to which one who is free is responsible".[21] Equilibrium in the values exchanged is "an unattainable chimera".[22] "[D]isequilbrium is the ransom price of liberty".[23]

Nevertheless, the reforms to the Civil Code of 2016 reinacted the traditional rule about relief for *lésion* in sales of land. In other situations, French courts have given relief from an unfair bargain supposedly for duress, fraud or mistake even though the disadvantaged party was not threatened, or lied to, and the only mistake was in the value of the other party's performance. In short, many French jurists are content with the 19th century approach which was to give relief in practice that one could not justify in principle.

3.2 *German Law: Relief for Unfairness Accompanied by Immoral Intent*

The German Civil Code of 1900 provided for relief from an unfair contract only if the unfairness was due to some weakness or disability of the disadvantaged party. Yet German courts have given relief even absent such a weakness provided the advantaged party acted with immoral intent.

An earlier draft of the German Civil Code, true to the will theories, abolished relief for *laesio enormis*. It provided that "[a] legal transaction that violates good morals (*gute Sitten*) is void", which became §138(1) of the Civil Code. The drafters had in mind cases such as contracts of prostitution. In the final draft, § 138(2) BGB was added to give relief when a contract is unfair. It provided:

> A legal transaction is also void when a person takes advantage of the distressed situation, inexperience, lack of judgmental ability, or grave weakness of will of another to obtain the grant or promise of financial

20 Laurent Aynès, 'La cause, inutile et dangereuse' (2014) 240 Droit et patrimoine 40.

21 Cyril Grimaldi, 'Les maux de la cause ne sont pas qu'une affaire des mots' (2015) Dalloz 814 at 815.

22 Romain Boffa, 'Juste cause (et injuste cause) Brèves remarques sur le projet de réforme du droit des contrats' (2015) Dalloz 335 at 339.

23 Denis Mazeaud, 'Protections des professionels contre les clauses abusives' (2012) Revue des contrats 276.

> advantages for himself or a third party that are obviously disproportionate to the performance given in return.

Beginning in 1936, the courts held that relief could be given when terms were unfair even though a party did not have any of the weakness mentioned in §138(2).[24] Relief could be given under §138(1) for a violation of good morals. The question arose, what was necessary, in addition to the disproportion in the values exchanged, for the transaction to constitute a violation of good morals? If nothing else was required, then §138(2) with its list of weaknesses would be superfluous. Since the intention of the drafters was to limit relief to the situations indicated in §138(2), any answer would be ingenuous. The courts' answer was that in the absence of one of these weaknesses, the advantaged party must have had the immoral intention (*verwerfliche Gesinnung*) of contracting on unfair terms. It is difficult to imagine that a party driving an unfair bargain without such an intention.

4 'Obvious Unfairness' and 'Unconscionability'

As the official commentary observed, the approach of Chinese Civil law was based on § 138–2.[25] A fellow drafter of the Civil Code, Wang Yi, traced the adoption the German approach to the 1929 draft Civil Code of Republic of China.[26] Even before the 1999 Contract Law extended full legal protection to private contracts, the General Principles of Civil Law (1986) had already introduced two doctrines that dealt with unfairness. They are: "obvious unfairness" (显失公平) and the "exploitation of one's vulnerability" (趁人之危). They are explained by Opinions of the Supreme Court on the Implementation of the General Principles of Law (1988):

Section 70 (Exploitation of One's Vulnerability) states:

> The conduct of a party is considered exploitation of one's vulnerability when he forces the other to make an untruthful declaration of intent and seriously harms the other party's interest by taking advantage of the other party's distress in order to obtain undue benefit.

24 Reichsgericht, 31 March 1936, RGZ 150, 1.

25 黄薇，中华人民共和国民法典总则编解读（中国法制出版社 2020）[Huang Wei, *Commentaries on the General Provisions of the Civil Code of Peoples Republic of China* (China Legal Publishing House 2020)] 491.

26 Wang (n 9) 56.

Section 71 (Obvious Unfairness) states:

> It is considered obvious unfairness when one party uses its strength or the other party's inexperience to achieve significantly unjust balance between rights and obligations that is contrary to the principle of compensation for equal value.

A contract is voidable either for "exploitation of one's vulnerability" or for "obvious unfairness" under article 54 of the Contract Law (1999).

As Han Shiyuan observed, obvious unfairness in both the General Principles and the Contract Law only required substantive unfairness or the unfairness of the content while exploitation of one's vulnerability focused on the subjective malice and required both exploitation and substantive unfairness.[27] Han concluded that this bifurcation relaxed the requirements of § 138(2) of the German Civil Code.[28] This observation was confirmed by many Chinese judges interviewed by one of the authors at City University of Hong Kong.[29] These judges acknowledged that most parties would opt for obvious unfairness unless there is clear evidence of exploitation. Even when there was such evidence, people would go for obvious unfairness simply because the bar is lower.

In 2017, these two doctrines were merged into a single doctrine of "obvious unfairness" by the General Provisions of Civil Law. In 2020, this revision was incorporated in article 151 of the Civil Code.

> When one party exploited situations such as the other's distress, vulnerability or lack of judgment and it resulted in the obvious unfairness of a civil juristic act at the time of its formation, the aggrieved party has the right to request people's court or arbitration agency to avoid such a civil juristic act.

Han praised this change as a positive development. As in Western scholars, he argued that obvious unfairness should not be a ground for vitiation.[30] The ground arises only when it is combined with exploitation.[31]

---

27 Han (n 4) 291.

28 *Ibid.*

29 Hao Jiang, interviews conducted between August 2018 and June 2019 (on file with the author).

30 Han (n 4) 291.

31 *Ibid.*

Some Chinese scholars, however, interpret their law in the same way as German courts have interpreted § 138(1) of their Code. The reason for giving relief from unfair terms is exploitation, which they regard as a special application of principle of good morals,[32] or a reflection of a combination of factors coming from other principles freedom of contract, fairness and good morals[33]. One cannot explain relief in Chinese law by borrowing the expression 'good faith'. It does not explain why relief is given in German law. As we have seen, to drafters of the German Civil Code, 'good morals' did not mean fairness in exchange. German courts said that an unfair exchange violated good morals only to escape the limitations of § 138(2) by applying § 138(1).

Nevertheless, the scholarly consensus is in agreement with the legislative commentary: "obvious unfairness" requires both subjective unfairness and objective unfairness,[34] a distinction like that drawn in the United States in discussions of the doctrine of unconscionability.

As we have seen, before the 19th century, courts of equity used this doctrine to give relief when a contract was severely unfair. In the 19th century, they continued to do so but the rationale changed. They said that the harsh terms were evidence of fraud. In the 20th century, in the United States, the doctrine was extended to allow both courts of law and equity to give relief for unconscionability. It was recognized that value was not purely subjective. There might be a 'gross disparity in the values exchanged'.

In 1952, § 2–302 of Uniform Commercial Code permitted relief for unconscionability in both law and equity.[35] In 1981, an equivalent provision was adopted in § 208 of the Second Restatement of Contracts.[36] § 208 of the Second Restatement of Contracts provides:

> If a contract or term thereof is unconscionable at the time the contract is made a court may refuse to enforce the contract, or may enforce the remainder of the contract without the unconscionable term, or may so limit the application of any unconscionable term as to avoid any unconscionable result.

---

32 He (n 2) 166.

33 贺剑, '《民法典》第151条评注', in 朱庆育 (ed), 《中国民法典评注》 (中国民主法制出版社 2021) [He Jian, 'Commentary on Article 151 of Chinese Civil Code', in Zhu Qingyu (ed), *Commentary on the Civil Code of China* (Publishing House of Chinese System of Democracy and Law 2021)] 1, 1.

34 Huang (n 25) 493; Han (n 4) 292.

35 Uniform Commercial Code § 2–302 (Am L Inst & Unif L Comm'n 1952).

36 Restatement (Second) of Contracts § 208 (Am L Inst 1981).

According to an Official Comment to the Second Restatement:

> Inadequacy of consideration does not of itself invalidate a bargain, but gross disparity in the values exchanged may be an important factor in a determination that a contract is unconscionable and may be sufficient ground, without more, for denying specific performance. Such a disparity may also corroborate indications of defects in the bargaining process, or may affect the remedy to be granted when there is a violation of a more specific rule. Theoretically it is possible for a contract to be oppressive taken as a whole, even though there is no weakness in the bargaining process and no single term which is in itself unconscionable. Ordinarily, however, an unconscionable contract involves other factors as well as overall imbalance.[37]

This approach is like that of the drafters of the German Civil Code. Relief is given where the there is a severe disproportion in the values exchanged that is due to some "weakness in the bargaining process". The Second Restatement, unlike § 138(2) BGB, acknowledges that relief may be given even when there is no such weakness. Yet it expects such cases to be rare.

Most American scholars believe that a disparity in the values exchanged is not enough to warrant relief. It must have been due to some weakness in the position of the disadvantages party. The Restatement Second mentions such weaknesses as "physical or mental infirmities, ignorance, illiteracy or inability to understand the language of the agreement".[38] American scholars use the terms "substantive" and "procedural unconscionability" to refer, respectively, to the unfairness of the terms and to the weak position of the disadvantaged party. According to most American scholars, a contract must be both 'substantively' and 'procedurally' unconscionable for a court to give relief.[39]

---

37 Id. comm. c.

38 Restatement (Second) of Contracts § 208 cmt d.

39 See Melissa T. Lonegrass, 'Finding Room for Fairness in Formalism – the Sliding Scale Approach to Unconscionability' (2012) 44 Loy U Chi L J 1 at 8–12 (describing the consideration of these two factors as the "conventional approach" and contrasting the "sliding scale approach" in "*strong* evidence of both prongs is no longer required to justify relief": Id at 11; emphasis by authors); see also Restatement of Consumer Contracts § 5 (Am L Inst, Tentative Draft, April 18, 2019) ("In determining that a contract or a term is unconscionable, a greater degree of one [form of unconscionability may offset] a lesser degree of the other element," but "in appropriate circumstances a high degree of substantive unconscionability is sufficient to find that a standard contract term [...] is unconscionable"). Our point is not only that substantive unconscionability is sufficient. It is

Chinese scholars use the terms 'objective' and 'subjective unfairness' in a similar way. As the official commentary to the Civil Code put it, objective unfairness concerns the "imbalance between the rights and obligations" which is measured objectively by only the disparity (or gross disparity) between price and value, which is deemed "a violation of the principle of compensation for equal value".[40] Subjective unfairness concerns a weakness on the part of the disadvantaged party. As we have seen, in 2017, the General Provisions of Civil Law article 151 created a unified doctrine of "obvious unfairness". The scholarly consensus is relief under this doctrine can be given only when there is both subjective unfairness (exploitation) and objective unfairness (significant imbalance or gross disparity) must be present to establish "obvious unfairness".[41] Chinese scholars are not necessarily borrowing from the American discussion. Like American jurists who require 'procedural unconscionability', they may be requiring 'subjective unfairness' or 'procedural unconscionability' because they do not believe that standards of fairness can be objective. Or they may believe that objective unfairness, in itself, does not warrant relief.

Some doubt that standards of fairness can be 'objective'. It is simply inappropriate, according to He Jian, to use principle of equal compensation for value (economic fairness) as the sole standard in determining obvious unfairness.[42] According to Han Shiyuan, value is subjective and mere judgment of man, and parties are the best judge of their own interest.[43] He has asked the courts to refrain from intervening contracts based solely on economic unfairness.[44] Chinese law should be primarily concerned with relief for subjective unfairness or injustice.[45]

As Han suggests, Chinese courts have considered only objective fairness in deciding whether to grant or deny relief. In *Jinding Corp. v Jirong Corp.*,[46] the Supreme Court denied relief because "[t]he supplementary agreement was the result of careful calculation and market risk allocation given the sudden and rapid increase of the cost of rare-earth magnet materials after the original contract was reached. It is within the range of normal market activities".

---

that procedural unconscionability should be relevant only as evidence of substantive unconscionability.

40 Huang (n 25) 493–494.

41 Huang (n 25) 493; Han (n 4) 292.

42 He (n 2) 156.

43 Han (n 4) 52.

44 *Ibid.*

45 *Ibid.*

46 (2014) 民申字第1072号 [(2014) Min Shen Zi No 1072].

In *Tong Xu v Liang ZF*,[47] the court gave relief even though the disadvantaged party could have protected itself and did not. The disadvantaged party agreed to pay RMB 3.9 million yuan for 49% of the shares of JZG Corp. The court found that "[t]he company had long been in deficit and had no commercial value and the asset value of the company did not exceed 100,000 yuan". The court said, "[t]he defendant either hid or did not properly disclose the true state of assets and finances of the company and so tricked the plaintiff into making the wrong decision in contracting". The evidence that the defendant did not make such a disclosure was that that the plaintiff had paid such a high price. The court added: "[e]ven when there is a disparity between the contract price and value, the contract is binding contract so long as parties reached the price after proper disclosure of the finances of the company". But one cannot conclude that the case would have been decided differently if the defendant had made a proper disclosure and the plaintiff agreed to pay such a higher price. If the defendant had done so, they plaintiff would not have agreed, and the case would never have arisen. What mattered was that in this case, unlike Jinding, the price was neither "the result of careful calculation and market risk allocation" nor "within the range of normal market activities".

Moreover, courts have been willing to infer that a party was not able to protect himself from the fact that the unfair result shows that he did not do so. In Yang v Zhang,[48] and in In Shi v Xia,[49] the driver of a vehicle negligently struck the plaintiff. In the first case, the plaintiff settled for RMB 90,000 and the damages turned out to be RMB 130,000 at the time of trail and further damages were anticipated. In the second case, the plaintiff settled for 24,000 yuan when the damages were 28,000 and nursing fee was 4,000 yuan. In the first case, in contrast to the second, the defendant was a medical doctor who had approached the family the next day and settled quickly. One might think that the result was different because, in the first case, the plaintiff settled too quickly and with less chance that the defendant, who was a medical doctor, to appreciate the harm he might have suffered. But that is another way of saying that the plaintiff, through his own ignorance, settled too quickly for too low a price. Whenever a party accepts an unfairly low price, he must have been either unaware or unable to get a higher one. The reason for giving relief is the unfair price. The party's ignorance was only the reason he did not receive a fair one.

In any event, relief from an 'obviously fair' contract in China, or an 'unconscionable' contract in the United States, would not be given at all if, as Han

47 (2017) 粤 01 民终 23863 号 [(2017) Yue 01 Min Zhong No 23863].
48 (2016) 宁03民终801号 [(2016) Ning 03 Min Zhong No 801].
49 (2016) 苏09民终3731号 [(2016) Su 09 Min Zhong No 3731].

suggests, there were no objective standards of fairness. That is the position of Anglo-American scholars such as Richard Epstein who doubt that such standards exist. He believes that unconscionability "should be used only [...] to police the process whereby private agreements are formed".[50] Similarly, Stephen Smith believed that relief for unconscionability was given where "cognitive asymmetry" between the parties gave the courts "good reason to be concerned about fraud, undue influence, duress, or a simple failure to agree, but in which they lack direct evidence of the defect".[51] "Cognitive asymmetry" means that one party had "little education, low intelligence, lack of knowledge, [or] lack of independence". Or, "the contract was difficult to understand, was in fine print, or dealt with difficult-to-estimate probabilities".[52] Yet the courts give relief in cases in which a party did not claim that the other party lied to him, unduly influenced him, or threatened him, and in which the only mistake concerned the value of the other party's performance. Substantive unconscionability matters in American law just as "obvious unfairness" matters under article 151 of the Chinese Civil Code. A harsh bargain may be due to a party's lack of education, intelligence, or knowledge. But in these cases, relief is only given when the bargain is harsh. Otherwise, a large number of people would be unable to enter into binding contracts.

Wang Yi also believes that although a contract can be objectively unfair, relief should be given only if it is subjectively unfair as well. It is objectively unfair when the "price differs greatly from the value", or the liability and the risk are "significantly unreasonable"[53] and subjectively unfair if the disparity in is due to "exploitation". According to a Supreme Court Judicial Interpretation, a contract price that is 30% higher or lower than the market price as a sufficient disparity to warrant relief following the guidelines set by numerous provincial high courts.[54] He believes that no relief should be given if the disparity is due to normal economic disadvantage.[55] The advantaged party must have

---

50 Richard A. Epstein, 'Unconscionability: A Critical Reappraisal' (1975) 18 U Chi J L & Econ 293 at 294–295, 315.

51 Epstein (n 50) 364.

52 Stephen A. Smith, *Contract Theory* (OUP 2004) 344.

53 Wang (n 9) 60.

54 Judicial Interpretation II of Chinese Contract Law, Article 19 (if the contract price does not reach 70% of the guiding price or market price at the place and the time of the transaction, generally, it may be deemed an obviously unreasonably low price. If the contract price exceeds 30% of the guiding price or market price at the place and the time of the transaction, generally, it may be deemed an obviously unreasonably high price).

55 Wang (n 9) 58.

exploited, for example, a pressing need for money or a solvency problem that threatens the survival of a party.

His example is a recent pre-Civil Code case in which the Shangdong High Court found both exploitation and obvious unfairness in an agreement that allowed one who had engaged contractors to pay them 5.86% less than previously agreed.[56] The agreement was concluded less five days before Chinese New Year. The reduction would have led the contractors to fall behind on payments for work done by migrant workers. The result, given the proximity of the Chinese New Year, could have been a massive protest that would imperil the contractors' solvency. The court found both obvious unfairness and exploitation.

In that case, however, it should not have mattered that the workers might have protested or the contractor's gone out of business as long as the price set by the new agreement was unfair. In the United States, relief would be given simply because there was no consideration – nothing given in return of the promise to reduce the price. This is one of the instances in which, as the authors have noted elsewhere, unfairness is prevented by the doctrine of consideration rather than unconscionability.[57] Civil law jurisdictions do not have a doctrine of consideration. Yet they will often refuse to enforce an unfair promise to pay more for a performance than was originally agreed.[58] Except in unusual circumstances,[59] if one party agrees to take less than he was promised for making the same performance, the other party is 'holding him up' by taking advantage of the fact that he has changed his position and will suffer if he refuses. In such cases, the new price would be unfair even if the contractor's solvency were not in danger. In any event, the evil to be remedied is the unfair price. If the original agreement had permitted the 5.86% reduction, then the contractors would have had to bear the risk that their workers would not be promptly paid.

---

56 *Ibid.*

57 James Gordley and Hao Jiang, 'Contract as Voluntary Commutative Justice' (2020) Mich St L Rev 725.

58 See national answers to case 9 in James Gordley (ed), *The Enforceability of Promises in European Contract Law* (CUP 2001) 219–238.

59 Section 89(a) of the Second Restatement provides that a promise modifying a duty is binding "if the modification is fair and equitable in view of circumstances not anticipated by the promisor when the contract was made". For example, in *Angel v Murray*, 322 A2d 630 (RI 1974), a garbage collector had contracted to pick up all the town's garbage for a fixed yearly fee. Unexpectedly, a developer built a new tract of houses in the town, adding greatly to the garbage collector's expenses. The court enforced the town's promise to pay him an additional amount as compensation for his extra expenses.

One is unlikely to find a case in which a contract is 'objectively unfair', or, as Americans would say, 'substantively unconscionable' when the disadvantaged party was not vulnerable. He may have been unaware that the advantaged party was taking advantage of him, as in *Tong Xu v Liang ZF* and *Yang v Zhang*, or he may have had no alternative to accepting a price he knew was unfair as in Yi's case of the contractors. The evil to be corrected, however, is the unfair price. If the price were fair, the vulnerability of one of the parties would not matter.

He Jian maintained that, in commercial transactions, the law should not worry about fairness of the contract because of the sophistication of the commercial parties.[60] The court would be underestimating the parties' sophistication if they were to use obvious unfairness to set aside a trade of non-performing assets. Parties know what they are doing and such a trade is by nature highly volatile.[61] However, such an argument only meant that fairness will be ensured by the market rather than that it is irrelevant. Again, the evil to be corrected is the unfair price.

This point is lost on American jurists who claim that there must be both substantive and procedural unconscionability for a court to give relief. The reason is that they have yet to escape the influence of the 19th century will theories. They regard procedural unconscionability as a ground for relief because, in their view, the disadvantaged party did not express his will freely. According to Hanoch Dagan and Avihay Dorfman (two Israelis who have contributed much to the American debate) and Michael Heller, "[p]rocedural unconscionability" means an absence of "self-determination"[62] or "meaningful choice".[63] If so, procedural unconscionability ought to be enough to warrant relief regardless of substantive unconscionability. It means a party could not make a meaningful choice. But, they say, there is procedural unconscionability when "[t]he weaker party suffers from 'physical or mental infirmities, ignorance, illiteracy or inability to understand the language of the agreement'".[64] If contract required a meaningful choice, and people with these qualities could not make such a choice, very many people could not contract at all.

---

60 He (n 33) 7.

61 *Id.*

62 Hanoch Dagan and Avihay Dorfman, 'Justice for Contracts' (2020) (on file with the author).

63 Hanoch Dagan and Michael Heller, *The Choice Theory of Contracts* (CUP 2017) 33, 86–87 (internal quotation marks omitted).

64 Dagan and Dorfman, 'Justice for Contracts' 48 (quoting Restatement (Second) of Contracts § 208 cmt. d.)

These scholars avoid that consequence by requiring the relief be given only when a contract is substantively unfair. But they also define substantive unfairness as an absence of autonomy. Terms are "substantive[ly] unconscionable" when they are "unreasonably favorable to the other party".[65] They unreasonably favor the other party when the parties did not "relate in a contract as equals either by assuming co-authorship of determining, or influencing the determination of, the terms of the interaction, or by satisfying reasonable expectations of typical term-takers".[66] So we go round in a circle. Terms are unfair when the parties would not freely choose them, and the parties are not free when the terms on which they agreed are unfair.

5 Conclusion

These problems are the legacy of the will theories. Contract was defined in terms of the will of the parties. Therefore, the parties were bound by terms to which they had agreed, fair or not. Western jurists rejected the idea that relief should be given because a contract is unfair, an idea that had prevailed for centuries. Since the 20th century, while acknowledging that relief is given, they still insist that the unfairness of a contract by itself is not enough to warrant it. Germans claim one party must have taken an 'immoral' advantage of another. If that were so, injustice of the terms of a contract would be reason in itself to give a remedy. American jurists have said that there must be procedural as well as substantive unconscionability, and explain them as infringements on parties autonomy or freedom to choose. But if all that mattered was freedom to choose, either contracts could never be made by parties whose choices are constrained, or, as the will theorists believed, all that should matter are the terms on which the parties actually agreed.

We have seen some Chinese jurists speaking, like Germans, about good morals, and others speaking about objective and subjective fairness as American speak about substantive and procedural unconscionability. In borrowing Western solutions, they have borrowed problems that only arose when Western jurists espoused will theories in the 19th century. In this instance Chinese jurists might do better on their own.

---

65 *Id.* 47.

66 *Id.* 47, 48 (internal emphasis omitted).

Expanded Table of Contents

PART 2

The Inner Contents of the Chinese Civil Code

PART 3

The Outer Significance of the Chinese Civil Code

Index